D0929936

DATE DUE

The Rape Case

The Rape Case

A Young Lawyer's Struggle
for Justice in the 1950s

Irving Morris

DELAWARE

Newark: University of Delaware Press

© 2011 by Irving Morris

Associated University Presses
2010 Eastpark Boulevard
Cranbury, NJ 08512

The paper used in this publication meets the requirements of the American National Standard for Permanence of Paper for Printed Library Materials Z39.48-1984.

Library of Congress Cataloging-in-Publication Data

Morris, Irving, 1925–
    The rape case : a young lawyer's struggle for justice in the 1950s / Irving Morris.
        p.   cm. — (Cultural Studies of Delaware and the Eastern Shore)
    Includes bibliographical references and index.
    ISBN 978-1-936249-36-7 (alk. paper)
    1. Curran, Francis J.—Trials, litigation, etc.   2. Maguire, Francis J.—Trials, litigation, etc.   3. Jones, Ira F.—Trials litigation, etc.
    4. Delaware—Trials, litigation, etc.   5. Trials (Rape)—Delaware—Wilmington.   6. Morris, Irving, 1925–   7. Defense (Criminal procedure)—Delaware—Wilmington.   I. Title.
    KF224.C87M67   2011
    345.751'202532—dc22   2010039362

I dedicate this book to Doris R. Morris who did not write or edit *The Rape Case* but, rather, lived it during the time I represented Curran, Jones, and Maguire, and when I wrote their story.

Cultural Studies of Delaware
and the Eastern Shore

Published by the University of Delaware Press

Series Editor: Carol E. Hoffecker, Professor Emerita

Among the titles in this series:

Contents

Contents 9

No free man shall be taken and imprisoned, or dispossessed, or outlawed, or banished, or in any way destroyed, nor will We proceed against or prosecute him, except by lawful judgment of his peers and through the law of the land.

Section 29 of the Magna Carta, 1215.

Foreword

Irving Morris has written *The Rape Case*, a gripping story for lawyers and non-lawyers alike, of how, as a young lawyer in his first case, he succeeded in overturning rape convictions and life sentences for three young Delaware men. The men served almost eleven years in prison before Morris won their release by showing the state had denied them a fair trial by its use of police perjury. Morris was, for many decades, the leading Delaware lawyer specializing in holding corporations accountable for misstatements or misconduct that injured shareholders. He also served, among other things, as President of the Delaware State Bar Association.

Writing more than sixty years after the trial, Morris says no success in his corporate cases ever brought him greater satisfaction.

One creative lawyer's perseverance against a system that failed miserably in its duty to do justice is particularly vital today when courts and legislatures seem more and more inclined to support finality rather than fairness, and toughness more than truth. Thus, the book teaches lessons for today's lawyers and citizens. And does so with graphic details and thoughtful analysis, coupled with charm and humor.

The Rape Case had elements of a fairly typical rape case. It turned on credibility. The young woman claimed she was raped. The three young men claimed she consented, and that there was no penetration. A jury sitting in Delaware state court found there was rape. The defendants could not afford lawyers to represent them on appeal. And Delaware did not provide counsel for appeals by indigent defendants, not even when they faced life sen-

11

tences. But there was no point to an appeal, even if they had had the money, since they lacked the proof of the police perjury which had destroyed their credibility at trial.

What was different from a typical rape case was that after the trial was over, a long-hidden police department report revealed that the police had committed perjury at the trial. How the report came to light is itself a fascinating part of the story.

But, even with the report in hand, Morris had to convince the courts that the police perjury made a difference. Not that the perjury proved the defendants were innocent, though they may well have been. What Morris had to show was that the perjury—coming as it did from officers of the state—rendered the trial so unfair that the guilty verdicts could not stand.

At first glance, the perjury does not seem stunning. Defendants testified that, after their arrests, they had made two statements to the police. This was true. But the police testified they had made only one. Then, after the convictions, and after the perjury was discovered, the prosecutors argued that the perjury was irrelevant because the defendants had not shown it mattered whether there had been one or two statements. The Delaware courts accepted this argument. Eventually, Morris persuaded a Federal Court otherwise.

Americans have become familiar with DNA evidence being used to win the release of convicted felons—including in rape cases. Innocence is often established by DNA. The Innocence Project has won the release of hundreds. But DNA had not been discovered when *The Rape Case* was tried. And DNA evidence was not first used to free an innocent person until years later.

What this book shows is that brilliant lawyering, perseverance, and, ultimately, a courageous Federal judge, matter. It was not enough "just" to show the police had lied. Convictions do not get reversed to punish policemen. What Morris had to show was that the perjury made the convictions fundamentally unfair, a denial of due process of law.

Morris recounts many memories of his periodic visits to the Delaware prison where his clients were held. Morris believes the main benefit of his visits was that he conveyed his confidence that their cause was just and they would prevail. Whether the clients themselves remained confident, we cannot know. But it must have been tough because, as Morris recounts, he suffered *six* defeats over the course of several years before the first victory.

Morris does not sugarcoat his defeats. Chapter headings summarize what happened. Thus: "My Failure to Research Leads to the First Defeat;" "the Importance of Civil Discovery (the Second Defeat)." Refreshing as candid self-criticism may be, Morris' early defeats were on procedural questions. So although they were defeats, they did not go to the substance of his attack upon the unconstitutional unfairness of the trial.

When Morris eventually did succeed in forcing the Delaware courts to consider the substance of his argument, he lost again. But now there is no self-criticism. Rather, there is a devastating attack on the squirming of Delaware judges to avoid reaching the fair result. Here is where Morris' book benefits from the passage of more than half a century. Time adds perspective and permits candor. Earlier, as a Delaware lawyer practicing before these same judges—and their colleagues—Morris never could have launched his critique of those judges, particularly his attack on their motives for preserving the unfair result.

When Morris finally succeeded in moving the case to Federal Court, Caleb Wright, Chief Judge of the Federal District Court, got it right. Morris then visited his clients in the Workhouse to report the news of the first victory in four and a half years of litigation. He writes: "They greeted my report of our success with what I thought was restraint. But as I walked away, I heard their whoops of joy as they returned to their cells."

As for the prosecutors, Morris pulls no punches in criticizing their behavior before and after the Federal Court threw out the convictions. For example, the prosecutors demanded that the defendants be handcuffed on the walk across the street from the Federal Court, which had reversed the convictions, to the State Court, where the prosecutors planned to announce they would not prosecute them again. The prosecutors' "real purpose" was to "humiliate [the defendants] by providing a photo opportunity for the press." (The Federal Court rejected the handcuffs.)

The prosecutor's churlish behavior was echoed in their public statements announcing the decision not to retry. There: "Instead of applauding the Federal Court for upholding the constitutional mandate of a fair trial," or expressing even one word about the importance of a fair trial in the courts of Delaware, the prosecutors used the defendants to promote their own political careers. Similarly, Delaware's largest newspaper attacked the Federal Courts in an editorial saying—without any basis—that the perjury could not "have reasonably influenced the jury" and that Federal Courts should avoid reversals on "technicalities."

Slurs about court enforcement of constitutional rights certainly did not disappear in the aftermath of *The Rape Case*. The Delaware prosecutors and the newspaper editorial gave only a foretaste of many demagogic attacks on Federal Courts that followed from the likes of President Richard Nixon and Alabama Governor George Wallace and sadly continue today.

Many lessons can be learned from *The Rape Case*. It was luck that led to Morris' involvement. But luck is the residue of desire. Thus, the lesson is always to be looking for opportunities to serve the public interest. Certainly the story also teaches the importance of perseverance. Or, as Robert the Bruce (my ancestor according to my grandfather) put it as he lay in a barn recovering from an initial defeat in his Scottish-led rebellion against the English: "If at first you don't succeed, try, try again." Finally, perhaps the most important lesson of Morris' book is what our constitutional protections mean for each one of us as a citizen and what it takes to insure them.

This is a first-rate book. While there are plenty of good movies involving trials, there are next to none about appeals. This book could be made into a gripping movie.

Frederick A. O. Schwarz, Jr.
Chief Counsel, Brennan Center for Justice at
New York University School of Law

Preface

The Wilmington, Delaware City Police arrested three young, white, native Wilmingtonians on October 30, 1947, claiming they had raped a young woman in Wilmington's Woodlawn Park during the early morning hours that day. The state subsequently indicted them and tried them in February 1948. The jurors found them guilty of the crime of rape with a recommendation of mercy.[1] Accepting the verdict, the three-judge court sentenced them to life imprisonment, the sentence Delaware law then mandated.[2]

At the midpoint in the twentieth century, as is still true sixty years later, neither Delaware's Constitution nor its government guaranteed an acquittal to an innocent person accused of a crime and brought to trial in the courts of the First State of the United States.[3] Nor did the United States Constitution so command under the Fourteenth Amendment, which Delaware did not adopt until February 12, 1901.[4] Then and now, Delaware did commit to provide and, indeed, both the Constitutions of the United States and Delaware compelled, a fair trial to an accused, a principle rooted in English history since the signing of the Magna Carta in June 1215.

What the jurors in *The Rape Case* did not know in rendering their verdict was that certain police officers had testified falsely at the trial. The police perjury in violation of the defendants' constitutional rights at their trial led inexorably to their convic-

15

tions and their sentences to life in prison. What the jurors' verdict would have been had they known the police were lying and the young men were telling the truth about a critical point, I cannot say. What I do know is the jurors would have heard the defendants' protestations of innocence free of the police perjury. By the time *State v. Curran* concluded in February 1959, it had become "Delaware's most famous criminal case of the past generation. . . ."[5] Anyone in Delaware who spoke of *The Rape Case* did not have to provide further identification.

What I have written is not a determination of the guilt or innocence of the three men. To the extent I discuss the prosecution's case and the defendants' response I do so only to emphasize how important the issue of credibility was at trial. While this book describes how the fundamental constitutional right to a fair trial fared in the First State in the middle of the twentieth century, it is essentially the story of a fledgling lawyer's struggle to overturn the result of a flawed trial by proving the police perjury.

The guarantee of a fair trial, the constitutional right of every citizen, is a hallmark of our legal system.[6] It is distinct from the issue of guilt or innocence. If it were otherwise, the government could charge an accused, torture a confession out of him, and convict him at a trial by introducing the confession. Such tactics do not and cannot meet the standards of either the United States Constitution or the Delaware Constitution. For me, the guilt or innocence of Curran, Jones, and Maguire was not the issue. The violation of their constitutional rights was paramount.

Many have questioned my willingness to serve as the lawyer for the three young men if I did not believe in their innocence from the beginning. My answer, that it was fundamental to our judicial system to afford all defendants the protection of their rights, usually was met with a lack of comprehension, or disbelief, or indifference. But the explanation is more complicated.

Surely how my parents raised me, my Jewish religion with its teachings of compassion and the pursuit of justice, and what my teachers through the years taught me all came together in the remarkable confluence of events compelling my decision to represent the three young men. Abraham and Katie Morris, Rabbi Jacob Kraft, Philip Cohen, Evelyn H. Clift, John H. Powell, John A. Munroe, Wesley Sturgis, Aaron Finger, Melvin G. Shimm, Francis A. Reardon, Chief Judge Paul Leahy, Bernard D. Fischman, and Edward G. Pollard, all of blessed memory, served as role models. Although I was not aware of it at the time, they exerted a profound influence.

I cannot reconstruct and then relate exactly what took place in Woodlawn Park in the early hours of October 30, 1947. To claim I can do so would mean I have the ability now, sixty years later, to determine the truth of events in which I did not participate. Almost five years passed after the trial, conviction, and sentencing before I became involved in *The Rape Case*. When I agreed to represent the defendants, my goal was to secure a new trial at which a new jury could determine their guilt or innocence without being misled by the police perjury the state introduced at the first trial.

I did not begin to write this story until more than fifty years after the events I describe. Consequently, even the events in which I personally participated are dimmed in the obscurity of memory, partially restored by the written record found in the trial testimony, depositions, court hearings, pleadings, newspaper articles, correspondence, contemporaneous notes, and by the recollections of other participants who survived and kindly submitted to interviews with me.

One might ask, "Why write *The Rape Case* now, years after the event setting it in motion?" My answer is severalfold. The story is compelling. The lessons it holds about our system of justice make it deserving to be told. Its telling, moreover, serves as a lesson about perseverance for young lawyers particularly and, perhaps, for everyone. Writing this book is, moreover, my attempt to contribute to the profession I practiced for over fifty years. But for me the need to relate *The Rape Case* is even more personal; it occupied my time and attention as a consuming passion for over six years. Serving as the lawyer for the three young men at the outset of my practice had an enduring effect on me and my career as a lawyer. No one else has come forward to tell the story. If I do not relate it, I fear no one else will. The result will be that only those who chance upon and read the reported opinions will know of the case, and even they will not know what you are about to learn.

Irving Morris
PALM BEACH, FLORIDA
February 2011

1

For Want of a Match

On Wednesday evening, October 29, 1947, the Lorraine Baseball Team held a party at the Labor Lyceum on Scott Street to celebrate the end of the semi-pro baseball season.[1] Although the participants consumed a considerable amount of beer, no one was boisterous. Afterward, Francis J. "Reds" Maguire offered Francis J. "Bud" Curran, Ira F. "Sonny" Jones, Edward J. Fahey III, John E. Masten, and Warren E. Schueler,[2] a lift home.[3] They all piled into his 1937 Plymouth, two-door sedan; Masten sat between Maguire and Curran in the front seat and Fahey, Jones, and Schueler sat in back.[4]

They stopped briefly for another beer at the Embassy Café across town on Lovering Avenue, between Scott and DuPont near the B&O Railroad bridge.[5] Reds, "red-haired, slight of build," just twenty-five, was the oldest of the six.[6] Sonny, "pallid faced, round shouldered," was twenty-three.[7] Bud, "swarthy, heavy-set," was the youngest, not yet twenty-one.[8] All three had served honorably in World War II.[9] Only Maguire was married, and his wife was pregnant.[10] They all came from working-class families and lived in the same neighborhood. None had ever had any involvement with the law. Except for Schueler, they were all Catholic. All but Curran attended Wilmington High School; he had gone to St. Elizabeth's and then Salesianum.[11] None went on to college. Reds Maguire was a fireman with the Wilmington Fire Department.[12] His older brother, Edward, was a Wilmington policeman.[13] Sonny Jones lived with his mother; he had four married sisters, two of whom, Virginia McKinley and Jayne Stigliano, were nurses.[14] Bud Curran's family was the largest. He had one brother and nine sisters.[15]

As Maguire drove out Fourth, Curran asked if anyone had a match.[16] Only he and Sonny Jones smoked.[17] When no one spoke up, Curran asked Maguire to stop if he saw anyone he could ask for a light.[18] After Maguire had crossed Union Street and passed the corner of Fourth and Bancroft Parkway, Curran yelled for him to stop.[19] He had noticed what he thought was a young man standing in the doorway of Skinner's, the general store whose front door faced Bancroft Parkway, a position from which the buses running on Union Street and the trolleys on Fourth were not visible.[20] As he got out of the car and walked back toward the person, Curran realized it was a young woman. He asked if she had a match. She said, "No," told him she didn't smoke, and started giggling and laughing. In answer to his question about what she was doing out so late, she replied she was waiting for her mother. He asked her where she lived, and she responded "Colonial Heights." Curran asked her if he could walk her home.[21] When she consented, so as to prove to himself "without a doubt, that she would go with [him]," he deliberately walked with her toward Fifth in the opposite direction of Colonial Heights.[22] She did not protest as they turned left on Fifth. They walked with his left arm about her shoulders and her right arm around his waist.[23] Bud Curran anticipated an easy score with the willing young woman at his side once they were in Woodlawn Park just past Bancroft Parkway.[24]

As Curran walked the girl toward Fifth, Maguire and the others watched. When the two were out of sight, Maguire, "[curious] to know who the girl was, and where they might be going,"

drove west on Fourth to Bayard. He then turned north on Bayard. As he did, he saw Bud and the girl at Fifth. "Curran was
kissing the girl and making love to her," Maguire subsequently
testified; he did not notice any protest on her part.[25] Maguire
then drove west on Fifth to Ferris, turned left and parked.
Through the car's rear window, he saw Curran and the girl enter
the park. After four or five minutes he drove south on Ferris to
Fourth, turned right and parked near Woodlawn Park across
from Ed Henry's auto body shop. There Jones and Fahey got out
of the car to watch Curran and the girl, leaving Maguire and
Masten in the front seat and Schueler in the back seat.[26] After a
few minutes Maguire made a U-turn, having decided he was
going to pick up his wife who was waiting for him at a friend's
house nearby on Ferris.[27]

After Maguire parked the car on Fourth, an off-duty policeman, Frank Johnson, passed the car while he walked from the
garage in the rear of 2380 West Fourth, where he had parked his
own car before heading to his home at 501 Bayard Avenue. Johnson had seen Maguire's car driving slowly west on Fourth without lights. The car had already stopped when Johnson got to it.
He saw two persons in the front seat as he glanced at it. He
looked around at the car and noted its registration number, Delaware 4–1047. As he neared Fifth and Ferris, he turned and saw
the car now moving slowly west on Fourth. Thinking "it was
strange for the car to act that way after being parked," he
thought he "had better remember the license and . . . wrote it
down."[28] After he stopped to make his note, he walked along
Ferris from Fourth to Fifth then on Fifth to his home, and entered it. During this time Officer Johnson did not "hear any calls
for help or any scream or any noise" from Woodlawn Park.[29]

As Maguire headed east on Fourth, he and Schueler and Masten "became very curious again as to what Curran might be
doing in the park, and they sort of convinced me," Maguire later

testified, "to stop the car and we would go back and see." Maguire parked "almost . . . in front of Sonny Jones' house at 432 Ferris Street."[30] There he, Masten, and Schueler got out and walked along the embankment behind the baseball backstop in Woodlawn Park to where Jones and Fahey were standing.

All five now entered the park, walking close to the fence. They could see Curran and the girl; she was leaning against a tree and Curran "was feeling her all over." She was "giggling and laughing."[31] When she realized they were being watched, she and Curran moved from left field, near Fourth, to deep center field. The five young men on the embankment continued to follow them. When the girl noticed the five again, Curran hollered "take off, 'Magwa'," a nickname for Maguire. When no one moved, Curran yelled again, "Take off, Jonesy." "And so all the other boys left the park," as Maguire later testified, "which left me in the park with Curran and the girl in deep center field."[32]

Fahey, Masten, Schueler, and Jones walked together back to Maguire's car. After waiting in the car for about fifteen minutes, they decided to walk to their respective homes. Jones, who lived nearby on Ferris, reached the door of his home, then turned around and went back to the park.[33] When Fahey, Masten, and Schueler reached Fourth and Union, they met and spoke to Everio L. Leonzio, another member of the Lorraine Baseball Team.[34]

Although Curran later admitted under oath he tried to have sexual intercourse with the young woman, he said he was unable, even with her help, because "[s]he was too tight."[35] He testified the only part of his person that went in her "was my finger."[36] Still, she had made no objection to his advances.[37] Maguire admitted he also tried to have sexual intercourse with the young woman; he testified he, too, was not successful.[38] Even so, he said there was "full consent" on her part.[39] When Jones approached, he said the first thing the young woman said to him was "Will

you take me home when you get finished?" Jones also later testified he tried unsuccessfully to have intercourse with her.[40] At this
time, according to Curran, a woman from a nearby house
shouted, "You had better leave the park and quit your carrying
on or I will call the cops."[41] Maguire also heard the warning.[42]

After the woman's threat, Curran and Maguire walked out of
Woodlawn Park to Maguire's car at Fifth and Ferris.[43] After driving Curran home, Maguire picked up his wife at her friend's and
drove her home.[44] He dropped her off before putting his car into
his nearby garage and returning to their apartment at 1330 West
Fourth.[45] But Jones stayed in the park with the young woman to
help her find and put on her clothes.[46] When she couldn't put
on her shoes, Jones assisted her in doing so.[47] Then, as she had
requested, he started to walk her home.[48]

At about the same time, the police dispatched a car to Woodlawn Park in response to a call from a woman who claimed
"there is a girl screaming down in the Park on Ferris Street, and
I think she is being raped."[49] The first officer on the scene at 1:45
a.m., Patrolman William Allen, saw Jones and the woman walking west on Fourth near the B & O Railroad bridge and stopped
them.[50] He asked Jones if there was any trouble. Jones said "there
was no trouble." Patrolman Allen persisted, telling them "we
have a complaint of some screaming." According to Allen, Jones
claimed "We just had a family argument, and I am taking her
home."[51] The woman also told Allen "that she did not have any
trouble."[52] Only after Patrolmen William Fisher and Christopher
McDermott arrived in a second police car and McDermott and
Allen separated the couple did the woman first claim, "This man
[Jones] and two others raped her down in the park."[53]

The police took Jones directly to the Central Police Station
where Detective John A. Rodenhiser and Patrolman Edward J.
Mazewski started to interrogate him at 2:15 a.m. on October 30,
1947.[54] At that hour Detective Rodenhiser was in charge of the

investigation of what he concluded, based on what he was told, was a rape case. Around 2:45 a.m., after learning from Jones the identity of Curran and Maguire, Detective Rodenhiser directed officers James A. Nagle Jr. and Angelo S. Delloso to bring them in.[55] With Sergeant John Emering, Nagle and Delloso first picked up Curran and then Maguire at their homes and brought them to Central.[56] By "about four o'clock" Rodenhiser and Mazewski had secured and witnessed a statement from Sonny Jones.[57]

At Central, Sergeant Emering, with Patrolmen Delloso and Nagle, questioned Curran beginning about 3:45 a.m. and secured a statement which Curran signed by 4:30 a.m. Delloso and Nagle signed as witnesses. Although there was a place for Emering to sign, he did not do so.[58] After returning to Central from the Delaware Hospital where she had been taken for examination, the young woman met with Sergeant Emering. He took her statement and witnessed it, as did Patrolmen Delloso and Nagle.[59] She claimed Curran, then Maguire, and finally Jones had sexual intercourse with her.[60] She said she protested their advances.[61]

Having finished with Jones, Rodenhiser and Mazewski then examined Maguire beginning around 4:10 a.m. Before 5:00 a.m. Maguire had signed a statement which the officers witnessed.[62]

Around 7:00 a.m., four other prisoners joined Curran, Jones, and Maguire in the turnkey's office for a line up. In the presence of Captain Thomas Buckmaster, Deputy Chief John Malloy of the Fire Department, Sergeant Emering, and Patrolmen Delloso and Mazewski, the young woman identified the three young men as her assailants.[63] Detective Rodenhiser then read the four statements to the three men and the woman. Neither the men nor the woman took any exception to what was read.[64]

Later that day, October 30, 1948, around 4:00 p.m., while Curran, Jones, and Maguire were still in the cell block of the Public Building, the police presented a second set of statements to them, saying they were the same as the first set, just retyped for "neatness." Each man signed his second statement without reading it.[65] Those second statements bore the same names and signatures as witnesses as were on the first set, but the police officers who signed did not actually witness the second signing.[66]

At the time of the arrests, no one told Curran, Jones, and Maguire of any right to see and speak to a lawyer before they made and signed statements. The United States Supreme Court had not yet declared as a matter of constitutional right that police must advise an accused of his right to remain silent and to have the advice of a lawyer upon arrest for a felony and did not do so for almost another twenty years.[67] And so, without the benefit of a lawyer's presence or advice, Curran, Jones, and Maguire each submitted to police questioning and each signed two statements.[68]

2

The Preliminary Hearing

When the Wilmington police placed Curran, Jones, and Maguire under arrest on October 30, 1947, and charged them with the crime of rape, Jenny Jones, Sonny's mother, knew she needed a lawyer for her son. A widow, she lived at 422 Ferris Street in a two-story house in an area known as "the Flats."[1] She and Sonny occupied the second floor apartment. Her four daughters were grown and married. The first two lawyers Jenny approached wanted no part of the case. Finally she turned to H. Albert "Hy" Young.

Young was as competitive as anyone could be.[2] In the opinion of most lawyers and the public, he was Delaware's consummate trial lawyer and assuredly so in his own judgment. An American success story, Young was born in Russia in 1904 with the family name Yanowitz and brought as a small child to the United States, first to Brooklyn, New York, and then, after twelve years, to Delaware. Starting from impoverished circumstances, he worked his way through the University of Delaware and the University of Pennsylvania Law School.[3] He always wanted to practice law in Delaware, his home state. At the time of Young's admission to the Bar in 1929, Delaware was the bastion of corporate protection. Only a few members of the Bar actually engaged in corporate litigation in Delaware's Court of Chancery. Young was not

among them. The legendary Aaron Finger, under the sponsorship of Robert H. Richards Sr., was the only Jew who had broken
the barrier to practice corporate law in Delaware as a member of
its Bar. The barrier did not come down for another two genera-
tions.

Criminal law became Young's métier. He rapidly honed his
skills in defending those accused of crime, becoming the lawyer
to retain in criminal cases.[4] He also represented plaintiffs in personal injury cases. When Jewish merchants in Wilmington
wanted a vigorous lawyer, they turned to him. Young thrived as
he reveled in his reputation as a "high charger." Samuel Han-
dloff, a contemporary of Young's, told me after he had successfully litigated a case on behalf of a client and recovered the
client's claim in full, he presented a bill of $1,250 for his services.
The client protested, saying for that kind of money he could have
hired Young. Sam's classic retort was, "Could he have recovered
more?"[5]

Young asked Jenny Jones for $5,000 to defend her son. If he
thought the staggering sum he set meant he would see no more
of Jenny Jones, he was mistaken. Unbeknownst to her family, she
had kept cash in bundles wrapped with rubber bands and se-
creted in shoe boxes on the top shelf of a closet in her bedroom.
Hearing the fee demand, she did not hesitate to take the cash
from the closet. After her son-in-law, Carmen N. Stigliano, her
daughter Jayne's husband, counted the money on the carpet of
her bedroom, she paid the amount the lawyer sought.[6]

At the time of their son's arrest, Nellie and Francis Curran had
eleven children, nine girls and another son besides Francis. They
all lived in a modest, three story, row house the parents rented
at 521 North Bancroft Parkway in the Flats.[7] Since Bud Curran
and his family had no money to hire a lawyer, he appeared at the
preliminary hearing unrepresented.[8]

Reds Maguire's parents, Edward and Susie Maguire, were people of modest means. They rented a house at 113 North Connell Street that was somewhat more substantial than the row houses where the Jones and Curran families lived.[9] They had three children, two boys and a girl.[10] With Edward Jr. a Wilmington policeman and Francis a Wilmington fireman, the Maguires were quite proud of their sons, both still in uniform after their military service in World War II. Both were married. Francis and his wife, Doris, lived nearby at 1330 West Fourth, with her parents.[11] Promptly after his arrest, the Maguires hired A. James Gallo, well-known for his divorce and criminal practice.

At the preliminary hearing on November 12, 1947, in the Municipal Court of Wilmington, only the young woman and the police surgeon, Dr. Paul R. Smith, testified.[12] The sole issue before the presiding judge, Thomas J. Herlihy Jr., was whether there was sufficient evidence to find probable cause, the legal test, to hold the three young men in custody without bail pending action by the Grand Jury.[13] The preliminary hearing provided the defendants and their lawyers with the opportunity to learn about the prosecution's case and, armed with what they could glean, to prepare for trial. It was important to have the prosecuting witness tell all she knew, not only to secure her complete story, but, moreover, to have her version of what happened in the record, thus enabling the defense at trial to exploit any deviation in her trial testimony in order to attack her credibility.

The City Solicitor's office deferred to Chief Deputy Attorney General C. Edward Duffy to conduct the preliminary hearing, as Assistant City Solicitor Charles L. Paruszewski told the Court, "[b]ecause of the notoriety which these cases have received in the newspapers and otherwise, and because the ultimate prosecution will rest with the Attorney General's Office. . . ."[14] Duffy took the young woman through her story. She told of taking a 4–1 bus from town, a bus that did not go to her home in Colonial Heights. She got off at Fourth and Union to transfer either

to a 4 or a Marshallton Bus. She walked across Fourth to Skinner's Market at the corner of Bancroft Parkway. Because she was
nervous, she said she walked up and down Fourth between
Union and Bancroft Parkway. A car approached and she claimed
she recognized Maguire in the car when it stopped at Fourth and
Bancroft Parkway. When Curran (she did not know his name
then) got out of the car, he asked her if she had a match; she said
"No, I didn't; I didn't smoke." In response to his questions, she
told him her name and where she lived, but demurred when he
asked her to walk to his house to get a match, telling him she
"did not know him well enough." He also offered to walk her
home. She thought "he was a nice boy" and started walking with
him up Bancroft Parkway toward Fifth in a direction away from
her home. She said Curran told her "he would take me home in
a taxi."[15]

At Ferris, Fifth Street dead ends at Woodlawn Park. They were
walking in the park when Curran pulled her to him. She claimed
he forced her to the ground and entered her with "his private
person." At that time she saw Maguire behind a nearby tree. He
joined Curran and she noticed another fellow who she identified
as Jones. She said Curran held her down while Maguire penetrated her, and then Curran had relations with her again. She
said she "pleaded with [Jones] to help me, but he wouldn't help
me." At that point she heard a woman hollering: ". . . leave that
girl alone, or else she would call a cop." Jones, she said "was having relations with me then. Maguire and Curran stood there."
When Jones got up, "the other two said, 'Here comes the cops,'
and ran." The young woman testified "[Jones] helped me with
my shoes, and he started walking up with me." She quoted Jones
as saying "they hadn't hurt me any" and ". . . they just had—
they hadn't had that for a long time, and they just wanted a
piece." With two further questions whose answers established
that "this occurred in this park—near Fifth Street and Ferris . . .

[t]hat is located in the City of Wilmington, New Castle County, State of Delaware," Duffy concluded his examination and turned her over for cross-examination.[16]

Over Duffy's objection, Young drew from the woman the fact she could have caught a trolley bus at Eighth and Market that would have taken her home without any need for a transfer. He further established she got off the trolley at Fourth and Union rather than the transfer point at Lancaster and Union, even though Fourth and Union was a much darker corner. She told Young she "just decided to get off at Fourth and Union." Then she crossed Fourth to wait on the north side of Fourth between Union and Bancroft Parkway.[17] Young specifically asked:

Q. As a matter of fact . . . you were standing in the doorway of the closed store of Skinner's at Fourth and Bancroft, were you not, when you first spoke to Curran?

A. Well, I was just walking down there. I just started to walk down to take the bus.

On this important point the young woman did not deny she was standing in the doorway of Skinner's grocery store.[18]

When Maguire stopped his car, she said she saw three boys in the car. Young asked: "Are you sure you only saw three?" "Well, I noticed Maguire," she answered. Even with Young's persistence she held to her testimony that there were "three boys altogether."[19]

Given her testimony, Young was on notice he would have to establish at trial that Fahey, Masten, and Schueler were present with the defendants that night. Their testimony not only would support the defendants' claim that the woman consented, but, in addition, it would attack the young woman's credibility in claiming there were only three persons in the car. Conversely, if her claim went uncontradicted, the testimony of the eyewitnesses would be repudiated and her credibility would remain intact.

Young was relying upon the testimony of the three eyewitnesses to carry the day.

During his cross-examination, Young twice suggested Jones did not attack the woman. In discussing probable cause and the possibility of bail if the intercourse was with consent, Young told Judge Herlihy: ". . . if I can show that there was intercourse with consent, then your Honor will have some problem, as far as Jones is concerned, as to whether or not it is a case that should be dismissed or whether it should be a bailable offense. Because, if your Honor please, I can immediately file a petition in the nature of a habeas corpus proceeding, in order to show that the presumption is not great or the proof positive."[20] Young's reference to a habeas corpus proceeding was clearly to the landmark Delaware case, State v. Hawkins, where Young sought to use, in Judge Richard Seymour Rodney's words, "the most important writ known to the law," to secure bail for his client accused of murder.[21]

Young later referred to the state's claim as "an atrocious, malicious charge against an innocent boy I represent," and, obviously catching himself, adding "and, in fact, against all three boys."[22] Clearly Young was making an effort to distinguish his client from the other two defendants.

Responding to Young's questions, the woman testified that (1) she knew the neighborhood; (2) she lived near that area all her life; (3) she went to a school only two blocks away from Wood-lawn Park; (4) she knew the location of left field and right field in the park. She walked with Curran because "I thought he was going to his home to get a match," although she admitted "I didn't know where he lived." She said she pushed Curran away when he kept trying to put his arm around her but explained "[h]e just put it inside of my arm like." She further admitted she didn't scream. As she entered Woodlawn Park with Curran, she knew it would not bring her to any house. When he kissed her, she pushed him away; she did not scream. When he drew her to him, she did not scream. When he pulled her over to a more secluded spot, she did not scream. She explained "I just was afraid he might harm me, he might kill me or something." When Young challenged her on this point, she admitted Curran did not threaten to kill her or do her any bodily harm; "[b]ut I knew what he was after." Although she did not remember asking Curran if he had a condom, she admitted she told him, "Protect me." When Curran and Maguire were having relations with her she said she did not scream "because they were all holding my mouth and everything, and I couldn't." Jones, she said, "still was in me" when a woman called, "Leave that girl alone. I will call the cops." She testified Jones did help her gather her clothes and put on her shoes and coat. They were walking together from the park when an officer arrived.[23]

She did not remember telling the officer, "This boy [i.e., Jones] did not hurt me or do anything to me; it was the other two." Nor did she remember "going to the hospital and telling them on [the] report that two boys attacked [me]."[24]

When Young concluded his questioning, Gallo, Maguire's attorney, examined her. She repeated that Maguire entered her and denied she played with him to help him get an erection.[25] To a further question from Young, she denied she was "getting some pleasurable excitement."[26]

After Duffy, Young, and Gallo completed their examinations, at Duffy's prompting, Judge Herlihy asked the unrepresented Curran: "Curran, are there any questions that you would like to ask this witness?" He answered: "Well, there is one thing." At that point Young interrupted, properly concerned that by his question Curran might incriminate himself. Young offered to advise Curran "acting in a sort of an amicus curiae," telling Judge Herlihy: "It just isn't cricket, under the Constitution, to

permit him even to ask a question at this time." Duffy took issue
with Young:

MR. DUFFY:I disagree with my friend entirely. This is not a final trial,
as I pointed out before. There are counsel representing two. There
might very well be a conflict in interest as between [sic] the three. I
don't know. That hasn't become apparent yet. But there isn't anything
different in this case, and in every other case, when it comes before this
Court, whether it be murder or any kind of a capital case. When it is
determined that he has to go on trial, it is going to try him; if he hasn't
got counsel, they appoint counsel so as to ably represent him.[27]

Judge Herlihy resolved the issue by first warning Curran of his
constitutional rights and then affording him "an opportunity to
ask any questions here" since, as Herlihy said, "I feel I am duty
bound" to do so. After listening to Herlihy's cautionary words,
Curran said: "I have no questions, your Honor."[28]

Duffy then called Dr. Paul A. Smith, the police surgeon, who
testified to having examined the young woman on the early
morning of October 30, 1947. He said her hymen had been ruptured "within a few hours" and that her vagina had been penetrated. Young's cross-examination was short:

Q. Doctor, how far from the vaginal opening is the hymen?
A. It is just inside the vulva, probably half an inch or inch; just inside
the vagina.
Q. And that can rupture, of course, with any woman or lady who is
having intercourse willingly, isn't that correct?
A. That's right.[29]

With the questioning complete, Duffy told the judge "the
State feels that they presented sufficient evidence to justify the
holding of these men for the action of the Grand Jury. We have
certainly presented a case to show probable cause." Young re-

sponded: "I think it is well understood we are not introducing any testimony, as we wouldn't have a right to do in a matter of this kind, since your Honor is sitting as committing magistrate, and that [the test the state must meet] is merely [to present] a prima-facie case for holding for the Grand Jury." After asking the defendants to stand, Judge Herlihy ruled: "The defendants are held without bail for action by the Grand Jury for a case in the Court of General Sessions, from where it will be transferred to the Court of Oyer and Terminer upon proper motion."[30]

Duffy did not mention or offer in evidence the statements the defendants had signed on October 30, 1947. Nor did the defendants have copies of what they had signed. In 1947 the state had no obligation to make copies available to them. A defendant was not even entitled to see a statement he gave to the police unless the state offered it in evidence at trial. Not until the Criminal Rules of the Superior Court became effective February 12, 1953, did a defendant have the right to secure a copy of any statement he had given to the authorities.

Hy Young had learned from Sonny Jones that he had signed two statements. What Young did not know, nor could he have reasonably anticipated, was how the police would use the written statements to destroy all three defendants' credibility.

On November 14, 1947, following the attorney general's motion, the Grand Jury indicted Curran, Jones, and Maguire on a charge of rape.[31]

3

The Trial

Delaware's law in 1947 mandated the punishment of death by hanging for anyone found guilty of rape. If, however, the jury recommended mercy and a majority of the three-judge court Delaware law then required to sit in a capital case accepted it, the court could impose the sentence of life imprisonment instead.[1] Beginning Tuesday, February 10, 1948, the state tried Curran, Jones, and Maguire in the Court of Oyer and Terminer of the State of Delaware in and for New Castle County, the court that then had jurisdiction over every crime punishable by death in the county.[2]

Chief Justice Charles S. Richards, of Sussex County, presiding, Resident Judge Charles L. Terry Jr., of Kent County, and Resident Judge James B. Carey, of Sussex County, made up the court at *The Rape Case* trial. All three were also members of Delaware's Supreme Court under Delaware's "leftover judges" system. Delaware's Constitution of 1897 had provided if a judge did not sit below, he sat on any appeal to the Supreme Court from a colleague's trial decision.[3]

The Rape Case trial took place in the cavernous, main courtroom on the third floor of Wilmington's Public Building. Each day spectators lined up early to attend. Assisted by police and Public Building guards, the sheriff's office exercised crowd control by keeping "all would-be spectators on the ground floor" until seats were available and only then permitting additional persons to take the elevators to the third floor to fill the vacant seats.[4]

The trial of a rape charge frequently comes down to "she says, he says." In *The Rape Case,* the defendants' denials of rape, supported by the testimony of three eyewitnesses, were set against the young woman's claim of rape.[5] The jurors' task was to determine what happened in the early morning hours of October 30, 1947, after Bud Curran walked the apparently willing young woman into Woodlawn Park. Their conclusion about the defendants' guilt or innocence would depend upon who they believed. If they accepted the woman's sworn testimony, they could conclude that first Curran and then Maguire and, finally, Jones forced themselves upon her against her will, penetrated her vagina, and thus committed the crime of rape. But if they accepted the defendants' protestations of innocence, supported by the three eyewitnesses' testimony under oath, they could not reach a verdict of guilty. The credibility the jurors assigned to the persons who testified was crucial to the outcome of *The Rape Case.*

Surely the defendants had the right to expect and, constitutionally, to demand that the jurors make their judgment without the state's attempting to prejudice the jurors against them.

When *The Rape Case* came to trial, all three men had lawyers. Only one of them, Hy Young, had participated at the preliminary hearing on November 12, 1947. By November 17, the Maguires had hired David J. Reinhardt to replace Gallo who had withdrawn after the preliminary hearing. The court appointed Leonard G. Hagner to defend Bud Curran who had no lawyer at the hearing.[6]

The Prosecuting Witness

Attorney General Albert W. James and his chief deputy, Ed Duffy, knew from the young woman's testimony at the preliminary hearing that they had their work cut out for them if they were to rely upon her to achieve their goal. To be sure, they wanted to convict Curran, Jones, and Maguire of the crime of rape. They considered their case strong enough to obtain a conviction. But more importantly they wanted to secure a death sentence conviction from the jury beyond the court's ability to alter: a jury verdict of guilty *without* a recommendation of mercy.

To that end they needed to present their chief witness as a shy, retiring girl, a naïve trusting person set upon savagely and violated by the three defendants. To accomplish their goal James and Duffy had to prepare the young woman to tell her story so convincingly and sympathetically as to cause the jury to believe her and without hesitation find the defendants guilty without a recommendation of mercy. They would also have to prepare her to withstand cross-examination. With their goal much in mind, James and Duffy met with her in numerous sessions between the mid-November preliminary hearing and the mid-February beginning of the trial, a fact freely, but perhaps inadvertently, Duffy admitted. Toward the end of the trail's first day when both the prosecution and the defense sought to adjourn despite the court's willingness to extend the trial day into the evening, Duffy, urging an adjournment, told the court: "Our experience in talking with her prior to this case, as you can realize, it has been necessary for us to have several conferences with her, and our experience has been that she tires pretty much after two or three hours in the office, and is much fresher when she started out again."[7] His comment disclosed the state's thorough preparation.

As the young woman's testimony would prove, James and Duffy concentrated the bulk of their preparation in teaching her how to thwart the anticipated cross-examination by Hy Young. By the time they called her as the state's first witness, they found the way for her to respond to Young's experience and mastery of the courtroom.

Following the practice that then prevailed in the conduct of the attorney general's office, Attorney General James nominally headed the prosecution team at the trial of this major case. Given their goal, the mild-mannered James knew he should defer to his far more experienced, hard-charging Chief Deputy Duffy to assume the lead role in prosecuting the state's case. They decided, however, it would be better for James to examine the young woman rather than Duffy with his aggressive style.

In his relatively brief direct examination, James gently guided her by leading questions, i.e., questions suggesting the answer, or questions reminding her about what to say if she strayed off the script she appeared to be following.[8] Shortly after taking the stand, she "broke down in tears and had to be led from the courtroom."[9] In her subsequent testimony, she added to what she had testified at the preliminary hearing. She told of attending a movie at the Arcadia Theater on Market between Fifth and Sixth with a girlfriend. After they left the theater, they walked six blocks to the Eagle Restaurant on Delaware Avenue near Orange where the young woman drank two bottles of beer.[10] They left the restaurant about 11:30 p.m. and walked back to Eighth and Market, where her girlfriend caught a 5 bus and she a 4–1 bus with a transfer. She got off at Fourth and Union where, using the transfer, she could catch the Marshallton or the Newark bus, either of which, unlike a 4–1 bus, would take her near her home on Gray Avenue in Colonial Park. She then crossed Fourth to Kiger's drugstore to wait for a bus coming down Union or Fourth.[11] As she had testified at the preliminary hearing, the number of passing cars made her nervous, so she decided to walk up and down the short block on Fourth between Union and Bancroft Parkway.[12]

In critical testimony about exactly where she was, James led the young woman to say what he wanted to establish:

Q. And did you start to walk up and down Fourth Street?
A. Yes, sir.

Q.   In which direction?
A.   That was Fourth Street.
Q.   Fourth Street, between Union and what other street?
A.   Bancroft Parkway.
Q.   Did you walk up and down there more than once?
A.   I walked there about one and one-half times—a couple of times, I
     would say.
Q.   A couple of times?
A.   A couple of times.
Q.   You walked up to Bancroft Parkway *or did you walk almost to Ban-
     croft Parkway on Fourth?*
A.   *Almost.*
Q.   *Almost?*
A.   *Yes, sir.*
Q.   And then did you come all the way back to Fourth and Union?
A.   Yes.
Q.   *And then did you go back to Bancroft Parkway?*
A.   *Yes, I did.*
Q.   *Or thereabouts?*
A.   *Yes, sir.*
Q.   And then did you start back towards Union?
A.   Yes, I was just starting back towards Union.
Q.   As you were just starting back towards Union Street *from some-
     where in the neighborhood of the Bancroft Parkway?*
A.   *Yes, sir.* [Emphasis added.][13]

Thus it was James, not the young woman, who first said she
walked "almost to Bancroft Parkway on Fourth" and "thereabouts" and "from somewhere in the neighborhood of the
Bancroft Parkway." But all of James' impermissible leading questions affirmed by the young woman's "Yes, sir" responses consti-
tuted *her* testimony. Despite the objectionable nature of James'
questions as leading and constituting testimony, neither Young
nor his colleagues rose to object, objections, I believe, the court
would have sustained. The effect of her testimony through James
was to place the woman on Fourth and not in the doorway of

Skinner's store fronting on Bancroft Parkway. Early in the trial where the young woman was standing may have appeared to be an innocuous fact; but was it?

Why was it so important for James and the state to have the jurors believe that the young woman was not standing in the doorway of Skinner's store? Unlike the defendants and their lawyers, James and Duffy and the state had in hand the statements the defendants had purportedly signed in the morning hours of October 30, 1947, as the police would testify, and the young woman's statement taken by Sergeant Emering that same morning upon her return from being examined at the Delaware Hospital. Curran had told Sergeant Emering and Patrolmen Nagle and Delloso that when he first saw the young woman she was "standing in the doorway of Skinner's store (Northeast corner) and I asked her for a match."[14] In Jones' statement to Detective Rodenhiser and Patrolman Mazewski he said "we [*sic*] noticed an unknown white woman standing on the northeast corner [at Fourth and Bancroft Parkway], and Maguire stopped the car and Francis Curran got out and asked the woman for a match."[15] Maguire's statement to Rodenhiser and Mazewski read: "And I drove my car to 4th and Bancroft Parkway and there was an unknown woman standing on the northeast corner, and Curran said he needed a match for a cigarette. I stopped the car and Curran got out and went over to the woman."[16] The statements the police secured from Curran, Jones, and Maguire were taken before they had had any discussion among themselves and before they had consulted with any lawyer. For her part, the young woman in her statement said: "at about 12.15 AM this date I was standing on the corner of 4th and Bancroft Parkway for about 2 minutes when a car drove up and stopped and a fellow fot [*sic*] out of the car and aked [*sic*] for [*sic*] me a match."[17]

Thus, immediately after the events in Woodlawn Park, the three men and the woman—each unprompted—were in agreement that the girl was at Fourth and Bancroft Parkway and not walking up and down Fourth when Maguire stopped his car and Curran approached her. If the young woman had been in Skinner's doorway, as Curran said, she would not have been able to see any bus on either Fourth or Union. With all four statements placing her standing at Fourth and Bancroft Parkway and not walking up and down Fourth, the conflict between her testimony and the four statements put her credibility in doubt. The apparently innocuous fact of where she stood was critical to the issue of credibility. James and Duffy did not want the defendants and their lawyers to have any of the statements contradicting the young woman when the defense cross-examined the prosecuting witness.

After placing the girl walking up and down Fourth "almost" to Bancroft Parkway, contrary to her statement, James asked his next question: "What, if anything occurred?" She replied:

A. Well, I noticed this car coming out, and I noticed these three boys in it, and one of them said, "Hello," and I didn't pay any attention at first. I looked in the car and I noticed that I could recognize this Maguire, and then I started walking down, and this fellow got out.[18]

Thus, in her first reference at trial to the number of persons involved, the young woman limited the number to "these three boys," a repetition of her testimony at the preliminary hearing.[19]

James then led her to talk about Maguire:

Q. And where did you know Maguire before?
A. He was a classmate.
Q. In which school?
A. In St. Thomas, and I seen him around high school.
Q. Around high school?
A. Yes, Wilmington High School.

Q. Had you seen him in St. Thomas Church?
A. Well, when I was younger, yes, sir.
Q. And you say, knowing Maguire, did you know him well or just knew him because you recognized him in school?
A. Because I recognized him in school.
Q. Where you in the same class with Francis Maguire in school?
A. Yes, sir, in the lower grades.
Q. You were younger?
A. Yes, sir.
Q. You were early in grades?
A. Yes, sir.
Q. And what happened then when the man jumped out of the car and came over to you, as you continued to walk after they had hollered "hello"?[20]

James' questioning, however objectionable as leading, was effective in establishing she knew Maguire, and that Curran "jumped out of the car," and that she "continued to walk after they [sic] had hollered 'hello.'" Clearly, James wanted the young woman walking on Fourth and not standing in the doorway of Skinner's store and so he placed her walking up and down Fourth even if he had to lead her by his questions as he did and thus testify himself.

In response to James' second query, "what happened" when the man got out of the car and came over to her, she confirmed her willingness to walk with Bud Curran toward Fifth, a direction away from her home:

A. Well, they [sic] asked me if I had a match, and I said, "No." I didn't smoke, and then he asked me my name and where I lived, and I told him, and he asked how about letting him walk me home, and so I didn't see any harm in that, and I told him I didn't know him well enough, and so then I thought it over and he said, "Well, I have seen you at St. Thomas' Church," and being that I recognized this Maguire, I thought it would be all right, I trusted him.[21]

James' continued questioning about seemingly innocuous matters was egregiously objectionable but still the defense lawyers made no objection:

Q. Did this man then ask you if you went . . . to St. Thomas' Church? [OBJECTIONABLE AS A LEADING QUESTION.]

A. He said he had seen me at St. Thomas' Church.

Q. And what was your reply to that?

A. I said, yes, I did.

Q. You said that you trusted him? [OBJECTIONABLE AS A LEADING QUESTION.]

A. Yes.

Q. You didn't know who he was? [OBJECTIONABLE AS A LEADING QUESTION.]

A. No.

Q. You didn't even know his name, then, did you? [OBJECTIONABLE AS A LEADING QUESTION.]

A. No, I didn't.

Q. But you did know Maguire? [OBJECTIONABLE AS A LEADING QUESTION.]

A. Yes, sir.

Q. And what did you think about Maguire when you saw him in school or recognized him when he came up, what kind of a boy did you think he was?

A. I thought he was a nice boy. He seemed like a nice boy to me.

Q. He did?

A. Yes, sir.

Q. And then did you agree to let this man walk you home? [OBJECTIONABLE AS A LEADING QUESTION.]

A. Yes. Being that he was a friend of Maguire's, I trusted him, and so I walked up Bancroft Parkway with him.[22]

As she walked with Curran along Bancroft Parkway toward Fifth, she claimed: "He said that—he told me these other two boys had been to a party and they were going home, and he told me he was a graduate of Sallies."[23] Thus for the second time at trial the young woman restricted the number of boys present to three. In explaining why she walked off with Curran, she emphasized she knew Maguire from high school, "recognized" him in the car, and "thought he was a nice boy."[24] Prompted by yet another leading question, she said she believed Curran was walking her to his home where he would get a match and call a taxi to take her home.[25]

James had a penchant for asking leading questions at critical times:

Q. What if anything did he say to you when he threw you down onto the ground and you were resisting intercourse? [OBJECTIONABLE AS A LEADING QUESTION.]
A. He says, "what kind of woman are you that you don't want this?" And I kept fighting him off, and that is when he really had relations with me.
Q. Did he take your pants off then? [OBJECTIONABLE AS A LEADING QUESTION.]
A. I don't know. At that time he tried to. I don't know when he pulled my pants off.
Q. You don't know when he pulled them off?
A. No. I was struggling.
Q. They were off when he was having relations with you, though, the pants off? [OBJECTIONABLE AS A LEADING QUESTION.]
A. Yes.
Q. Now did Curran throw you down on the ground with force? [OBJECTIONABLE AS A LEADING QUESTION.]
A. Yes.[26]

Young finally objected but it was too late. The damage was already done since she had already answered the question:

MR. YOUNG: Just a moment. Just a moment. I have let it go on, and so have my colleagues, because we have as much regard for every witness in this case as does the State Attorney-General, but when it comes to leading questions of this kind, where the defendants are all tried for their lives, and we permit [it] to go on, we must object to it. Did he use force? And that sort of thing; throw you down; that is for the jury to determine when this case is over.

RICHARDS, C.J.: Mr. Attorney-General I think that is very leading, and we feel you should be very careful with a witness of this kind in this kind of a case.

MR. JAMES: I withdraw the question, sir.[27]

Moreover, throughout his questioning, in addition to asking leading questions, James had the irritating habit of repeating the witness's answer to the previous question before asking his next question. The young woman's answers about what clothes she left in the park illustrates both points:

Q. Now did you leave any clothes in the park when you came out? [OBJECTIONABLE AS A LEADING QUESTION.]
A. My pants I left; my pants I had left there; there was a sanitary belt I had on.
Q. Anything else?
A. And pads.
Q. What are pads?
A. Well, you wear them inside your shoes in place of stockings.
Q Well now, with respect to the sanitary belt, do I understand you say that the sanitary belt was not on you when you walked off out of the park? [REPEATING THE ANSWER AND OBJECTIONABLE AS A LEADING QUESTION.]
A. No.
Q. And your pants were not on? [REPEATING THE ANSWER AND OB-JECTIONABLE AS A LEADING QUESTION.]
A. No, they were not on me.
Q. Your pads were not on you? [REPEATING THE ANSWER AND OBJEC-TIONABLE AS A LEADING QUESTION.]
A. No. [28]

Exasperated by James' repetition of her answers and his continued use of leading questions, Young interrupted:

MR. YOUNG: Just a minute. It is very hard to determine whether you
are testifying or [the young woman].
MR. JAMES: I am repeating what she is testifying.
MR. YOUNG: I can hear her, and when I can't I will make an objec-
tion.
MR. JAMES: All right.[29]

As she had at the preliminary hearing, she again claimed that
first Curran, then Maguire, and finally Jones assaulted and attacked her in Woodlawn Park on the morning of October 30,
1947, penetrating her vagina despite her struggle.[30] For the first
time in court she further asserted that when Curran was having
relations with her, Maguire "came in front of me and straddled
some way, and . . . finally forced his person in my mouth."[31]
When Maguire subsequently testified on the sixth day of the
trial, he vigorously denied the charge.[32] She further testified she
wore a sanitary belt under the panties as she expected her period.
She said she menstruated two days afterward.[33] Before concluding her direct testimony, at James' direction, she identified Curran, Jones, and Maguire as her assailants.[34]

Cross-examining the young woman presented a delicate problem for the defense. If the examination were harsh, the defense
attorneys ran the risk of alienating the jury. Apparently by agreement, Hy Young, the most experienced among them, assumed
the responsibility. His task was to attack the young woman's
credibility so as to cause the jurors to believe what the defendants and the other defense witnesses would testify. Young was
not without evidence to demonstrate that the prosecuting witness was less than truthful. He had available to him what his client, Sonny Jones, had told him. He had the transcript of the
preliminary hearing with its contradictions to what she had testified in her direct testimony. He knew from his interviews with
the three eyewitnesses that their testimony would contradict the

young woman about where she was standing. And he had the hospital report with its critical comment, "Vaginal smear, no semen."

When he rose to examine the young woman, however, Young did not have the most important weapons he needed to effectively cross-examine her: the statement she gave to Sergeant Emering on October 30, 1947, and the statements the police had taken from the three defendants. In 1947 the state had no obligation to make copies available to them. A defendant was not even entitled to see a statement he gave to the police unless the state offered it in evidence at trial. At the time the prosecution called the young woman as its first witness on February 10, 1948, the state had not offered any of the defendants' statements in evidence. Not until the Criminal Rules of the Superior Court became effective on February 12, 1953, did a defendant have the right to secure a copy of any statement he had given to the authorities prior to trial and then only if the state offered it in evidence.[35]

Along with the defendants' statements, the woman's statement was part of the police file available and accessible to the attorney general's office and thus known to James and Duffy. I now believe they deliberately did not introduce her statement at trial. Unlike her testimony that she recognized Maguire in the car when it first stopped, her statement is silent. Unlike her testimony that there were only three men in the car, her statement is silent. Unlike her testimony that she had waited about "ten minutes" before the car stopped, her statement said "about 2 minutes." Unlike her testimony that she was walking up and down Fourth between Union and Bancroft Parkway while waiting, her statement said: "At about 12:15 A.M. this date I was standing on the corner of 4th and Bancroft Parkway. . . ." If Young had had her statement he could, and undoubtedly would, have examined her on the inconsistencies between her testimony and her state-

ment, an examination that would have seriously undermined her
credibility.

Withholding the young woman's statement from the defense,
the jurors, and the court was in keeping with the prosecution's
goal of securing a conviction without a recommendation of
mercy. But assuredly the withholding conflicted with the inter-
ests of fairness and justice which should mark a trial where the
lives and freedom of the defendants are at stake. In 1948 trial by
ambush was the accepted procedure.

The defendants and their attorneys did not learn the woman
had given a statement until the third day of trial. With Rodenheiser on the stand, Duffy asked him about the 7:00 A.M. line-
up and what took place after the woman identified the three defendants:

Q. What was then done by you?
A. [The woman] was brought into the turnkey's office and with the
    three defendants, Patrolmen Mazewski, Nagle, Delloso, and Ser-
    geant Emering there present, and I read the statements of the de-
    fendants.
Q. The statement of each of these defendants was read in the presence
    of all three defendants?
A. That is right.
Q. And was [the woman's] statement read, also?
A. It was.
Q. And in the presence of these three defendants?
A. It was.
Q. Was any statement made by either of the defendants or any denial
    made by either of them?

MR. YOUNG: I object. Are we going to have that statement of [the
woman's]?
MR. REINHARDT: I would like to have the statement of [the woman's], if it was in writing.

Q. Was any exception taken by Jones or Maguire to the statement of Curran?

RICHARDS, C. J.: (Interrupting) Just a minute.

MR. REINHARDT: It has already been offered in evidence in this case. It is immaterial.

MR. DUFFY: If the Court please, it is done all the time. Where you have more than one defendant and separate statements are made, it is important to show that the defendants are brought together and the statements are read, to give them an opportunity to voice any protest or make any disagreement, if they have any, and that wasn't done.

MR. REINHARDT: And who was there to warn the defendants of their rights and their legal duty?

MR. DUFFY: There was nobody here to warn them.

MR. REINHARDT: Let us try to be fair about the case.

RICHARDS, C. J.: That is an improper remark, Mr. Reinhardt. We don't think that you should make a remark like that.

MR. REINHARDT: I apologize to the Court.

RICHARDS, C. J.: I assume that that was preceded by a statement that was read to them.

MR. DUFFY: In their presence.

RICHARDS, C. J.: In their presence, yes.

MR. DUFFY: Yes, sir. That testimony is already in.

RICHARDS, C. J.: We overrule the objection.

Q. Will you answer the question.
    (Exception noted for all defendants.)
A. There was no exception taken by any of the defendants after the reading of the statements.[36]

From the foregoing it is clear the defendants and their attorneys would have been entitled to see the woman's statement and cross-examine her about it on recalling her as a witness for the precise reason Duffy urged upon the court to overrule Young's objection. But Duffy ignored Young's and Reinhardt's request for the woman's statement and Young and Reinhardt did not pursue it. Perhaps they thought the court ruling precluded a request for it. The failure to secure the statement was a body blow to the defense.

Apart from their entitlement to see the young woman's statement based upon its having been read at the October 30, 1947 line-up, the defendants and their lawyers could not have compelled the state to produce it since they had no way of proving there were any inconsistencies between what she told Sergeant Emering on October 30, 1947, and what she testified at the preliminary hearing on November 12, 1947, and what she said at the trial which would have entitled them to demand production.

What Young had to overcome in his cross-examination was the woman's testimony that there were only three people, the three defendants, in Maguire's car. If he did not rebut her testimony, the jurors would not believe the critical testimony of the three eyewitnesses yet to be heard. From Jones and the other defendants and the interviews of Fahey, Masten, and Schueler, Young and the other defense lawyers knew that the eyewitnesses were there and would testify about what they saw and heard.

Young's cross-examination of the prosecuting witness was almost three times as long as James' direct examination.[37] He began in a direct but deferential manner. He elicited the name *Variety Girl* as the movie she and her friend had seen but not what the movie was about. He drew from her the name of the girlfriend who accompanied her to the movie and then to the Eagle Restaurant, but neither the state nor the defendants ever called the girlfriend to testify. Young had her confirm she drank two bottles of beer during the one hour she and her girlfriend were at the Eagle.[38] At this point Chief Justice Richards interrupted:

RICHARDS, C.J.: Are we to understand—is the jury to understand that this witness had two bottles of beer or that the witness and her friend had two bottles of beer?

MR. DUFFY: I think that the testimony was that she had two bottles of beer.

RICHARDS, C.J.: That is what I understand.[39]

Duffy's comment was a violation of Delaware's practice that when one lawyer examines a witness, as James had of the young woman, no lawyer on the same side is permitted to participate in any further examination of that witness. Young did not object to Duffy's participation, perhaps because what Duffy said again confirmed that the young woman within one hour "had two bottles of beer."

Young then asked the young woman to retell how she took a 4–1 trolley after waiting at Eighth and Market where she could have waited a few minutes more for a 4 bus which would have taken her directly home. She explained: "I thought that, beings [sic] it was nearer to my home, I was afraid to stand there in town. I thought I would get to my home quicker." Young then asked: "Is it fair to say than that the reason you did not want to wait around Eighth and Market is because you were afraid to stand there alone?"[40]

Young's question elicited an objection, not by James but rather by Duffy, again a violation of Delaware practice.

MR. DUFFY: If the Court please, I think that is restrictive of what she said. She did say she was afraid; she also said that the 4's didn't run so often at that hour during the week. She also said she thought she could get home quicker by going to Fourth and Union, because she had the gas bus and the 4 bus.[41]

Without waiting for any argument from Young, Chief Justice Richards ruled: "We don't think the present question is proper. Objection sustained." The ruling is questionable since Young asked his question on cross-examination where fairly large latitude is given to an examiner. But within a page in the transcript

the astute Young elicited the answer he wanted: "Q. Did I understand you to say that you were afraid to wait at Eighth and Market? A. Yes, I was afraid."[42]

Step by step Young tried to establish with the witness that
Eighth and Market was well lighted compared to Fourth and
Union:

Q. Was it bright at Eighth and Market Street?
A. No, it was dark.
Q. It was dark?
A. At that hour.
Q. At that hour. And that was about what time?
A. About twenty minutes of twelve, I think.
Q. Now when you got off at Fourth and Union was it light or dark
    on the corner there?
A. Well, it was light there.
Q. It was light?
A. There were lights around—
Q. Were any of the stores open?
A. —on the street
Q. Were any of the stores open?
A. There were street lights down there. I did not notice whether any
    stores were open but it was light there. It was a bright moonlight
    night.
Q. It was a bright moonlight night, yes. Was the drug store open or
    closed on the northwest corner of Fourth and Union?
A. Closed.[43]

Young tracked with her the fact that after she alighted from the
bus, she crossed Fourth to the drug store. In answer to Young's
further questions, she repeated her earlier direct testimony about
walking up and down the short block between Union Street and
Bancroft Parkway, "[n]ot right away, but after awhile."[44]

He then turned to her testimony: "I noticed three boys and I
noticed Maguire."[45] What Young wanted was for her to admit

the presence of Fahey, Masten, and Schueler. In the process, he drew from her that, although she claimed to recognize Maguire, she had not seen him for "three or four years." Her answer to his question about when she had last spoken to Maguire was: "I don't know. I don't remember. I recognized him." By his follow-up questions Young further elicited from her that Maguire did not say anything to her nor did she to him. Neither acknowledged the other when she said she recognized him.[46]

In the face of her insistence that she saw only Curran, Jones, and Maguire in the car, Young countered by calling first Fahey and then Schueler, both in the courtroom, to stand up, and asking the young woman in each instance: "Did you recognize him in the car?" Each time the young woman answered: "No, I didn't."[47]

In order to avoid responding to many of Young's questions on cross-examination, she frequently answered, "I don't remember" about several important issues:

Q. Isn't it a fact that it was an officer who said to you, "Do you wish to press any charges"?
A. I don't remember.
Q. Now . . . you don't remember anything you said to the officers, you don't remember anything that the officers said to you, but you distinctly remember, in answer to Mr. James, that Jones said to you, "Don't press the charges"?
A. Yes.
Q. You do remember that?
A. Yes.
Q. That is the one thing in your hysteria that you do remember, is that correct?
A. Yes, sir.[48]

Her alternatives to "I don't remember" were her responses "I must have misunderstood you," "I was mistaken," or "I was hysterical." Each frustrated Young. Neither in her statement to the

police nor in her direct testimony did she claim she was hysterical. When he tried to confront the young woman with the contrasts between her trial testimony and her prior testimony in
Municipal Court, she showed herself to be well-prepared. Beside
the issue of where she was standing at Fourth and Bancroft Parkway, there was also the issue of how dark it was:

Q. Yesterday . . . I asked you whether it was quite dark at Fourth and
     Bancroft Parkway and your reply was "No." Do you recall that?
A. Yes.
Q. Did you not say, in answer to my question propounded to you on
     November 12, 1947, in the Municipal Court where you testified at
     page 27, you walked up Fourth and Bancroft. "It was quite dark
     there, wasn't it?" Answer, "Yes."
     Did you say that?
A. I must have misunderstood you.
Q. My question . . . is, did you say that?
A. Well, if I said that, I was mistaken.
Q. My question is did you say that? I have been patient with you and
     considerate. That is a simple question and a simple answer.
     Can you explain it any way to us?
A. Yes.
Q. Did you say that?
A. Yes.
Q. Why did you say that?
A. I must have misunderstood you.[49]

About her knowledge of the neighborhood, there was a flat-
out contradiction between her testimony at trial and her testimony at the pretrial hearing:

Q. Did you ever live near that neighborhood?
A. No.
Q. You went to Church how far away from that playground in the
     park, or went to school; how far away from that park?
A. What was that?

Q. Did you go to school near that neighborhood?
A. Yes.
Q. What was that answer?
A. Yes.
Q. How long did you go to that school?
A. How long did I go to school?
Q. Yes.
A. Eight years.
Q. I refer to page 33 of the record of testimony, in the Municipal Court, on November 12, 1947. You were asked:
    "Do you know that neighborhood; don't you?"
    "Answer: Yes."
Q. Did you not also answer this: "You have lived near that neighborhood all your life, is that correct?"
    "Answer: Yes."
    "Question: You went to school only two blocks away from that playground or park, isn't that right?
    "Answer: Yes.
    "Question: Is that right?
    "Answer: Yes."
Q. Did you so testify?
A. Yes.[50]

Whether the young woman was coached on how to answer at trial by James and Duffy or whether she came upon the techniques on her own, I cannot say with absolute conviction. But having studied the young woman's statement to the police, her testimony at the preliminary hearing and at the trial, I can only conclude her ability to thwart Young in his cross-examination was remarkable. She fell back on responses "I didn't understand" and "I was hysterical" and "I don't remember" so many times that it strains credulity to believe she came up with these responses on her own. Young's cross-examination on the first day of trial further illustrates the problem she gave him:

Q. Did Jones have his arms around you while he was walking out of the park with you?

A. I don't remember that.

Q. You wouldn't say that he did not?

A. I don't remember, because I was exhausted by that time.

Q. Did you have your arms around him?

A. I don't remember that.

Q. Do you recall when you got out of the park—by the way, was he taking you home?

A. No, he was—I was going with him, I was heading for home; but when I found out that they were the cops, I wasn't scared then. I wasn't as scared.

Q. When you saw the cops did you run away from Jones?

A. No.

Q. Did you say, "Jones, there's one of the boys that attacked me"?

A. No I didn't.

Q. In fact, weren't you asked whether there was any family trouble between you and Jones?

A. No, I wasn't asked that. I was asked was there any trouble, what was the trouble, but I don't remember anything else.

Q. Didn't you say, "No, no trouble"?

A. I don't remember.

Q. Then wasn't it after the officers separated you from Jones that you then said that the boys attacked you?

A. What was that? I didn't understand.

Q. Wasn't it only after you were separated from Jones by the police officers that you then stated to the officer or officers that three boys had attacked you?

A. I still don't understand that, I am sorry.

Q. I will withdraw that and try to get that in simpler language, if I can. Maybe I'm at fault.
    . . . When Jones was about to have sexual relations with you, didn't you say to him "Will you take me home when you are through"?

A. I don't remember. No, I never said that.

Q. Now, instead of "I don't remember", you would definitely know whether you said that or not, wouldn't you?

A. No, I don't remember.[51]

Young also tried to establish where she was standing when Curran got out of the car and talked to her and she decided to accept his invitation to walk her home. A Latin expression well known to lawyers, falsus in uno, falsus in omnibus (false in one thing, false in everything), would definitely have been on the minds of Young, Reinhardt, and Hagner and their opponents, James and Duffy. If a lawyer could demonstrate that one or more of the defendants or the young woman was not telling the truth, even on a minor point, he could argue the errant defendant or the chief prosecution witness, the young woman, should not be believed in all of the other matters to which he or she testified. The fact of where the young woman was standing when Bud Curran first spotted her was such a point of conflicting testimony.

In her direct testimony the young woman claimed, in response to James' leading questions, that she was walking "up and down Fourth Street . . . between Union . . . and Bancroft Parkway" when the car carrying Curran came out Fourth.[52] Adopting James' word in his leading question, she said she walked "almost" to Bancroft Parkway. Thus if the woman's testimony were truthful, she was not standing in Skinner's doorway.

Mindful of the importance of where she stood when Maguire stopped his car, Young asked:

Q. Could you tell us where the car stopped when you first saw him?
A. It stopped right along Bancroft Parkway—on Fourth Street.
Q. Was it on the other side of Bancroft Parkway or was it right near Skinner's store?
A. Near that side, near that store.
Q. Near Skinner's store?
A. Yes.
Q. At the time that you saw the car were you standing in the doorway of Skinner's store?
A. No.
Q. Where you anywheres [sic] near the door of Skinner's store?
A. No.[53]

A few questions later, Young, apparently trying to catch the young woman in a lie, asked her: "Did you have to turn around the corner in order to get to Bancroft Parkway?" She answered "Yes," meaning she was claiming she was on Fourth and not on Bancroft Parkway in Skinner's doorway when she talked with Curran before walking north with him on Bancroft Parkway toward Fifth.[54] Initially Young ignored the young woman's affirmative answer to his question. He never questioned her about her failure in her direct testimony to say anything about turning "around the corner" to walk north on Bancroft Parkway with Bud Curran.[55]

Young did return to the issue whether the young woman was standing in Skinner's doorway toward the end of his continued examination of her on the second day of the trial. He confronted her with the difference between her testimony at the preliminary hearing in the Municipal Court with her claim at trial that she was about a quarter of the way down Fourth from Bancroft Parkway when Curran got out of the car and started talking to her:

Q. Did you not say in answer to my questions, page 31 of the record, in the Municipal Court, at a hearing in this case, "Where did you finally—where did you talk with Curran when he got out of the car?

　"Answer: He was there at Bancroft Parkway.
　"Question: What corner?
　"Answer: A little ways down.
　"Question: A little ways from the corner? North or south?
　"Answer: North."

Did you not so testify? What?

A. Yes.

Q. And north of Bancroft Parkway would have been in front of Skinner's closed grocery store, isn't that correct?

A. Is that north?

Q. Did you understand north and south when we were in City Court . . . ?

A. Yes.

Q. I won't press it further.[56]

In reading her answer to his question in the Municipal Court about where she and Curran talked, Young omitted one key word, "right." Her complete answer was: "He was *right there* at Bancroft Parkway." [Emphasis added.] It would have helped his case if Young had established on the record precisely where "right there" was.

By his questions and her answers, it is obvious Young thought he had established from the young woman that she was standing in the doorway of Skinner's store when Curran first saw her and they talked. Young's decision not to "press it further" had to reflect his unwillingness to have the witness return to her earlier denials of standing in the doorway. He knew that the testimony of the three defendants and two of the three eyewitnesses—yet to come—would place the woman in the Skinner doorway. Under oath, Curran said that when he first saw the "woman" she was "in front of the doorway . . . not on the step, but right in front of the step," confirming what he had told Sergeant Emering on October 30, 1947.[57] Fahey said he also saw Curran talking to her when she was standing "in the doorway" of Skinner's store. From where she was standing, Fahey testified: "[s]he could never see Union Street."[58] Masten's testimony was that after Curran got out of the car he saw "a young lady standing in the doorway [of Skinner's store]." He too said she could not see buses at Fourth and Union from where she was standing.[59] Jones also placed her in the doorway, as did Maguire.[60] Schueler, who sat in the rear on the left side, did not see any woman walking on Fourth and did not pay attention when Curran got out of the car until he noticed Curran and the girl: Curran's "arm was around her and her arm was around him" as they walked north on East Bancroft Parkway toward Fifth.[61]

But if she were walking back and forth between Fourth and East Bancroft Parkway and Fourth and Union, the headlights of Maguire's car would have picked her up and she would have been seen by all the occupants in Maguire's car as he drove west on Fourth across Union and then stopped at the west side of Bancroft Parkway at Curran's command.

Thus the trial went forward with the issues of where the young woman was standing and for how long to be determined by the jurors on the basis of whose testimony they would believe. But they would do so without the benefit of the young woman's statement. Without her statement to the police, Young did not have the facts he needed to successfully confront the woman about precisely where she was standing at Fourth and Bancroft Parkway and the amount of time she was there before Maguire drove up and, indeed, if she had been walking up and down Fourth as she claimed.

In concluding his examination, Young, abandoned his earlier approach and attacked the woman, starting with her claim that she "struggled all the time":

Q. Did you say . . . that you struggled all the time?
A. Yes, I did.
Q. Tried to get away?
A. Yes.
Q. Tried to resist each and all of these three boys?
A. Yes, whenever I had a chance; yes.
Q. Did you scratch any of them?
A. I kept pushing them away with my hand.
Q. . . . did you scratch any of them?
A. I did not notice it. No, I didn't.
Q. Did you bite any of them?
A. No.
Q. Did you pull the hair of any of them?
A. No.
Q. Did you kick any one in his groin?

A. I was kicking all the time.

Q. Did you kick any one of them in his groin?

A. No.

Q. Were any of the shirts of any of these boys torn?

A. I did not know.

Q. What?

A. I don't know.[62]

Young then aggressively examined the young woman:

Q. Isn't it true that when you went into the park you knew what Curran wanted?

A. No, I didn't.

Q. You also knew what you wanted?

A. No, I didn't.

Q. Isn't it true that you willingly and voluntarily submitted to sexual intercourse with each of these three boys?

A. I did not.

Q. Isn't it also true that you did not have any sexual relations with Jones at all?

A. No, that isn't true.

Q. And isn't it true that because you voluntarily and willingly submitted to sexual relations with these three boys that when the police came on the scene in order to defend your honor you said you were attacked?

A. No.

Q. And isn't it true that in order to explain this matter to your mother and to your family and to the entire State of Delaware when you came out of the park walking arm in arm with Jones that to cover your shame you said you were attacked?

A. No.[63]

With that answer, Young ended his examination. James said he had two questions to ask but he did not want to do so unless Young's cross-examination of the young woman spoke for all three counsel. Thereupon Hagner asked for a brief recess. After the recess it became abundantly clear that Reinhardt and Hagner had agreed to look to Young to lead the defense. Reinhardt told the court, ". . . so far as I am concerned, I have no questions to ask. . . . I think that Mr. Young has covered the situation very thoroughly." Hagner concurred: "I feel the same way that Mr. Reinhardt does. I feel that the examination has covered all of the points which I could bring out, and I have no questions."[64] Their judgment confirmed the community's assessment that Young was Delaware's best criminal defense attorney.

James then asked his questions correcting two errors he had made in his direct examination of the young woman when he had referred to the "night" of October 30 instead of the "morning" and called the park "Woodland" instead of "Woodlawn."[65]

Absent from Young's cross-examination and unasked by Reinhardt and Hagner was any question about the young woman's having given a statement to the police. Three police officers were involved in the taking and witnessing of her statement. Two of them, Sergeant Emering and Patrolman Nagle, testified at the trial; the third officer, Patrolman Delloso, did not. Neither the young woman nor the two officers made any reference to her statement when they testified. The trial went forward with the defense handicapped.

With the young woman still holding to her claim there were only "those three boys," Young knew he had not succeeded in his effort to destroy her credibility.[66] He also knew he still had to convince the jurors that Fahey, Masten, and Schueler had been present. Thus, the defendants and their lawyers would have to rely upon the three eyewitnesses to refute the prosecution witness and support the defendants' version of the facts and their claim of innocence.

As the trial continued, the defendants and their lawyers were not yet aware they faced as great, if not a greater problem than whether or not the jurors would believe the three eyewitnesses.

The police officers' testimony about the number of statements the defendants signed and when they did so was still unheard, unanticipated, and ahead of them.

The Police Commit Perjury

The three young men had not expected to be arrested. Sonny Jones had remained with the woman in Woodlawn Park to help her find and gather up her shoes and other articles and help her put on her shoes and coat.[67] He said she requested he walk her out of the park and toward her home in Colonial Heights.[68] Jones' behavior—staying with the alleged rape victim, assisting her, and then accompanying her toward her home—was at odds with that of an alleged rapist. Certainly he did not expect to be arrested. Nor did Bud Curran and Reds Maguire, who were in bed when the police arrived at their homes a few hours after they left the park.[69] From the time the police took them into custody until they first signed their individual statements, the record does not reflect that the three young men were ever together. Thus they were unable to discuss among themselves what they would or should say.

Late in the afternoon on the second day of the trial, after the testimony of the prosecuting witness was over, the state moved to introduce the first statement ascribed to Bud Curran. According to its first paragraph, Curran had made it to "Sergeant Emering and Patrolmen Nagle and Delloso on October 30, 1947." Under Attorney General James' questioning, Patrolman Nagle testified Curran "freely and voluntarily" gave a statement and signed the paper that morning "in the absence of threats or promises." Three times he swore he, Emering, and Delloso were present when Curran signed. Nagle asserted and the paper showed he and Delloso signed as witnesses. Although there was a place for Sergeant Emering to sign, that line was blank. Apart from Nagle's admitting he did "talk with Francis J. Curran at the police station on the morning of October 30, 1947," neither the paper nor Nagle's brief testimony provided the exact time of signing. Twice Nagle said he personally "typed" or "recorded" the Curran paper in Curran's presence.[70]

After the prosecution offered the Curran paper as State's Exhibit No. 10, claiming it was Curran's statement signed the morning of October 30, 1947, Hagner, Young, and Reinhardt read it for the first time. Young spoke first, telling the court: "In so far as the defendant Jones is concerned, there is no objection whatever to the admission of this statement of Curran's." Reinhardt followed Young's lead, using almost the exact words: "In so far as the defendant Maguire is concerned, there is no objection to the statement and no questions." When the Chief Justice called upon Hagner to respond, the record reflects: "RICHARDS, C.J.: Mr. Hagner? Oh, Mr. Hagner is reading it." Hagner, finally responding, also followed suit even adopting some of Young's words: "I have no objection whatever, your Honor please, to the admission of this statement." Thereupon Richards ruled: "The statement is admitted without objection."[71] At that point Attorney General James read the Curran paper to the jury, prefacing his reading with the following words to drive home the significance of State's Exhibit No. 10: "With deference to the Court, and ladies and gentlemen, I am reading to you now a statement signed by Francis Curran on October 30, 1947, and which has been admitted in evidence as State's Exhibit No. 10."[72] During direct examination Nagle neither was asked nor did he volunteer about having typed a second statement on October 30 and Curran's signing it that afternoon.

After reading the Curran paper, James ended his examination of Nagle with the traditional invitation to the opposition: "Cross-examine." Hagner responded: "No questions." Reinhardt and Young were silent.[73] Thus neither Hagner nor Young nor Reinhardt cross-examined Nagle about the exact time Curran signed, the voluntary nature of the Curran paper, the number of papers/statements Curran had signed, or the fact the paper lacked Emering's signature as a witness.[74] At the time State's Exhibit No. 10 came into evidence and Nagle's testimony concluded, Bud Curran and the other two defendants had yet to testify.

On the third day of trial, February 12, the state turned to the Jones paper, calling Detective Rodenhiser, who, with Officer Mazewski, had interrogated Jones.[75] Duffy's examination and Young's cross-examination of Rodenhiser differed markedly from the examination and the lack of any cross-examination of Nagle about Curran's statement.

Duffy's first substantive question was: "What if anything did [Jones] say to you as you started to question him?" Young reacted immediately: "I object. If it was reduced to writing, I think the statement could be introduced. As I understand it, this was the time."[76] In the ensuing colloquy before and with the court, and with the jury in the courtroom, Young and Duffy spelled out their disparate positions:

MR. YOUNG: If your Honors please, during the course of the examination by police officers of a defendant, all the statements that are made during either the course of an examination or a grueling examination when reduced to writing represents the statement he made, and then it is for the jury to believe or disbelieve any portion of that statement they wish to believe or disbelieve. But it is the statement, when it is finally reduced to writing, as a result of that examination, that is admissible.

If your Honors will grant me the opportunity, I believe we can show authorities that when a statement made by a defendant in connection with a case, particularly of so serious a consequence as in this case, is reduced to writing, the writing is the statement.[77]

In response to Richards' effort to clarify Duffy's position, Duffy explained himself:

RICHARDS, C.J.: . . . Now you want to show, as I understand it now, certain other statements which he made in the police station which are not in accordance with the written statement.
MR. DUFFY:That is correct. If the Court please, in the charge I am sure that you will charge the jury that signed statements are confessions if such they be, and submitted to them for such credit as they see fit to give to them, and they may ignore those things they think are not worthy of belief, and statements that are self-serving may be ignored by them, and admissions indicating guilt may be considered by them. *That being true, I think by the same token that is all for the purpose of enabling the jury to test the credibility of the defendant.* That being so, I think we should be permitted to show before this final statement was made, there were other conflicting statements as indicated. It is not so much to tell them actual facts immediately. [Emphasis added.][78]

For fifteen pages in the transcript Young and Duffy battled until the Chief Justice made a suggestion to which Duffy reluctantly agreed:

RICHARDS, C.J.:Don't you think it would be well to put the statement in?
MR. DUFFY:I beg your pardon?
RICHARDS, C.J.:Don't you think it would be well to put in the statement first, if you have one? It might eliminate this whole thing.
MR. DUFFY:It won't eliminate.
RICHARDS, C.J.:How do you know it won't? You can't say it won't.
MR. DUFFY:No, I can't; it is only my view. But I will be glad to offer it in evidence at this time, and that might help solve the problem.[79]

The entire colloquy took place with the jury in the courtroom. When Duffy spoke hypothetically of the state's right to show a defendant made "three different statements" and "that goes directly to his credibility," Young immediately said: "Of course, I object to that. And if the argument is going to carry on any further about his having made three different statements. . . ." Here the trial transcript does not refer to any sidebar conference with the court. Accordingly, the fair inference, especially from Young's comment, is that the jurors heard the lawyers as they argued. Young did not want Duffy to continue as he had within the jury's hearing.[80] The record reflects that Duffy promptly backed off:

MR. DUFFY: I wasn't applying that to this case.
MR. YOUNG: I am glad that you made that clear.
MR. DUFFY: I wasn't applying that to this case. I have no right to do that at this point.[81]

Significantly, Duffy twice argued that part of what he was attempting was to bring out from Detective Rodenhiser that Jones made contradictory statements that went to the issue of the credibility the jurors should give to Jones' testimony.[82]

With Rodenhiser still on the stand, Duffy, acting on Richards' suggestion, laid the basis to offer the Jones paper:

Q. I hand you a document and ask if you can identify that?
A. I can.
Q. What is it?
A. It is a statement of Ira F. Jones that I took on October 30 at 2:45 A. M. in the Detective Bureau in the presence of the defendant and Patrolman Mazewski.
Q. And is that the signature of Ira F. Jones?
A. It is.
Q. One of the defendants in this case?
A. It is.
Q. Did he sign that in your presence and in the presence of Patrolman Mazewski?
A. He did.
Q. Is that your signature?

A.   It is.
Q.   I ask if that statement were [*sic*] freely and voluntarily made by Ira
     F. Jones?
A.   It was.
Q.   Were any threats made to him or hope of reward held out?
A.   There were not.
MR. DUFFY: I offer it in evidence.[83]

Young asked to see the Jones paper and, not having seen it before, he read it. When he rose to cross-examine, Young had just learned from Rodenhiser's testimony for the first time that the police claimed his client had signed the statement offered in evidence "on October 30 at 2:45 A.M." From Jones, however, he knew that Jones signed two statements, one in the morning of October 30 and the second that afternoon. But Rodenhiser made no mention of the second one. From his questions, it is not clear whether Young knew if the offered document was the first or second paper Jones signed. But as his cross-examination shows, Young set out to prove that there was another statement. He told the court: "Your Honor, I will request a preliminary examination on the admissibility of this thing, which I understand has been the rule, to be without the presence of the jury."[84] Young's reference to the proffered statement as "this thing" showed his disdain. The Chief Justice granted permission and the jury retired.[85]

Young did not get far in cross-examining Detective Rodenhiser before Duffy objected to a question that was quite similar to the one Duffy had asked Rodenhiser and to which Young had objected:

Q.   What was the first thing that you said to Jones?
MR. DUFFY: If the Court please, I object as not being the proper question. The testimony here is, was the statement made freely and voluntarily without any threats.

MR. YOUNG: I am coming to that.
RICHARDS, C.J.:*Well, of course, that is the real purpose, as I understand, from this examination.*
MR. YOUNG:*That is right.*
RICHARDS, C.J.:I think you should get right to it. [Emphasis added.][86]

Duffy's objection and Young's comment, "That is right," were both based upon a ruling by the court a year earlier in a notorious murder case, *State v. Norris,* where the defendant had killed a city policeman. In *Norris* the court ruled that the objection to the introduction of a defendant's statement was restricted to whether it was freely and voluntarily given and without any threats. By his comment, however, Young conceded that he was confined by the *Norris* ruling, which did not include showing there were multiple statements. Four more times Young agreed he had to so confine his cross-examination.[87] But the ruling did not cause Young to abandon his effort to prove the existence of another statement, one different from the one the state had offered. Again and again Young attacked the police denial that Jones had signed more than one statement.[88] In further examining Detective Rodenhiser while the jury was out, Young specifically asked:

Q. Officer, I will ask you, was that the last statement that you secured from Jones and had him sign?
A. Yes.
Q. Do you know whether he signed another statement?
A. He did not.
Q. You say that as a fact under oath that he did not sign another statement?
A. I do.[89]

In response to Duffy's objection that Young was "going far afield on the voluntary character of the [offered] statement," Young argued, "If your Honor please, if I can show that later statement, which I am prepared to show, was obtained at four o'clock and signed, and the selection of this statement without that other statement, I am going to ask that it be ruled out."[90] This was the first time Hy Young asserted there was a later statement "obtained at four o'clock and signed." Young did not specify the date.

Before Young put Jones on the stand, Duffy called Officer Edward Mazewski. Under Duffy's brisk examination, Mazewski testified he was a member of Wilmington's Police Department and on October 30 he was assigned to the Detective Bureau from midnight to eight to work with Detective Rodenhiser. Mazewski supported Detective Rodenhiser about the proffered Jones paper. After Mazewski testified that Jones freely and voluntarily made the statement, Duffy concluded his examination.[91]

In his cross-examination of Mazewski, Young was no more successful than he had been with Rodenhiser. Again he attempted to establish that the offered Jones paper was not what the state claimed it was, prefacing his final question before he asked it:

MR. YOUNG: Your Honor, I do want to ask this question, although your Honor has asked me to limit it as to this particular point. I think it is important as to whether this was the one and only or the last statement that was made.
Q. Officer, do you know whether this is the only written statement taken of Jones?
MR. DUFFY: I object.
RICHARDS, C.J.: Just a minute. We sustain the objection at this time.
MR. YOUNG: May I have an exception?[92]

Reinhardt and Hagner, going along with Young's leadership of the defense, joined in Young's exception thus reserving the right to raise the issue on appeal.[93]

Having introduced all his testimony in support of his claim that the offered Jones paper "was freely and voluntarily made,"

Duffy rested. The court then permitted Young to introduce evidence to contradict Duffy's claim.[94] The only witness he called was Sonny Jones. Under Young's direct examination, Jones testified: Rodenhiser did not advise him of his constitutional rights when he was first questioned; he gave the names of Curran and Maguire only after Rodenhiser threatened him; about Schueler, Masten, and Fahey, the three eyewitnesses, Rodenhiser said, "We don't want to hear any thing about them. We are just interested in you." Young directed his final questions to Jones about multiple signings:

Q. Did he take your full and complete statement?
A. Yes, sir.
Q. At that time?
A. Yes.
Q. Do you know whether he had reduced it to writing?
A. No, I don't.
Q. Did you sign any other statement after that?
A. Yes, sir, I did.
Q. What time?
A. Four o'clock the next afternoon.
MR. YOUNG: That is all
THE WITNESS: Down in the cell block.[95]

In his brief cross-examination Duffy did not ask a single question about Jones' claim he signed a second statement on October 30, 1947, "Down in the cell block."[96]

Chief Justice Richards then ruled: "The statement is admitted into evidence, or will be when the jury come [sic] back." When Hagner said "Exception," Judge Carey said, "We can't admit it until the jury is in. You better take your exception then."[97]

When the jury returned to the courtroom, Duffy recalled Rodenhiser who repeated his testimony that the paper Duffy put before him was "a statement of Ira F. Jones, which I took on

October 30, [1947] at 2:45 A.M., in the Detective Bureau, with Patrolman Mazewski." The reference to "2:45 A.M." was the time he swore he started "to reduce [the statement] to writing." He said the signature was that of Jones and "that [it was] affixed to that paper in [his] presence and in the presence of Officer Mazewski." After he identified his own signature, he said Jones "made and signed [the statement] freely and voluntarily." He denied that "either [he] or Mazewski or anyone else [made threats] to induce Jones to sign that statement." Rodenhiser further denied that "any promises or hope of reward [were] held out by [him], through [him] or anyone else to induce [Jones] to sign this statement." With that Duffy said he would offer the statement after cross-examination.[98]

During Young's cross-examination, he tried to establish that the statement was Rodenhiser's rather than Jones': "Did you do [the statement] in narrative form or did you do it by putting questions and securing answers?" After the court overruled Duffy's objection, Rodenhiser answered: "Why, I asked the defendant a question and as he dictated his answer it was typed on the paper; the question was not typed." Rodenhiser admitted he did not advise Jones of his constitutional rights, but he denied threatening him.[99] Young again specifically questioned Rodenhiser about the Jones paper:

Q. Did you read any other statements to him?
A. We had none to read to him.
Q. Do you know whether he signed any other
    statement?
A. No. I did not-
MR. DUFFY: I object.
Q. Were you present when he signed a statement about four o'clock?
MR. DUFFY: I object.
RICHARDS, C.J.: Just a minute. You object to what, Mr. Duffy?
MR. DUFFY: The question was asked, "Do you know whether he

signed any other statements." And I object, I ask that the answer be stricken.

RICHARD, C.J.: We sustain the objection and order the answer stricken out.

BY MR. YOUNG:

Q. Were you present when he signed a statement at four o'clock in the morning?

A. Yes. He signed a statement in my presence.

Q. At four o'clock in the morning?

A. *That is when I finished his statement that's here before the Court now.* [Emphasis added.][100]

Given Rodenhiser's emphatic testimony, there is no doubt he was referring to the particular piece of paper the prosecution was offering as Jones' statement, State's Exhibit No. 11.

When Young again turned to whether Jones signed another statement, the record reflects Young's confusion about the date of the second signing and Rodenhiser's denial of Young's focused question and, as well, Young's persistence in his effort to prove there were multiple written statements:

Q. Did he sign another statement?

MR. DUFFY: I object.

Q. Between 2:15 and four o'clock?

MR. YOUNG: *If the Court please, I didn't know he had him until four o'clock. That is when we claim he signed another statement.*

MR. DUFFY: *That is the only statement I am offering.*

RICHARDS, C. J.: *We are only concerned with this particular statement.*

MR. YOUNG: I am naturally going to abide by your Honor's ruling.

TERRY, J.: It is at this time, Mr. Young.

RICHARDS, C.J.: We sustain the objection.

BY MR. YOUNG:

Q. Were you present when the defendant signed another statement the following day?

MR. DUFFY: I object.

RICHARDS, C.J.: That has been objected to, I think, on two occasions, Mr. Young.

MR. YOUNG:*If the Court please, it is a question of whether or not there were two statements.*

RICHARDS, C.J.: Yes. We sustain the objection. [Emphasis added.][101]

Duffy's comment, "That is the only statement I am offering," clearly emphasized the false police assertion that State's Exhibit No. 11 was signed by 4 a.m. on October 30. The exceptions Young and then Reinhardt ("to all three") took saved the defendants' objections for an appeal.

Duffy then called Mazewski to the stand. He supported Rodenhiser in all to which he had sworn. The most telling was Mazewski's unequivocal testimony about the Jones statement:

Q. And were you present with Detective Rodenhiser when Ira F. Jones was questioned?
A. I was.
Q. I hand you this paper and ask if you can identify it?
A. Statement given us by Ira Jones that morning.
Q. Morning of October 30?
A. The morning of October 30. Four o'clock it was completed.
Q. Is that the signature of Ira F. Jones?
A. It is.
Q. Was that paper signed by him on your presence and in the presence of Detective Rodenhiser?
A. It was.
Q. Is that your signature?
A. It is.[102]

Having completed the direct examination of Mazewski, Duffy reoffered the Jones paper in evidence. Young then briefly cross-examined Mazewski but did not ask him whether Jones signed another statement. On Duffy's offer of the Jones paper, Reinhardt objected because the document "mentions Maguire and

Curran, and they were not present at the time the statement was taken." Hagner joined in Reinhardt's objection. Young's objection was broader:

My objection, if the Court please, goes to the fact—in view of the preliminary hearing permitted by the Court on the question of law that it isn't a voluntary statement; *and, also, on the ground that there were questions put to the effect that there is a later statement, and there can't be a selection of one against the other.* [Emphasis added.][103]

Richards overruled the objections and admitted the Jones paper as State's Exhibit No. 11. Reinhardt sought an exception; Hagner chimed in "an exception for all of us." Duffy then read State's Exhibit No. 11 to the jury.[104]

I infer from Young's cross-examination that he did not realize the paper the prosecution offered and the court admitted as State's Exhibit No. 11 was the second statement Jones signed. Nor did Young know Rodenhiser had destroyed Jones' first statement.

The state next turned to the Maguire statement. Duffy called Rodenhiser to the stand, handed him the Maguire paper, and asked him if he could identify it:

A. I can.
Q. What is it?
A. It is the statement given me by Francis Maguire, in the presence of Patrolman Mazewski, at 4:10, A.M., on October 30, 1947.
Q. When you say 4:10, A.M., is that the time you started or the time you completed the statement?
A. The time I started.
Q. Is that the signature of Francis J. Maguire?
A. It is.
Q. Made in your presence?
A. It was.
Q. In the presence of Mazewski?

A. It was.

Q. Is that your signature (indicating)?

A. It is.

Q. Was that statement freely and voluntarily made by Francis J. Maguire?

A. It was.

Q. Were any threats made by you, Mazewski, or anyone else, to induce him to make that statement?

A. There were none.[105]

Duffy then offered the Maguire paper in evidence.[106]

Unlike the fight over admitting the Jones paper, Reinhardt neither questioned Rodenhiser about the time of signing nor did he make any attempt to show Maguire had signed twice. In fact, Reinhardt embellished his lack of objection by adding "and, as far as my client, Maguire, is concerned, I cannot see where this statement does any harm and I have no objection." Neither Young nor Hagner asked any questions or objected to the admission of the Maguire paper.[107] So the Chief Justice ruled: "The statement is admitted in evidence, without objection, we understand, gentlemen." After it was marked as State's Exhibit No. 12, Duffy read it to the jury.[108]

Rodenhiser then testified to the 7:00 a.m. line-up on the morning of October 30, 1947, of the three defendants and four other prisoners. The complainant identified the defendants. Rodenhiser then read "[t]he statement of each of these defendants . . . and [the woman's] statement in the presence of all three defendants" and the young woman. He swore that the defendants did not take any exception to what was read to them.[109]

Thus by the end of the morning session on the third day, the state had secured the admission into evidence of the three papers the police asserted were the statements Curran, Jones, and Maguire made and signed "freely and voluntarily" and "without any threat or promise of reward" on the morning of October 30,

1947. Of the five police officers who were present at the interrogations of the three defendants (Detective Rodenhiser and Officer Mazewski for Jones and Maguire; Sergeant Emering and Officers Nagle and Delloso for Curran), James and Duffy only called Rodenhiser, Mazewski, and Nagle to testify in moving the admission of State's Exhibits Nos. 10, 11, and 12. The testifying policemen each said the documents offered in evidence were the statements the defendants made and signed early in the morning on October 30, 1947, prior to 5:00 a.m. The police did not admit to or testify about a second signing. About the other two police officers whose names appear as witnesses on the Curran paper, Sergeant Emering's signature was missing, and Delloso was not called as a witness.

During the course of the defendants' case, each man testified and swore he signed two statements: the first signing by 5:00 a.m. on October 30 and the second around 4:00 p.m. the same afternoon without reading the second statement.[110] When Curran testified in the afternoon on Saturday, February 14, 1948, he was the last witness on the fifth day of trial.[111] In cross-examination Curran swore for the first time he had signed two statements.[112] Maguire testified as the first witness on the sixth day of trial, Monday, February 16, following the Sunday recess.[113] Both on direct and again during cross-examination Maguire swore he, too, had signed two statements, mistakenly placing the second signing on the afternoon of "the following day."[114]

With the completion of Maguire's cross-examination, instead of putting Jones on the stand as the next witness, Young called Detective Rodenhiser:

Q. I hand you State's Exhibit No. 11. Is that the statement that you took from Ira Jones?

A. It is.

Q. At what time?

A. At 2:45 A.M., starting at 2:45 A.M.
Q. Did you type it yourself?
A. I did.
Q. How long have you been typing?
A. Oh, about five years, I guess.
Q. Are you what we know as the one-finger artist? I mean do you
    type—
A. Partially; in between.
Q. I want you to look at that statement and see how many mistakes
    you have there.
    Mr. Duffy:If the Court please—
Q. Or erasures.[115]

At that point Duffy objected arguing "The statement is in evidence; it speaks for itself." Duffy added "mistakes in typing are [not] material to this case."[116] But Young's intent in calling Rodenhiser to the stand before Jones was to show, as Young told the court, "there isn't a single mistake outside of a little crossing out of one name," and therefore it is impossible for Rodenhiser to have typed Jones' statement as he claimed.[117]

Duffy's objections and comments from the judges frustrated Young to the point he finally said "I want to get on with the trial and I want to proceed as quickly as possible. I will withdraw this witness. . . ." Judge Terry then said, "Don't be in that much of a hurry on account of the Court." Young's response with the jury listening was: "I don't think it is of too great significance. Nevertheless, I don't want to leave anything unturned that should have been accomplished in the course of the defense."[118] The reason he said the number of statements was not of "too great significance" was this experienced trial lawyer's way of trying to tell the jury to ignore the fact he had failed to expose the police perjury. If, however, the jurors took him at his word, he ran the risk of making the situation not only worse for Jones but for all the defendants. If multiple statements were not of "too great significance" to the lead defense lawyer, why should the jurors believe otherwise and conclude the police were not telling the truth? Young most certainly knew the issue was of "great significance" since he returned to attack it, again unsuccessfully, when the prosecution on rebuttal recalled Rodenhiser as its last witness.[119]

The state certainly realized the significance of the disparity between the police officers' testimony and that of the defendants. In arguing for the admissibility of the Jones paper, Duffy had stressed the issue of credibility. On the last day of testimony, after the defendants testified and closed their defense, the state brought forth in rebuttal Sergeant Emering and Detective Rodenhiser as the final witnesses the jury heard.

When Hagner and Reinhardt objected to Emering testifying about the Curran statement with the jury present, Duffy made clear he had recalled Emering to rebut Curran's claim that he had signed two statements:

BY MR. DUFFY:
Q. Sergeant Emering, I show you State's Exhibit No. 10, being the statement of Francis Curran. At what time approximately did Francis Curran sign that statement?
MR. HAGNER:I object.
MR. REINHARDT:I object.
MR. DUFFY:If the Court please, it has been testified by Curran that he signed two statements, and he did not know whether that was the statement that he signed in the morning or at 4 o'clock in the afternoon, and I am showing what statement it is.

At the time it was presented originally we had no knowledge that any contention would be made that one was signed at 4 o'clock in the afternoon.
MR. REINHARDT:Well, if the Court please, it is still not in rebuttal, because Curran said he didn't know which statement it was. He didn't say whether it was the morning statement or the afternoon statement. He simply said he didn't know. Therefore, it is not in rebuttal.
MR. DUFFY:If the Court please, they have made an issue as to whether

or not this is the statement taken in the morning, and I think I am entitled to show that.

RICHARDS, C. J.:We think he is and we overrule the objection.

(Exception noted for all of the defendants.)[120]

Under Duffy's examination, Emering then testified about State's Exhibit No. 10:

Q. About what time did Francis Curran sign that particular state-
    ment?
A. Around 4:00, A. M.
Q. On October 30?
A. That is right, sir.[121]

Although the three defense lawyers were aware of Curran's testimony when Duffy cross-examined him and he volunteered that he had signed two statements, neither Hagner nor Reinhardt nor Young questioned Emering about a second statement.[122]

For the same reasons the state had recalled Emering to testify about the Curran statement, Duffy then recalled Detective Rodenhiser to testify first about the Jones statement:

BY MR. DUFFY:
Q. Detective Rodenhiser, I show you State's Exhibit No. 11, being the
    statement of Ira F. Jones, and I will ask you about what time that
    particular statement was signed by Ira F. Jones (handing same to
    the witness)?
A. About 4:00, A. M. on October 30.[123]

Duffy then asked Rodenhiser a similar question about the Ma-guire statement:

Q. I hand you State's Exhibit No. 12, being the statement of Francis
    J. Maguire, and I will ask you what time he signed that (handing
    same to the witness)?

A.   About 5:00. A.M. on October 30.

Q.   Is that the particular statement that he signed at that time?

A.   It is.[124]

Duffy's explanation removes any doubt that the state considered the defendants' claim of two signings significant and germane to the issue of whose testimony the jurors should believe.

In cross-examination Young pinned Rodenhiser down about the number of statements Rodenhiser took from Jones:

BY MR. YOUNG:

Q.   How many statements did he sign?

A.   One, to the best of my knowledge.

Q.   Don't you remember? How many statements did Jones sign?

A.   One.

Q.   Are you sure that you did not give him two statements?

A.   I did not.

Q.   When did he sign the one statement?

A.   About 4:00, A. M.

Q.   And how many statements did you type of Jones?

A.   One statement in triplicate,—three copies.

Q.   And how many did you bring to him?

A.   All three copies.

Q.   Did he sign all three?

A.   He did.[125]

With that testimony, Young ended his spirited but unsuccessful effort to prove that the police were lying when they claimed State's Exhibit No. 11 was the only paper Jones had signed and it was the one he had signed about 4 a.m. on October 30, 1947. Again, Rodenhiser's testimony remained impervious to Young's attack.

The truth was State's Exhibits Nos. 10, 11, and 12 were not the papers read to the defendants at the line-up and, indeed, did not even exist until after the 7:00 a.m. line-up on October 30, 1947.

Thus the police testimony that the papers in evidence were the only statements the defendants signed and that they were signed in the early morning hours on October 30, with their signatures witnessed by the interrogating officers, went to the jury without any indication—let alone an admission by Detective Rodenhiser or Sergeant Emering or Patrolman Mazewski or Patrolman Nagle—that the testimony each had given under oath was false and each of them knew it was false.[126] The state's case, both initially and in rebuttal, withheld material facts.

The police testimony about the number of statements had to have had a devastating effect upon the defendants' credibility. When the jurors compared the testimony of the three men, each claiming he had signed twice, with the police testimony on direct and then in rebuttal that each defendant had signed only once, the jurors could only infer that each defendant had deliberately lied about the number of statements he signed since—so far as they knew—the police had no reason to lie. The conclusion flowing inexorably from the inference was if Curran, Jones, and Maguire were lying about the number of statements they signed, then why should the jurors believe them when they denied raping the woman? Furthermore, there was no need for the police or the prosecuting attorneys to claim the defendants were liars or for the prosecuting attorneys to assert that claim in summation. All the police had to do was testify that State's Exhibits Nos. 10, 11, and 12 were the only statements the defendants had signed and that the signing took place early in the morning on October 30, 1947, and hold to those lies. And they did. The blue wall of silence held.

Before the end of the trial Curran, Jones, and Maguire knew the police lied. So did the family members with whom they shared the facts and who believed them. Their lawyers knew, as is shown by the fact each defendant testified to the second signing. Young particularly knew before Jones first testified, so he acted vigorously to prove that Rodenhiser and Mazewski lied about Sonny Jones' statement. But none of the lawyers attacked the police lies about the Curran and Maguire statements. So the trial went forward with the truth deliberately hidden from the jury by the police and with the defendants' lawyers unable to prove that their clients were telling the truth.

The Three Eyewitnesses

State Exhibits Nos. 10, 11, and 12 now in evidence as the defendants' statements were even more revealing of police misconduct. Only one, Bud Curran's, referred to "three men whom I did not know."[127] But Fahey, Masten, and Schueler were with Curran, Jones, and Maguire in Maguire's car that night.[128] All six, as each testified at trial, had traveled together from the Labor Lyceum to the Embassy Café and then out Fourth Street to Bancroft Parkway where Maguire stopped the car and Curran alighted to get a match from the "young man" he noticed standing in front of Skinner's store at the corner of Fourth and Bancroft Parkway.[129]

Neither State's Exhibit No. 11 (Jones) nor State's Exhibit No. 12 (Maguire) refer to Fahey, Masten, and Schueler or even to "three men whom I did not know," the words attributed to Curran in State's Exhibit No. 10. Although Fahey, Masten, and Schueler watched what went on in the park, the police never made any effort to find and interrogate them.[130] In fact, when Curran started to talk about the three eyewitnesses, he testified Sergeant Emering told him: "We will not worry about those three. Don't worry about the other three and we don't want to hear about them."[131] Jones testified he told Rodenhiser "six of us left that party" but Rodenhiser would not "accept the names" despite the fact Jones was prepared to give him the names of the other three.[132] Rodenhiser told Jones: "I am not interested in them. I am interested in you three."[133] Maguire's testimony was equally emphatic. He testified he told Rodenhiser that three others were present, but Rodenhiser said, "I don't want to know about them, I want to know about you."[134]

At the trial, Fahey, Masten, and Schueler, called by the defendants, appeared and testified on direct.[135] Not one of the three wanted to get involved, let alone to testify. Young had to threaten them that he would seek their indictment as co-conspirators unless they came forward and testified truthfully to what they had seen and heard.[136] Under the state's cross-examinations, Fahey and Masten testified they saw the woman enter Woodlawn Park arm-in-arm with Curran.[137] All three eyewitnesses testified they saw and heard the woman's assent to Curran's advances.[138] All three saw them move about willingly in the park.[139] All three saw the caressing, hugging, and kissing.[140] Even after they with Jones walked away leaving Maguire and Curran behind in the park, they each testified they heard no screams, no cries for help.[141] Under oath they said they did not see any struggle.[142] Moreover, in the first recorded report, the record of the woman's admission to the Delaware Hospital, she claimed two, not three, men attacked her.[143]

The woman's own actions prove the presence of the eyewitnesses. Twice, when she realized there were people nearby looking at them, she told Curran, as he testified, they should move.[144] The first time they walked farther into the park.[145] The second time Curran hollered for Maguire and Jones to "scram."[146]

In Young's opinion, as he told me years later, the jurors did not give the three eyewitnesses' exculpatory testimony any credence. Their names do not appear in State's Exhibit Nos. 10, 11, and 12. By the absence of their names, the police made it appear Fahey, Masten, and Schueler were not even present and, therefore, were not credible.

From the time the young woman had testified at the preliminary hearing that there were only "these [three] boys altogether"
in Maguire's car, Young, resourceful lawyer as he was, knew he
had to do more to buttress the fact of the presence of the three
eyewitnesses. Consequently, on the fifth day of the trial, he called
Everio L. Leonzio, the teammate from the Lorraine Baseball
Team about whom Schueler had testified.[147] The record reflects
that Duffy and Young as well as the court understood the importance of Leonzio's testimony:

Q. Were you within the vicinity of Fourth and Union Streets on the
    night of October 29 or early morning October 30?
A. Yes, sir.
Q. And when you were there did you see Warren Schuler?
MR. DUFFY: I object.
A. Yes, I did.
MR. YOUNG: I withdraw that.
Q. Whom if anyone, at that time did you see?
MR. DUFFY: I object. If the Court please, the issue here is what occurred at Fourth and Ferris, in that vicinity, and Woodlawn Park, not
what occurred or who this man saw at Fourth and Union Street. *Pre-
sumably this is the attempt to corroborate other witnesses as to their identity at Fourth and Union.* I submit it is not relevant here. The issue here
is what occurred, what took place in Woodlawn Park, which is several
blocks west of Fourth and Union Street. *This is presumably an attempt
to corroborate another witness in corroboration of the defendants.* [Em-
phasis added.]
MR. YOUNG: It merely attempts to—I won't even go that far.
MR. DUFFY: If the Court please, I don't think that we are concerned
with whether Warren Schuler was at Fourth and Union at any particular time on that date. That isn't our issue.
MR. YOUNG: If the Court please, I think you are concerned with
whether Schuler, Masten and Fahey were at Fourth and Ferris at about
that time. It is only a few blocks away.
MR. DUFFY: That is my objection.
MR. YOUNG: *The examination was made and cross-examination of*

these witnesses made with an attempt to show that they were not there, and we are going to prove through someone else that they were there. [Emphasis added.]

RICHARDS, C. J.: This man is going to say he met them some distance from there after that, some distance away from there after that.

MR. YOUNG: I want to show that Schuler and Masten and Fahey, who testified that they were at Fourth and Ferris and left at a certain hour, were walking in the direction from which they said they were coming at about that time. Unless my friend is going to admit that we are correct in that contention, and there is no objection to the testimony of those three witnesses, there is no point in having it.

MR. DUFFY: I am [not] saying I admit it. One of these witnesses testified that he stopped for ice cream.

MR. YOUNG: Bought at Fourth and Union.

MR. DUFFY: Front and some other street.

MR. REINHARDT: Fourth and Scott.

MR. DUFFY: He stopped for ice cream. Is it material? Is Mr. Young to be permitted to call witnesses to testify that he was in an ice cream parlor at Fourth and Scott, if that is where it was? I don't see that that has anything to do with the issue in this case.

MR. YOUNG: My question had nothing to do with an ice cream parlor. I merely asked this question since what—

Richards,C.J.: We understand that. *We think this testimony corroborates the fact, or corroborates the testimony of the three witnesses who said they were there in that area about that time.* And we overrule the objection. [Emphasis added.][148]

Leonzio then testified he saw Fahey, Masten, and Schueler while he was walking out Fourth between Union and the west side of Bancroft Parkway. He placed the time as "between five minutes of one and five after." They were walking toward him from the direction of Fourth and Ferris. Thus Leonzio's testimony corroborated the earlier testimony of the three eyewitnesses about their presence in the area.[149]

Could Young and the other defense lawyers have done more? Perhaps the testimony of members of the baseball team or others who saw the six young men either leave the Labor Lyceum or the

Embassy Café together would have helped. It is possible the lawyers made the effort to secure such testimony but were not successful. Or the lawyers could have thought such testimony was not germane to what occurred in Woodlawn Park.

The state had another objective in recalling Sergeant Emering and Detective Rodenhiser: the state wanted to rebut the testimony of Curran, Jones, and Maguire about the presence of the three eyewitnesses.[150] The state's aim was to convince the jurors that Fahey, Masten, and Schueler were not present so the jurors should disregard their testimony as untruthful and worthless. Duffy's false suggestion provided the basis for his outrageous claim in his summation that the three eyewitnesses were not even there.[151]

Why would Curran, Jones, and Maguire each give statements to the police and *not* identify three eyewitnesses who could corroborate their claim of the woman's assent and their own innocence? Curran, Jones, and Maguire each testified to knowing Fahey, Masten, and Schueler and to their presence.[152] Why did the police fail to interrogate Jones and Maguire about the three men Curran said he did not know in his statement as the police admitted? Moreover, once Curran had referred to three other men, why did the police fail to look for them? Surely they had an obligation to follow this lead. And if they had found these three readily available men, the police and the prosecution had the further obligation to interrogate them and then share their exculpatory accounts with the defense. Instead, what the police did was to ignore the three eyewitnesses and then in State's Exhibit Nos. 10, 11, and 12 emphasize only the presence of the three defendants.

The Use of the Word "Moaning" in the Statements

Although the police interrogated each of the defendants separately in the early morning hours of October 30, 1947, the word "moaning" appears in all of the statements the state introduced at trial, State's Exhibits Nos. 10, 11, and 12.[153] According to the Curran paper: "This girl was moaning during both attempts."[154] In Jones' paper there appear the words: "The woman was moaning and her clothing was above her waist."[155] "I heard the woman moaning, 'You're hurting me,'" is the version ascribed to Maguire.[156] But in the woman's own statement given that same morning, October 30, 1947, to Sergeant Emering, she did not use the word "moaning."[157] Moreover, at trial each defendant under oath denied using the word "moaning."[158] If the defendants did not use the word, what is the explanation for its presence in each of the statements in evidence, statements proven after the trial not to be the statements the defendants first gave and signed?

The Failure to Object to the Admission of the Curran and Maguire Papers

Young's rigorous objection to the admission of Jones' paper contrasts sharply with his and Reinhardt's and Hagner's lack of objections to the admission of the Curran and Maguire papers. Moreover, none of the defense lawyers asked any questions of the police witnesses about either State's Exhibit No. 10 (Curran) or State's Exhibit No. 12 (Maguire).[159] The question arises: Did the lawyers not know at the time the state offered Curran's and Maguire's statements in evidence early in the trial that each one had signed two statements, as each of the men subsequently testified?[160] From his cross-examinations of Rodenhiser and Mazewski it is a certainty Young knew that Jones had signed twice before he called Jones to testify as part of his objection to the admission of State's Exhibit No. 11. The state offered the Curran paper before the Jones paper; thus, Hagner did not have the ben-

efit of Jones' testimony or of Young's cross-examinations of Rodenhiser and Mazewski. But Reinhardt sat through all three
examinations. Having heard Jones' testimony about signing
twice, Reinhardt was well aware of the issues: the number, the
time, and the signing of the Jones statements.[161]

What accounts for the disparity between Young's objection to
the introduction of the Jones paper, in which objection Reinhardt and Hagner joined, and all three attorneys' lack of objection to the introduction of the Curran and Maguire papers and
their collective failure to examine Curran and Maguire as well as
to cross-examine the police officers about the number, the time,
and the signing of those papers? My speculation is that the defense lawyers, not having seen the statements before the state offered them in evidence at trial, and not anticipating the police
perjury about the statements, never discussed the statements
among themselves and never agreed upon a common defense to
their admissibility. As Young made clear in the course of arguing
to the court, the lawyers *had agreed* upon a common defense to
the charge of rape: "The defense . . . in this case is . . . consent."[162]

But the lawyers prior to their clients' testimony apparently did
not share with each other what they knew or what they thought
about the number, the time, and the signing of the statements.
As hard as it may be to believe in hindsight, Curran and Maguire
clearly did not tell their lawyers as they prepared for trial that
they had signed twice nor did their lawyers extract the information from them.

About Curran, Hagner never asked Patrolman Nagle a single
question about whether there was another statement when Curran's statement was offered in evidence nor did he object to its
admission.[163] Nor did he ask Curran a single question about a
second statement when Curran testified in direct examination in
his own defense.[164] It was not until Duffy's cross-examination of

Curran late in the afternoon on the fifth trial day that Curran first testified to signing twice.[165] Only then did the Curran family learn Bud Curran had signed two statements.[166] Nonetheless, Hagner again did not ask a single question about the second signing nor did Young or Reinhardt.[167]

About Maguire, Reinhardt was present when Young cross-examined Rodenhiser and Mazewski about Jones' statement and when Jones testified he signed two statements.[168] Despite the testimony Young had elicited, Reinhardt asked no questions of Detective Rodenhiser and made no objection when Duffy, with Rodenhiser on the stand, offered Maguire's statement in evidence as State's Exhibit No. 12 in the afternoon of the third day of trial.[169] Nor did Young or Hagner ask any question or make any objection.[170] On the sixth day of trial, Maguire in passing in direct examination testified that he had signed twice. When he did, his testimony startled Reinhardt:

Q. And did they question you and get you to sign a statement?
A. Yes, they did question me.
Q. *And did you sign a statement?*
A. *I signed two statements.*
Q. *You signed two statements?*
A. *Yes, sir.*
Q. Is one of those statements in evidence here?
A. I believe so, sir.
Q. Now, does that statement contain everything that you told the detectives?
A. No, it does not, sir.
Q. Is that a true statement of your activities of the evening?
A. No, sir, it is not. [Emphasis added.][171]

I say Maguire's testimony "startled" Reinhardt not only because Reinhardt repeated Maguire's words as his next question, but, moreover, because Reinhardt did not ask a single follow-up question to explore what so obviously was news to him; it was

Duffy who asked the few follow-up questions.[172] If Maguire's testimony that he had signed twice had been known to Reinhardt before Maguire testified, surely Reinhardt would have asked Maguire obvious questions: when did he sign the second statement; where did the signing take place; who witnessed the second signing; and whether the statements were the same. Reinhardt's failure to inquire is all the more remarkable given his knowledge of Young's effort when the state offered the Jones statement.

If Reinhardt first heard on the sixth day of trial Maguire's claim that he had signed twice, as I think is the fact, it meant Reinhardt had not discussed the signing issue with Maguire either in preparing him to testify at trial or at the time Maguire's statement came into evidence. Similarly, if Hagner first heard on cross-examination at trial Curran's claim that he signed twice, it meant he also had no prior discussion with his client about the signing of two statements.

Young's lack of objection to the introduction of the Curran and Maguire statements earlier in the trial meant he did not know that they, like Jones, had signed two statements. Late in the trial, Young heard both Curran and Maguire testify to having signed twice, yet he did not question them to draw out details. Nor did he question the police officers about Curran and Maguire signing twice even though he had questioned Rodenhiser and Mazewski about Jones signing twice.

In trying to understand why the three defense lawyers did not object to the admission of the Curran and Maguire statements and why they did not question Curran and Maguire and the police officers about their statements, a reader of the transcript cannot ignore the separate representation of the three men. Young wanted to prove Jones was innocent. He may not have thought it was in Jones' interest for him to share the fact Jones had signed twice. Since it appears likely that neither Hagner nor Reinhardt knew prior to their clients' testimony that their respective clients had signed twice, they had nothing to share with Young. Lacking proof of a second signing by either of them, Young had no reason to make the effort to object to the admission of the Curran and Maguire papers as he had with Jones'.[173] But if Young, prior to trial, did share what he knew from Jones, it was a serious error for Hagner and Reinhardt not to have checked with their clients and then gone after the police officers about the number of statements their clients signed, as Young had done when he questioned Rodenhiser and Mazewski about the Jones paper. Hagner and Reinhardt, having joined in Young's objection to the admission of the Jones paper, had nothing to lose by following Young's lead when the prosecution offered the Maguire paper. For Young not to have questioned Curran and Maguire *after* they each had testified about signing twice is equally inexplicable.

Neither the lawyers nor their clients had any reason to anticipate the police would perjure themselves in securing the introduction of State's Exhibit Nos. 10, 11, and 12, documents that did not exist before 7:00 a.m. on October 30, 1947, by which time, according to the police testimony, the defendants had signed the offered statements in evidence. The officers did not admit destroying the first statements. To the contrary, they denied there were any statements other than those offered in evidence.[174] About the timing, Jones initially said he signed a statement "the next afternoon."[175] Maguire testified he signed a statement "[a]bout four o'clock the next day in the afternoon."[176] Curran testified he signed two statements, "In the morning and in the afternoon."[177] When he examined Rodenhiser, Young asked: "Were you present when the defendant [i.e., Jones] signed another statement the following day?" But Chief Justice Richards sustained Duffy's objection to the question on the ground the cross-examination was limited to the issue of whether Jones' statement was voluntary.[178]

The final factor bearing upon the absence of objection by the lawyers to State's Exhibit Nos. 10 and 12 may have been that they underestimated how the police perjury would undermine their clients' credibility.[179] Or, they could have understood the attack but had no way to combat it. For his part, Chief Deputy Attorney General Duffy well understood the issue of credibility arising from the conflicting testimony about how many statements the defendants signed. In arguing to the court about the admission of the Jones paper with the jury present, Duffy twice referred to his purpose in putting in testimony to show conflicting oral statements as "enabling the jury to test the credibility of the defendant."[180]

Apart from Young's cross-examinations of Rodenhiser and Mazewski, where he struggled to show they were not telling the truth when they denied the existence of a second statement by Jones, neither he nor the other defendants' lawyers addressed the issue of credibility during the trial, including in their summations.

Sonny Jones' Shorts

The story of Sonny Jones' shorts illustrates the difficulty of writing about events years later. When I spoke to Carmen N. Stigliano by telephone in November 2002, I thought I had come upon a dramatic occurrence demonstrating both Sonny Jones' innocence and police corruption. Carmen, the husband of Jayne Jones Stigliano, one of Sonny Jones' four sisters, told me that on October 29, 1947, he and Jayne and his sister-in-law, Virginia McKinley, and her husband, William, were visiting the sisters' mother, Jane "Jenny" Jones, with whom Sonny lived.[181]

Carmen recalled that before Sonny went out that night, he complained to his sisters, both nurses, of a nasty, painful wound on his rump, the result of a back injury while in service. Carmen said Sonny's older sister, Virginia McKinley, covered the infected area with a bandage. Following Sonny's discharge from service, he had gained weight and his pants were tight, so he was more comfortable without undershorts. Carmen was certain Sonny was not wearing undershorts when he left home on October 29 because the bulge in his pants from the dressing was visible.[182]

Late in the afternoon on October 30, 1947, a Wilmington police officer came to Jenny Jones' apartment and asked for shorts and a pair of trousers for her son.[183] At Jenny Jones' direction, Carmen went to Sonny's room, secured the articles the policeman sought, and turned them over to him. The innocuous request for shorts became a major issue for Carmen when Detective Charles F. McCool and the attorney general's chemist and toxicologist, Dr. Harold E. Tiffany, testified for the state at the tag end of the third day of trial.[184]

Detective McCool testified he examined both Curran's shorts and Maguire's shorts at the time of their arrests and observed, using the same words about both: "Soiled marks and spots about the flies."[185] About Jones' shorts, according to what Jones had told him, McCool testified that they were "the same shorts which [Jones] wore that night."[186] *In contrast to his testimony about Curran's and Maguire's shorts, McCool twice testified, both on direct and cross, that when he examined Jones' shorts, he did not "notice any spots or soiled marks on the shorts of Ira Jones."* [Emphasis added.][187] In cross-examination, Young for Jones drew from McCool that he had examined Jones' shorts by holding them up "to the window or the light or something" and, noticing nothing, initially gave the shorts back to Jones. He then changed his mind and retrieved them.[188] Young did not ask McCool what prompted him to change his mind about collecting Jones' shorts. Thus McCool's trial testimony was, at least in part, consistent with Carmen Stigliano's recollection that there could not have been "spots or soiled marks" on shorts Jones was not wearing.

Dr. Tiffany testified shortly after McCool. As Duffy asked Dr. Tiffany questions to qualify him as an expert witness, Young interrupted: "If the Court please, I am willing to admit the qualifications. *I think we all studied under Dr. Tiffany.* [Emphasis added.]"[189] Young's comment was unnecessary and only went to enhance the doctor's credibility in the eyes of the jury. Perhaps his intention was to remind the jurors of his familiarity with Dr. Tiffany from his extensive experience in criminal defense work. In any event, Dr. Tiffany's testimony about the result of his examination of Sonny Jones' shorts differed sharply from McCool's: "There was much blood on the back and on the fly of these shorts. There was semen and there were spermatozoa. Now, some of the blood on these shorts was in the shape of a clot, showing that there was considerable blood on those shorts at the time."[190] How could anyone square Dr. Tiffany's findings with McCool's testimony that he had noticed nothing about Jones' shorts? Moreover, both McCool's and Dr. Tiffany's testimony contradict Carmen Stigliano's recollection that Sonny was not wearing shorts when he left home on the night of October 29, 1947. Carmen also recalled that as soon as the court session ended on the afternoon of February 12, 1948, he rushed over to tell Young that Sonny had not worn shorts on the night of October 29, 1947. He said he also told Young about the police visit to pick up clean shorts and trousers for Sonny. Although Carmen's facts cast doubt on McCool's and Tiffany's testimony, Carmen told me Young had shrugged his shoulders and said it was not important.[191] Young's response in 1948 was as inexplicable to Carmen then as it was in 2002 when I spoke with him.

Did Young not hear what Carmen had to tell him? Was his mind focused on another aspect of the case? Did the stress of the trial, already having consumed three days full of tension as he struggled to prove the existence of a second statement, cause Young to fail to comprehend what Carmen had told him? Did

Young, a seasoned lawyer, really shrug off critical evidence? The fact he subsequently called Virginia McKinley to the stand suggests Young did hear Carmen on February 12 and, of even greater significance, supports Carmen's recollection.

Moreover, Dr. Paul R. Smith, the police surgeon, testified he did not find any semen or sperm in the woman's vaginal tract when he examined her around 4:00 a.m. on October 30, 1947, at the Delaware Hospital, assuredly a major point helpful to the defendants.[192] The hospital report itself corroborated Smith's testimony: "Smear—No sperm seen."[193]

Carmen Stigliano testified on Saturday, February 14, the fifth day of the trial, but Young only asked him about the woman's appearance when he saw her at the police station around 9:00 A.M. on October 30, 1947.[194] If he had been asked, he could have testified, based on his own knowledge, that his brother-in-law was not wearing shorts when he departed the apartment on the night of October 29, 1947. But Young did not ask him.

Virginia McKinley, Jones' sister, who, according to Carmen, had applied a dressing to Jones' posterior before he went out on October 29, 1947, also testified later on the fifth trial day. Her entire testimony follows:

BY MR. YOUNG:
Q. Mrs. McKinley, where do you live?
A. 3121 West Second Street.
Q. And do you have a profession?
A. Yes, sir, I am a graduate nurse.
Q. Is Sonny Jones your brother?
A. Yes, sir.
Q. In the early evening of October 29, of last year, did you have occasion to see him?
A. Yes, sir, I did.
Q. Did he complain about any condition?
A. Yes, sir.

Q.   What was that condition?
A.   He had complained, I would say, before.
Q.   Yes.
A.   And he asked me to examine his back at the end of his spine and his coccyx.
Q.   What did you see there?
A.   He had a cyst at the end of his spine and there was a small opening of the cyst and it was draining a small amount of bloody serum.
Q.   And did you recommend anything?
A.   Yes, sir, I told him that he should see a doctor about it, *but it wasn't draining enough at that time to put a dressing on it.* [Emphasis added.][195]

With Virginia's last answer, Young abruptly concluded his examination and turned her over to Attorney General James for cross-examination. James simply said, "No questions."[196]

What was Young's purpose in calling Virginia to the witness stand if not to rebut Dr. Tiffany's testimony by asking her to tell about the bandage and Sonny's not wearing shorts on October 29, facts Carmen Stigliano had told him? His initial questions were leading up to establishing the fact of a dressing and the absence of shorts. If Young *knew* Sonny Jones was not wearing shorts on the night of October 29, his brief examination of Virginia without any reference to what Sonny was wearing makes no sense. The thought that Young called Virginia to testify as his witness without first interviewing her and confirming what Carmen had told him is beyond belief. There is another possible explanation for the abrupt ending, although it is admittedly speculation on my part. Her answer to Young's last question, in which she volunteered "it wasn't draining enough at that time to put a dressing on it," was unexpected and startled him. Since he had called her to testify, she was his witness and he could not impeach her. In any event, Young abandoned any further examination of Virginia McKinley.

Had she forgotten? Did she misspeak? Was Carmen Stigliano's distinct recollection a figment of his imagination? Even if it was, it still remains difficult to square Detective McCool's direct trial testimony affirming, after his close inspection, he did not "notice any spots or soiled marks on the shorts of Ira Jones" with Dr. Tiffany's testimony about his findings.[197]

When Young called Jones to the stand to testify in his own defense on the sixth day of the trial, although Young asked him about the war wound on his buttocks, he neither asked Jones about any dressing nor whether he was wearing shorts when he left home on October 29. Given Virginia McKinley's testimony, there was no point to establishing a conflict between Jones' and his sister's testimony.

The Summations

Even before the start of the trial, the lawyers for the state and for the defendants knew they would have to sum up their respective cases to the jurors after the evidence was in and before the court charged the jury. Accordingly, one would think they would plan what to say well before they rose to speak. Indeed, all the lawyers had to realize as the trial progressed that what they would say to the jury would be circumscribed by what the witnesses had said under oath. The state's lawyers' task was easier. Since they had thoroughly prepared the young woman to testify, all they needed to do was follow the script. The defendants' lawyers confronted a harder task, but only one of them took the right approach.

After the Sunday recess, the trial resumed on Monday, February 16, 1948, the sixth and longest day of the trial.[198] It must have been an exhausting day for the jurors. They heard Maguire and Jones deny raping the young woman, joining in Curran's denial as the last witness on Saturday, February 14. They heard each defendant swear he had signed two statements. Finally, from the state's last two witnesses in rebuttal, the jurors heard the emphatic, but, unknown to them, perjured testimony of Sergeant Emering and Detective Rodenhiser reaffirming the state's claim that the defendants' statements in evidence were the only ones they had signed and that they had signed them in the early morning hours of October 30.

When the testimony concluded late in the afternoon, it was time for the lawyers to summarize their cases. In a civil jury case, the plaintiff bears the burden of proving his case by a preponderance of the evidence and makes the opening and closing statements to the jury. In a criminal case, the state opens and closes since the state bears the burden of proving the guilt of the defendant beyond a reasonable doubt. Thus, in *The Rape Case* Attorney General James spoke first.

James outlined the state's case against Curran, Jones, and Maguire. In the course of his thirty-three minute address, he described the young woman as a "shy girl considerably embarrassed" who gave a "distinct impression of sincerity." His description of the defendants' conduct was that it was "brutal and savage" and that the young woman offered "all the resistance a little thing her size could offer," referring to her weight as 106 pounds. At length he discussed "the medical testimony which indicated specimens from each of the three men had been found in damaging places. He told of the abrasion at the base of her spine, of multiple bruises, of internal injuries that could have been caused only by sex relations." James told the jury:

There is a great responsibility on the part of the state of Delaware to see that our laws are enforced and that each and every citizen be protected by those laws. Our citizens have the right to walk on the streets, highways or byways anytime [sic] of the day or night without molestation or harm.

Our womanhood has the right to be protected against any molestation and to be protected against savage and brutal attacks. [The prosecuting witness] had that right when she stood on the corner of Fourth Street and Bancroft Parkway but her right was violated by these three defendants.[199]

When James finished, it was the defendants' lawyers' turn. They had agreed about the order in which they would speak. Since during the trial Len Hagner's role, as reflected in the trial transcript, was the least significant of the three, his colleagues assigned to him what they must have regarded as the least important of the three summations; he was the first to speak.

Hagner started by telling the jurors he would be brief, "after which my colleagues, Mr. Reinhardt and Mr. Young will also speak to you."[200] In his measured, quiet voice, Hagner turned to the merits: "Mr. James has painted a picture to you which is, indeed, a serious one, if it is true. I shall try to comment on some of the things that he has said, and also to paint a somewhat different picture."[201] His summation, which takes up only eight, double-spaced pages of the court reporter's notes, demonstrated his close following of the testimony and his mastery of the salient arguments favoring the defendants.

He first spoke of the seriousness of the charge. "This is, of course, as you Ladies and Gentlemen know, a very serious case. As you were asked before you were seated in this jury whether you had any conscientious scruples against finding a verdict of guilty in case the evidence should so warrant you, as that was asked time and time again, certainly no one in this court room could fail to appreciate how very serious it is." He told the jurors: "It is a very serious thing for [the young woman] and her family, and a very, very serious thing for the family of these young men who are accused of this crime. . . . Mr. Curran is 20, and the other boys are still in their early youth,—men who all have served this country in the navy of the United States and who, up to this time, have borne a good reputation in the community in which they live."[202]

Thus, without making reference to the possible death penalty his clients faced upon conviction, he made plain to the jury the impact of the charge on all concerned: first on the young woman and her family and then on the defendants and their families. By what he said he covered the youth of Curran, Jones, and Maguire; their honorable service in World War II; and their good reputations. While showing sensitivity to the young woman and her family, there was neither confrontation nor overstatement in what Hagner said.

Using the conversational "we," he raised the central question the jurors would have to deal with: ". . . we ask ourselves how could this unfortunate event have happened,—how could it have happened? I have asked that of myself many times. I don't know whether I have the right explanation of it." His hesitancy was a perfect, self-effacing transition to his explanation for what had happened:

But if we go back to that evening of October 30 and follow the course of events before this meeting which, it seems to me, to be occasioned by a cruel chance of fate, these three boys had been attending a dinner for their baseball team. They were having a jolly evening and there was considerable beer consumed, I take it. Then, they went to the Embassy, where they had more beer, including Mr. Curran, Francis Curran, who is under 21 years of age and shouldn't have had any beer at all. We see them there celebrating the end of the baseball season.

At almost the same time, Ladies and Gentlemen of the Jury, [the young woman] was in the Eagle Café, the Eagle Lounge, on Tenth Street. She was also enjoying some beer. I think that the testimony is that she had two bottles of beer.[203]

Leaving the jury to conclude the obvious—that the drinking had impaired the judgment of the defendants and the young

woman and doing so without condemning any of the participants—Hagner set the context for the events that ensued. He
pointed out how the young woman could have taken a number
4 bus at Eighth and Market "which would have taken her directly
to her home." "I wonder why she didn't," Hagner mused. He
then followed her to Fourth and Union where she got out of the
number 4–1 bus and walked to the northwest corner of Fourth
and started walking back and forth between Bancroft Parkway
and Union. "She went down to the corner of Fourth and Bancroft Parkway, which is a much darker place, and it was a place
where there were no buses that came by that point, no motor
coaches, . . . and, for the second time, we wonder why [she]
chose to stand at that corner, and particularly when the buses
were running freely. I think that the evidence was that there were
five or six buses that went by between 11 and 11:30. She was perfectly free to get a bus, it seems to me. There was nothing at all
preventing her from getting one. . . ."[204] By placing the young
woman at the corner of Fourth and Bancroft Parkway, an incontrovertible fact, Hagner avoided the contentious issue whether
she was standing in the doorway of Skinner's Market.

Hagner continued: "and then these boys came by in the car."
He emphasized that "at that point again the testimony of [the
young woman] and all of the witnesses for the defendants and
the defendants themselves is completely in agreement." Always
referring to the prosecuting witness by name preceded by a re-
spectful "Miss," Hagner stressed areas of agreement as he raised
doubts about her testimony: "The car in which the boys were
traveling passed the intersection where [the young woman] was
standing, a short distance, and then Francis Curran, who had
been wanting a match, came back and he said he saw this person
in the doorway and he knew it was a girl after he had gotten out
and he asked her for a match. He said he asked [the young

woman] for a match. [She] said he asked her for a match. So that at that point the testimony is in agreement."[205]

Hagner then turned to the young woman's claim that "Before that time she said she had recognized one of the persons in that car." Yet again, Hagner gently took issue: "Now, I wonder if that is correct. A short distance further up the street, you will remember the testimony of the officer who passed the car close enough to read the license number, and said that he couldn't tell how many were in the car, he couldn't tell whether they were men or women. The only testimony that he could give was that he saw two people on the front seat of the car, and he couldn't tell whether they were men or women."[206] Without calling her account a lie, Hagner raised a doubt about her claim that she had recognized Maguire.

He then drew the jurors' attention to the most significant argument in the young men's defense: ". . . Francis Curran said to [the young woman], "Can I walk you home?", and [she], after some, perhaps, demurrer, apparently assented; and they started up toward Fifth Street." Hagner continued: "Now, we must remember that [she] lived at Colonial Heights, which was in a very different direction. [She] apparently was willing to allow Francis Curran to walk her home; and, not only that, she was perfectly willing to walk with him, even though he started out in a direction which was quite opposite from where she lived. Now, how can it be that [she] would do that at approximately half-past twelve in the morning? That is a question which might present some difficulty."[207] There was nothing strident in Hagner's summation either in tone or content.

He quietly but pointedly continued to raise doubts about the charge of rape by turning next to the testimony of the three eyewitnesses. "Then, the testimony of all of the defense witnesses followed that as they walked along, Francis Curran put his arm around [her], as they walked up Bancroft Parkway; and there again both the defense witnesses and [the young woman] are in agreement. She testified that Francis Curran did have his arm around her as they walked up Fifth Street towards the park, and she testified that she made no effort to leave him, and, if my memory is correct, that she did not protest at that time."[208]

Hagner then drove home his case. "Now, it seems to me that the kindest thing, perhaps, that might be said is that [the young woman] had felt the effects of the two bottles of beer that she had had. Certainly, I think that Francis Curran had felt the effects of the beer that he had had that night, and that combination, Ladies and Gentlemen of the Jury, in this particular case, added up to tragedy—tragedy upon tragedy and sorrow upon sorrow for the families of all these people who are involved in this very, very unfortunate case."[209] Thus Hagner identified for the jury the real culprit: the drinking of too much alcohol.

In reviewing the testimony, Hagner emphasized the young woman's voluntary acts that the state could not contradict. "It is not disputed that [the young woman] walked into the playground at around 12:30 in the morning, and that she walked in that playground alone. Ladies and Gentlemen of the jury, you have seen the playground, although I assume you haven't seen it at night. It is not a well lighted place. It is a place that you wouldn't expect a young lady to enter with a young man that she had never met, did not know, and had never seen before, at that time of the night."[210]

Yet again Hagner returned to the young woman's act of walking with Curran into the park without objecting:

. . . the evidence is that she did go into that park without making an objection at a time, Ladies and Gentlemen, when the slightest objection and the slightest effort to attempt to run from the direction in which Curran was going would have been successful, insofar as the evidence in this case shows. There was nothing to prevent [her] simply to tell Francis Curran that, "Here, I am not going into that park with you." As a matter of fact, she could have told him in the very first instance, "I haven't any match and I don't want you to bother me," and that would have been the end of it.[211]

Hagner ended his recitation of the facts by again referring to the drinking: "When the venture first started, she was within a very short block from Fourth and Union Streets, which was well lighted, well populated, and there were plenty of people around there at that time. She didn't have to embark upon this venture, and it seems to me that the kindest thing that can be said for [the young woman] is that perhaps she did feel the effects of these two bottles of beer."[212]

His submission was free of rhetorical flourishes with the single exception of quoting the famous soliloquy from *Othello*, first reminding the jury of the context:

. . . You remember that Othello had been driven almost frenzied by this bit of evidence and that bit of evidence . . . which had led him to the conclusion that his wife was unfaithful to him, and in the last act of that play we see Othello in his wife's darkened bedroom. He is determined that he will destroy her, that he will kill her, and he is in that darkened bedroom, and his wife is asleep . . . , and beside the bed there is one single candle burning, and as he thinks of the murder of his wife, he says to himself,
Put out the light, and then put out the light:
If I quench thee, thou flaming minister,
I can again thy former light restore,
Should I repent me:-but once put out thy light,
Thou cunning'st pattern of excelling nature,
I know not where is that Promethean heat
That can thy light relume,
and he proceeded to do that very thing, only to find in almost the very next moment that the evidence of his wife's infidelity upon which he

relied was fragile, undependable, and not to be acted upon; but here it was too late.[213]

Hagner intended the quotation to be instructive—to emphasize the reasonable doubt about the young woman's story and thus in the state's case without calling her names or condemning her in any way. What Hagner said was in direct contrast to Attorney General James who in his summation had called for the death penalty—"to put out the light of these three men." Hagner concluded "that on the evidence in this case there is no justification for your doing so; and I feel that when my colleagues have completed their addresses to you, Ladies and Gentlemen of the jury, you will feel that the proper verdict in this case is not guilty for Francis Curran, and also for the others."[214]

In Hagner's view, the culprit was the alcohol all the participants had consumed. It affected their judgment and led to a tragedy for all. Finally, quoting the passage from *Othello* enabled him to warn the jurors that if they rushed to a judgment of guilty, the result would be irreparable. Thus, he addressed the death penalty in a subtle but effective way. His task was not to prove that the defendants' were innocent but, rather, to demonstrate there were reasonable doubts about the young woman's story and thus the state's claim of the defendants' guilt. Hagner's summation contains not a single argument with which the state could take issue.

Maguire's attorney, Reinhardt, then spoke. His summation was both repetitious and confrontational. Although Hagner had told the jurors each of the three defendants' lawyers would speak, Reinhardt thought if necessary to repeat it, thereby doing what he had told the jurors the defendants' lawyers would not do: "[To avoid repetition] we have agreed among us that Mr. Young is to carry the burden of the submission to you members of the jury."[215] By emphasizing Young's role, Reinhardt diminished Hagner's sensitive summation.

Reinhardt then told the jurors "I do not condone [Maguire's] actions as a married man. You saw his wife on the witness stand. If he had been charged properly or indicted properly and charged with attempted adultery, I wouldn't be here, that is, if he followed my advice, he would plead guilty to a charge of that sort. But the State has seen fit to have him indicted on a charge wherein his life hangs in the balance and, Folks, he just isn't guilty as he is indicted, and that is all there is to it, and that goes for the other two defendants, also."[216]

But Reinhardt's personal view was of no moment. It did not help Maguire for his lawyer to admit, as Reinhardt did, that Maguire was guilty of "attempted adultery," an admission of wrongful conduct. Moreover, unlike Hagner, he attacked the woman's honor thus challenging the jury to defend her: "It is unfortunate that in a case of this sort it is necessary to discredit the testimony and discredit the person of . . . the prosecuting witness. But not only is she discredited, in my eyes, at least, by her own testimony and certain other mute testimony which lies before you."[217] Whereas Hagner had "doubts" about the young woman's testimony, Reinhardt implied she was a liar, the only meaning the word "discredited" could have in these circumstances.

In tracking the same facts Hagner had covered so effectively, Reinhardt was strident. When he referred to the contrast between the testimony of the off-duty policeman who passed the car and that of the young woman, he disparaged the prosecution's claim "that she thought that Curran was all right because she recognized Maguire, but a few minutes later a police officer [who] was closer than Maguire and [he] didn't recognize him; pretty thin trusting Curran whom she had never seen before."[218] Instead of Hagner's explanation that the events were "occasioned by a cruel chance of fate" brought about by the drinking, Reinhardt asserted that the explanation for what had occurred was that the young woman "was an ordinary, every-day pick-up." Reinhardt claimed her actions were not "those of a normal person under such circumstances." His name calling challenged the jurors to brand her a "pick-up" and an "abnormal person."[219]

When Reinhardt presented the defendants' strongest point, that the young woman had willingly gone off with Curran, he did so in a way that again challenged—and may even have offended—the jurors. "Would you want your daughters or your sisters or your wives to wait one block away from where she could get a bus, at Fourth and Bancroft Parkway, where there is no bus, at a place that she couldn't see a bus if it was coming, and to pick up and go off with the first person that came along? Are those the actions of a normal woman? I say to you, no."[220] In saying she was "at a place that she couldn't see a bus if it was coming," it is obvious Reinhardt was convinced the young woman was standing in the doorway of Skinner's Market. That may have been the fact to Reinhardt and everyone else on the defendants' side, but not necessarily to the jurors.

About drinking, Reinhardt attacked the young woman's claim she had "two bottles of beer." "I have never yet known a case where a person admitted having so many beers, when the fact of the matter was that actually they had many more."[221] Reinhardt referred to the movie, *Variety Girl,* which the young woman and her friend had attended that night. When he claimed it was "probably sexy," for which there was no testimony in the record to support his description, Duffy immediately objected. Before the court could rule, Reinhardt retreated saying "I will go no further on that point." But having done so he could not resist adding a further repetitious reference to her drinking: "Having seen that picture, she had at least two bottles of beer, and how many more I don't know."[222]

In summing up, Reinhardt returned to the fact of the young woman's walking off with Curran in a direction away from her home, repeating what he had already said and what Hagner had effectively covered. Ignoring the two women on the jury, Reinhardt's language became offensive and sexist:

Now, what was Curran to think about that? Weren't these other boys showing perfectly normal curiosity? You men, at that age, if there had been three or four of you together, and one of you had gotten out of the car and picked up a girl and started up the street together, what would you have done? Would you have followed along to see what happened, and after you saw that it was there and free and easy, and maybe you would have wanted a little yourself. Maybe you won't admit it today, but look back to when you were twenty years old and see how you would have acted. Think it over, you men, and think it over carefully.[223]

Reinhardt then picked up State's Exhibit No.s 20 and 21, the young woman's panties and sanitary belt, claiming the "two articles of clothing" discredited her story and her. He hammered his point home:

I say, how could any man remove those panties or that sanitary girdle without tearing them without hurting them, if a woman was kicking and hollering and biting and scratching all the time? It couldn't be done. With these in evidence, and I thank the Lord that they are in evidence, because you can see that they are not torn, you can see that they are not damaged, and I say that they could not have been gotten off that girl without her consent.[224]

His assertion directly challenged the prosecution to prove by these exhibits that the young woman had not cooperated.

Reinhardt challenged the prosecution yet again, this time for its failure to introduce photographs to support the claim that the prosecuting witness' "face was terribly swollen and bruised and bleeding": "The State is handy . . . with its Police Department and with a camera. If that were the picture of her face, why didn't they take a picture of it and put it in evidence here? Why didn't they do it? They took pictures of everything else in the place. . . . There is no picture put before you. That would be evidence."[225]

Reinhardt then turned to Dr. Smith's testimony and the documentary evidence about the young woman's condition. He reminded the jurors "she was allowed to leave the hospital just as soon as Paul Smith had finished his examination. She waited for some time until Dr. Smith got there, and what does the hospital report say about her condition? Good. That is what it says. I read it to you the other day."[226]

About the ruptured hymen mentioned in the hospital report, Reinhardt was again combative, speaking to the jury as if the two women serving on it were not there: "She had a ruptured hymen. That does happen in a woman's life at some time or other, sometimes after marriage, sometimes before. You men all know that. But that isn't a sign of rape. That isn't a sign that it was against her will. They found it chafed. That is no sign of rape. The presence of blood there, that is no sign of rape. Her first intercourse,—it is perfectly normal,—or if she had squirmed a little bit. That is normal. That is not a sign of rape. So that the evidence brought before you doesn't prove the crime of rape."[227]

When Reinhardt took up the testimony of the three eyewitnesses, Fahey, Masten, and Schueler, he could not let go of his willingness to challenge the prosecution yet again. After noting they were "three nice looking boys," he asked the jury "do you believe that they would take a chance of a penalty of perjury and come up on this witness stand and perjure themselves just for the sake of these three boys? I don't believe that they would." Reinhardt went on to claim "that had they not been telling the truth," Chief Deputy Duffy and Attorney General James by their skillful and grueling cross-examinations "would have broken them down, and I challenge my two friends, Mr. James and Mr.

Duffy, to show me one material point where the stories of Fahey, Masten, and Schuler, or, so far as that is concerned, where any of these three defendants were shaken on that, and they are good at cross-examination. But they haven't been able to on one material point."[228]

Reinhardt wound up his summation by first talking about "both reasonable doubt and the presumption of innocence," and then concluding with yet another challenge to the state about imposing the death penalty upon Curran, Jones, and Maguire: "I say to you, what good will it do the State of Delaware, the citizens at large, if you take three young lives?" His logic was, if Maguire's wife, who testified for him, "is confident and believes in him, can't you have that same belief, and if you have that same belief in him, you should have it in his companions, and you should realize that this case contains that real element of reasonable doubt and you are duty bound, bound by your oaths as jurors, to bring in a verdict of not guilty as to all three."[229]

As soon as Reinhardt finished, Chief Justice Richards told the jury that, by agreement with counsel, "we have decided to have a session tonight." He assured the jurors the arguments "will be finished tonight" and estimated the arguments "this evening will consume from two to three hours." He then excused the jurors until seven o'clock.[230]

Neither James nor Hagner nor Reinhardt had any time between the conclusion of the testimony and the beginning of the summations to prepare what they were going to say. Hy Young had slightly more time to prepare what he would say between the time Reinhardt finished and the jury returned at 7:00 p.m. But he knew as soon as he had completed his examination of the young woman on the morning of the second day of the trial that he faced the problem of showing the jury why they should question her truthfulness.

By the time he rose to speak, Young knew he could not rely

on the jurors to accept the testimony of the defendants as true. Try as he could and did about Jones, he had been unable to prove the police were lying when they claimed the defendants had signed only one statement. The three eyewitnesses had been of help since they had supported significant portions of the defendants' testimony. But there was one area where he could demonstrate why the jurors should not accept the prosecuting witness' claim, namely, the multiple contradictions between her testimony at the preliminary hearing on November 12, 1947, and her testimony at the trial on February 10 and 11, 1948, where on cross-examination Young had tracked the contradictions with her.[231] Young had the transcript of the preliminary hearing and he, Reinhardt, and Hagner each received the transcript of that day's trial testimony. All Young had to do was enumerate for the jurors the instances where she swore one way at the preliminary hearing and differently at the trial. But that is not what he did.

Instead, Young began with a personal reference that never before had he "been charged with so grave a responsibility and so important a duty as I have been charged with in this case. . . ."[232] The personal point only reminded the jury of his long record of representing criminal defendants, a fact of little, if any, importance to the jurors in this case. He then tried to charm the jury while emphasizing the importance of the facts: ". . . It is in this fortress of justice where our refuge lies. And during the entire proceedings we have felt reasonably sure that idle gossip and rumor have been laid aside and that you have been weighing only facts and evidence in the case."[233]

He first played down his lack of success in his cross-examination of the young woman: "*And while I had the opportunity, members of the jury, and I could have pursued more thoroughly than I did the questioning of the complaining witness,* it was because of my feeling for the complaining witness, although she sought refuge in just two statements: 'I was hysterical,' 'I don't remember,' 'I hollered and screamed all the time.' It sounded like a record. [Emphasis added.]"[234]

He then went on to explain: "*But I felt sorry for her, and I did not pursue the questions further because I knew that there would be independent testimony introduced in the case that would show you exactly what did happen,* and whether she did in fact holler and scream all the time, and whether she was in fact hysterical all the time and didn't know what was going on. [Emphasis added.]"[235] Clearly, Young questioned her veracity.

Young also gave the impression, or at least wanted to, that he was so satisfied with the "independent testimony introduced in the case" that when he referred to it there was no need to repeat it:

"Dynie" Fahey and Jones got out of the car to see what was going on, and later they were joined by Maguire and Masten and Schuler. *They told you what they saw. I am not going to repeat it. You heard it. You will remember it.* And afterwards they heard Curran say, "Scram Magwa," or "Scram Lash," I don't recall the exact words; and Jones and Masten and Schuler and Fahey left the park, so that it left in the park Maguire, Curran and the complaining witness. [Emphasis added.][236]

Should Young have repeated the testimony of Fahey, Masten, and Schueler rather than rely on the jurors' memory? I doubt it, since they departed with Jones, leaving Curran, Maguire, and the woman in the park, as Young noted. The three eyewitnesses thus were not present when the never-identified woman called out or when Jones returned to the park. Should Young have referred to Leonzio's testimony corroborating the presence of the three eyewitnesses? Although he knew that Duffy had tried to suggest in his cross-examination the three were not there, Young did not remind the jurors of Leonzio's corroborating testimony about their presence. But I doubt even Young anticipated how Duffy in

his summation, yet to come, would talk about the three eyewitnesses.

Reiterating the same point Reinhardt had made, Young too
noted the absence of photographs of the young woman's face.
He then issued an implicit challenge to the prosecution to address in the rebuttal summation:

> If she was in this horrible condition, members of the jury, do you
> think that the hospital would let her go without medication, without
> treatment? And I say if that face was in the condition that it was—we
> have had all of the dirty underwear in this case—you would have had
> photographs in this case, if it showed anything of any consequence.
>
> And don't let my friend say that the pictures would not have been
> taken, or were not taken because of the certain intimacies and private
> parts of the complaining witness. There was no hesitation in bringing
> all this in, there wouldn't have been any hesitation in bringing the
> other things in.[237]

By including a reference to "private parts," Young expanded
upon what Reinhardt had said about photographs. Reinhardt
only spoke of facial photographs. Young suggested more than
that, providing yet another opportunity for the state to seize.

Young, as had Reinhardt, specifically challenged the state to
explain "how the underpants could have been gotten or taken
off [the young woman] without a single tear . . . , and how the
sanitary belt, with all that rubber and all that paraphernalia here
could be taken off without a single tear."[238]

He then turned to discuss other evidence. Unlike Hagner's approach—explaining what had occurred was the result of the
drinking by all the participants—Young adopted Reinhardt's
confrontational assertion, asking the jurors to blame the young
woman: "That under the evidence I am firmly convinced and I
believe you will be of the same mind, that the sorrow and the
tragedy was initiated and motivated by the complaining wit-

ness."[239] The basis for his charge was in effect, that the young woman had control of what happened. He illustrated his point by the following facts: (1) she could have taken a number 4 bus directly to her home from Eighth and Market but, instead, chose a different bus; (2) she could have changed at Lancaster Avenue and Union, the regular transfer point, but, instead, she chose to get off at Fourth and Union; (3) she could have waited at Fourth and Union, but, instead, chose to cross Fourth and then walk the short block to Bancroft Parkway "and stood in the dark recess of a doorway, where there is no bus stop and there is no transfer point"; (4) when Curran asked to walk her home, she could have told him "No" but, instead, she chose to walk off with Curran, "a boy she had never seen . . . [or] talked with in her life before," in a direction opposite from her home.[240]

With one exception, Reinhardt and Young repeated what Hagner had already said. The exception was their placing the young woman standing "in the dark recesses of a doorway."[241] But Hagner placed her at "the corner of Fourth and Bancroft Parkway . . . where there were no buses that came by that point, no motor coaches, no buses of any kind. . . ."[242] The significant difference in tone between the two versions is that Hagner's was not confrontational while Young's and Reinhardt's were. Hagner did not confront the young woman's claim that she was not standing in the Skinner doorway. But the state could not dispute the accuracy of Hagner's description.

If Reinhardt and Young wanted the jurors to discredit the young woman's story that she was walking on Fourth between Bancroft Parkway and Union, they could and should have cited to the fact that no one in Maguire's car saw her there. Had she been walking where and when she claimed, she would have been visible in the headlights on Maguire's car. Yet neither Reinhardt nor Young made this point, a point that simultaneously would have attacked her credibility and buttressed the defendants'.

Reinhardt's and Young's emphasis on placing the young woman standing in Skinner's doorway did not help the defense; it only distracted the jury's attention.

The more significant fact, of course, is not where she was standing, but rather her willingness to go off with Bud Curran, a boy she did not know, in a direction opposite to her home, after accepting his offer to walk her home, a point first Hagner, then Reinhardt, and, finally, Young, repeatedly made. In short, Young added nothing to what had already been said, effectively by Hagner and crudely by Reinhardt.[243]

In his summation Young made no mention of Sonny Jones' shorts. To corroborate the testimony of the three defendants that they had "no complete intercourse," Young did refer to "the findings, spermatozoa over the clothes, over the pants, and everywhere, except in the vaginal tract, according to Dr. Smith, the police surgeon, and the mute testimony in the case, the hospital record 'Vaginal smear, no semen.'"[244] But he did not refer to the conflict between the testimony of McCool and Dr. Tiffany about Jones' shorts.

Nor did Young address the number of statements. To have done so would have underscored the disparity between the three defendants' truthful testimony that they signed twice and the police officers' lying testimony that each defendant had signed only once. There was no point in emphasizing in his summation what he was not able to establish at the trial.

At the preliminary hearing, Young suggested his client, Jones, was unjustly accused.[245] At trial, he tried to secure an admission from the woman that she "did not have any sexual relations with Jones at all."[246] Her denial ended Young's effort to differentiate Jones from Curran and Maguire. The claim did not surface in his summation.

Young did have to address the black cloud overhanging the case. With all the testimony in, the police lies cast doubt on the defendants' credibility. He knew the woman's credibility had not been destroyed either by the testimony of the defendants and the three eyewitnesses or by his cross-examination. The record was clear: the three eyewitnesses had departed the park before the woman from a neighboring house yelled, threatening to call the police. Given the record, Young was compelled to consider and mention the possibility, if not the probability, that the jurors would conclude the defendants were guilty of rape. In what he said he had to tread a fine line to avoid suggesting that was the case. Saving this point for last, Young told the jury: "I could go on and on and on and show you the inconsistencies between what the complaining witness said and what was introduced in evidence by the defendants and by the witnesses on behalf of the defendants." He referred to the fact, ". . . I have stood up before juries on many, many occasions, but in this particular case . . . I had the feeling that there were twelve jurors, that they were going and are going to weigh the evidence in this case." Young claimed: "I did not come here tonight to steal your hearts. I merely am performing my duty in summing up what I believe the crystal-clear evidence in this case, and . . . according to the evidence in this case it would be one of the greatest miscarriages of justice if the lives of these three boys . . . if their lives are to be taken for what the complaining witness did and instigated on the night of October 29, and, more than that, it is just as serious a punishment if forever . . . the door of freedom, should be shut in the faces of these three boys. . . . It is not the punishment that these boys deserve."[247]

Young then turned to yet another point Reinhardt had already made, a point neither should have made since it conceded wrongdoing by the defendants:

If you were to ask me did they do anything wrong that night? I openly and honestly and sincerely say to you of course they did. They did things that night that could be called lewdness, which is punishable in this State, or adultery, which is punishable, or attempted adultery, which is punishable in this State. There was indecent exposure in a public place, yes, that is true, but it was not rape which justifies the hanging of three boys.[248]

Young repeated what Reinhardt had said about "reasonable doubt" and "the presumption of innocence." Finally, he told the jurors:

And we hope in view of the evidence in this case, because the case, notwithstanding what anyone may say, has had a salutary effect, and you and I have performed the great service in bringing to light the fact that it is true that women shall have the right to walk the streets, but that it is also true that when women invite the attentions and the liberties of the promiscuity that was invited in this case, those are the consequences.

And under the evidence, and in view of the facts of this case, I know that you members of the jury, on the evidence and the evidence solely, will return with a verdict that is courageous and honest and proper, and that is a verdict of not guilty as to all three.[249]

Young had no proof of the police perjury beyond the testimony of the three young men. His rhetoric and showmanship were no substitute for the proof he lacked. One can only imagine what he could and would have done to restore their credibility and to establish they had not committed the crime of rape had he had the woman's statement the prosecution deliberately withheld and the post-trial McCool's Report buried in the police department files despite its proof the police had lied.

When Young finished, it was the state's turn to sum up. Chief Deputy Duffy rose to make the state's rebuttal. He began by sympathizing with the jury, but quickly made clear he wanted to eliminate sympathy as a factor in the jurors' deliberations:

We are now drawing to an end this long tedious trial. I know you are tired. You have been patient. I wish it were so that it could be submitted to you now without consuming any more of your time, but as representing the State I do have a duty to perform and that is to discuss these facts with you for a few minutes. I shall make it as brief as possible, but I must of necessity do what I think is necessary in order to discharge my obligation. *We are trying facts, gentlemen, and only facts. We are not trying personalities. We are not trying families. We are not to be swayed by sympathy, and I know you won't be, and what I shall do is, at every turn, present and discuss with you nothing but facts, because after all they are what will determine your ultimate verdict.* [Emphasis added.][250]

Duffy immediately turned to the challenges Young and Reinhardt had made: "Before I forget it, I want to answer the challenge of Mr. Young and Mr. Reinhardt. [They have] challenged me to explain to you how these spots, how those leaves, how the dirt, how the semen, how the spermatozoa, got on these pants, *how they got off that girl without being torn.*" [Emphasis added.] To Duffy the explanation was simple. After noting the elasticity of the undergarments, Duffy told the jurors: "That the only natural inference and conclusion that you can draw from the facts, that the blood, semen, and spermatozoa are on the pants, that *Curran, at the outset, in his frenzied, beastial attack, attempted to have intercourse with this girl with her pants on and, being unsuccessful, ripped them off.*" [Emphasis added.][251] In addressing the jury, Duffy, as had Reinhardt, spoke to the "gentlemen," and ignored the two women on the jury, perhaps out of habit since the presence of women on juries occurred for the first time in Delaware in *The Rape Case.*[252]

The explanation for the removal of the sanitary belt, Duffy asserted, was the same: "[it] came off with the pants." He explained: "Where is the sanitary belt? There is the answer to your attack, gentlemen, when [Curran] ripped off those pants, he

ripped off the sanitary belt at the same time, and he was so frenzied, so excited, that he did not even know he had done it. I
think that is sufficient to answer Mr. Young's challenge."[253]

Duffy then took up Reinhardt's challenge "to show one instance on any material point where there is a conflict between
the testimony of Masten, Fahey, and Schuler, and these three defendants. Gentlemen, I will mention just one." But Duffy used
two illustrations: the testimony about who sat where in Maguire's car coupled with Curran's telling Maguire and Jones to leave
the park without mentioning any of the eyewitnesses. His conclusion was that the testimony proved not only that Fahey was
not there, but neither were Masten and Schueler.[254] Although
Curran placed Jones in the front seat, the testimony of Maguire
placed Masten in the front seat. Fahey, Jones, and Schueler
agreed with Maguire. Masten was not asked where he sat.[255] The
fact Curran only called out to Maguire and Jones does not negate
the sworn testimony of Curran, Jones, Maguire, Fahey, Masten,
and Schueler that they all were in the park.

Duffy boldly told the jurors: "Those three defendants were
cruising around to find the first girl they could see, and when
they found one it was going to be too bad."[256] Although Duffy's
claim had no support in the record, his assertion, if true, eliminated the presence of Schueler, Masten, and Fahey. The jurors
could accept Duffy's statement only if the police testimony had
destroyed the credibility of Curran, Jones, and Maguire. And
that the police had done. Duffy's outrageous charge that Fahey,
Masten, and Schueler were not even there were the last words
the jurors heard from the lawyers on the point before the charge.

Duffy directly took issue with the defense claim by Reinhardt
and Young that the young woman stood in the doorway of Skinner's store. He relied upon the testimony of Jones and Maguire,
both of whom noticed the young woman standing on the northeast corner of Fourth and Bancroft Parkway, without saying any-

thing about her standing in the doorway of Skinner's store.[257]
But in making his claim Duffy said nothing about Curran's statement to the police which Duffy himself introduced in evidence
where Curran, without coaching from anyone, said he first saw
the young woman standing in the doorway of Skinner's store.
Nor did Duffy say anything about Curran's sworn testimony that
"as we passed the intersection at Fourth and Bancroft Parkway I
seen someone standing in front of the store. I told Maguire to
stop the car and I would get out and get a match, and he stopped
the car on the other side of the plot [dividing Bancroft Park-
way]."[258] Nor did Duffy say anything about the testimony of
Jones, Maguire, Fahey, and Masten, all four of whom testified
they did not see the young woman until after Curran got out of
the car and walked back to where she was standing in front of
Skinner's store; Schueler testified he did not notice.[259] Nor did
Duffy refer to the young woman's October 30, 1947 statement to
the police where she said she was standing on the northeast corner of Fourth and Bancroft Parkway when Maguire stopped his
car and Curran approached her. And, finally, Duffy said nothing
about the fact that she did not assert in her statement she was
walking up and down Fourth between Bancroft Parkway and
Union. The state had neither produced nor put the statement in
evidence.

About the defendants' most telling defense, stressed repeatedly
by all three defense lawyers in their summations, that the young
woman willingly went off with Curran to the park in a direction
opposite from her home, Duffy's answer was that "she made a
horrible mistake in going with Curran. . . ." "But you heard the
girl testify," he told the jurors, "she is a shy, timid, naïve, trusting girl . . . here is a shy, trusting girl twenty-three years old,
obviously an inexperienced, naïve girl, you can tell that from her
manner on the stand, and she went with Curran. True, it was a
tragic mistake for her to make, but the girl never had one

thought that he was going to do anything such as he did. I am not going to dwell at any length on it, but you remember the testimony of some of these witnesses."[260] In not dwelling "at any length on it," Duffy avoided dealing with the fact that *Curran was walking the young woman in a direction away from her home without any protest on her part.*

Duffy referred to the alleged attempt to have oral sex to which the girl had testified: "And then, ladies and gentlemen of the jury, the testimony of that—as I characterize it—dirty, filthy act, do you suppose for one instance that that shy girl would have told you of . . . the bestial act that Maguire perpetrated on her while Curran was having intercourse with her, if it were not true? Do you suppose it was any pleasure for that girl to give you that horrible testimony? I am not going to dwell on that any more, ladies and gentlemen."[261] Duffy did not refer to Maguire's vigorous denial: "I never did such a dirty, filthy thing."[262]

Duffy did not lack for an answer to the challenge Reinhardt and Young had posed about the absence of photographs the police could easily have made to support their claim of injury to the young woman:

And my friend asks about pictures. I am surprised at him. Hasn't [the young woman] suffered enough? He told us about her personal garments being brought in, and if it is not too pleasant for anybody, it is not too pleasant for us, but there are bits of evidence that we have to have in order to prosecute the case. I don't have to send a photographer out to [the young woman's] home and ask her to expose herself to photographs of the most intimate nature and bring them in this courtroom. I think that you members of the jury can learn just as much, and are intelligent enough to take the testimony of a doctor, and yet Mr. Young would have me bring in photographs. The poor girl can't even rest now.[263]

Despite Duffy's implied disclaimer, the fact was the police, by Lieutenant Charles E. Bryan Jr. of the Identification Division, on the morning of October 31 beginning at about 9:30 a.m., *did take* "five photographs of the face and body of [the young woman]" at her home. The photographs were "numbered in [the police] records as No. 1 to No. 5, inclusive."[264] Yet the state did not call Bryan as a witness.[265] The defendants and their lawyers were unaware of the photographs. Worse yet, in his summation Duffy was careful not to claim that *he* sent a photographer to take photographs. The fact was the police on their own took the photographs. Given their accessibility to the police records, Attorney General James and Chief Deputy Attorney General Duffy undoubtedly knew of the photographs. Given the facts that the police took the photographs and had them on file, for Duffy to deny their existence is shocking and his disclaimer disingenuous if not an outright lie.

In his references to the defendants, Duffy described a "frenzied, beastial attack" and said Curran was "a sex maniac and a beast." He concluded with a reference to the "savage, wicked attack" by "three maniacs."[266] In contrast, he depicted the prosecuting witness as "a shy, timid, naïve, trusting girl," "a shy, trusting girl twenty-three years old, obviously an inexperienced, naïve girl, you can tell that from her manner on the stand. . . ."[267]

Before ending, Duffy directly raised whether the jurors should make a recommendation of mercy if their verdict were guilty, provided, in their opinion, the facts of the case so justified which was the law of Delaware. He first commented on what a verdict of guilty would mean. In doing so he, perhaps inadvertently, put in context the issue of credibility. "If your verdict is guilty, you will have believed the testimony of [the young woman], you will have believed that these three defendants raped her."[268]

Duffy then fell back on a prosecutor's typical urging to inflame the jurors: "If you think that Francis Curran showed [the young woman] any mercy, you are at liberty to recommend it." He used similar words about Maguire and Jones, telling the jurors, "I am satisfied that under no circumstances, no stretch of the imagination, that you [can] find it in your heart to show mercy to any of these three."[269] His final words made clear his goal: "I am satisfied that there can't be any possible doubt in your mind, and that you will be convinced beyond a reasonable doubt that Curran, Jones, and Maguire did rape [the young woman], and that your verdict will be guilty."[270]

Duffy had made an effective summation without explicitly using the words "death penalty" or "death sentence." There was no question, that Duffy, for himself and James, sought a guilty verdict without a recommendation of mercy which meant a death sentence. The following morning the newspaper account trumpeted the state's position in its headline: "State in Summation Leaves No Doubt of Its Desire for Verdict With Hanging Penalty."[271]

The summations took three hours and three minutes in all. The state used one hour and twenty-nine minutes, and the defense consumed a total of one hour and thirty-four minutes. The state's time was divided thirty-three minutes for James and fifty-six minutes for Duffy. The defending attorneys divided their time fourteen minutes for Hagner, nineteen minutes for Reinhardt, and one hour and one minute for Young.[272]

In hindsight one can only wonder how the defendants would have fared had the jurors heard only Hagner's summation. Hagner had not claimed the young woman stood in Skinner's doorway as Reinhardt and Young had; all he claimed was she was standing on the dark corner of Fourth and Bancroft Parkway. He did not issue a challenge, as Reinhardt and Young had, for the prosecution to explain the absence of any tear in the young woman's underwear or sanitary belt, providing Duffy the opportunity to talk about the elasticity of the garments and Curran's "beastial frenzy." He did not challenge the prosecution, as Reinhardt had, to show an instance of a material point of difference between the testimony of the three eyewitnesses and the three defendants, thereby enabling Duffy to seize upon Curran's error in memory about who sat to his left in the front seat of Maguire's car. Nor did Hagner challenge the prosecution, as first Reinhardt and then Young did, about the absence of photographs, giving Duffy the opening to claim the defense would deprive the young woman any rest even now by insisting she expose her private parts for photographs despite the existence of such photographs in the police records.

By what Reinhardt and Young said they permitted Duffy to explain and excuse the young woman's walking off with Curran, a boy she did not know and had never seen, in an opposite direction from her home. Duffy did not have to address the doubts Hagner had pointed out in her story. Duffy never had to address Hagner's on-point explanation of the tragedy: the consumption of alcohol which affected the judgment of the participants. In short, if Reinhardt and Young had said nothing and left Hagner's studied, nonconfrontational approach as the defendants' last word, the result might not have changed, but Duffy surely would not have had so many opportunities to exploit what Reinhardt and Young offered him. Given the withholding of the woman's statement from the defense, the jurors, and the court, and the successful attack on the defendants' credibility by the police, coupled with Duffy's summation, there probably was no way the defendants could have avoided their convictions.

The Charge

Chief Justice Richards began his charge to the jury the next morning, Tuesday, February 17, 1948. He summarized the outstanding counts of the indictment, first setting forth the state's arguments.[273] He then separately stated the defendants' contentions with one exception.[274] Starting with the defendants' claim concerning the presence of three eyewitnesses, Richards charged:

All of the defendants contend that on the evening of October 29, 1947, they went to the Labor Lyceum on DuPont Street, between Fourth and Fifth Streets, where they stayed until about 11:15; that *they left there in an automobile of the defendant, Maguire, accompanied by John E. Masten, Edward J. Fahey and Warren Schuler, and went to the Embassy Cafe, staying till about 12:05, when they went to Fourth and Union Streets.* [Emphasis added.][275]

Although he identified the three eyewitnesses who provided the critical testimony supporting the defendants' denials of raping the young woman, never once in his twenty-seven page charge did Richards refer to their corroborating testimony.[276]

The Star of the Trial

The Rape Case, of course, was about the guilt or innocence of Curran, Jones, and Maguire. But if there was a star at the trial it was H. Albert Young, "a colorful figure," as Ellen H. Crossman, the *Sunday Star* reporter, described him after the fifth day of trial:

The faultlessly tailored, silver-thatched lawyer is a showman. His theatrics in the courtroom are well known. He is managing, by his adroit questioning, to instill doubt in the audience, and perhaps in the minds of the jury—though no one can tell that until the verdict is rendered.

Mr. Young is a past master as everyone knows from his reputation as a criminal lawyer. He is wearing a different suit every day of the trial.[277]

Reinhardt and Hagner deferred to Young, the more experienced lawyer by far in defending a criminal case, and willingly let him man the laboring oar. It was Young at the outset of the trial who spoke for all the defendants concerning the introduction of maps and photographs of the scene as exhibits.[278] It was Young who cross-examined the prosecuting witness, after which Reinhardt and Hagner first conferred and then told the court they had no questions.[279] It was Young who made the opening statement for all three defendants.[280] It was Young who examined eyewitnesses Masten and Schueler as well as the corroborating witness, Leonzio.[281] It was Young who made the longest summation to the jury.[282] And it was Young who made the main argument in support of the motion for a new trial.[283]

The deference Hagner and Reinhardt paid to Young was their recognition of his preeminence in defending a criminal case. Although both Hagner and Reinhardt had served as deputy attorney generals shortly after their respective admissions to the Bar, neither could match Hy Young's extensive experience in criminal defense work. The reported cases reflect that from 1922, the year of Hagner's admission to the Bar, to the time of his appointment in the fall of 1947 to represent Curran, there is not a single reported criminal case where Hagner represented a defendant. Similarly, between his 1927 admission and *The Rape Case,* Reinhardt appeared in only one reported criminal defense case, and in that one Young also appears for the defendants. In contrast, between Young's 1929 admission and *The Rape Case,* he represented defendants in sixteen reported criminal cases including four capital cases in the Court of Oyer and Terminer.[284]

The responsibilities he bore at trial and his persistence in seeking the truth about the two sets of statements, the only lawyer to do so, clearly established Young from the start as the star of *The Rape Case.*

The Verdict

On Tuesday, February 17, 1948, "the seventh day of the longest criminal trial in the court for many years," the court convened late after meeting with the lawyers about the charge.[285]

Following Richards' charge, the twelve jurors retired a few minutes after 11:30 a.m. to take lunch and deliberate.[286] Including time for lunch, they were out less than three hours before returning at 2:39 p.m. with their verdict.[287] The Chief Justice warned the audience in the crowded courtroom not to demonstrate when the jurors announced their verdict.[288] Deputy Clerk of the Peace John L. Malone then conducted a roll call to reflect in the record the presence of all twelve jurors, and proceeded with the ritual still observed today:

MR. MALONE: Ladies and gentlemen of the jury, have you agreed upon a verdict?
THE FOREMAN OF THE JURY: We have.
MR. MALONE: Who shall answer for you?
JURORS: Our foreman.
MR. MALONE: How say you, Madam Foreman, do you find the prisoner, Francis J. Curran, guilty in manner and form as he stands indicted in the first count or not guilty?
THE FOREMAN OF THE JURY: Guilty.[289]

When the forelady, Isabelle Booth, spoke the single word "guilty" about Curran, "There was an electrifying silence while the word penetrated through the courtroom."[290] Because the jury had not recommended mercy, the guilty verdict meant an automatic sentence of death. The lawyers had not merely lost a case; their clients were going to die. Reinhardt was the first defense lawyer to react: "I ask that the jury be polled."[291]

What then ensued was as dramatic a scene as had ever occurred in a Delaware courtroom. With a nod of assent from

Richards, Deputy Malone went forward to poll the jurors one by one. In response to the question, "Is that your verdict," the first eight jurors confirmed it was. The ninth juror, Richard E. Porter, answered "It is, with a recommendation of mercy." Porter's different response did not register with Malone as he continued with the same question to the tenth juror, Louis H. Talley. Talley responded "It is. We couldn't hear Mrs. Booth, with a recommendation of the mercy of this Court." Whereupon Mrs. Booth interjected: "I did not know whether I was to give that now or when you finished, but we do make that recommendation."[292]

The recommendation of mercy, provided two of the three judges accepted it, meant the court would impose the statutorily mandated sentence of life imprisonment upon Curran, Jones, and Maguire.[293] Without the polling, there would have been no recommendation, and the issue of the trial's unfairness might well have died with the three accused.

Although there was no outcry, "Maguire's wife and mother, Curran's mother and other women in the courtroom wept. Jones' mother, who was not in the courtroom, was said to have been home in a state of collapse."[294]

But the accused were not to die by the jury's verdict and the court order. On March 16, 1948, after denying the defendants' motions to set aside the verdict, the court unanimously accepted the jury's recommendation of mercy and sentenced the three young men each to a term of life in prison, a sentence, Chief Justice Richards said, "is sufficient punishment to meet the ends of justice."[295] "The three men took the sentence without display of emotion, and soon after were led from the courtroom."[296]

No appeal followed their sentencing. The now-convicted defendants and their families did not have the money to pay lawyers for an appeal. Neither their trial lawyers nor any other lawyer at Delaware's Bar volunteered to take an appeal. Moreover, there was then no history in the Delaware justice system requiring the appointment of counsel to seek the review of a life sentence. The sentiment many held was that the defendants were lucky to be alive. From the time of their arrest on October 30, 1947, with the exception of the one night they had spent in the lockup deep in the basement of the Public Building, the state had held them at the New Castle County Workhouse at Price's Corner, southwest of Wilmington. And there they remained. In the years that followed, only family members (and not all of them) thought about helping. But neither the convicted young men nor their families knew what to do.

When the *The Rape Case* trial ended, I was just two months past my twenty-second birthday—about the same age as the defendants—and in the second semester of my first year at the Yale Law School. Immersed in my studies and miles away in New Haven, Connecticut, I was unaware of the arrests, the trial, the convictions, and the sentences of my hometown contemporaries, none of whom I knew.

4

The Families Suffer

Bright, petite Marie Curran was in the fourth grade at St. Thomas Roman Catholic School. Years later her classmate, Joseph Matassino, remembered her as always raising her hand to answer questions the teacher posed. Marie knew the answers. But then her brother Bud was arrested and charged with rape. The Curran family had never known the stigma of public disgrace. They had faith in Bud's innocence. After all, the woman had entered the park willingly with him as she herself testified. They believed Bud when he told them she consented to his attentions. Moreover, Bud denied he had ever physically entered her, an essential element of the crime of rape. Following the arrest, Marie withdrew into a shell and ceased to raise her hand in class.[1]

Helen Curran, twenty-one at the time of the trial, had gone to work at age eighteen for Joseph Bancroft and Sons, the Wilmington mill where her mother had worked for many years. Following the arrest of her brother, some of her coworkers made nasty comments.[2] Learning of them, W. Ralph MacIntyre, vice president of Bancroft and superintendent of the mill, called a meeting of all the employees.[3] He pointed out that a number of employees at the mill were related to the three arrested men. In his stentorian voice, he set forth the policy: "We will not discuss this case!" He went on to say if he learned that anyone did discuss the case, that person would be fired. The nasty comments ceased. Helen's immediate supervisor, Alf R. Valentine, Bancroft's assistant treasurer, took her aside and offered money to help if she and the family needed it.[4] Helen thanked him but declined his sensitive offer.

Catherine "Kitty" Curran, seventeen at the time of the trial and the closest sibling to Bud both in age and friendship, worked in production at Address-o-graph. Her talent quickly brought her to the post of production supervisor, where she trained not only the Address-o-graph staff but also the personnel of companies who purchased the equipment. The boss, Alex P. Ardito, laid her off when the case broke, claiming Address-o-graph could no longer send forth Kitty Curran as its representative.[5] Charles Hitchens in Personnel had worked with her father at the Dravo shipyard in Wilmington during World War II. Empathetic as Hitchens was to Kitty and as much as he valued her as an employee, he could do nothing. He told her were he to intervene, he would lose his job. She immediately looked for work elsewhere and answered an ad for a job at the Diamond Ice and Coal Company. During the interview with Harry West, she told him she was Bud Curran's sister and would need time off to attend the trial when it took place.[6] West's supportive response was immediate: "When can you start?"

One of Nellie Curran's brothers, Joseph McHugh, stopped talking to his sister after the arrest. Early one evening Kitty found her mother in tears in the kitchen. Kitty drew out of her the reason for the tears: Joe had passed Nellie on the street without acknowledging her. Kitty took off to Uncle Joe's house where she told him he should be ashamed of himself and, moreover, if he ever brought tears to her mother's eyes again, he would answer to her.

On the day after the trial ended, Bud's not-yet-sixteen-year-old sister, Margaret Josephine ("Peggy") Curran, incensed by a letter from "E. K. H." the *Journal* published on February 18, 1948, wrote to the paper. She made abundantly clear the family's view of Bud's accuser and her testimony:

From a Defendant's Sister

TO THE EDITOR: Concerning a letter written by E. K. H. published in "Letters to the Editor" column, Feb. 18, I quote, "I waited one night for one hour and 20 minutes (11:30 p.m.–12:50 a.m.) at Fourth and Market Streets for a No. 4 while only one bus (Newark) and three 4–1s passed by." Perhaps if E. K. H. would tell the date she waited for that trolley, I could check with the coach company and satisfy myself as to how many No. 4s really passed. She seems to forget that an official from the Delaware Coach Company took the stand and testified that [the alleged victim], on the night of Oct. 29, 1947, had her pick of "three trolleys and two buses" and this is gospel truth and I'm willing to stake my life on it.

Furthermore I quote: "Incidentally, what has a late hour got to do with a girl's decency?" Let me ask you, E. K. H.? Would a "decent" girl wait on a very dark corner in a store doorway where she could neither see not hear a trolley or a bus and then go off with the first man (unknown) that spoke to her? . . .[7]

At about the time of the trial, Francis and Nellie Curran conceived a child. During the entire pregnancy, Nellie suffered the torment of concern about her oldest son, now convicted of rape and sentenced to life imprisonment. On October 18, 1948, she gave birth to a boy, Richard. He was a large, handsome baby, weighing eleven pounds, Helen and Kitty recalled years later. He lived only an hour. As his father washed the little baby's body, he tried to soothe him with words of love while the sisters who had gathered around wept. Richard was the thirteenth and last child born to the Currans.

Jenny Jones, Sonny's mother, believed in her son's innocence. Before her death in 1949 at the age of sixty-one, just months after her son began his mandatory life sentence, Jenny asked two of her daughters, Virginia McKinley and Jayne Stigliano, to promise they would continue to do all they could to get their brother out of jail. It was a promise they never forgot. In contrast, Jenny's oldest daughter was so mortified by Sonny's arrest that she and her husband moved to Baltimore, Maryland. A fourth daughter distanced herself from the family.[8]

The arrest and subsequent conviction of their son, Reds Maguire, brought shame upon the Maguire family. Nonetheless, they remained convinced of his innocence, especially after his brother Ed told them of the scuttlebutt in the Police Department about perjury at the trial and about his subsequent exchange with Superintendent Andrew J. Kavanaugh, who promised to investigate. Even when time passed without word from Kavanaugh, they did not despair. Doris' later divorce action against Francis was yet another blow to the family.

The three families soldiered on in the effort to find some way to help their sons. They were held together by the common bond of belief that their sons were innocent and had not had a fair trial. The bond was sorely tested as the weeks stretched into months and the months into years while the three men continued to serve life sentences.

5

Searching for a Lawyer

With her son in jail and her family in disgrace, it was a dark time for Nellie Curran. She believed Bud was innocent and his incarceration unjust. But who would help prove it? She could not and would not turn aside from the teaching of her faith that God would not forsake her or her family.

Shortly after the trial she sat in her living room reading an article entitled "He Frees The Innocent" by Frederic Sondern Jr. in the January 1948 issue of *The Reader's Digest*. Wilmington City Councilman Walter Brady had called the article to her attention. His sister, Gertrude, was married to Nellie's brother, Joseph McHugh. From the article Nellie learned of Herbert L. Maris, an uncommon lawyer. Years earlier, Maris had turned aside from his Philadelphia practice in corporate law. In his new career he worked to free persons accused of crime or already convicted and incarcerated. The decision in one case reduced the stays in prison of some 700 prisoners.[1] His conscience placed few limits on his willingness to help others, a stark contrast to his fastidious protection of his pocketbook. His lifelong frugality enabled him to afford his new practice with its low overhead. Brady urged Nellie Curran to call or write to Maris.

After a telephone conversation with Maris, Nellie Curran sent her husband, Francis, to meet him in Philadelphia. With his secretary, Samuel Thompson, and his investigator, George S. Corbeil, present, Maris listened as Bud's father told the story of his son's conviction and the claim of innocence by all three. Maris said he would look into the matter to determine whether the youths received a fair trial.

But before Maris would act, he wanted to read the trial transcript, which the families did not have because of its cost. So he guided them in securing it. The Curran family bought the 1,086 page transcript one section at a time. Years later, R. Harry Brown and Leon Ackerman, the court reporters, told me that Chief Justice Richards resisted their typing the transcript and selling it to the families. (I was also to learn from Harry, after I promised not to use the information in my effort to free my clients, that Richards made changes in the transcript before he permitted its delivery. Neither Harry nor anyone else told me what the changes were.)

Maris assigned Corbeil to go to Wilmington and ferret out the facts. After he received Corbeil's report covering Corbeil's reading of the transcript and interviews with Curran, Jones, and Maguire in the New Castle County Workhouse, Maris believed an injustice had taken place. At Maris' urging, Corbeil also interviewed several jurors in an effort "to find out why the 'Weight of evidence' in trial testimony did not militate in favor of the defense and thus satisfy ourselves that some elements did, in fact, destroy the credibility of not only the defendants, but of their eye-witnesses as well."[2] According to Corbeil, one of the jurors, Louis H. Talley, told him "the jury agreed the eyewitnesses were not only lieing [sic] but in fact were not eyewitnesses at all."[3] Talley's statement confirmed the success of Duffy's trial tactics. Over time, Corbeil became close to the families, particularly the Currans. His frequent visits buoyed their spirits when they still did not have the required Delaware lawyer to move the admission of the Philadelphia lawyer willing to help. Corbeil believed not only in the unfairness of the trial but also in the defendants' innocence. Relying on Corbeil, as he knew he could, Maris came to believe in their innocence as well. He was the first lawyer to hold out hope for their release.

During the time Corbeil conducted his investigation for Maris, the Currans received anonymous telephone calls. One caller urged them to "tell that Philadelphia lawyer to lay off the case." Some callers threatened them. Years later I learned from one of the Curran daughters that even their family physician had come to their home and urged them to take Maris off the case, telling them: "A man high up in this town asked me to tell you this." But not all the calls were negative. A woman who did not identify herself told Nellie Curran the prisoners' statements had been retyped and the typist, Officer Nagle, "would talk." That there was a second set of statements was not news to Nellie and her family nor to the other families and surely not to their sons. What they needed was proof of what they knew.

Mrs. Curran shared the information about Nagle with Maris and Corbeil. New to the police force as of April 16, 1947, Nagle had gone to pieces emotionally after *The Rape Case* trial. The Wilmington Department of Public Safety dismissed him in January 1949 after he was accused of being drunk on duty. Following Nagle's dismissal, Bud Curran's father arranged to meet with him. The two rode around in Nagle's car and talked. Nagle gave Francis Curran veiled information and agreed to talk further with George Corbeil, the investigator.[4]

On February 13, 1949, Corbeil met with Nagle. In his report, Corbeil related that Nagle appeared "nervous and worried." Initially, all Nagle would admit was that the statements Maguire and Jones gave at the police station "might have been retyped." He claimed if the defense attorneys had asked him one more question when he was on the witness stand, "and if that question was the right one regarding the statements, the truth would have come out."[5]

Early in September 1949, Nagle arranged to meet the Reverend Francis X. Burns, a young priest who lived at the rectory of St. Elizabeth's Roman Catholic Church on South Broom and who served as chaplain at the New Castle County Workhouse.[6] They met on a Sunday morning in the rectory office to discuss the case. It was not "in the relationship of Priest and Penitent."[7] Nagle told Father Burns "he had typed two sets of statements and he hadn't come out and said that [at trial], and he felt that perjury had been committed, and that he was a part of it as a typist." Nagle explained to Father Burns "that, in [*The Rape Case*] trial, it was indicated that there was one set, and he seemed to attach an awful lot of importance to that fact."[8] Father Burns "had the impression that [Nagle] was speaking of three [sets] but I don't recall any numbers being mentioned."[9] Although he did not "remember distinctly that [Nagle] said that the sets were different," Nagle did not tell him the sets were the same.[10] Father Burns asked Nagle to come back, but the second meeting never took place.[11] On September 15, 1949, Nagle committed suicide by turning on the gas and putting his head into his kitchen oven.[12]

Based on Corbeil's reports and his own judgment, Maris told the families he would go forward with the case but would not travel to Delaware personally. As energetic as he was at age seventy-three, Maris did not consider himself up to the task. He had already determined he would ask Charles F. G. Smith to undertake the thankless, substantially unpaid task of representing his new clients. Like Maris, Smith was a Philadelphia lawyer, but much younger and thus better able to assume the responsibility of trial. Since Smith, like Maris, was not a member of the Delaware Bar, he too could not appear without a local lawyer to move his admission. Securing a Delaware lawyer proved a far more formidable task than anyone had foreseen.

Maris began by explaining to the families the need for a local lawyer. He did not have to tell them members of the Delaware Bar were not rushing forward to assist. Maris' reputation in Philadelphia failed to give him access to a Delaware firm willing to undertake the cause even on the modest scale Maris needed. The then three largest Delaware firms, Richards, Layton & Finger, Southerland, Berl & Potter, and Morris, Steel, Nichols & Arsht, were immersed in lucrative corporate work. They had no history of ever having represented alleged rapists, let alone convicted rapists, on any basis, either for a fee or pro bono. The families' frustration mounted. Although in Maris they now had a lawyer willing to help, the Delaware Bar seemed deliberately blind to assisting.

The families had little hope of securing a Delaware lawyer on their own. All previous attempts had been unsuccessful. Now Maris and Corbeil tried. In mid-1950, Maris wrote to Joseph Donald Craven, a seasoned Delaware lawyer, requesting his help.[13] Nellie Curran then met with Craven. Thereafter Corbeil wrote to Craven in an attempt to clarify a misunderstanding Craven apparently had about Maris' position: ". . . Mr. Maris has admitted in the past that grounds for normal appeal are absent, as a matter of procedure. He is concerned with grounds for appropriate action based on unfair trial and denial of due process of the law, for which he is most hopeful there is [a] remedy." Corbeil went on to explain to Craven what he considered the "unfinished task; an examination of the set of statements signed by the defendants immediately after arrest, not introduced in evidence, their existence denied by the police in testimony, and why they were not introduced in evidence by the prosecution."[14]

At that time in his investigation, Corbeil believed the first set of statements was in the attorney general's office and if he produced them, they would prove the unfairness of the trial and command the clients' release. Corbeil and Maris had turned to Craven to help them secure the all-important first set. "Mr. Maris, as you know," Corbeil wrote on August 12, 1950, to Craven, "cannot go into Delaware and do it himself, especially without [an] associate." The same letter includes a remarkable paragraph: "I might mention here that Mr. Maris has expressed himself as not being interested in exposing the false testimony of the police witnesses in regard to these statements. If, after an examination of such statements, he found that the false testimony did not militate against the defense unfairly, the matter of the false testimony would be a closed incident from his point of view."[15]

What Corbeil wrote meant he and Maris had ignored the effect of the police perjury on the jurors. Even if the language of the first set of statements were identical to the statements introduced at trial, the police testimony, falsely denying the existence of any such earlier statements, had given the jurors reason to believe the defendants were lying about having signed two sets of statements and, accordingly, were lying when they claimed they did not commit rape.

Failing to obtain Craven's support, Maris and Corbeil turned to Thomas J. Healy Jr., an able young lawyer who came to the Bar in 1946.[16] His livelihood derived primarily from searching titles for real estate transactions, a fact that did not differentiate his practice from that of most Delaware attorneys at that time. One lawyer claimed three-quarters of all Delaware lawyers made seventy-five percent of their income searching titles. I thought the percentages were low in both categories. The fact Healy's practice was not in trial work was not a factor against turning to him, since Maris and Corbeil always contemplated the Delaware attorney's role would not be substantive.

Corbeil delivered a packet of papers concerning the case to Healy for review. Some time passed without any response. Finally, Healy wrote to Corbeil declining to represent Curran, Jones, and Maguire and offering this explanation: "After a thorough investigation of the facts and law . . . it is my opinion that there is not sufficient [reason] for me to undertake the proposed action. I have not taken this matter lightly and this is the reason for the delay in reaching a conclusion. I am returning herewith the papers which you left with me."[17]

Corbeil responded graciously on November 6, 1950, expressing his disappointment in Healy's decision, "especially because there was nothing in your letter to indicate your findings as to the facts I submitted to you." He closed his letter assuring Healy the effort to secure relief would continue "until somebody can and will show that our facts are wrong. . . ."[18] The same day, Maris forwarded a copy of Healy's letter and Corbeil's response to Mr. Curran, writing: "We are disappointed in Mr. Healy's decision, and I must concur with the reply Mr. Corbeil sent to him. It would have been most helpful had Mr. Healy given his reasons, but it was a matter he had to determine himself. . . . I am now in the position of not knowing whether Mr. Healy's decision was based on his finding of fact, or of law, or of both." Although he assured Mr. Curran he would explore "other efforts," he concluded with words that had to be discouraging for the Currans to read: "it does seem impossible to secure [a] legal associate in Wilmington."[19]

The search continued. The families almost secured William E. Taylor Jr., an experienced Delaware lawyer, quite confident in his own ability and harshly deprecating of those he did not like.[20] He had started with Richards, Layton & Finger, then tiny in size compared to what it was to become. After he reviewed all the materials Corbeil sent to him, Taylor did express a willingness to represent the three defendants. His conditions to serve, however, were beyond what Maris was willing to meet. An even greater obstacle was his proposed fee of $7,500, an amount the families could not afford. In early 1951, Maris summarized the situation in a letter, in which he first expressed his pleasure that Taylor was "the first Delaware attorney who showed willingness to co-operate in the case." But Taylor's proposed "fee of $7500.00 . . . is so far beyond the possible resources of the Currans that neither it nor any substantial fraction of it would be paid." Maris asked Taylor to return the papers either to the Currans or to him.[21]

Taylor quickly answered, writing he "was anxious to handle this case." He thought there had been ". . . an error of Mr. Curran's relating to my fee for handling this case." In setting the $7,500 amount, he intended "to insure that once this case was started it could be carried as far as necessary to obtain the result we all desire."[22] In explaining he only "intended" a retainer of $1,000 to $1,500, he made a passing reference to an application to Delaware's Pardon Board.[23] It struck the wrong note with Maris as his reply made clear: "I note your mention of the Board of Pardons, but I have always told Mr. Curran that I do not consider this case a proper one for clemency, but one where acquittal is the aim." Maris went on to explain his approach was to bring "the matter to the attention of the Attorney General . . . and then . . . to . . . the original trial court by appropriate procedure." Since Maris believed the "apparent false testimony on the part of the prosecution witnesses . . . amount[s] to what I believe apparently was a fraud on the court," he thought the judges would want to undo the convictions. Maris believed the case would be settled in the "original trial court."[24]

Maris shared his thinking with Taylor: "If we cannot prove the allegations [in the original trial court], I see no hope of proving them in any higher court. This is not a question of disagreeing with a verdict on the evidence in the record; rather it is a question of seeking anew [*sic*] verdict on evidence which would have gone into the record but for the apparent false testimony, which testimony defense counsel apparently suspected as being false." Accordingly, Maris told Taylor the only course was to "seek remedy in one court at this time the original trial court, in fairness to that court." Maris concluded by telling Taylor to "arrange . . . a conference with the Attorney General to apprise him of the plans and the evidence, for which I expect you to charge a nominal fee."[25]

Given what subsequently happened, Maris' hope that the attorney general's office and the Delaware judges would act promptly to grant relief was optimistic in the extreme. Taylor's response made it unlikely the two men would ever work together. He resented Maris telling him how to practice and what to charge. He concluded what could have been a gracious and conciliatory letter by writing he was "still quite willing and anxious to handle this matter on the terms which I have suggested in my letter of March 2. Otherwise, I am not interested in being a messenger boy or a mechanical associate in what might easily develop into a farce when the various aspects of this case are correctly appraised in terms of local precedent and practice in the *habeas corpus* actions."[26]

In an equally testy reply Maris made it clear he had no use for Taylor: "I purposely delayed answering your letter of the 23rd, since had I answered it at once, I am afraid that my letter would have been couched in language even less temperate and professional than was yours." In detail he took up each point Taylor had made. Paragraph by paragraph, he emphasized his role as the attorney for the clients, the work he had done, the cooperation he offered and expected, and the willingness to compensate Taylor reasonably within the modest means of the families. He concluded by telling Taylor "it would be best if you handed all documents to Mr. Curran, and then try to forget that you were

even spoken to in the case."[27] The letters they exchanged termi-
nated any chance Maris had of securing Taylor as local counsel,
an arrangement that might have accelerated the release of Curran, Jones, and Maguire, since the habeas corpus petition, a civil
proceeding, could have gone forward prior to the adoption of
the Criminal Rules with its Rule 35, effective February 12, 1953,
which the Superior Court compelled the defendants to use first.[28]

However disappointing the failure to engage Taylor's services
was, neither the families nor Maris nor Corbeil desisted from the
effort to secure a member of the Delaware Bar to serve as local
counsel to Maris. They came close in Newton White. White was
able and thorough. For several years, he was an associate in the
office of William Prickett, acquiring there the training in the per-
sistent methodology of the practice of law Prickett followed. No
one could have served under Prickett's mentoring, as White had,
without learning well the habits of good lawyering. When White
could no longer confine his personality within the strictures
Prickett insisted upon, he went out on his own and earned a reputation as an accomplished solo practitioner. After Corbeil had
met White and delivered to him a fair amount of material, White
wrote to Maris on August 13, 1952, pointing out he had attended
most of *The Rape Case* trial.[29]

Maris responded two days later, expressing the same thought
Corbeil had written to Craven two years earlier and and continuing to underestimate the significant adverse effect the police perjury at trial had on the defendants' credibility:

I believe Mr. Corbeil told you that if it is found that the first set of
statements are materially the same as the ones which were introduced
in evidence, I shall discontinue my active interest in the case. I am sure
that the court would not be impressed if the only difference shown
were typos and grammatical errors and neither would I. I have often
told persons interested that *I am not concerned primarily with the possible perjury,* but with the substance of the statement which was illegally

obtained, illegally introduced in evidence, false, and which contributed
to conviction. [Emphasis added.][30]

Weeks passed before Maris wrote asking, "Can you advise me
at this time as to the probability of your decision in the near future?" In my search of the available records I found no reply
from White. Despite the months of hard work the families,
Maris, and Corbeil had expended, Curran, Jones, and Maguire
were still without a Delaware lawyer.

6

Serendipity

In September 1952, United States District Court Chief Judge Paul Leahy slipped and fell from the rear steps at his home on Burnt Mill Road in Centreville. The blow to his head in the short fall caused a blood clot to form within his skull and press against his brain. With his strong constitution, he continued to work for several days before headache pain and drowsiness finally forced him to visit a physician. The history of the fall and the physical signs yielded the diagnosis: a blood clot pressing on his brain would kill him unless immediately removed. At the time of his fall, I was serving, as I had from February 1, 1951, as his law clerk.

Looking back almost sixty years, I still cannot say if Judge Leahy's fall, with its subsequent effect upon my life, was fortuitous or providential. At the time all I could think of was that this good man was near death. At the Delaware Hospital I listened with Frances Leahy, his wife, as Dr. Philip Gordy, Delaware's preeminent neurosurgeon, told us what was wrong, what had to be done, and how he would do it. After he removed the clot and thus the pressure on the Leahy's brain, Dr. Gordy assured Mrs. Leahy her husband would recover without any aftereffects. Subsequently I learned from the judge, who had extracted the information from Dr. Gordy, that the surgical procedure was an ancient one. Three thousand years ago the Egyptians knew to drill a hole in the skull to remove a blood clot by suction, thus relieving pressure on the brain.

While recuperating, Judge Leahy had unexpected visitors. Jayne Stigliano and her older sister, Virginia McKinley, two of Sonny Jones' sisters, were nurses at the Delaware Hospital, but not his attending nurses. Quiet, shy Virginia was hesitant to join when Jayne suggested they ask him to provide the assistance they needed. Neither knew him, nor did they have any assurance he would help. They knew he could not avoid seeing them, confined as he was to his room. They also were aware they faced disciplinary action for disturbing a patient not under their care should he protest their approaching him. Brash Jayne's service as a World War II army nurse in New Guinea, where she earned a Bronze Star, had hardened her to any reprimand she might receive for talking to Leahy in her brother's interest.[1] She decided they had nothing to lose compared to what they might gain if he agreed to the help they sought for their brother and his two friends. To them, it was not a major request. They just needed a Delaware lawyer to serve as local counsel for the Philadelphia lawyer who had already agreed to represent their brother. In turning to Leahy, Jayne was keeping the promise she and Virginia had made to their mother.

Judge Leahy had no problem with either the sisters' approach to him or their request. His sense of fairness required him to act affirmatively. After all, they were not asking him to free their brother from a conviction in a case over which he had no jurisdiction. All they sought for their brother and the other men was a Delaware lawyer to serve as local counsel in the contemplated state court proceedings. On the next of my daily visits to Leahy, he directed me to find such a lawyer. I was now well into the second year of my clerkship. As with every assignment, I set about accomplishing the task immediately.

Judge Leahy had told me none of the families could afford to pay a lawyer. He was right. In 1952, more than four years after their brother's conviction, Virginia McKinley and Jayne Stigliano lacked Jenny Jones' secret stash of closet money now long gone. Young, their lawyer at trial, had become Delaware's attorney general and was unavailable. Only the newspaper articles about the case Jayne clipped and saved remained, along with the belief they shared with the Currans and Maguires that Maris would help.

Years later Jayne's husband, Carmen N. Stigliano, told me the Maguire family paid David J. Reinhardt approximately $2,000 to represent Reds at the 1948 trial. Reinhardt's assignment was the most difficult, because Reds gave the impression of being a wise guy. As a fireman, he had a police officer's authority and responsibility to arrest a person committing a crime.[2] At trial on cross-examination, Chief Deputy Attorney General Duffy successfully baited him about this power and drew a response more helpful to the prosecution than to the defense:

Q. You are also sworn in as a city policeman, aren't you?
A. Yes, sir.
Q. And you were a city policeman at the time of this occurrence, weren't you?
A. Yes, sir.
Q. And all of this occurred in the presence of you, as a city policeman?
A. There was nothing there to cause me to lock anybody up. If so, it would have been the girl.
Q. You would have locked up the girl?
A. Yes, sir.
Q. You would have locked up the girl?
A. She was contributing to the delinquency of a boy who was not 21.
Q. You mean, Francis Curran?
A. Yes, sir.

Q. If you thought this was wrong, why didn't you stop him?

A. I was giving them all a break. I didn't intend to lock anybody up.[3]

However amusing Maguire thought he had been, the trial transcript does not reflect any laughter from the jurors or the spectators in the courtroom. The jurors already had before them the
woman's testimony accusing him of trying to force her to have
oral sex, a charge Maguire heatedly denied.[4] Whether true or not,
the charge tainted the defense of all three men.

Like the Joneses, the Maguires did not have the money to hire
another lawyer for their son. Nellie and Francis Curran, with
their large brood, could not afford a lawyer either in 1947 or in
1952. At trial they depended upon Sonny's court-appointed lawyer, Leonard G. Hagner. Some thought shy, gentle Len Hagner
was in over his head. Others thought Hagner's quiet way made
him the most effective of the three defense lawyers at trial. In
contrast to Young's $5,000 fee and Reinhardt's approximate
$2,000 for his service, the court authorized the payment of only
$500 to Hagner after Curran's sentencing.[5]

From the start I knew any Delaware lawyer willing to serve as
local counsel would have to do so with the foreknowledge he
would receive little or no compensation. Since my understanding
was Maris would do all the substantive work, I did not regard the
arrangement as unfair to the Delaware lawyer who would play a
role, however minor and modest, in Delaware's most celebrated
criminal case. Moreover, there was no reason to think that press
coverage of an attempt to reopen the case would be less intense
than it had been five years earlier. The Delaware lawyer would
benefit from the exposure while bearing whatever vilification the
public might harbor against anyone who represented the three
men.

Thus, the men needed a defender who cared neither about the
money he would not receive nor about the criticism he most as-

suredly would receive. They also required a lawyer who commanded respect. Neither the judges who would hear the matter nor the public who would read about it should regard the effort to reopen *The Rape Case* as anything other than the serious matter it was.

Overriding all the factors was one mandating acceptance: the opportunity to serve three men who claimed their constitutional rights had been violated by perjurious police testimony at their trial, a violation resulting in life sentences, demanded a remedy. I believed lawyers went to law school not merely to represent corporations or to do title searches or just to make money; they went to learn how to help those who needed help, even if it meant working for little or no compensation. The chance to represent the three men seemed to me to have the potency of a magnet to a lawyer with any mettle. I thought I would readily find such a person among those capable young men (no woman had clerked for a Delaware judge as of that time) who had served as law clerks to judges in Delaware's federal courts.

The first person I approached was H. James Conaway Jr., who had clerked for Judge Richard S. Rodney in the District Court shortly before I became Chief Judge Leahy's law clerk. I knew he enjoyed an excellent reputation. Even before I spoke to him, I thought I had found my man. But I overlooked a disqualifying factor he brought to my attention after first saying he would consider taking the assignment. He was then with the firm of Morris, James, Hitchens & Williams. Albert W. James, one of the firm's founders, had served as attorney general at *The Rape Case* trial. Although Chief Deputy Duffy had borne the major burden of the prosecution, conducting all of the critical examinations both on direct and cross-examination, James had participated throughout the trial.[6] After the evidence was in, James made the opening summation to the jury and Duffy made the rebuttal summation before Chief Justice Richards charged the jury. Conaway pointed out, quite correctly, reopening the case might place him in conflict with James, his senior partner. But for the possibility of a real conflict of interest, I think Conaway would have taken the case.

Forced to look for someone else, I turned to Andrew D. Christie, who had clerked for John Biggs Jr., then the Chief Judge of the United States Court of Appeals for the Third Circuit. Christie's credentials were impeccable. His father was the Reverend John Christie, the preeminent Presbyterian minister in Wilmington. The son, my contemporary, was a graduate of Princeton and the University of Pennsylvania Law School with an outstanding academic record. But by early December 1952 Christie turned me down. He too had a conflict of interest, since he had agreed to undertake the post of chief of the Legislative Reference Bureau in Governor J. Caleb Boggs' administration. I think Christie was relieved. My impression was he really did not want the assignment.

By the time I knew Conaway and Christie would not serve, my own plans had changed. In a few months I would complete a second year of clerking for Judge Leahy. The Judge and I had no understanding about when I would complete my service. My impression was if I never elected to leave, he would never encourage me to do so. As rewarding and enjoyable as the clerkship was, I knew it was not something I wanted to do year after year. I knew I wanted to practice law. And while Judge Leahy permitted me to conduct a modest, private civil practice, I could not mount an active practice while I remained a clerk.

In late November 1952, Philip Cohen invited me to become his partner starting January 1, 1953. It was the right offer at the right time. Initially he proposed a 60–40 arrangement. When John Kane and his company, The North American Life Insurance Company, signed on as a client with a $10,000 annual retainer in December 1952, Mr. Cohen altered our arrangement to a 65–35 split. I did not object. Absent starting my own practice, I knew of no other opportunity that would provide the latitude I saw in practicing law with Mr. Cohen. I did not expect to make a great deal of money, but I knew I would be my own boss.

Judge Leahy approved of the partnership with Mr. Cohen. So after Christie turned me down in December 1952, I felt comfortable in asking him if he had any objection to my representing Curran, Jones, and Maguire. Knowing my attempts to secure a lawyer had failed, he told me he had none, but warned I should not let the Philadelphia lawyers take advantage of me. He said his own experience was that out-of-town counsel would not hesitate to load upon any Delaware lawyer serving as local counsel whatever work they could. I assured him I would not allow that to happen. I did not expect to receive any money for my work. Compensation was not my concern. Nor was the expected criticism. Any such criticism evinced ignorance of how our system works and how lawyers function in it.

Nor was my focus on whether Curran, Jones, and Maguire were guilty of the crime for which a jury had convicted them. I was focused on the police perjury that destroyed the young men's credibility and denied them a fair trial. My concern about finding a lawyer with "standing" no longer loomed as large. Still, I realized I lacked the experience to command the respect and attention of judges, much less the public, but that no longer was an impediment to my serving.

In undertaking *The Rape Case,* I had no idea of the work I would eventually do. My expectation was I would participate under the leadership of Maris and Smith, lawyers more experienced and knowledgeable than I, in securing a new trial at which the police perjury would be exposed and the issue of innocence or guilt resolved. From Judge Leahy I knew the claim they were asserting was that the 1948 trial had been constitutionally unfair because of police perjury. If their claim were valid, the defendants were entitled to a new trial.

After making a telephone call to set up the appointment, I took a train on December 16, 1952, to meet Maris. It was the first of my trips to Philadelphia about *The Rape Case*. Later that day, Maris wrote to Bud Curran's father: "This is to inform you that we have secured satisfactory Wilmington legal counsel, and that he has been in conference with us today in Philadelphia, in the offices of our Philadelphia associate, Charles F. G. Smith, Esq. . . . Mr. Smith will be in charge of handling the case."[7]

By my presence Curran, Jones, and Maguire finally had a local lawyer. Now they could go before a Delaware court. Years later, I learned the Curran family regarded my coming into the case as the answer to all their prayers.[8]

During this same time another event of consequence occurred. Through a blind date arranged by my sister, Sylvia Levy, I met Doris Richter. Sylvia, nineteen years older than I, lived in Plainfield, New Jersey, with her husband, Harry, a pharmacist, and their two daughters. Doris, four years and four months younger than I, was the adviser to a youth group at the Plainfield Jewish Community Center, a part-time job she held while she was a graduate student at Rutgers University. Sylvia's youngest, Carol, belonged to the group. For our first date, Doris and I, and my niece Evelyn and her husband, Irving Altman, drove to New York to see the movie *A Clouded Yellow*, a spy thriller starring Trevor Howard. Upon my return to Delaware, I told Judge Leahy I had met the girl I intended to marry. Soon Doris and I were engaged. When *The New York Times* on January 25, 1952, carried the announcement, identifying me as law clerk to Chief Judge Paul Leahy, he joked he had always known when he made *The New York Times* it would be in the society section.[9] On December 25, 1952, nine days after taking my first step in *The Rape Case,* Doris and I were married in Temple Shalom in Plainfield by Rabbi Sidney Nathanson. We had a one-week honeymoon to Bermuda and returned on January 1, 1953. After purchasing a set of bone china, I had twelve dollars to my name.

As a law student, I thought if I could earn as much as $5,000 a year, I could buy all the books I wanted to read and all the records I wanted to listen to and still have ample funds to sustain myself. By the time I departed the post of law clerk, I was earning slightly in excess of $5,000 a year, because Judge Leahy endorsed every pay raise as soon as I became eligible. With my entry into marriage and active practice, I quickly found my achieved goal of $5,000 fell short of meeting my obligations as a husband, let alone allowing me to buy books and records.

When I began the practice of law, on January 1, 1953, Curran, Jones, and Maguire languished in jail at the tag end of the fourth year of their life sentences and the fifth year of their imprisonment.

7

My Colleagues and My Clients

O n December 16, 1952, I met Maris and his unusual
staff, George Corbeil, his investigator, and Samuel
Thompson, his secretary, at Maris' office in Philadelphia. Maris had white hair and a pinkish face with a benign expression.[1] Corbeil was an affable, gnome-like fellow with dark
features who had a penchant for playing golf. Through the years
as we worked together for our clients, our friendship flourished.
Early on he told me of his plan to retire to Australia and own
a sheep station. George often spoke of his plan with increasing
anticipation, but there always was a reason to postpone the Aus-
tralian adventure, mostly because of the needs of a daughter and
her children in upstate New York. He never realized his ambi-
tion.

Samuel Thompson was a thin, slight fellow in his thirties, with
an aesthetic face and sandy hair. He was the first male secretary
I ever knew. Sammy sported another "first" in my experience:
he was a convicted bank robber. I did not become privy to his
criminal past immediately. Not that he withheld the information; indeed, he proclaimed it. He always credited Maris with securing his freedom. He not only served Maris with his shorthand
and typing skills, he also acted as a sounding board for Maris'
ideas. Sammy had a host of unusual resources from his criminal

past that he relied on to assist Maris in his work. He was as well a reality check on Maris' willingness to accept as true an outlandish claim of innocence. His most important role, I thought, was his presence in the office reminding Maris of how important it was to reach out to undo an injustice.

Sammy and George coupled their loyalty to Maris with an equal commitment to justice. They both had street smarts. Neither stayed with Maris in expectation of financial reward; they knew they could not achieve either the action or the satisfaction found in his unusual practice at any other firm. No lawyer in Philadelphia matched Maris.

From Maris' office, Corbeil and I walked to the office of Charles F. G. Smith, the lawyer Maris had secured to represent the clients. Charlie was a phlegmatic, stolid Philadelphia lawyer who had agreed to assume responsibility for pressing the habeas corpus application Maris had decided was the tack we should take. I never thought Charlie held a passionate commitment to our clients' cause. My impression was he was involved because of an obligation to Maris, the nature of which I never learned. It was understood Smith would man the laboring oar, and I would be the local counsel. From that day forward, Maris did not participate in the preparation of the papers, nor did he sign the pleadings.

Unlike Smith, George Corbeil had met the clients and their families. He was the one who pursued the hands-on investigation of *The Rape Case* in Delaware. He passionately believed in our clients' innocence. As I became more involved, he and I made common cause in our shared conviction of the unfairness of the 1948 trial. My initial concern was the defendants' entitlement to a Delaware lawyer so the Philadelphia lawyers could address the issue of fairness. Guilt or innocence was beside the point. Even when I learned more, the fairness of the trial remained the heart of the matter. But the innocence of Curran,

Jones, and Maguire was never beside the point to Corbeil; *to him it was always the point of the effort.*

With the lawyers in place, the next step was to file an appropriate application for our clients' relief from their unlawful imprisonment. Maris had urged we proceed by a writ of habeas corpus. Judge Richard S. Rodney had clearly recognized the importance of the writ in Delaware law in *State v. Hawkins* where Hy Young sought the setting of bail for his client accused of murder. Judge Rodney wrote:

Of course this Writ of Habeas Corpus which has been designated as the most important writ known to the law and which is preserved by express Constitutional provision cannot be displaced by any mere statute in the sense that the Writ of Habeas Corpus would not remain available as a remedy whenever needed.[2]

Judge Rodney, however, thought that Young should first seek relief under Section 3980 of the 1935 Code since it "presents an adequate, convenient, economical and proper remedy for the present application." Judge Rodney thereupon ruled: "I do not say that the Writ of Habeas Corpus does not lie in any proper case, but I do say that ordinary remedies are primarily applicable to ordinary cases, leaving extraordinary remedies to those cases which they alone can meet. Without definitely determining that Habeas Corpus would not lie, I do believe that the proper initial application is under the statute."[3] Young had then withdrawn the application, presented a motion under Section 3980 which the court granted and admitted the defendant to bail.[4] Young's experience in *Hawkins* should have served as a warning to me.[5]

Consistent with his promise, Charlie Smith turned to drawing the petition for the court to issue a writ of habeas corpus commanding the authorities to release Curran, Jones, and Maguire. There are at least two schools of thought about what a lawyer should include in a pleading. Some prefer a shotgun approach setting forth every theory of recovery with the hope one of them will resonate with the trier of the facts or the judge and carry the day. At the opposite end is the rifle-shot approach. There the lawyer analyzes his case and generally settles upon one theory, but not more than two, upon which he relies to succeed for his client. My preference has always been the rifle shot. I cannot claim the shotgun approach is wrong or even that my narrower, less-is-more tactic is superior. I have seen both work. Smith belonged to the shotgun school.

In the habeas corpus petition, Smith asserted eight grounds.[6] Smith's seventh point was: "Were the voluntary statements initially signed by the relators and witnessed by the police illegally suppressed at trial and otherwise excluded from evidence by the perjury of the police witnesses, in violation of the due process clause of the Fourteenth Amendment to the Constitution of the United States?" Only this point was at the heart of what I thought was the constitutional violation of our clients' rights at trial. But my judgment did not mean much. Later, when it fell to me to take charge, I placed the emphasis upon the police perjury and its nondisclosure, arguing they destroyed the credibility of Curran, Jones, and Maguire and thus violated their constitutional right to a fair trial.

Claiming police perjury, of course, does not prove it occurred. Based upon what Corbeil learned in his investigation, Maris' thinking was that another set of statements as well as an internal police report existed. If these documents could be produced, they would prove the defendants had told the truth at trial and the police had lied. Accepting the clients' trial testimony about signing statements twice as true, the key to proving the claim might surely be found in the rumored internal police report. Securing the document was the goal in this early stage of the litigation.

Before filing the petition for habeas corpus relief, I visited

Curran, Jones, and Maguire at the New Castle County Work-house at Prices Corner where they were serving their life sentences. It was the first of many visits. I saw as my first task in *The Rape Case* the need to explain to my new clients my assessment of their perilous position. Although *The Delaware Code of 1953* with its sixteen volumes had replaced the one-volume *1935 Code* containing all the statutory law of Delaware, the law applicable to the penalty for rape had not changed. Even if we succeeded in wiping out the convictions because of the false police testimony, the defendants still would face a retrial on the rape charge with its possible death penalty.[7] I discussed with them what they faced if the state retried them and again secured a jury verdict against them. To go forward and succeed in wiping out the convictions from the unconstitutional trial meant they would have to place their lives at risk in a new trial. Nevertheless, neither at our first meeting nor on any subsequent session did Curran or Jones or Maguire ask that I not do everything I could to set aside the convictions. They knew full well they had no say in the state's determination whether or not to retry them. Nonetheless, they held fast to their quest for full exoneration because they were convinced a new trial would make clear their innocence. Their perseverance despite the risks convinced me all three surely believed in their innocence.

The Workhouse, with its twenty-foot high, blue-granite, fortress-like wall, was a forbidding structure.[8] Beyond the wall, metal fences topped with barbed wire encircled the grounds, obstacles to unlawful entrance or exit. All visitors entered through a small, brick building, the guardhouse. Both the outer and the inner fences were connected to the walls of the guardhouse. Once inside the guardhouse, visitors presented themselves, provided their names and addresses, signed the log inserting the time of arrival, identified the prisoner they had come to see, and stated their business. If visitors carried packages for prisoners, the guards opened them and searched for contraband. Lawyers, especially those whose clientele made them frequent visitors, passed through the screening process easily without even a search of their briefcases. Upon leaving, all visitors, including the lawyers, signed out in the log, noting the time of departure.

To leave the guardhouse and proceed to the Workhouse proper, all visitors had to pass through a steel door which opened at the press of a button by the guard in charge. A loud buzzing sound followed and ended only when the door clanged shut. Once past the steel door, one followed a concrete walkway to the steps leading to the main building with its red brick exterior. At the top of the steps was an ordinary wooden front door with half windows. The door opened upon a wide hallway with offices on both sides. At the far end was the first of two heavily barred inner steel doors. For security reasons it was forbidden for both inner doors to be unlocked at the same time. The second inner door led to the central area known as the hub, off of which corridors led like spokes of a wheel to the prisoners' cells. On my frequent visits to Curran, Jones, and Maguire, we would meet in a high-ceilinged room to the right and between the steel doors. When what I regarded as the lawyers' room was already occupied, we met in the Workhouse's tiny library in the hub area. The library easily held its few books.

My visits were depressing. An offensive odor I have always associated with poorly run institutions pervaded the place; but my clients had been confined so long they did not appear to notice it. They endured "the abominable toilet facilities" and the eating area with its "bullet-proof pillbox in one corner . . . [where] a guard would sit . . . armed with a tear gas gun just in case the prisoners became riotous."[9] My clients welcomed me always; my presence broke their dull daily routine. Moreover, and of greater significance, I personified to them the possibility of release—the reality that someone was actively working to upset their conviction, proving they were right in continuing to hope.

With all clients I tried to present as accurate a report as I could about what I was doing. In *The Rape Case* my policy yielded one disheartening report after another as I told Curran, Jones, and Maguire of the unbroken string of defeats during the first four years of my effort to upset their conviction.[10] Looking back on those sessions, I believe the only comfort my visits brought was my absolute conviction the state had not given them a fair trial.

I am certain I never said I could guarantee upsetting their conviction. At the same time, they had to have inferred from my conversations with them my expectation of success because of my confidence our system of justice could not, should not, and would not sustain a conviction based upon as flawed a trial as the state had provided them. As far as I was concerned, their release was only a matter of time. Despite my optimism, they continued to serve the life sentences the state had imposed. There was no groundswell for their release.

Immersed as I was in my practice and *The Rape Case,* I was also concerned for my young family. The responsibility for attending to the needs of our then only child, Deborah Lynne, fell almost exclusively upon my wife Doris. She continued to take the major role in making our home and caring for our children as Jonathan Abraham (may he rest in peace), Karen Lisa and David Paul came along after Deborah Lynne. Why I thought this division of parental responsibility appropriate, I cannot fathom, but Doris did not protest.

On some weekends, Doris entrusted me with the care of our children so she could attend to other tasks at home. If I planned a visit to the Workhouse, I sometimes brought Debbie with me when she was four or five. Since she could not go beyond the guardhouse, she remained there with the guards with a book or a toy or two as I went about my business. The time I spent inside varied but was never short. Not until she was an adult with children of her own did Debbie tell me the terror she felt when the buzzer sounded like an electric shock, followed by the clanging of the steel door as it firmly shut behind her departing father. She sat alone, ignored by the guards, until I returned. Because she never complained, I always assumed she enjoyed going to the Workhouse. So much for my perceptiveness as a parent.

8

Picking a Judge

A sea change occurred in Delaware's judicial system three years after the 1948 trial that is best summarized in the *Delaware Bar in the Twentieth Century:*

In 1951 extensive amendments of the 1897 Constitution established a three-member Supreme Court with appellate review as its primary function. Thereafter, the title of "chief justice" no longer applied to a trial judge and the new head of the Superior Court was designated "president judge." The Courts of Oyer and Terminer and of General Sessions were abolished and their functions were incorporated into the Superior Court.[1]

These changes became effective on May 9, 1951, when, on the motion of Chief Deputy Attorney General Vincent A. Theisen, Associate Judges Caleb R. Layton, III and Daniel L. Herrmann ruled: "all indictments, proceedings and matters of a criminal nature pending in the former courts and all books, records, and papers of [those] former courts be transferred to the Superior Court. With approval of that motion, Delaware's ancient Courts of Oyer and Terminer and General Sessions passed into history."[2]

In early 1953, knowing we were headed to court, I gave thought to the judge or judges who would preside. My Yale Law School professors had taught me I should know as much about the presiding judge or judges as I knew about the facts and the law applicable to my case. They had little difficulty in pointing to similar cases with disparate results where the only explanation was the judge who made the ruling. I needed a judge who was committed to the importance of civil rights and thus empathetic to my claim that an injustice had taken place in *The Rape Case.* As I looked at the roster of judges sitting in the Superior Court, I quickly concluded the only one before whom I would want to bring the petition for habeas corpus seeking relief for Curran, Jones, and Maguire was Daniel L. Herrmann.

My reasons for picking Herrmann were not complex. First of all, he was known for his fairness, and I thought he would have compassion for a person incarcerated in violation of his constitutional right to a fair trial without regard to guilt or innocence. Moreover, I thought he would have the courage to grant relief even though public opinion would not agree. I shared my thinking about Herrmann with Corbeil and Smith.

Smith's position was we should seek a hearing before a single judge and, moreover, any judge who had participated in the prior proceedings should not evaluate our petition. He was convinced that involving the 1948 trial judges, Richards, Terry, and Carey, would harm our cause. His thought was, if only a single judge were to be available, and it was Judge Herrmann, so be it. Neither Smith nor I recognized the reality that the court itself controlled the selection of the judge or judges who would hear our case without regard to our preferences.

Smith prepared the petition for the issuance of the writ of habeas corpus with some assistance from me.[3] It was a hectic time. Upon entering the partnership with Philip Cohen I was swamped with work, as I wrote on January 20, 1953, to Smith, "all of which seems to be underscored 'Rush'. To top it off Mr. Cohen leaves this Thursday morning for a month's stay in Florida." I further explained: "After Mr. Cohen leaves Thursday I hope to get things on a more even keel and be able to do some research work in the library next week and have a report to you within the week. I am giving the Curran matter top priority for next week so that real estate settlements will just have to wait."[4]

Smith was similarly slowed in his work by his practice's demands: "Thank you for your letter of January 20th relative to the Curran case. I sympathize with your situation as I am undergoing the same pressure. I am hoping, however, to get down to the Curran matter this weekend. Any efforts in this direction by you will, therefore, be greatly appreciated."[5]

While Smith worked on the petition, I spoke to Leonard Hagner, Curran's trial attorney, about *The Rape Case*. Not only did he turn over his entire file to me, but he also said he would cooperate in every way he could. I so reported to Smith.[6] On February 4, 1953, Smith wrote to tell me he "was now entering into the active preparation" of the petition.[7] A month passed. Finally, on March 2, Smith sent me the original and three copies of the petition he had prepared following the procedure applicable in Pennsylvania.[8] In his letter, he asked me to check the Delaware procedure carefully before filing "as it is quite technical." Smith also included a note of urgency: "In any case, it is quite important that the writ be filed without delay as the parents of the boys are becoming quite impatient and further delay would be therefore inadvisable."[9]

With Smith's agreement, I arranged an appointment with Judge Herrmann for both of us. We brought a copy of the petition to the March 10, 1953 conference in chambers. The meeting did not last long. After I introduced Smith, I explained our need for discovery of certain documents and a prompt hearing. He listened to us, accepted the courtesy copy of the petition, and ended the meeting by telling us he would send it to President Judge Richards, assuring us we would hear from the court. He was silent about what the Superior Court would do.[10]

On March 17, 1953, Judge Herrmann called me to his office

and told me Judge Richards thought the petition deficient since it lacked a copy of the commitment papers directing the imprisonment of our clients. He also said he thought the petition would come before the same three judges who had sat at the trial.[11] On March 19, 1953, I redelivered the petition with copies of the commitment papers attached to Herrmann.[12] While we waited for word from the court, I prepared a Motion for Production of Documents under Rule 34 of the Superior Court and sent it to Smith for review.[13]

On March 31, President Judge Richards summoned me to a meeting where he suggested a minor change in the caption from "the Warden" to "the Board of Trustees" as I reported to Smith.[14] In early April, he told me by telephone he would call me on April 13. He didn't. Finally, on April 15, I met him in the Public Building. He looked at the revised petition now designating the defendants as the Board. On April 22, 1953, more than six weeks after Smith and I first presented the petition, I called President Judge Richards in Georgetown. He told me the papers were "OK" with him and said I should present them to Judge Herrmann. I did so and waited. The Superior Court judges did not share my sense of urgency.

At last, by a July 13, 1953 letter from Associate Judge Caleb R. Layton III of the Superior Court to me, I learned Judge Richards had assigned "the *habeas corpus* proceeding involving Francis Curran et al to [Judge Layton] for hearing." It had taken more than four months for the Superior Court judges to select a judge to hear the petition—more time than had passed between my clients' arrest on October 30, 1947, and their conviction on February 17, 1948. So much for the Superior Court's compliance with its Rule 1 proclaiming the purpose of the Rules was "to secure the just, speedy and inexpensive determination of every proceeding."

In his letter, Judge Layton said he would schedule a hearing "as promptly as possible and will be glad to hear from counsel for both sides what hearing date they would prefer." Judge Layton then raised two issues, neither of which boded well for my cause or our clients. Each made clear Judge Layton's desire the case should go away, or at least away from him:

However, preliminarily I would appreciate it if counsel for the State and for the Relators could enlighten me on one point. Does not the provision in Section 28, Article 4 of the Delaware Constitution (since reenacted as Section 25) grant to a prisoner the right of appeal so long as he is incarcerated and six months thereafter? Its plain language seems so to do. If this is true, then these Relators all have the right of the appeal to the Supreme Court of this State from the verdict of guilty which was found against them some years ago in the Court of Oyer and Terminer.

Is it not a fact, also, that most, if not all the issues raised in the Relators' Brief, were raised and decided adversely to Relators at the trial? To the extent that this is true, it would seem to me that this whole proceeding is invalid for failure to pursue the appeal which, superficially at least, seems not only available to the Relators but mandatory upon them before a proceeding in *habeas corpus* could possibly be entertained.

I would like prompt consideration of these questions to be given by counsel prior to a formal hearing on the issues raised by Relators' Brief.[15]

So ended my effort to orchestrate who would decide our clients' habeas corpus petition. The case was now in the hands of the Delaware judges. As was readily apparent from the questions in Judge Layton's letter, relief would come neither easily nor quickly.

9

My Failure to Research Leads to the First Defeat

Instead of spending my time thinking about which judge might hear the case, I would have better served my clients if I had researched the newly promulgated *Criminal Rules of the Superior Court,* adopted November 6, 1952, effective February 12, 1953. As I would learn from the state's motion to dismiss our petition for the issuance of the writ of habeas corpus, I had failed my clients and Maris and Smith as well. Hy Young, now Attorney General of the State of Delaware, as the former lawyer for Sonny Jones had turned over responsibility for the state's role to Chief Deputy Attorney General Vincent A. Theisen and Deputy Attorney General Stephen E. Hamilton Jr.

I hardly knew Theisen, who was nominally in charge. Although Hamilton was much older than I, I knew him fairly well. He led the state's case opposing the relief I sought. He was an able, keen adversary, whose small, slight physique belied the championship game of tennis he played in his youth.[1] He worked best at night, using the daylight hours for sleeping. His work habits drove his colleagues to despair. The law was Hamilton's jealous mistress, and he guarded her secrets zealously. When he learned I owned and had read Frederic Bernays Weiner's *Effective Appellate Advocacy,* he asked me not to tell other lawyers about this excellent treatise lest they too learn its road map for success in the law. In response I told him the difference between Harvard Law School (his school) and Yale Law School (my school): at Harvard, if a student found a good case, he would hide the book; at Yale, the student would share the case with everyone. Knowledge of the law was not the key; it was how you used the knowledge.

From 1951 to 1955, while Hamilton served part-time as a deputy, he moved in his civil practice from Young to Albert L. Simon.[2] He then left Simon to become a senior associate at Richards, Layton & Finger. After a row with Robert H. Richards Jr., for whom he worked exclusively, Hamilton departed to do freelance work for other lawyers. I thought he was the finest brief writer at our Bar, an opinion many other knowledgeable members shared. Hamilton never lost any of the battles we had in *The Rape Case.*[3]

On June 19, 1953, Hamilton filed the state's motion to dismiss the habeas corpus petition Smith and I had formally submitted two months earlier. In the motion, Hamilton made three arguments, two of which were substantive, for dismissing the petition. In the first he argued the petition had no merit since the evasive, false police testimony—asserted but not proven—was not known to the prosecuting attorneys. In the second he claimed such police conduct as we alleged was insufficient to warrant relief as a constitutional violation of the defendants' right to a fair trial.

Hamilton's third argument was procedural. He claimed my clients had to exhaust all available state remedies under the new Criminal Rule 35, which had become effective February 12, 1953, a month before Smith and I first presented the habeas corpus petition to Judge Herrmann.[4] Hamilton argued unless we first sought relief under Rule 35, we had no right to attempt to seek, let alone to secure, relief through a habeas corpus proceeding.

As a Commonwealth of Pennsylvania lawyer, Smith had no reason to know about Delaware's new criminal rules. As a Delaware lawyer, I was mortified, not only by my lack of knowledge but also by my failure to do any research. I never thought to do so. Now, from Hamilton's motion to dismiss, my colleagues and I learned I had not done my homework. I had no choice but to put aside my embarrassment and help Smith prepare for the argument of the state's motion to dismiss.

The writ of habeas corpus was a civil remedy and therefore not subject to the coverage of the criminal rules. That I was correct on this point was of no solace. Since the Superior Court, with the Supreme Court's approval, had designed Criminal Rule 35 to provide relief for those in custody in place of habeas corpus and other civil procedures, Hamilton argued I had to use the new rule *before* I could file a habeas corpus petition. His argument was akin to the one Hy Young confronted in *State v. Hawkins*.[5]

On June 17, 1953, almost two months after I formally filed the petition and before the argument on the motion to dismiss, the *Morning News* publicly awoke to the fact we had filed the habeas corpus petition. The headline that morning covered four full columns on the front page. Without noting the April 23 filing date, the article's sixth paragraph did say: "The petition, accompanied by a brief, was filed several weeks ago."[6]

Maris and Corbeil believed the attorney general had a set of the defendants' first statements.[7] Charlie Smith, prompted by their thinking, thought we should ask for a formal acknowledgement from the state about the existence or non-existence of the first set of statements. At his urging on June 25, 1953, I wrote to Hamilton:

In answer to our motion and Judge Herrmann's order of June 9, 1953, in reference to statements or confessions signed by the petitioners, we have received from your office statements which were introduced at the time of trial. We believe that these statements are not the first set of statements which were given by Curran, Jones and Maguire. I should be grateful if you would produce the first set of statements for us or give an account to me as to the destruction or loss of the original set.[8]

On July 9, 1953, Hamilton responded:

Pursuant to your request I inquired of the Police Department as to whether the petitioners signed any written statements other than the ones introduced at the trial. *The Police Department informs me that the written statements introduced at the trial are the only ones that were ever signed by the petitioners.*[Emphasis added.][9]

Thus, the Police Department continued with the same falsehoods its officers, led by Detective Rodenhiser, had testified to at trial. Surely the Police Department records and the memories of its officers contained the proof that the initial set of statements Curran, Jones, and Maguire signed no longer existed because they had been destroyed. Steve Hamilton's letter showed he accepted the Police Department's falsehoods.

The argument went forward on August 3 before Judge Layton. Local reporters were present. Hamilton spoke first. He claimed the police conduct at the 1948 trial could not bind the state because policemen were not representatives of the state and, therefore, their acts did not constitute state action under the Fourteenth Amendment to the United States Constitution. According to Hamilton, only if *the prosecuting attorneys* actually knew of the perjury could there be a constitutional violation. As I listened to him cite cases to support his argument, I thought he could not be right. In my view, *the Wilmington City Police did represent the state.* Moreover, if the prosecutors could close their eyes and ears to what the police knew, the result of Hamilton's argument was approval of behavior that deserved repudiation, not endorsement.

Although I had no proof at this early stage, I subsequently learned from *Morning News* reporter John A. Gibbons that Chief Deputy Attorney General Duffy had told him he knew of the police perjury at the time of the trial. Because Duffy wanted a conviction and the imposition of the death penalty, he ignored what he knew. When Gibbons confided this, he also said if I ever tried to use the information to free my clients he would deny telling it to me. I never used what he told me.

While Smith argued, I sat at the counsel table, smug and reveling in my importance as a young lawyer taking part in the most notorious and well publicized case any Delawarean could remember. Sitting in the rear of the courtroom were Bud Curran's parents, Sonny Jones' sisters, Virginia McKinley and Jayne Stigliano, and Reds Maguire's parents and his older brother, Edward Maguire Jr. The family members appeared so trusting of the lawyers who had come forward to help them and their loved ones. They may even have thought we were doing well for their sons and brothers.

Listening to Hamilton and Smith make their disparate arguments and responses to Judge Layton's questions, I did not think the argument went well for us. At lunch at the Town House on Shipley Street, both Smith and Corbeil told me they thought we had done better than I thought we had. I was particularly concerned because of Hamilton's claim that police action was not state action. The thought that police officers could take the witness stand and lie with impunity was anathema to me and to the bedrock principle of fairness underlying our system of justice.

On September 23, 1953, we received Judge Layton's opinion deciding against us.[10] He responded affirmatively to Hamilton's procedural argument. Holding "Rule 35 seems to furnish all the relief previously known under the writ of *habeas corpus*," Judge Layton dismissed the habeas corpus petition on a procedural ground. Because he avoided ruling on Hamilton's two substantive arguments, Judge Layton had no need to address either. Thus, he did not pass on the merits of my clients' substantive claims.[11]

10

The Importance of Civil Discovery (The Second Defeat)

Maris' judgment to file a habeas corpus petition was studied. He knew the power of the Great Writ and had used it frequently in seeking relief for his clients. When I first sat with Charlie Smith in the Superior Court before Judge Layton, I did not understand the important difference between moving under habeas corpus and filing a motion under Rule 35 of Delaware's newly enacted Criminal Rules. By the time Judge Layton denied the petition for the issuance of the writ, however, I realized the distinction. The key difference was the use of depositions, interrogatories, requests for production, requests for admission—in short the discovery critical to *The Rape Case*. Since habeas corpus was a civil proceeding, I would have had free access to the broad, liberal discovery provisions the Civil Rules provided in contrast to the far more restrictive Criminal Rules.[1]

Under habeas corpus, I could demand and receive documents, including, if it still existed, the rumored report of the police department's 1948 investigation of *The Rape Case*. I could direct interrogatories, receive answers, and depose the police officers whose testimony under oath I needed to prove their perjury.

174

Without the ability to use the various civil discovery methods, I feared I would not be able to gather the proof I needed. Because the existence of a post-trial police report was still only a rumor, I would need broad discovery powers to secure it. Rule 35, on the other hand, was a criminal rule and the Criminal Rules had no comparable provisions about discovery. In the few areas where they permitted discovery they were most restrictive.

Thus, when Judge Layton ruled we must first exhaust the remedy Rule 35 provided, his ruling left in place the state's unfairness to my clients.[2] I thought I could set it right. I also knew I could no longer content myself with the role of local counsel on the team. Since Hamilton's argument about police perjury was wrong and Judge Layton's opinion in forcing us to use Rule 35 was an error, I decided to match my conviction with my action. If success were to elude me, it would not be because I did not play an active role. When I approached Smith and Corbeil, they readily agreed to let me seek reargument. Although not obvious at the time, the petition for reargument marked the point where I began undertaking responsibility for the case.

My motion for reargument and supporting brief did not change Judge Layton's thinking. Without any further oral argument, he held to his prior ruling in a Supplemental Opinion.[3] In a note, however, he recognized the point I was trying to make: "Presumably, an application for habeas corpus, being a civil remedy, relators would clearly have the right to the discovery proceedings under our Civil Rules."[4] Knowing Rule 35 would not provide me with the discovery I needed, I rejected his ruling.

Even when the state proffered the use of discovery, it was less than what I thought I was entitled to in a civil proceeding. I believed Judge Layton misunderstood my reasons for insisting on discovery as provided in a civil proceeding when he wrote:

Secondly, relators' counsel argue very strenuously that they should not be forced first to exhaust their remedy under Rule 35, because (1) these remedies are not so broad as under habeas corpus and (2) being remedies granted by the Criminal Rules, they would be sharply limited in their efforts to obtain pre-trial discovery. My answers to these arguments are these—first, the remedies afforded by Rule 35 are as broad as under *habeas corpus* and secondly, it is the effectiveness of the remedy, not the difficulties inherent in pursuing it, which should be the governing factor. In this connection, the State has stated on the record that it will not oppose relators' attempts to obtain discovery pursuant to a proceeding under Rule 35. And, regardless of the effectiveness of this waiver, these relators are not precluded hereafter from applying for *habeas corpus* should their petition under Rule 35 fail.[5]

Judge Layton's dismissal of the petition, even without prejudice, seemed to me disingenuous, elevating form over substance. No legal principle barred him from regarding the habeas corpus petition as a Rule 35 Motion. The same words would appear in both and the same issues would come before the Superior Court for resolution no matter what the caption. But he postponed any consideration of the merits since the habeas corpus petition was "premature," his justification for further delay.

Judge Layton interpreted Rule 35 to require an "application to the original trial Court."[6] When the case eventually did come before the Superior Court on the merits, the original trial judges, Richards, Carey, and Terry, were all alive and active. To this day, I remain curious about the discussions that resulted in the same three trial judges sitting again on *The Rape Case* more than five years after the February 1948 trial.

The steps I took differed markedly from Hy Young's in *State v. Hawkins.* He promptly withdrew his petition for the issuance of a writ of habeas corpus and moved successfully under Section 3980 of the 1935 Code. Doggedly I clung to my view because of the substantial difference in discovery. Rather than accept a watered-down discovery, I appealed Judge Layton's adverse ruling. The Delaware Supreme Court, however, was no less adamant than Judge Layton in affirming that we first had to use Rule 35. In Associate Justice Daniel F. Wolcott's unanimous opinion, dated May 6, 1954, the fact there existed liberal discovery under the Civil Rules applicable to a habeas corpus proceeding was of no moment to him, Chief Justice Clarence A. Southerland, and Associate Justice James M. Tunnell Jr.[7] It was a low point for me. Either I had to abandon the thought of securing the discovery available to me only under the liberal Civil Rules, or I had to seek a petition for certiorari in the United States Supreme Court. The likelihood of the High Court's agreeing to hear the issue of discovery differences was remote, if not nonexistent.

My friend and opponent, Steve Hamilton, asked what I intended to do. I told him I intended to seek review before the United States Supreme Court. He asked why I wanted to do that. I then shared with him what I had learned from George Corbeil. Following the trial, Reds Maguire's older brother, Edward, a Wilmington policeman, complained to Wilmington's Superintendent of Public Safety, Andrew J. Kavanaugh, that the police trial testimony about having taken only one set of statements from Curran, Jones, and Maguire was "a pack of lies." Kavanaugh promised he would investigate. But Kavanaugh never told Ed Maguire what he did as a result of Ed's complaint. Finally, I told Hamilton, I learned from an informant that there existed a police report about the number of statements.

What was rumor to me was fact to Hamilton. Much to my surprise, he readily confirmed the rumored report existed and offered a trade. He proposed that if I would agree not to seek certiorari from the United States Supreme Court, he would make the report available to me and, moreover, not object to my taking depositions of the police department personnel. I think Hamilton was convinced I was entitled to see the report. His agreement to turn over a copy would obviate the need for me to appeal. In addition, giving me access to the report could possibly meet yet another critical purpose. It might well serve as a road map for the depositions I intended to take. The report could break open the case. I was so delighted at the prospect of receiving it I did not anticipate how costly the trade-off—replacing my habeas corpus petition with a motion under Rule 35—would prove to be.

I kept my end of my bargain with Hamilton by filing a motion for relief under Criminal Rule 35 on June 22, 1954, the first motion ever filed under the new rule. In return, he agreed to deliver a copy of the report to me.

During the time I struggled to convince the Delaware judges of the correctness of my position, I frequently talked about *The Rape Case* with my friend, Louis J. Finger. At the time, Hamilton was at Richards, Layton & Finger. One night in my living room, after I had again tried to persuade Lou how *right* I was, he finally said: "You know, when I listen to you, I think you're right. Then when I listen to Steve, I think he's right." How my astute, learned friend could think Hamilton correct was disturbing.

11

The Buried Report Surfaces and the Depositions Begin

As he had agreed, Steve Hamilton delivered Detective Charles F. McCool's Report on July 26, 1954. I promptly read all seventy-seven pages. The existence of McCool's Report proved Superintendent Kavanaugh had acted on what Red's brother had told him, but not because he was altruistic in the pursuit of justice. As Kavanaugh subsequently explained when I deposed him in preparation for the hearing on the Rule 35 Motion:

Well, there was [sic] a lot of rumors going around the building and a lot of rumors outside and I was asked by several people about two statements that were taken and I wanted to satisfy myself, so I wanted a thorough investigation made because I have a reputation, you know, 46 years of it, and I don't want to sacrifice that reputation. That is all I have got left out of my career.[1]

Kavanaugh said he heard the first rumor from Ed Maguire. He knew Ed since he had interviewed and hired him for an office job in the Police Department, "because he was a typist and we needed him badly at that time."[2] Kavanaugh recalled being in his office when he heard a commotion outside his door. He walked

out and found Ed Maguire holding his mother; ". . . he was fin-
ishing a sentence which he had started with reference to 'a son-
of-a-bitch going down the hall,' which was Rodenhiser and Mc-
Cool and they walked back and I stepped out into the hall at the
time. It seemed quite a disturbance over a statement he made
that Rodenhiser had perjured himself. That was the first that I
had any knowledge of what was wrong with Maguire."[3]

Kavanaugh then talked to Ed Maguire and asked him for
"some proof" to support his claim there had been two statements. "The only proof he could give me was the fact that he
said his brother signed one in his presence and that his brother
had signed others before that and he only knew that from hearing it from somebody else." This meant Ed Maguire had witnessed his brother's second signing after 8:00 a.m. on October
30, Kavanaugh explained, "because . . . he didn't come to work
until that time."[4]

A day or so after his conversation with Ed Maguire, Kavanaugh met with Detective Rodenhiser to question him about the
signing of a second statement. Kavanaugh "was anxious to find
out from Rodenhiser" since his recollection from having attended *The Rape Case* trial was "that during the cross-examination [of Rodenhiser] at that time Attorney Young was talking
about a second statement quite a little while he was on the stand
and producing a statement and asking him to identify it and if
that was the same statement that he typed."[5] As Kavanaugh recalled, in response to Young's questions "Rodenhiser then answered that there was only one statement taken and that was the
statement that he took."[6]

At that point in Kavanaugh's deposition Hamilton said, "I am
a little bit lost here," and interrupted to question Kavanaugh. I
did not object. Hamilton then elicited from Kavanaugh the following confirming testimony: "[Rodenhiser] definitely denied to

me that there were two different physical statements. That is definite. I wouldn't go wrong on that, because that was the thing that I was interested in, because there was going to be some trouble."[7] In answer to Hamilton's further questions, Kavanaugh emphasized he was interested in whether there were changes between the two statements; the fact that retyping had taken place, thus producing two sets of statements, was not significant to him.[8] Right after Superintendent Kavanaugh finished with Rodenhiser, he spoke to Patrolman James A. Nagle Jr., who had retyped the statements, and to Officer Edward J. Mazewski who was with Rodenhiser during the interrogation of Sonny Jones on October 30, 1947.[9] Kavanaugh concluded "there wasn't any doubt in my mind when I got through with Rodenhiser and with Nagle that the statement that [Nagle] took from Maguire wasn't changed in substance from what Rodenhiser took. [Nagle] told me definitely all he did was spell the words properly."[10]

The critical distinction—the fact that Rodenhiser and other officers had unequivocally denied at trial that there were two sets of statements—was of no significance to Superintendent Kavanaugh. Relying on Rodenhiser, Kavanaugh—not the jury—determined there were no changes in the two sets. *At the time he reached his conclusion, he knew Rodenhiser had destroyed the first set of statements; Rodenhiser had told him so.*[11]

Despite accepting Rodenhiser's claim there were no differences between the statements he destroyed and those introduced at trial, Kavanaugh went forward with an investigation. He placed Captain Charles F. McCool in charge, because he thought McCool was "an A-1 detective." Chief of Police James C. Riley concurred. Both men agreed McCool was "the best man to do the job."[12]

When I subsequently deposed him, McCool testified he immediately began work on the assignment. Although he could not recollect the exact period he conducted his investigation, he said "I would go so far as to say it was shortly after the [February 1948] trial."[13]

McCool's Report opened with a chronological synopsis followed by the twenty statements he secured from those involved in the arrests, the investigations, and the interrogations. Each person he interviewed signed his or her statement McCool typed, and McCool witnessed each one, with one exception: John Rodenhiser. Only Rodenhiser did not sign his statement, dated March 9, 1948.[14] As part of his report McCool attached copies of State's Exhibits 10, 11, and 12, along with a copy of the woman's statement that the state did not introduce at trial.[15]

In my judgment, Patrolman Nagle's signed statement in McCool's Report proved the claim I had made on my clients' behalf and entitled them to relief. The critical portion of Nagle's statement read:

6.15 A.M.
During this time Detective Rodenheiser came to me with the statement of Ira Jones (signed) and the statement of Francis Maguire (does not remember if it was signed or not) and asks me to re-type them because of the mistakes in the names and other typographical errors. I agreed to do this but told him that I did not know when they might be completed as it was a lot of typing and I was already very busy.
7.00 A.M.
I had completed the typing of the [woman's] . . . Statement and the re-typing of Jones' statement but had not started on the Maguire statement. I went to the Turnkey's Office to see this line up. . . . I did not stay for the reading of the statement but returned to the Radio Room where I was working.

I do not know when I completed the retyping of the Maguire statement other than it was getting close to 8 A.M. as the day shift men were around the office and I was particularly concerned because I was using the typewriter at the desk of Pat. Edward Maguire and I did not want him to see his brother's statement which I was then re-typing. I do not know when this statement was signed as I finished it and gave it to Detective Rodenheiser.

Signed   *James A. Nagle, Jr.*

Charles F. McCool[16]
Witness

McCool's Report laid bare the facts. It showed Rodenhiser took the original statements from Jones and Maguire and secured their signatures, Jones around 4:00 a.m. and Maguire around 5:00 a.m. Later, as Patrolman Nagle told McCool, Nagle typed a second set of statements for all three defendants.[17] The papers read at the line-up were the first statements; obviously, the second set Nagle typed did not exist until after the line-up. After the police told the three men the second set was identical to the first, each then signed his second statement without reading it around 4:00 p.m. on October 30.[18] None of the men could identify the policemen who brought the second statements to them.[19] In his signed statement in McCool's Report, Officer Mazewski wrote: "Sometime later [on October 30, 1947], but I cannot recall the time, Detective Rodenhiser discovered that Maguire had not signed one of the copies. Rodenhiser then detailed me to go down to the cell block and have this signed."[20]

The significance of McCool's Report was its corroboration of the testimony my clients gave under oath at their trial about signing two statements. From Emering's, Mazewski's, and Nagle's detailed signed statements and Rodenhiser's unsigned statement, McCool's Report provided incontrovertible evidence that the police trial testimony and the Police Department's claim in Hamilton's July 9, 1953 letter that the defendants' statements in evidence were "the only ones that were ever signed by the petitioners" were lies. Set in juxtaposition to the defendants' claim they each signed two statements, the police testimony effectively destroyed the defendants' credibility before the jurors.[21]

Kavanaugh claimed to have read McCool's Report twice in 1948, but he apparently never considered the effect the false police testimony had on the defendants' credibility. Even though Detective Rodenhiser admitted to Kavanaugh tearing up the first statement Maguire signed, Kavanaugh failed to recognize how wrong he was in accepting Rodenhiser's explanation of "neatness" for the retyping and believing Rodenhiser's assertion there were no differences in the two sets of statements. Nor did he recognize the seriousness of Rodenhiser's decision not to tell the court or the lawyers for the state or the defense of the police perjury at trial.[22] Although he gave a copy of McCool's Report to each of the then three Directors of the Department of Public Safety, he never had a conversation with any of them about McCool's Report.[23] The directors never returned the copies to Kavanaugh.[24] Thus, McCool's Report remained buried in the Police Department's records protecting its mendacious officers to the detriment of the accuseds and their constitutional right to a fair trial.

Kavanaugh never responded to Ed Maguire. Moreover, neither Kavanaugh nor the Police Department took any action against Detective Rodenhiser. By the time of the hearing on the Rule 35 Motion, the Police Department had promoted Rodenhiser to the rank of lieutenant.[25]

On July 28, 1954, I began taking the depositions Hamilton had agreed not to oppose. The first deponent I called was McCool. By arrangement with the attorney general's office, my clients were present with me in the Public Building where the depositions went forward.[26] Deputy Attorney General Clarence W. Taylor represented the state at the first day of depositions and Hamilton at the rest.[27]

The depositions I took exposed Hamilton's strategy to defeat the relief I sought for my clients. Despite the Police Department's denial in Hamilton's July 9, 1953 letter to me, Hamilton had to have known by July 1954, when he gave me a copy of McCool's Report, that the statements introduced at trial were not the only statements the three defendants signed.[28] To get around this master fact Hamilton developed his theory: if there were no differences between the second set of statements, the ones the state introduced in evidence, and the earlier destroyed set, as he argued, Hamilton could and did claim, "no harm, no foul." But, as I saw it, the real harm was the police perjury's adverse effect on my clients' credibility. To counter my point, Hamilton needed to create confusion to mask the testimony of the police officers almost seven years after the events to which they testified. Thus arose Hamilton's "two pieces of paper" defense.

It was his contention the same words appeared on both statements and thus there had been no harm to the defendants. But the only proof the second statements were identical to the first came from Rodenhiser. Hamilton, however, could not prove there were no differences by producing the first set because Rodenhiser had destroyed the first set, and then compounded his dishonesty by denying there was a first set as the defendants testified. To accept the argument one had to ignore the fact that Hamilton's claim of "no differences" came from police officers who lied at trial and deliberately concealed the truth from the jury.

Neither the individual statements nor McCool's Report carried the date of preparation. At his deposition, I marked McCool's Report as Exhibit A.[29] Under oath McCool claimed he had no recollection of any conversation with Kavanaugh concerning his report and did not know of any action Kavanaugh or the Police Department took after he delivered it. When he submitted the report, he said his "job was completed." And he testified "I received no further orders after submitting the report."[30]

In deposing Captain McCool I had to go through an exercise

akin to pulling teeth without anesthesia to get him to admit the obvious police perjury.[31] He testified repeatedly he had no recollection of many of the matters that had taken place and to which his report bore witness. He said he only "casually glanced through" a copy of the report prior to his deposition on July 28, 1954.[32] He frequently fell back on the fact that the events it covered had occurred almost seven years earlier.[33] Before he finished testifying, he volunteered his opinion concerning the statements and Rodenhiser's trial testimony: he was satisfied the second set of statements was not changed substantively from the first set.[34] He did finally admit, however, that Jones and Maguire had signed two statements.[35] Given Nagle's statement to McCool in McCool's Report, there was no question that there were two Curran statements as well.[36] McCool concluded his deposition: "I agree with you that Patrolman Nagle typed the statements" submitted in evidence.[37]

Still he could not get around the fact of the destruction of the first set.[38] Although McCool said it was wrong for Rodenhiser to have done it, he offered an explanation for the destruction: at the time, in the fall of 1947, each detective was free to follow his own practice concerning the retention of documents. It only became mandatory to retain copies of all statements after the Police Department placed McCool in charge of officer training.[39]

Because of McCool's explanations, it fell to me at his deposition to prove the perjury by referring to specific passages in the trial transcript and in McCool's Report. I persisted and drew from McCool the admissions I needed to establish the existence of the first set of statements and, further, the nonexistence of the second set at the time of the police line-up between 7:00 a.m. and 8:00 a.m. on October 30, 1947.[40]

McCool said he was called on the afternoon of October 30, 1947, around 2:00 p.m., to take charge of the investigation. When I quoted another police officer who said Rodenhiser had bungled the investigation, McCool would not confirm he ever heard that statement or, indeed, any criticism of what Roden-hiser had done. But it was McCool—not Rodenhiser—who se-cured the clothes of Curran, Jones, and Maguire for delivery to the chemist for analysis. He also assembled the evidence from the scene of the alleged rape for safekeeping. After McCool handed all five copies of his report to Kavanaugh, his involve-ment in the trial and its immediate aftermath ended.[41]

There is not a single reference to the eyewitnesses Fahey, Mas-ten, and Schueler in McCool's Report. The fact was the police never interviewed them. Although they testified under oath at the trial to being onlookers near the fence separating Woodlawn Park from the railroad tracks at the time of the alleged rape, Mc-Cool did not recollect interviewing them prior to trial. He said he thought he must have since the state called them as witnesses. When I pointed out it was the defendants who called them, Mc-Cool claimed the Police Department probably did not consider it important to have their testimony as part of the state's case. Superintendent Kavanaugh at his deposition went further. He testified under oath "these boys weren't there."[42]

What the depositions would have been like without McCool's Report is easy for me to suggest. Given that almost seven years had passed since October 30, 1947, when the Wilmington police had taken my clients into custody, and given the silence police-men typically show toward outsiders—the so-called "Blue Wall of Silence"—I doubt any of the involved officers would have ad-mitted there were two sets of statements. The examinations themselves were excruciatingly slow and difficult. Not one of the deponents was a willing, forthcoming witness.

Detective Rodenhiser personified the difficulties. Throughout his deposition testimony, there was a familiar refrain: the first set of statements was exactly like the second set of statements with the exception of the spelling of Curran's last name, corrected from "Kern."[43] In addition, Rodenhiser claimed he destroyed the first set of statements only after that single change was made. He regarded the destruction of the first statements and his trial testimony as "some little technicalities or details about retyping." His arrogant position was that the jury's verdict of guilty meant, as he testified at his deposition, ". . . I wasn't far off cover, you can bet that."[44] But if Rodenhiser's story were true, why did he and the other police officers fail to tell the court and the jury at trial and, even before the trial, to tell the attorney general's office, about the existence and destruction of the first set?

Thus sixty years later the question remains: why did Rodenhiser and other police officers claim there was only one set of statements? Before they testified and perjured themselves they had to have anticipated that if the defendants took the stand they could and would testify to having signed two sets of statements. The police also had to have anticipated that the jurors would give no credence to the defendants' testimony after hearing what the police had to say on the stand and so would conclude the defendants were liars. On the other hand, if Curran, Jones, and Maguire had not taken the stand, the wrongdoing of the perjury would never arise as a disputed matter. Either way, the police must have thought they were safe. As long as the officers did not break rank, their perjured testimony could withstand any attack—as it did at *The Rape Case* trial.

By the time of the depositions in July and August 1954, knowing McCool's Report was in my hands, Rodenhiser and the others had to come up with an explanation for the unexplainable. And they did. Whether their fall-back position was the result of Hamilton's artful advocacy or whether they conjured up the story themselves, I do not know. It was an aggressive defense: Rodenhiser claimed I was confusing two pieces of paper with two sets of statements.[45] According to him, the second set was the same as the first with the single exception of the misspelling of

Curran's name.[46] Thus to Rodenhiser and the others, the fact there were, indeed, physically two pieces of paper was of no moment. As Rodenhiser put it: "I regarded this thing as light, just simply retyping for the benefit of neatness and correction, not changing these boys' statements in any way at all. There was nothing, no entrapment on my part that I thought I was changing anybody's statements."[47] But if the existence of the first set was not material, why did Rodenhiser destroy them and then lie on the witness stand instead of disclosing what he had done?

Moreover, accepting Rodenhiser's post-trial explanation of "two pieces of paper" would mean ignoring his trial testimony. At trial Hy Young had cornered Rodenhiser and covered that precise point in trying to pin him down in an explicit cross-examination:

Q. I hand you State's Exhibit No. 11. Is that the statement that you took from Ira Jones?
A. It is.
Q. At what time?
A. At 2:45 a.m., starting at 2:45 a.m.
Q. Did you type it yourself?
A. I did.[48]

By willfully committing perjury, Rodenhiser was able to fend off the need to explain the destruction of the first set of statements and the claims of Curran, Jones, and Maguire under oath at trial that the first set differed in substance from what was in the second set, the statements in evidence. His lies thwarted Young's effort to prove the police duplicity.

12

The Offer I Should
Have Refused

With the depositions behind me, I prepared for the Superior Court hearing already scheduled for December 1, 1954, before the same three judges who had sat at the 1948 trial. Meanwhile, I contended with the usual demands of the fledgling firm of Cohen and Morris. I also committed to working for my party at the polls on Election Day, November 2. Along with other young, volunteer lawyers for the Democratic Party I was to be available to go to any polling place where there was a problem. Upon arrival, we would contend with the young, volunteer lawyers the Republican Party fielded.

The vote was heavy despite rain, thunder, and lightning. United States Senator J. Allen Frear Jr. led the Democratic ticket to victory by nearly 20,000 votes, the Democrats' greatest sweep in modern times. Harris B. McDowell Jr. won Delaware's single seat in the House of Representatives. Joseph Donald Craven won the office of attorney general, thus placing it in Democratic control for the first time since 1912. Craven's victory meant the departure in January 1955 of all the Republican lawyers, including Steve Hamilton, from the attorney general's office. It also meant Hamilton's departure from *The Rape Case*.

The 1954 election was the first in Delaware following the enactment of legislation, effective July 1, 1953, to permit the use of automatic voting machines. The legislation was quite specific about how to respond to voters requesting instructions and about who could enter the voting booth. An election officer had to give instructions using sample ballots posted in the polling place. If a voter entered the voting booth and then asked for additional instructions, two election officers of opposite political parties "shall give such instructions to him; but no person assisting a voter shall in any manner seek to influence his vote." The officials were to retire before the voter cast his vote.[1] The statute was equally precise about the single exception it provided for the presence of a nonelector in the voting booth: only if the voter was blind or physically disabled. Any election officer who knowingly or willfully violated the law faced a fine for as much as $200 or imprisonment for not more than two years.[2]

Early in the evening on election day I stood with several others across the street from 231 Tatnall Street, the polling place for the Second District of the First Ward of Wilmington. Through the storefront window we could easily see the voting booth and those going in and out. The Republican Party designated as its Second District election officer a Wilmington city councilman who was also his party's leader in the First Ward. He carried a clipboard he constantly checked, presumably noting who among the Republican faithful had voted. We watched him repeatedly reach behind the drawn curtain of the voting booth to pull the lever, ostensibly to assist the voters who needed "help." The physical infirmities of First Ward voters were altogether remarkable, defying reality.[3]

The *Morning News* issued a special election "EXTRA" edition, dated November 3, but also bearing the time "10:00 p.m." meaning it was prepared November 2, the night of the election. The front page carried a picture of the poll-watching lawyers, including me, standing in the rain, observing the councilman hold forth. The accompanying article reported in detail how "he occasionally went into the voting booth, where he was seen to point to the levers, and then retired before the curtains closed." The article went on to report: "To the observers this appeared to be in violation of Section 5021 of the Election Law which specifies that if a voter requests instructions on the manner of voting after entering the voting machine, 'two election officers of opposite political parties shall give such instructions to him.'" The article continued: "On other occasions the same election official . . . was plainly observed going into the voting machine with voters and remaining after the curtains were closed."[4]

The councilman delivered the First Ward for his party by a vote of approximately 500 to 400. Despite his questionable efforts, the 1954 election was a Democratic victory of outstanding proportions overall, if not in the councilman's district. The Democratic candidates for "the row offices" in New Castle County each won by majorities of more than 8,000 votes.[5] In the afterglow of this sweeping victory, no Democrat thought it worthwhile to come forward and challenge the councilman's clearly illegal conduct.

The Democrats celebrated their triumph with a parade on Thursday, November 4. As the cavalcade of cars wound through downtown Wilmington, Joe Craven in his open touring car spotted me in the crowd in Rodney Square and called me over. While the car rolled slowly forward, he told me he wanted to see me and asked me to call him. When we met, he asked me to be one of his deputy attorney generals, telling me I was the only deputy he was insisting upon naming. He added he did not care who else the party leaders wanted to designate as deputies; he wanted to know he had on his staff one honest, able lawyer who knew how to try a case. Perhaps my appearance on the front page of the *Morning News* had sparked Craven's interest. Or perhaps it was my well-known work in *The Rape Case* talked about by members of the Bar, most of whom—if not all—did not think I had a chance of succeeding.

I immediately accepted Craven's offer without consulting either of my mentors, Mr. Cohen and Judge Leahy. The honor of the appointment and the modest, but guaranteed, salary of $3,000 a year easily turned my head. To my discredit, I do not think I even paused to consider rejecting Craven's offer. The fact I would have to surrender participation in *The Rape Case* did not cross my mind until later. And when it did, it did not occur to me to renege on my promise to serve as one of Craven's deputies, even though accepting meant I would be reneging on my promise to serve Curran, Jones, and Maguire. Given my commitment to them and their families, I should have refused Craven's offer out-of-hand.

After accepting Craven's offer, however, I continued preparing for the December 1954 hearing. Although I did not yet have a favorable decision for my clients from the Superior Court, I was convinced, given the proof of the police perjury I now possessed, I had already won the case. In my opinion, the relief I sought for my clients was imminent.

13

Winning the Newspaper Decision

On February 5, 1954, the Delaware Supreme Court, in a unanimous opinion by Justice Tunnell, decided *Equitable Trust Co. v. Gallagher,* holding: "[it] is the duty of a court, in . . . a case of willful destruction of evidence, to adopt a view of the facts as unfavorable to the wrongdoer as the known circumstances will reasonably admit. The maxim is that everything will be presumed against the despoiler." The court went on to say: "This attitude of the law is in truth no more than the application of a rule of common sense, based upon the characteristics normally found in human nature."[1] The holding fit *The Rape Case* perfectly.

The hearing on my application for relief under Rule 35 took place on December 1–2, 1954, in the Superior Court before the same three judges who sat at the 1948 trial. Armed as I now was with McCool's Report and the transcripts of the depositions, I elicited from the police officers under oath that they had willfully destroyed the first set of statements on October 30, 1947, and had prepared a second set for my clients to sign late in the afternoon the same day. The admissions proved beyond doubt the statements placed in evidence at trial were tainted. Surely the Superior Court would apply the Supreme Court's unequivocal holding in *Gallagher* "that everything would be presumed against the despoiler," and that meant my clients' trial testimony about the number of statements and what the first statements said would compel the Superior Court to set aside the convictions and grant a new trial. Or so I thought.

Now in the final days of his service, Deputy Attorney General Hamilton, picking up the false police claim, again argued that I was confusing two statements with two pieces of paper. His argument adopted as true the police assertion that the second piece of paper each accused signed was simply "a copy" of the contents contained in the first piece of paper, the same assertion Captain McCool had urged in the first deposition of police officers I had taken on July 28, 1954.[2] But Hamilton's contention was based on the police lies at the February 1948 trial. Even assuming, contrary to my clients' trial testimony, that the second statements were identical to the first, his assertion did not address the critical impact that the police lies had upon Curran, Jones, and Maguire's credibility before the jury.

Certainly the colloquy between Hamilton and Judge Terry on the first day of the hearing demonstrated the impact of the proof I presented upon Judge Terry. Hamilton argued that *Gallagher* did not apply since in *Gallagher* "everything was destroyed. There wasn't anything left. There is no inference that can be drawn here if you once believe that the two statements are the same." Terry saw the fallacy in Hamilton's claim immediately, responding: "But you have got to believe that."

Hamilton, still relying on the false police testimony, answered: "There is testimony here and the testimony was before the jury. The statements were the same." Terry said: "At the trial, as I recall the trial, I was under the impression that only one statement was signed by the boys." Hamilton tried to blunt Terry's meaning by conceding: "Well, that is still everybody's impression."

Terry persisted: "Well, when I say that, I mean, they signed their name once. I understand how the officer is attempting to explain the situation. But I was under the impression that the statement was signed by them early in the morning, and they placed their signature to one paper, and it appears now that they placed their signatures to two papers, but the officer said that the language was the same in both papers and the boys say, 'No, that isn't the truth.'"

Hamilton, continuing to base his argument on the police lies, claimed Rodenhiser's rebuttal testimony, after the defendants had testified, meant "the only thing that he [was] talking about [was] whether the substance is the same, and that is the only thing that is of significance and that is the only thing that could be before the jury. If the statements were not changed, then there is no materiality." Terry again rejoined: "Of course, the boys testified that the statements were changed." Hamilton agreed and agreed again when Terry added: "And that they signed two statements."

What Hamilton chose to ignore was that the police never admitted at trial there were two signings and thus two pieces of paper as Curran, Jones, and Maguire had testified. Terry noted the police could have cleared up the discrepancy at trial but did not. Moreover, Judge Terry took up the point that the second papers contained the word "moaning" but the first papers did not. He summed up the dispute: "Therefore, they said they signed two statements, one containing the language, but the other didn't contain it at all, and, when the officer was brought back, it was cleared up and he said they didn't sign but the one paper and they didn't sign any other, and they said that the statement[s] that they [first] signed didn't have the 'moaning and the groaning'."[3]

On December 2, 1954, the *Morning News* carried a lengthy account of the proceedings of the first day of the hearing. It highlighted my calling Captain McCool and my cross-examination of Rodenhiser. The most significant feature was the reporter's reference to what Judge Terry had said:

Judge Terry late yesterday afternoon told Mr. Hamilton and Mr. Morris from the bench that at the trial of the case, as he remembered it, there was only one statement signed by each of the three defendants. Now it is brought out there were two statements, the Judge said. The police, Judge Terry continued, say the statements were substantially the same, the defendants that they were not.

At another point, Judge Terry, speaking for the court, said that since there were clear implications of perjury on the part of police who testified at the trial, and since the court had imposed life sentences on the defendants, he and his associates on the bench intend to look into the matter thoroughly.[4]

When the hearing ended, there was a discussion with the court about the waiving of post-hearing briefs. Since I had already accepted Attorney General-elect Craven's invitation to serve as one of his deputies, effective January 1, 1955, the need to attend to other matters in my practice before I embarked on my new part-time public duties made time precious. Still, the thought of submitting the issue on a record that clearly established the perjury was tempting. If counsel wrote briefs it would be the first time my clients and I and the state would submit briefs specifically addressing the merits of my claim for the release of my clients because of police perjury. I was loath to give up that opportunity. Surrendering the right to submit briefs and argue would be at my peril and to my clients' disadvantage. So I prepared and on December 23, filed a brief emphasizing that the hearing testimony established beyond any doubt the police perjury and its adverse effect upon my clients' credibility. Charlie Smith had no part in this decision. By the time of the hearing we had already agreed there was no point in my continuing to take the train to

Philadelphia or to send him materials to review.⁵ Uniformly he approved of what I did and what I wrote. I was already signing all our pleadings and briefs without him. He did not protest, nor did Maris. Probably Smith was relieved I was willing to do the substantive work. But for the longest time I was no more successful than he had been.

In boxing matches years ago, if a bout did not end with a knockout or the inability of one of the fighters to continue, the local newspaper declared the winner. I thought the December 2 *Morning News* article had clearly declared me the winner. I had made my point: the police had perjured themselves and thereby had destroyed my clients' credibility rendering the 1948 trial constitutionally unfair. I was confident it was only a matter of time before the Superior Court would order the relief that the proof of the perjury now required: vacating the sentences while leaving the state with the right to try Curran, Jones, and Maguire again.

The Superior Court could not restore the more than seven years of hard time my clients had spent in the New Castle County Workhouse. Nevertheless, I was certain they would—in prison parlance—"hit the bricks" within weeks. I would not be their lawyer then, because accepting Craven's offer meant I had to withdraw as their attorney. The fight was not over, of course, but given the proof of the perjury now in the record, I thought relief was just a matter of time. After all my hard work, my one regret was someone else would receive the credit for being the lawyer who finally upset their convictions. In wanting that credit I was no different than Hy Young.

14

Young's Name and
My Capacity for Work

It must have been frustrating for Hy Young, as proud a man as he was, to read in his morning paper that what he tried so hard to prove at the February 1948 trial was finally, in December 1954, publicly acknowledged as fact. Judge Terry's comments at the hearing reported on December 2 meant at least one judge of the trial court recognized "clear implications of perjury" in the police trial testimony.[1] Terry's comment clearly implied Rodenhiser had testified evasively and, indeed, deliberately failed to give full and truthful answers to Young's questions.[2] In 1948 all Young had to go on was what Jones had told him and all three defendants had testified to at trial. His persistence in trying to prove that Jones had signed two, separate statements elicited the police denial and laid the basis for the claim I asserted and proved years later: that the police had committed perjury at *The Rape Case* trial. And now that he had been vindicated by what the newspaper quoted Judge Terry as saying, another lawyer, a younger one without Young's experience or savvy or standing, would receive the acclaim that would have come to him had he been able to prove the perjury at the trial.

In 1950, "after a stormy Republican state Convention in

which he bested . . . C. Edward Duffy," his nemesis at *The Rape Case* trial, Young became his party's candidate for the office of attorney general.[3] The Democrats nominated Thomas Cooch, the direct descendent of a colonial family for whom Cooch's Bridge is named. It is the site of the only Revolutionary War battle fought on Delaware soil.[4]

The election campaign between Cooch and Young was bitterly contested. The Democrats successfully insisted the ballots carry Young's first name, "Hyman," even though he was known professionally as H. Albert Young and called by his nickname, "Hy." The Democrats would have preferred to have had his original last name, "Yanowitz," appear on the ballot as well, but Hy had changed it legally many years before. The Democrats thought— and so did Young as he later told me—the use of his full first name told the voting public he was a Jew and therefore not someone they should choose when a native son, Tom Cooch, was also running. Only after conducting a spirited campaign throughout the state did Young prevail in a close vote. He was the first Jew to win a statewide post in a Delaware election.[5]

As attorney general, Young had the responsibility to enforce the state's election laws to ensure a clean election in 1952. At the time, I was still Chief Judge Leahy's law clerk. I volunteered to work for my party on election day. One of my tasks was to accompany Edwin Hensel, the Chairman of the Democratic Party in Wilmington, as he traveled to trouble districts.[6] Several weeks after the 1952 election, Young made a point of telling me he had prevented my arrest on the charge of violating the Hatch Act, a Federal Act prohibiting employees in the executive branch from participating in partisan politics on pain of prosecution. Young wanted me to believe he did this as an act of kindness. I told him the Hatch Act did not apply to the judiciary and its staff and, thus, he avoided embarrassing himself.

Young and I never discussed *The Rape Case* and his role in it before I filed the habeas corpus petition in 1953. By the time I began serving as local counsel, Young was already attorney general. Given his conflict of interest as Jones' former lawyer and his current post, I think he thought (correctly in my opinion) it would have been inappropriate for him to assist either the prosecution or me in any way. Recognizing his position, I thought it was inappropriate for me to turn to him. The silence between us ended on December 3, 1954, the day after the close of the hearing before the three-judge court.

William Prickett and his son, my contemporary who bore his father's name, had invited me and many other members of the Bar to a cocktail party that evening to celebrate their move to newly renovated offices at 1310 King Street. At that time few lawyers, and certainly none of Prickett's standing, had offices in the row houses along King Street. I readily accepted the invitation as did many other members of the Bar curious to see what the senior Prickett had accomplished by moving from an office building to a residential structure. Unlike my mentor and partner, Philip Cohen, who declined to attend, I got along well enough with the senior Prickett in the trials I had with him. Mr. Cohen did not respect Prickett; he considered him a pettifogger and said so in a brief he filed in the *Fortner Will* case.[7] Mr. Cohen viewed Prickett as a man who regarded the law as a game lawyers play to win. To Mr. Cohen the law was the passionate pursuit of truth and justice. It was far too serious to be anyone's—let alone a lawyer's—game.

When Hy Young approached me that evening, it was the first time he ever sought me out to talk about *The Rape Case*. I had yet to achieve any judicial success in it.[8] All I had to show for my efforts so far was the notable achievement of having proved the police had lied at the 1948 trial, my "newspaper decision." Still, I believed the release of my clients was imminent. I think Young thought so too. His comment that evening evinced the confidence he had in himself and the opinion he held of others in relation to himself: "Why didn't you wait for me to get out of office?" he bristled. "With my name and your capacity for work, we could have these men out in no time." His bluntness startled me. I do not recall responding before he turned aside without a word of praise for my work, my legal theory, or my advocacy skills. Since my clients were still in jail, I thought his comment was critical. Clearly his view was that if I had exercised patience and deferred to him, then he, upon leaving office, would have secured the men's freedom promptly. So far as he was concerned and despite the 1954 newspaper accounts, *The Rape Case* was still "his" case. He was still the center of attention when it came to *The Rape Case.*

In 1948, Young had not sought to appeal for Jones although, as he told me years later, he believed his client and the other defendants were telling the truth. An appeal in 1948 would have been pointless. Delaware did not yet have a separate Supreme Court. There was little likelihood that the judges who would have heard the appeal would have reversed their chief justice and his and their colleagues, Terry and Carey. Moreover, what error of law or fact could Curran, Jones, and Maguire have raised on appeal from the verdict? Proof of the unfairness and unconstitutionality of the trial was beyond the ability of the defendants and their lawyers to establish in 1948, when the police deliberately concealed the proof and McCool's Report did not exist and when McCool delivered his report, it was buried in the Police Department files.

Following the sentencing, Young turned aside from his client and *The Rape Case.* Judge Leahy's comment to me about his classmate and friend was that once a case was over "Hy was on to the next one." The Judge thought Young's ability to put aside any past defeats (they were few and far between) made him the outstanding advocate he was. I was the opposite. When Vice

Chancellor William Marvel in open court one day insisted I respond to his comments critical of my unwillingness to regard trials as if they were cricket matches on the playing fields of Eton, I told him: "When I lose a case I bleed."

Young gladly and proudly entered the political arena with its unpredictability and secured the high office of attorney general. Years later I learned from Kitty Curran that her family and Jones' two sisters thought Young had been "bought off" by the offer to run for the post of attorney general. Neither I nor anyone else professionally involved with me in the effort to prove the unfairness of the trial found any support for such a charge.

But I, not Young, was the lawyer who went forward to prove the unfairness of the trial. Now I, like Young, was about to enter public office and put *The Rape Case* behind me.

Even if there had been merit to Young's suggestion and I had been willing to wait for his availability, I cannot imagine Curran or Jones or Maguire or their families in December 1952, when I said I would enter the case and serve as local counsel, assenting to a delay until 1955 when Young was out of office before putting into motion the effort to free them from their unlawful incarceration. Just as I did not have the impression Young gave a moment's thought to the clients' view of what was in their interest, so it never occurred to me to delay acting to set aside the convictions. They were entitled to the fair trial I sought for them and then to their freedom if they were acquitted at a fair trial. I thought I had proved their entitlement to a new trial. But I underestimated the myopia of the state court judges.

15

The Original Talk Show Host

Although Mr. Cohen and I were partners, the office of Hart Cooper, the insurance adjuster, separated our respective quarters. Given my habit of getting to work not later than 7:00 a.m., I was already at my desk around 8:00 a.m. one morning when my unlocked door suddenly swung open and, without any greeting, in walked my benefactor, Francis A. Reardon, who years before had urged Judge Leahy to employ me as his law clerk. Reardon's office was across the hall. He asked, "What time was it last night when you punched him in the nose?" I had no idea what he was talking about. Realizing he had brought me news, Reardon proceeded to explain.

The previous evening, one of my contemporaries had appeared as the "mystery guest lawyer" on *The Joe Pyne Show*. Pyne was the first talk show host in Delaware and among the first in the nation to invite listeners to call in and express their opinions on the air. Each weekday evening he held forth on WILM from 7 to 11 p.m. from a table in the back room of the English Grill, a bar and restaurant on Market Street between 9th and 10th Streets. Pyne had served as a Marine during World War II. As he strode through life, he carried himself with the air of authority a Marine learns early on. A one-word description of him was "opinionated." His colorful, provocative, raucous style quickly made *The Joe Pyne Show* the best known radio broadcast in northern Delaware. He was not in awe of the local establishment and never lacked for a quick riposte to a caller's stupidity.

Although Pyne had not identified his mystery guest, those who knew him could not mistake his voice. On the night he appeared, *The Rape Case* was again in the news because of the hearing before the three judges. At the same time, the *Sheppard* case in Ohio, the case in which F. Lee Bailey made his national reputation, was also in the news. Ohio had charged Sheppard with the murder of his wife. Sheppard swore he was innocent, claiming that a stranger had entered his home and committed the crime. Bailey's work secured a new trial for Sheppard after the United States Supreme Court held that pretrial publicity had deprived him of a fair trial.[1]

When Joe Pyne sought his guest expert's opinion on both *The Rape Case* and the *Sheppard* case, the guest lawyer responded without hesitation that my effort to secure a new trial for my clients would prove unsuccessful because of their obvious guilt. His private view was thus broadcast to Delaware listeners, some of whom might eventually find themselves called as jurors if I succeeded in setting aside my clients' conviction and if the state then decided to retry them. Ironically, the guest lawyer declined to answer Joe's questions about the *Sheppard* case, since, he said, all he knew about it was what he read in the newspapers.

The guest expert's responsible answer about the *Sheppard* case could easily have given listeners the impression that his opinion about my clients' guilt was accurate and informed, since his prompt expression of their guilt was in such sharp contrast to his properly declining to opine about Sheppard's guilt. In fact, he had no knowledge of *The Rape Case* either, other than what he may have read in newspapers. He had never discussed *The Rape Case* with me. He had never read the transcript of the trial. He had never interviewed witnesses. He had never sought the opinion of experts on the critical medical testimony. He had never researched the law applicable to *The Rape Case*. His knowledge of *The Rape Case* was no better than his knowledge of the *Sheppard* case. In short, given his ignorance, his opinion about the guilt or innocence of my clients was meaningless. I knew that, but Joe Pyne's listeners did not.

Reardon's solution, to punch the "expert" in the nose, however inviting, would not help my clients. Moreover, I knew the mystery guest well enough to conclude there was no point in trying to convince him to retract his remarks. There was every reason, however, for me to speak to Joe Pyne.

Although an infrequent listener to *The Joe Pyne Show*, I thought Joe was fair once all the facts were placed before him. I called to arrange to talk to him at the WILM studio, then located only a block from my office. He agreed to see me immediately. Upon arriving, I wasted no time in getting to the point.

I told Joe I had no intention of censoring whatever he wanted to say or do on his talk show, but I made it clear that uninformed opinions of the kind his guest expert had expressed could poison a radio audience, some of whom could and, indeed, probably would be chosen as jurors at a new trial. Joe asked if I wanted to appear on his program to express my opinion. I told him that would be inappropriate. The place for the trial was in a courtroom, not on radio from the English Grill. Joe heard me out and told me he thought I had a point. He then said he would make it known that the guilt or innocence of Curran, Jones, and Maguire was not a subject for discussion on his show for the reason I had suggested. Several callers thereafter tried to discuss the case, but Joe discouraged them, and soon *The Rape Case* faded as a topic on his program.

16

My Short-Lived Public Service

Accepting the appointment as a deputy attorney general meant I would have to withdraw as the lawyer for Curran, Jones, and Maguire and find someone to represent them. By December 23, 1954, I had prepared and filed my brief urging the Superior Court to grant the Rule 35 motion following the hearing earlier that month. On January 3, 1955, on behalf of the state, Hamilton, as one of his last acts in office, filed a well-written answering brief arguing the court should deny the motion. About Maguire's statement, Hamilton emphasized Reinhardt's comment: "as far as my client is concerned I cannot see where this statement does any harm, and I have no objection."[1] When Hamilton attacked Jones' testimony in his brief, he seized upon Young's remark when he withdrew Rodenhiser as his witness that his line of questioning to prove there was another statement: "I don't think it is of too great significance." Hamilton argued Young's comment was "undoubtedly the case."[2]

After the 1954 election, when Joseph Donald Craven succeeded Hy Young as attorney general in January 1955, he assigned Deputy Attorney General Frank O'Donnell Jr. to *The Rape Case* to replace Hamilton. Among the short list of persons I considered to replace me, one name stood out. I thought John Merwin Bader, a conscientious, knowledgeable lawyer, would press the case. He was older than I and in practice since 1948. We were professional friends. He had been an associate at Killoran & VanBrunt, occupying the North American Building's sixth floor, when I worked with Mr. Cohen on the eighth floor. In my early years of practice, I frequently saw John engaged as I was in searching titles in the offices of the Recorder of Deeds or the Prothonotary or the Register of Wills.

Convinced of the rightness of my cause, I was optimistic about the outcome of *The Rape Case*. The proof of the police perjury found in McCool's Report and established at the hearing, the strength of my legal arguments, and Judge Terry's comments at the hearing, made me think I was turning a sure winner over to Bader. When I explained my need for a successor lawyer, he immediately understood the task and the responsibility. His "Yes" meant his prompt involvement, since the reply brief had to be filed by January 14, 1955, in accordance with the schedule Hamilton and I had agreed upon. John set about his work. Neither of us then recognized the depth of the Superior Court's opposition to the relief we sought.

In his approach to his brief, Bader proved to be as naive as I had been optimistic. At the outset, he attempted to distance himself from the hard-fought proceedings that had preceded his advent into the litigation, writing: "The writer of this brief is in a rather fortunate position to assay the contentions of both Petitioners and State in this matter. Coming into the case at the eleventh hour, he gains a better perspective, albeit a less detailed familiarity, than those who have 'borne the burden of the day's heat.'"[3] Bader thus tried to align himself with the three members of the Superior Court. One could infer from his words that he and the three judges, disinterested as they all were, would decide the case together. Judges Richards, Terry, and Carey, however, were as impervious to Bader's novel approach as they were to my substantive arguments.

Although Bader was unsuccessful in convincing the Superior Court to favor his clients, his summary of the main points was right on target:

Rodenheiser's perjury—his testimony is susceptible of no other characterization—had a three-fold effect: (1) it concealed the destruction of the earlier statements which differed from those in evidence; (2) it discredited the veracity of the defendants on a point which, from all that appeared at that time, Rodenheiser had no reason but to tell the truth; and (3) it destroyed the defendants' opportunity of cross-examination.[4]

Bader's comments on the applicability of *Equitable Trust Company v. Gallagher*,[5] the case involving the destruction of material documents where the Delaware Supreme Court held all reasonable inferences should be found against the destroyer of the documents, were less wordy and more focused than mine had been:

To follow the State's reasoning it is necessary to assume that Rodenheiser's testimony is true. Yet, under the cited case, this Court should adopt a view of the facts as unfavorable to Rodenheiser (the despoiler) "as the known circumstances will reasonably admit." Rodenheiser is attempting to tell us that the destroyed statements were word-for-word identical with the ones in evidence. There is ample direct and circumstantial evidence pointing the other way, all of which, under the *Gallagher* case, is to be accepted in preference to Rodenheiser's version of the facts.[6]

Hamilton's assertion that the court should deny relief relied on *Bowen v. United States* and *United States v. Moore*, post-conviction cases where, years after trial, defendants complained a constitutional violation had brought about their convictions and the courts held that in order to secure relief the defendants must demonstrate "a retrial would result in a different judgment."[7] In response, Bader said the state's argument ignored both reality and the law. To accept the state's position would impose a burden beyond the ability of the petitioners to prove. Moreover, the court's acceptance would insulate the state from accountability for serious constitutional violations. Bader concluded: "It is only in the most clear-cut case that one can say, from a reading of the record, whether the prejudicial matter did or did not affect the verdict. This is for the obvious reason that no one but the jurors themselves know how delicately the question of guilt or innocence was balanced in the jury's mind."[8] By suggesting there existed an exception to the effect of perjury, "only in the most clear-cut case," Bader unnecessarily tempered his point that only *The Rape Case* jurors could decide how the perjured testimony affected their judgment of the accuseds' guilt or innocence.

While Bader struggled to move *The Rape Case* forward, I turned to my tasks as a deputy. I soon learned one of newly-elected Attorney General Craven's goals was to secure pay raises for the attorney general and his deputies in order to attract able lawyers. Although he personally stood to gain from the increases, Craven's concern was genuine. For years under Republican attorneys general, the larger firms placed their young associates in the office as deputies to gain trial experience. Unlike the prior administration of Hy Young, most members of Craven's staff were solo practitioners or from small firms. They needed the money and Craven fought hard to secure the increases. On one occasion, he brought me with him to Dover to confront Speaker of the House James R. Quigley, demanding Quigley explain why he had not permitted the pay-raise bill to come to the House floor for a vote. Quigley, who had as foul a mouth as anyone in public office I ever met, told us between four letter expletives that the bill would not come before the House until his dog-track bill was out of committee.[9]

Toward the end of its 1955 session, the General Assembly finally enacted the increases Craven sought. When it did, my salary for my part-time job as a deputy attorney general for the State Tax Department jumped from $3,000 to $6,000 a year. Craven now feared members of the General Assembly would pay a surprise visit to the New Castle, Kent, and Sussex attorney general's offices to determine whether or not the deputies were working harder, given the doubling of their compensation. He thought if the deputies were physically at their desks, it would justify the General Assembly's action. Without telling any of us what he was doing, Craven directed his secretary to keep track of the hours we each were in the office.

The time Craven chose for the surveillance was the week of June 27, 1955, when the Superior Court turned to civil trials after completing that term's criminal trials. Understandably, criminal cases had priority over civil litigation. That same week was the one in which, on June 29 and 30, I tried a civil claim after I had completed my criminal trial assignments and was up-to-date on all the other matters Craven had laid on me. I went forward with the trial, my mind entirely focused on its result, which was a success for my client and me. During recesses and at the lunch hour with my client and his wife, I did go from Courtroom No. 1 of the Superior Court to the room I shared with Deputy Attorney General Wilfred J. Smith Jr. in the attorney general's office on the floor below. I was not there to work on matters as a deputy. By the end of the week, I had learned of Craven's checking exercise. I was incensed.

On the following Monday, Craven's secretary called and said he wanted to see me, a request I expected. I immediately responded, walking the short distance from my private office to his public office.[10] Seated across the desk from Craven, I listened to his short prelude about how he had checked everyone's time. He concluded by noting mine, only a few hours in total, and said it was unacceptable considering the doubling of my salary. I told him I regretted he had not asked me how much time I had spent in the office. The facts were, I went on, I had not spent any time on attorney-general work that week. I took pleasure in telling him that when I was in the office that week and his secretary recorded my time, I was there working on my civil case and not on any state assignment.

I then asked Craven whether he was satisfied with the quantity of my work. He replied he was. I asked him if the quality of the work I did met with his approval. He again assured me it did. Whereupon, I told him I quit. He appeared shocked. He said that was not necessary; all I had to do was spend more time in the office. I responded that when he hired me he had hired a lawyer and not an elevator operator. (I meant no offense to elevator operators; it slipped off my tongue, since I was making an analogy to a typical nine-to-five worker.) The facts were I spent whatever time was necessary to complete my assignments promptly and with the same striving for excellence I brought to whatever I did. I told him I resented his surreptitious checking and would not continue to serve under him.

Back in my private office, I dictated to Sadie Golden (Mr. Cohen's and my secretary) a letter of immediate resignation, and delivered it to Attorney General Craven's office. The letter contained no reference to what I considered his deceitful conduct. For my part, I kept my own counsel. There was no need to embarrass Craven. He put his best face upon the matter when in a gracious letter he publicly explained that my departure was motivated by my desire to return to private practice. Neither of us wanted to, nor did we, air dirty linen in public.

To the best of my knowledge, I was the only state employee who ever resigned from public office following the doubling of his compensation. For some reason—it could have been a slow news day—my resignation made the front page of the *Morning News* on July 9, 1955, together with my University of Delaware graduation photograph taken in 1947. Not yet thirty, I thought the unlined, youthful face staring back at me was now beyond recapture. The article stressed the close relationship between Craven and me, quoted my letter in full, and included a biography that could have served as a resume were I embarking on a job search. But I already had a career in place with Philip Cohen.

The abrupt end of my public-service career meant I could return to *The Rape Case;* I had no problem reclaiming it from John Bader. From the filing of his reply brief on January 14, 1955, through my six month tenure as a deputy attorney general and into the autumn, the three judges had the Rule 35 Motion "under advisement." Nothing had taken place to advance the freedom of the clients. Bader never had a full opportunity to demonstrate his considerable talents. Maris, Corbeil, the families, and the clients were all delighted I was back on the case, once again caught up by my infectious optimism readily conveyed by everything I said and did in *The Rape Case.*

When the summer passed without any word from the court, I thought I had to "spark" the three judges to act. "Sparking" a court, even in a long delayed matter, almost always redounded to the disadvantage of the clients and their lawyer who sought court action. Aware of the risk, I nonetheless requested a meeting to find out when the three judges would decide the issue put before them at the December 1954 hearing.

It was a bold step, but I thought there was nothing to lose. If the judges were going to decide for us, as I thought they should, they should do so sooner rather than later so my clients could prepare for another trial or secure their release. If the judges were going to decide against my clients despite the proof, again they should do so sooner rather than later so I could appeal to reverse such a ruling. I did not share my thinking or impatience with the judges. Although judges may show impatience with lawyers, only a foolish lawyer shows impatience with a judge, and the client generally bears the cost of a lawyer's failure to control himself.

In September 1955, I came before the three judges in their chambers in the Public Building. After noting the now nine months since the hearing, I respectfully offered to submit additional materials, orally or in writing, if the court thought it would help in deciding the pending motion. It was unnecessary to ask when they expected to rule, since my request for the meeting and my presence implied the question.

During the short session, the deputy attorney general present, having no need to say a word, said nothing. President Judge Richards, speaking for the court, assured me I would receive the opinion promptly. Although he gave me no reason to expect a favorable result, I remained optimistic.

17

Something More Needs
To Be Said
(The Third Defeat)

O n October 3, 1955, ten months after the hearing, the
Superior Court finally filed an opinion and a concurring opinion. Both writings denied relief to Curran,
Jones, and Maguire.[1] The result was not surprising to those who
did not know what I knew, but it was shocking and upsetting to
me.

President Judge Richards' opinion appeared first.[2] It ignored
the effect the police testimony had on the defendants' credibility
and expressed his slant on the evidence. As proof of the trial's
fairness, he pointed to the "experienced trial lawyers" for the accused: "The defendants Jones and Maguire were represented by
counsel of their own selection, H. Albert Young and David J.
Reinhardt Jr., both of whom were experienced trial lawyers, and
the Court appointed Leonard G. Hagner, an experienced trial
lawyer and former Deputy Attorney General, to represent the defendant Curran."[3]

Despite holding a number of public positions, Len Hagner
never considered himself "an experienced trial lawyer." He
served as assistant city solicitor of Wilmington, as a deputy attor-

ney general in the 1920s, and as a part-time judge of the Family Court in 1947. I could only conclude from Richards' description that he really did not know Len. The mild-mannered Hagner had done what he could, but he had not overcome Duffy's forceful prosecution. Although Reinhardt, like Hagner, had served as a deputy attorney general, he was not considered among the outstanding practitioners in criminal defense work. Young was the only one of the three who could claim the status of an "experienced trial lawyer" in a criminal case. Surely Hagner and Reinhardt realized that, given their deference to Young to lead the defense at every significant turn in the case.[4]

To Judge Richards, another critical element in showing the trial's fairness was the trial court's permitting the defense lawyers to ask additional questions during jury selection "to determine whether they were entitled to challenge for cause." He cited yet other facts to prove the trial's fairness: "The trial lasted seven days and counsel were given ample opportunity to examine and cross-examine the witnesses. In addition they were allowed to take any course in conducting the defense permissible under the constitution and laws of this state."[5]

But Judge Richards was silent about how any of his claims of fairness were of use to Curran, Jones, and Maguire. Clearly their lawyers' right to broad examination had not caused the police to tell the truth. The length of the trial ignored the effect of the police perjury upon the jurors. Counsel's freedom in the conduct of the defense was of no avail in the face of the obdurate police perjury. Richards conceded that Rodenhiser failed to testify he had destroyed "the original statements."[6] His use of the term, "the original statements," was in keeping with his belief the statements the state put in evidence were merely "retyped copies" of the first set, as Detective Rodenhiser had claimed to Superintendent Kavanaugh shortly after the trial.

Richards further downplayed the significance of Rodenhiser's conduct by falsely claiming Rodenhiser's destruction of the first statements "was the only information in reference to the statement [*sic*] made by the defendants which was not brought out before the jury." To him, Rodenhiser's action was "not sufficient to justify this Court to grant the relief prayed for in this motion." In reaching his conclusion, Richards distorted the record. He inaccurately claimed: "All of the testimony in reference to the statements, the number signed, where they were signed, when they were signed and what they contained was before the jury and was doubtless given consideration.All of the material evidence in connection with the statements of the defendants was before the jury at the time it rendered its verdict."[7]

Richards' sweeping generalizations ignored three master facts that made false his assertion that the jurors knew everything about the statements when they rendered their guilty verdict: (1) the jurors did not know the police had lied about the existence of the first set of statements; (2) the jurors did not know the police had destroyed the first set of statements; and (3) the jurors did not know Curran, Jones, and Maguire had told the truth about the number of statements they each had signed.

Richards adopted Hamilton's argument and its distortion of the facts when he wrote:

There seems to be no doubt that two statements were signed by the defendants Jones and Maguire, or that the second statements were a re-typed copy of the first. It is true that Detective Rodenheiser testified at the trial that they signed only one statement. The defendants testified that they signed two statements and contradicted the testimony of Detective Rodenheiser. The defendants also testified that the statements introduced in evidence were not the same as the first statements they signed because they contained the word "moan" or "moaning" which was not in the first statements. [Emphasis added.][8]

As was true of Hamilton's claim, the only support for Richards' assertion that "the second statements were a retyped copy of the first," was Detective Rodenhiser's claim. Like Hamilton, Richards relied on Rodenhiser, the same person who destroyed the first statements and kept that fact secret from the defendants, their lawyers, the jurors, and the court. Given the facts now proved, Richards' conclusion strained both credulity and logic, compounding the deliberate withholding of information by police officers six years earlier so that the defendants were made to appear as liars.

Moreover, Richards adopted Hamilton's argument that Curran, Jones, and Maguire were "confusing two statements with two prior pieces of paper."[9] Neither Hamilton, who urged the argument, nor Richards, who accepted it, addressed the impact of the police perjury itself and how it destroyed the credibility of the defendants' repeated assertion that they had not raped the woman. Richards ignored the obvious, as illustrated in his erroneous assertion:

The fact that the original statements were torn up by Detective Rodenheiser after they were re-typed was not brought out at the trial, and did not become known until it was brought out in the depositions and the evidence taken at the hearing on this motion. The only explanation given by Detective Rodenheiser for having the statements taken and written by him re-typed, and destroying the originals, was his desire to have his work present as good an appearance as possible, and his lack of experience in work of that nature.[10]

Richards' conclusion that Rodenhiser's destruction of the first set of statements "did not become known until it was brought out in the depositions and . . . at the hearing on this motion" is not true. He again ignored critical facts. The other police officers who gave perjured testimony at the trial surely knew they had not told the truth, a fact made clear by the colloquy between Judge Terry and Hamilton at the hearing:

TERRY, J.: The Police Department knew that two statements were signed.

MR. HAMILTON: Yes.

TERRY, J.: But it wasn't told to the jury in this case?

MR. HAMILTON: That is right. There is no dispute about that.

TERRY, J.: The only statement given by the witness is that one statement was signed, is that right?

MR. HAMILTON: That is right. But whether he knew anything about it, what did that have to do with it? He wasn't in control of the case.

TERRY, J.: But it was brought to the attention of Detective Rodenhiser that he shouldn't have done what he did.

MR. HAMILTON: He admits it.

TERRY, J.: He didn't indicate in the trial what he had done on the trial.

MR. HAMILTON: That is admitted. The trial speaks for itself. Of course, the evidence is in there. Of course, he didn't admit it.[11]

Within weeks after the trial, Superintendent Kavanaugh had in hand McCool's Report confirming in detail that there were two sets of statements; a police officer had destroyed the first set; and the police had concealed the facts at trial. Moreover, prompted by what Ed Maguire told him, Kavanaugh confronted Rodenhiser, who denied any difference between the two sets, claiming he was a new detective and unaware of the need to retain the first set. Relying on what Rodenhiser had said, Kavanaugh chose to ignore the wrongdoing and its effect on the defendants' credibility.

It was the state, and not Curran, Jones, and Maguire, who concealed the truth. Yet none of the three trial judges, now sitting as the judges on my clients' Rule 35 Motion, mentioned, let alone expressed concern or, indeed, outrage, about Kavanaugh's immediately burying McCool's Report with its proof of police perjury.

In a single sentence, in a stand-alone paragraph, Judge Richards summarily disposed of my reliance on *Equitable Trust Co. v. Gallagher*,[12] holding in a conclusion lacking any explanation:

"The case of *Equitable Trust Co. v. Gallagher*, Del.Supr., 102 A.2d 538, is not applicable to the case now before the Court."[13] Under the unequivocal language in *Gallagher*, the Superior Court should have given credence to the sworn testimony of Curran, Jones, and Maguire about what the first set of statements said, but it did not do so.

Neither Richards nor Terry nor Carey ever asked: "Why should the police lie about how many sets of statements Curran, Jones, and Maguire signed?" If the police typed the statements for "neatness," why would they not readily say so at trial? The inexorable response to the unasked questions was that the police needed to cover up the truth. They had to have known if they admitted that each defendant's testimony about signing two statements was true, the police claim that the second set was simply retyped for the sake of neatness would have exposed them to questions about the differences the defendants claimed existed between the first set and the statements in evidence. To prevent exposure, all the officers who testified about the admission of State's Exhibits 10, 11, and 12 deliberately concealed the existence of the first set of statements and their subsequent destruction. *Gallagher* mandated accepting what Curran, Jones, and Maguire had testified: the statements in evidence differed from the first set.

If Judge Layton in 1953 and the Delaware Supreme Court in 1954 had not compelled the use of a Rule 35 Motion, a criminal proceeding, I could have argued *Gallagher* and the habeas corpus petition as civil cases stood alike and, therefore, the *Gallagher* rule applied.[14] The only distinction I knew of then or now between *Gallagher* and my Rule 35 Motion was that *Gallagher* was a civil case involving money while my motion arose in the setting of a criminal case involving freedom.[15]

The destruction of the first set of statements and the police perjury about doing so was one issue. Another was my contention that the police officers' testimony had destroyed my clients' credibility in the jurors' minds. Although the two issues were intertwined, I always thought the negative effect of the police perjury on the defendants' credibility was the stronger point. From childhood I regarded policemen with great respect. I knew the officers in our neighborhood, and my parents inculcated in their children faith in a policeman's word. I think the jurors in *The Rape Case* brought to their jury service a similar belief. They too were victims of the police mendacity.

The effect of the police perjury upon the jurors went beyond the police claim that there was only one set of statements and, indeed, beyond the issue of changes from the first to the second set. If the jurors believed my clients lied about the number they signed, "the seemingly innocuous fact," the jurors surely could infer they lied in denying, as each had under oath, that they had committed rape.

Judge Richards, however, neither had the agreement of his colleagues in what he wrote nor did he have the last word. Judges Carey and Terry were unwilling to endorse Richards' acceptance of Detective Rodenhiser's lying and his explanation for doing so. Neither Carey nor Terry let Rodenhiser escape condemnation. At the hearing, Terry made clear his impression that, at the time of the trial, there existed only one set of statements signed by the defendants, and they were the ones in evidence.[16] Judge Carey concurred in Richards' conclusion but set forth his own reasons: ". . . something more needs to be said concerning the testimony of Detective Rodenheiser at the original trial." Carey noted that although Rodenhiser "was on the stand for a considerable length of time, he said nothing about the fact that the original written statements were destroyed after they had been retyped and that the papers actually put into evidence were the second ones not typed by him but signed by Jones and Maguire." About Rodenhiser's effort to excuse his conduct by now claiming "he thought the matter was unimportant, and that the proper questions were not asked of him so as to give him a chance to tell about the episode," Carey's view was clear: "A witness, of course, has no business deciding upon the importance of any particular question or line of testimony; his sworn duty is to answer the questions put to him truthfully and fully."[17]

Carey's response to Rodenhiser's claim "that no opportunity was given to him to explain this matter," was to note "it seems plain to me that there were at least three places in the questioning when a full and truthful answer would necessarily have included this information." Judge Carey quoted "only one of those instances, which occurred during examination by Mr. Young:

Q. I hand you State's Exhibit No. 11. Is that the statement that you took from Ira Jones? A. It is.
Q. At what time? A. At 2:45 A.M., starting at 2:45 A.M.
Q. Did you type it yourself? A. I did."[18]

Judge Carey then hit hard on Hamilton's two pieces of paper defense. "I cannot understand," Judge Carey wrote, "how he could possibly have understood the questions above quoted to refer to anything other than the piece of paper that was then shown to him and identified by him." He continued: "while [Rodenhiser] was still on the stand, a lengthy colloquy took place between counsel and the Court, the nature of which could only indicate to him that the matter was of importance and so considered by counsel. Immediately after he left the stand, a recess was taken. Notwithstanding this, he admittedly made no effort to tell the Attorney General or any one else about the retyping episode."[19]

In concluding his scathing critique of Rodenhiser's trial testimony, Carey wrote: "Regardless of the category into which this testimony should be placed, nevertheless the witness was certainly guilty of conduct of a censorable [*sic*] character, regardless of its actual effect upon the outcome of the trial. If we pass this sort of thing in silence, we may be thought to give our sanction to such conduct."[20]

The fact that Judge Carey agreed with the facts I had gathered and placed before the Superior Court at the hearing was, at last, a victory, but it came without any relief. He denounced Detective Rodenhiser's evasive trial testimony and reprehensible conduct in unmistakable terms. Yet despite his factual findings of the police misconduct at trial, he concurred in Richards' denying of relief. Adopting Hamilton's argument, Judge Carey justified the result on a basis different from that of Judge Richards:

This does not mean that petitioners are entitled to a new trial because of that evasive testimony of this witness. To warrant such relief [*i.e.,* a new trial] under Rule 35(a) there must be a showing that a retrial could reasonably be expected to result in a different verdict and judgment. *United States v. Bowen,* D.C., 94 F. Supp. 1006 (N.D. Ga.), *affirmed,* 5 Cir., 192 F.2d 515, *certiorari denied* 343 U.S. 943. . . . , *rehearing denied* 343 U.S. 988 . . . ; *United States v. Moore,* 7 Cir., 166 F.2d 102. Under all the evidence in this case, no such likelihood appears. . . . In short, I cannot believe that there would have been any difference whatever in the outcome of the trial had the full facts concerning the aforesaid retyping been disclosed to the jury.[21]

Judge Carey concluded: "I am authorized to say that Judge Terry concurs with what has been said herein."[22] Thus, Judge Carey's concurrence was really the majority opinion of the three judges who heard the Rule 35 Motion for Relief.

In adopting the *Bowen* and *Moore* test, the concurring judges neither said nor suggested how my clients would or could mount the proof to meet it. Requiring my clients to show "a retrial could reasonably be expected to result in a different verdict and judgment" would mean they would have to prove their innocence on their motion when the issue was the fairness of the trial and not their guilt or innocence.[23] The test placed an impossible burden on my clients. The two cited cases, *Bowen* and *Moore,* could not, would not, and should not carry the day. Once the violation of a constitutional right is shown, the burden of showing innocence is irrelevant. My clients' entitlement to a new trial would be a will-o'-the-wisp if they had to meet the standard Carey and Terry laid down. Moreover, in concluding as they did, they ignored the thrust of my claim: the adverse effect of police perjury on the defendants' credibility before the jurors determined their fate. For the trial to be fair in a constitutional sense, it would have to have been free of police perjury.

Yet again, the difference between Rule 35 and habeas corpus was critical. Unlike the holding in *Bowen* and *Moore,* a habeas corpus petition only required showing that keeping the person in custody violated his rights. To continue Curran, Jones, and Maguire in custody for convictions obtained at a trial in which police testimony adversely affected their credibility certainly was a violation of their constitutional right to a fair trial.

Whether or not my September 1955 sparking of the three judges to decide the Rule 35 Motion propelled the adverse ruling, I do not know. Given the result, my reminding the Court of the existence of the Rule 35 Motion illustrated and, perhaps, proved the point I knew even before I sought the conference. Except as a necessary step on the way to eventually bringing the case before judges who would listen to my arguments and rule impartially, the denial of relief was a stunning defeat, especially after Judges Carey and Terry both concluded Rodenhiser had not told the truth. Although disheartened, I was still certain of the correctness of my claim. I knew what I had to do.

My next move was to the Supreme Court of Delaware. I was optimistic. With Judge Carey's majority opinion, I thought that once I showed how wrong Judges Carey and Terry were in their legal test, the Supreme Court surely would reverse the Superior Court and order the lower court to grant a new trial.

One day, while my appeal was pending, I was waiting for the elevator to come to the third floor of the Public Building. As I stood there, Carey and Terry came along on their way to lunch. After we exchanged greetings, Judge Terry, a tall, broad-shouldered, heavy set, kindly man, looked down at me and said, "We didn't hurt you, did we?" A smile was the only response I could muster. If I were correct, as I thought I was, and successful in convincing the appellate judges of my view, as I expected to be, I could look forward to a retrial before Judge Terry and his colleagues.

18

The Optimistic Brief

In pressing the appeal to the Delaware Supreme Court, I took into account the recent creation of the separate Supreme Court effective June 1, 1951.[1] Its first three members were Chief Justice Southerland and Justices Wolcott and Tunnell.[2] In the first eighteen months of its existence, there were twenty reversals, entirely or in part, among the reported decisions. This figure almost equaled the total number of comparable reversals reported over the previous ten years.[3] With the new Supreme Court's willingness to subject cases on appeal to independent analysis, I thought I had a good chance to reverse the Superior Court's denial of relief.

Having shown the importance of the defendants' credibility at trial, I culled from the record and analyzed the material facts and fair inferences, in each instance citing to the pages in the record, including McCool's Report, or where I had included the relevant pages in the appendix to my brief. My goal was to show how important the issue of credibility was at trial: whether the petitioners had raped the woman, as she claimed, or whether she had consented, as the petitioners claimed.[4] In accordance with the Supreme Court rules, I set forth the questions involved on the appeal. They required affirmative answers:

I.   Where The Issue At A Criminal Trial Is The Credibility Of The
     Accused As Against The Credibility Of The Prosecuting Witness
     And Where A Police Officer Deliberately And Knowingly Testifies
     Evasively And Falsely Thereby Destroying The Credibility Of The
     Accused, Is The Accused Denied His Constitutional Rights And,
     Therefore, Entitled To Relief Under Rule 35(A) Of The Superior
     Court Rules Of Criminal Procedure?
II. Where Police Destroy Evidence Favorable To An Accused, Sup-
     press The Fact At Trial That They Have Destroyed The Evidence,
     And Deny Further At Trial That Such Evidence Ever Existed, Have
     The Constitutional Rights Of The Accused Been Violated?[5]

At the outset in the "Statement of Facts," I stressed the significance of my clients' trial testimony juxtaposed with that of
their accuser. The woman testified she did not consent; Curran,
Jones, and Maguire each testified she consented.[6] Thus, immediately the Supreme Court justices could see how important the
issue of credibility was to the jurors.

I referred to my clients' trial testimony that each had signed
two statements, citing to the pages of the appendix to the brief
where I quoted from specific transcript pages of the trial and the
hearing.[7] I thought the record I placed before the Supreme Court
demonstrated beyond any reasonable doubt how Rodenhiser's
deliberately false trial testimony adversely affected the defendants' credibility, destroyed their defense, and made it impossible for the jury to reach an impartial verdict. In my judgment,
the undisputed facts, impressive and persuasive, supported the
relief I sought.

I began the argument section of my brief by claiming the hearing established to the satisfaction of a majority of the three Superior Court judges that Curran, Jones, and Maguire had told the
truth when each testified he had signed two statements and thus
the police testimony to the contrary at trial was untrue.[8] I

pointed out that the Superior Court judges heard Rodenhiser's explanations for his false trial testimony, and that while Judge Richards did not find Rodenhiser's perjury unacceptable, Judges Carey and Terry did.[9]

About Rodenhiser's second excuse, that he had not been asked the proper questions, the majority judges noted "that there were at least three places in the questioning when a full and truthful answer would necessarily have included this information." But even they did not label Rodenhiser's trial testimony as perjury.[10]

When Judges Carey and Terry in their October 9, 1955 opinion relied upon *Bowen* and *Moore* to support the legal test they thought I had to meet, they ignored *United States v. Morgan*, decided May 19, 1955, over four months earlier.[11] In *Morgan*, Judge Jerome Frank of the Second Circuit, speaking for a unanimous court, repudiated *Moore:*

> To hold that [a] defendant can be relieved of an unconstitutional conviction only if he makes a showing of innocence (or a showing that probably he would be acquitted at a constitutionally conducted trial) would be to compound the unconstitutionality of his conviction, for it would shift to him the burden of proof, deprive him of the presumption of innocence, and leave the determination of his guilt or innocence to a judge, thus denying him a jury trial. Surely one unconstitutional deprivation cannot justify still others.[12]

Although Hamilton had cited to *Bowen* in the state's answering brief, he filed his brief before the Second Circuit decided *Morgan* and thus was unaware of its ruling.

In summarizing the petitioners' legal position, I emphasized how other federal courts had expressly rejected the legal test the Superior Court majority had applied. I argued that under the facts and the applicable law, petitioners were entitled to relief because of Rodenhiser's perjury.

Rule 35, like its progenitor, habeas corpus, raised the question of whether the state had obtained a petitioner's conviction by violating his constitutional rights. Neither a petition for habeas corpus relief nor a Rule 35 Motion determined a petitioner's guilt or innocence of the crime charged against him.[13] A judgment of conviction, void because of a denial of constitutional rights, is not made valid by the fact the accused was actually guilty, for the law presumes innocence until a *valid* finding of guilt is made.[14] The law also requires the state to prove an accused's guilt beyond a reasonable doubt. To require an accused to prove his innocence shifts that burden and violates his constitutional rights.

The test the *Moore* case sanctioned and Judges Carey and Terry applied in deciding my Rule 35 motion teaches by implication that as long as a person is guilty, it makes no difference how the state obtains the conviction. Such a theory has no place in the American system.[15] In the Superior Court proceedings, my clients and I did not attempt to make a "showing" of their innocence, since we believed, as is plain from *Morgan* and the other cases, the law does not permit a retrial to determine their innocence or guilt under Rule 35. Instead, Rule 35 confined the motion and proof at the hearing to the issue of whether the 1948 trial violated the defendants' constitutional rights. Although I told the Supreme Court that the petitioners asserted their innocence at trial, asserted it again on the appeal, and were prepared to prove it if granted the relief to which they were entitled, the only requirement they had to meet was to prove Delaware had deprived them of due process.[16]

The answer to whether the state violated the petitioners' constitutional rights involved a consideration of the factual circumstances and the applicable law. I argued that the facts brought to light in the hearing held almost seven years after trial plainly showed the constitutional violation. Before concluding the brief, I turned to Judge Carey's holding: "The only basic issue in the case was whether the victim consented."¹⁷ My clients and I agreed with his statement but disagreed with his further comment that the full facts concerning the execution of two sets of statements would not have made any difference in the outcome of the trial.¹⁸ Whether there would be a different result on a new trial or whether there would have been a different result had all the facts been disclosed at the first trial is not the test the law applies to a petition under either habeas corpus or Rule 35. In considering whether the State of Delaware violated petitioners' constitutional rights at their trial, we believed the lower court's legal opinion was in error.

Even though Curran, Jones, and Maguire claimed critical, harmful changes were made in the second set of statements, the significance of their own and the police trial testimony concerning the statements was not about the extent the statements in evidence differed from those the police destroyed. *Rather the significance of the police officers' testimony is the effect it had on the jury.* The majority opinion of the Superior Court considered only the question of variation and thereby missed the essential fact: at trial the police and the prosecuting attorneys, by relying on police perjury, created the impression all three defendants were liars. Once the police testimony destroyed the defendants' credibility, the trial lost the intrinsic fairness guaranteed to every accused by the words "due process."

One can only speculate about the jury's reaction if, for example, after the petitioners swore under oath they had signed two statements, Rodenhiser had testified, "Yes, it is true, I destroyed the initial statements, but they were the same as those here in court." The petitioners would, of course, have had the right to cross-examine Rodenhiser about why he destroyed the initial statements and whether the statements in evidence were, indeed, identical to those he destroyed. More importantly, the jury would have known the petitioners were not liars when they testified they signed two statements.

Even if the legal test to be applied to petitioners' Rule 35 Motion was what Judges Carey and Terry held, that there must be a showing that a retrial could reasonably be expected to result in a different verdict and judgment, I argued the petitioners met this test. Upon a new trial, the state would have to admit the defendants told the truth about signing two statements. Further, the state would have to admit the deliberate destruction of the initial set of statements. Finally, the state would have to admit the police lied under oath. Given these three admissions, my argument went, a jury would surely have to place greater weight upon the petitioners' trial testimony that the woman consented.

19

Unexpected Help and Surprising Praise

I n reading the state's reply brief Deputy Attorney General
Frank O'Donnell Jr. filed, I had the impression Hamilton
had not departed *The Rape Case*. In a note at page 9, O'Donnell acknowledged Hamilton's role: "The work done by Mr.
Hamilton has been found very helpful in presenting the matter
to this Court." O'Donnell's gratitude to Hamilton was appropriate since he lifted almost word for word large sections from
Hamilton's answering brief in the Superior Court, including
Hamilton's use of the Reinhardt and Young trial comments as
noted above in Chapter 16.[1] He also relied on President Judge
Richards' opinion, seizing upon Richards' erroneous assertion
the petitioners had contended "the trial was improperly conducted."[2] In my main brief, I specifically denied Richards' claim;
he read into the Rule 35 Motion "something that does not
exist."[3]

O'Donnell deliberately did not challenge the point-by-point
factual analysis my brief set forth. Nor did he refer to the factual
conclusion so straightforwardly presented in Judge Carey's opinion condemning Rodenhiser. O'Donnell went so far as to argue
"[t]here was no perjury," since "the same words appeared on

both pieces of paper."[4] The only support O'Donnell had for this claim was that "Rodenhiser was strenuously questioned [at the hearing] on this point and replied that he had compared the two pieces of paper."[5] O'Donnell also patently ignored Rodenhiser's original trial testimony that Jones and Maguire each signed only one statement.[6]

O'Donnell's brief also ignored my attack on *Moore* and *Bowen*, the two cases Judge Carey had cited, relied upon, and accepted as the standard my clients had to meet before they could secure relief. Although O'Donnell did not refer to either, he did cite *Morgan*, but in an odd way: "The petitioners cannot prevail upon their motion because they were not denied a Constitutional right. *United States v. Morgan*, 222 F.2d 673 (2nd Cir. 1955)."[7] O'Donnell failed to mention Judge Jerome Frank's condemnation in *Morgan* of a test "that [a] defendant can be relieved of an unconstitutional conviction only if he makes a showing of innocence . . . [Such a test] would compound the unconstitutionality of his conviction. . . ."[8]

What I had not expected was O'Donnell's extra effort to support Judge Richards' conclusion that Rodenhiser's trial testimony was "not sufficient to justify this Court to grant the relief prayed for in this motion."[9] For the first time for the state, O'Donnell claimed Rodenhiser's testimony did not "so permeate the trial as to constitute an injustice."[10] In support, he turned to the record: "The prosecution put twenty-one (21) witnesses on the stand. The defense called thirty-eight (38) witnesses (including character witnesses). The trial took seven (7) days. Over a thousand pages of testimony was [sic] taken. Ten (10) police officers were called by the State (included in the twenty-one (21) mentioned above)."[11]

O'Donnell must have thought his recital of the number of witnesses, the number of trial days, and the number of pages of the transcript would be persuasive. I did not disagree with his numbers. But O'Donnell's facts told the Delaware Supreme Court justices nothing about the importance and effect of the police perjury. Until O'Donnell set forth undisputed numbers, I had not thought to count the pages myself and use the count to demonstrate the materiality of the police perjury, as obvious an exercise as it then seemed. Now, sparked by O'Donnell's counting—his unexpected help—I counted the pages of the trial transcript referring to the statements and the police denial of the existence of any statements other than those in evidence, despite the testimony of the defendants. My count included every page where the prosecutors, defense lawyers, witnesses, including the defendants, and the judges talked about the statements. The exercise established the materiality of the police perjury and proved that it had permeated the trial. I concluded no objective person could read the trial transcript and find Curran, Jones, and Maguire guilty, taking into account the extent of the police perjury and its effect on their credibility. I was convinced the Supreme Court would regard my recital of the facts and references to the statements in the record as the basis for reversing the Superior Court's failure to grant relief. As I wrote in my reply brief:

The State tests the extent to which Lieutenant Rodenhiser's lying permeated the trial by noting the number of witnesses called, the total pages of the record and the length of the trial. Petitioners do not agree that there is such a thing as a slight violation of constitutional rights which is the logical conclusion of the State's argument. Petitioners are willing, nonetheless, to meet the State factually on the record on its argument. Of the 1085 pages of the trial record, 175 pages concerned the statements. Tr. vol. 1, 173, 245–252, 254, 276–368, 450–461; and Tr. vol. 2, 783–784, 810–814, 818–821, 824–827, 830–832, 853–855, 889–896, 898–904, 930–932, 934–942, 945–948, 969–970, 1007–1012, 1063–1064. What is of greater significance is that of the 1085 pages of the trial record, 920 pages represent testimony or remarks by counsel or court with the jury present before the case was closed. Of these 920 pages, 124 concerned the statements.[12]

By the time I filed my reply brief on December 23, 1955, I was confident I had established my clients' entitlement to relief. The police perjury was now beyond dispute, and the trial transcript proved the materiality of that perjury. The case law as exemplified by *United States v. Morgan* provided the legal test for the relief my clients had to meet and which I sought for them. Had I counted the pages for the Superior Court, I doubt my effort would have made any difference. From the separate Supreme Court, however, I expected it would grant the relief to which my clients were entitled.

The Delaware Supreme Court heard argument on Monday, March 12, 1956, on my second appeal in *The Rape Case*.[13] This appeal was the fourth time I had argued before the court in my three years in private practice.[14] The entire complement of the Supreme Court, Chief Justice Southerland and Justices Wolcott and Howard W. Bramhall, participated.[15] Because no member of the bench asked a question to which I did not have an answer, I thought I had removed all factual and legal obstacles to relief.

Ten days after the argument, the Delaware State Bar Association held a formal dinner at the Gold Ballroom in the Hotel Du-Pont. Doris and I attended, and I was in particularly good spirits. My law practice was going well. I was secretary of the association. In *The Rape Case*, I thought I had matched my convincing reply brief with an equally convincing oral argument. Doris was pregnant with our second child, our son Jonathan, and we were planning a summer vacation in Florida. The trip would be our first time away since our honeymoon more than three years before.

Among the attending members of the Bar, I stood out by my attire: only Chief Justice Southerland and I wore tuxedos with wide lapels. He surely had purchased his tuxedo when wide lapels were in vogue. Mine, on the other hand, was a hand-me-down from my brother-in-law, Harry Levy, my sister Sylvia's husband. I promised myself I would buy a new one, tailored to fit me, just as soon as I could afford it; my pocketbook, however, did not catch up with my desire for many years.

Before dinner, in the duBarry Room above the Gold Ballroom, the drinks from the open bar flowed freely for the usual excessive time, enabling many members to test their imbibing capacity. The association's get-togethers in those days were a far cry from the Annual Bench and Bar Conferences Chief Justice Daniel L. Herrmann inaugurated many years later, larded as they were with study sessions and lectures for preceptors. Chief Justice Herrmann made attendance mandatory and it was actually recorded until the Bar members' numbers exceeded the fire-code capacity of the available sites, forcing the association to secure larger accommodations and the bench to abandon compulsory attendance.

I picked up a nonalcoholic drink for Doris and a scotch for myself and was on my way back to Doris. Standing in my path were Justice Bramhall and J. Caleb Boggs, then Governor of Delaware and a member of the Bar, and a third person whose identity I no longer recall. As I tried to pass them, Bramhall stopped me. "You know Governor Boggs, of course," he said. "Of course," Boggs replied before I could say anything. But Justice Bramhall did not use my name nor did the Governor. At the time I did not think Boggs knew me. He had no reason to. He was one of the most popular politicians in Delaware history, securing election as governor twice, its sole representative in the United States House of Representatives three times, and twice as senator. On election day in 1950, I was introduced to him on three separate occasions; each time he greeted me enthusiastically, expressing delight in making my acquaintance.

It was obvious Justice Bramhall wanted to say something to the others but he wanted me to hear it as well. Without identifying *The Rape Case,* he said, in substantially these words, "Irving here has just made an argument before the Supreme Court and

I wouldn't want him to make any untoward inference from what I am about to say that it predicts the result the court will reach. The fact is Irving made the finest argument I have ever heard since I've been a judge." His words were high praise, indeed. My response was immediate and in substantially these words: "Well, Mr. Justice Bramhall, I don't want you to draw any untoward inference from what I'm about to say, but a remark of the kind you have just made generally precedes an adverse result." I smiled, Bramhall and the others laughed, and I returned to Doris.

20

Unfairness Affirmed
(The Fourth Defeat)

In the end, perhaps Justice Bramhall, whose opinion I was
prepared to believe, and I were both right. Putting aside the
merit of his observation, the Supreme Court's prompt decision left no doubt about the accuracy of my comment. The court
was unanimous in denying relief and artful in the way it did so
in the opinion filed April 16, 1956, five weeks to the day after the
March 12 argument.[1] From the outset of Chief Justice Southerland's opinion for himself and his colleagues, Justices Wolcott
and Bramhall, it was clear that the Supreme Court could not,
and did not, take issue with the factual finding in Judge Carey's
concurrence, with which Judge Terry agreed: police officers had
not told the truth at *The Rape Case* trial, particularly Detective
Rodenhiser who testified each of the defendants had signed only
one statement. Even President Judge Richards had conceded,
"There seems to be no doubt that two statements were signed by
the defendants Jones and Maguire. . . ."[2] On the evidence at the
hearing, Judges Carey and Terry had found Rodenhiser guilty of
"conduct of a censorable [*sic*] character."[3] To take issue with
Carey and Terry, the members of the Supreme Court would have
had to find the facts about the perjury for themselves without

having heard the evidence. Thus, after reviewing the facts in the record, the Supreme Court unequivocally adopted Carey's condemnation of Rodenhiser's trial testimony and found Rodenhiser had "failed" in "his sworn duty to answer the questions put to him truthfully and fully." In accepting Carey and Terry's finding, Southerland and his colleagues were content to condemn Rodenhiser severely, calling "his conduct on the stand highly reprehensible."[4] The condemnation rang hollow since it did nothing for my clients.

In passing upon the state's response to the Rule 35 Motion, the Chief Justice rejected "the two pieces of paper" defense, writing: "This is mere equivocation. Counsel was entitled to the facts, and entitled to make such use of the facts as he saw fit."[5]

The Supreme Court ignored the reason Carey and Terry gave for concluding Rodenhiser's false testimony did not warrant relief, namely, to secure relief, my clients would have to meet the burden of "showing that a retrial could reasonably be expected to result in a different verdict and judgment. [Citations omitted.] Under all the evidence in this case, no such likelihood appears."[6] As was true in a habeas corpus proceeding, Rule 35 did not contain any requirement for the granting of relief as the Superior Court had imposed. Moreover, beyond proving the police perjury as they had already done, what additional showing did my clients have to make to secure relief? Sensing that Carey and Terry's false premise of law would not withstand close examination, Chief Justice Southerland was unwilling to adopt the Superior Court's reasoning and its cases. He had to find another way. And he did.

Southerland avoided both the effect of Carey and Terry's unequivocal finding of false police testimony, with which he and his colleagues agreed, as well as the suspect legal principle Carey and Terry had relied upon in denying relief. *Without acknowledging what he was doing, Southerland convened himself, Wolcott, and*

Bramhall as belated jurors at the trial of Curran, Jones, and Maguire.[7] As Southerland reported in his opinion: "Each member of this Court has read the entire record of the trial for rape. The Court has also been furnished with a transcript of the addresses to the jury of all three counsels for the defendants, and of the closing address for the State."[8] Thus, without so asserting, Southerland, Wolcott, and Bramhall, having read the trial transcript and the summations, convened themselves as "judicial jurors" and considered themselves to be in the same posture as the trial jurors. *But the master fact was that the judicial jurors knew more than the 1948 trial jurors had known.* The judicial jurors knew that Rodenhiser and other police officers had lied at trial; the trial jurors did not. The judicial jurors had the post-trial McCool's Report with its statements from participants setting forth a contemporaneous account of the police wrongdoing; the trial jurors did not. The judicial jurors had the depositions I took confirming the police wrongdoing; the trial jurors did not. The judicial jurors had the testimony of the December 1954 hearing making an official court record of the police perjury before Richards, Carey, and Terry; the trial jurors did not. The judicial jurors had the condemnation by Carey and Terry of the police perjury; the trial jurors did not.

When Southerland convened himself, Wolcott, and Bramhall, as jurors, they had all of the additional facts unknown to the trial jurors. Nonetheless, the judicial jurors denied relief. *In doing so they missed the critical point that the proof of the police perjury meant that the defendants were telling the truth when they each claimed to have signed two statements.* The defendants' credibility was the critical factor at trial. Had the prosecution admitted that the police perjured themselves, the truth would have restored the defendants' credibility. Had the trial jurors known that Curran, Jones, and Maguire—and not the police—had testified truthfully, thus restoring the defendants' credibility, no one can assert with certitude years after the 1948 trial what the result of that trial would have been. So far as the judicial jurors were concerned, their "verdict" was that Curran, Jones, and Maguire were guilty and, therefore, not entitled to relief. In support of their "verdict," Chief Justice Southerland mounted what he must have considered a withering attack on the substantive evidence I had adduced.

What did Southerland do? In summarizing the state's evidence at trial, Southerland seized upon testimony concerning the call to the police whose content had not been known by the trial jurors, but which the judicial jurors accepted as true:

Two witnesses living in nearby houses heard screams. A woman in another nearby house called out to them: "You had better leave that girl alone or I will call the cops." At about a quarter of two a telephone call from an unknown woman was received at police headquarters. She said: "Please send the police quick, there is a girl screaming down in the Park on Ferris Street, and I think she is being raped."[9]

Although the opinion noted that the last "statement was not before the jury," the court quickly went out of its way in a footnote to add "but it appears to us to be admissible as a part of a spontaneous exclamation."[10]

The court's purposeful focus upon the "screams" dovetailed with the opinion's treatment of the fact that each of the defendants' statements in evidence "said in varying forms, that the girl was 'moaning' and added, while one or more of the men was attempting intercourse."[11] A full page later the opinion noted that each defendant denied using the word "moaning" and added "but this is of little significance."[12] The court's view was: "As to this point, the important issue was not whether the girl was 'moaning' but whether she was screaming."[13] Immediately following this observation there was a reference to the three eyewitnesses, Fahey, Masten, and Schueler: "The defendants called three witnesses who said they were in the car with the defendants, followed them to the park, and heard no outcry."[14] I infer from what Southerland wrote that he and the other judicial jurors, like Duffy at trial, did not believe the three eyewitnesses Young had to threaten with indictment before they agreed to appear and testify and tell what they knew.

For their part, the defendants' lawyers had tried to lessen the impact of the girl's testimony about screaming. Fahey, Masten, and Schueler, as well as each defendant, swore to the lack of screaming; they each testified she consented. When the state called Frank Johnson, the police officer who, on his way to his home after garaging his car, walked past Maguire's car parked on Fourth near the railroad overpass, stopped, and noted the license number, it was Young in cross-examination who brought out that Johnson had heard no screams from the park.[15] Young cross-examined the girl after she claimed she had "struggled all the time" and resisted each and all of these three boys "whenever I had a chance." He established that she did not scratch or bite or pull the hair or kick any of the defendants.[16] Yet Southerland made no reference to that testimony by Johnson or by the young woman.

The master fact is that whether or not the girl was screaming goes to the question of whether or not the defendants were guilty of raping the young woman. But guilt or innocence is *not* the issue on a Rule 35 Motion or on a habeas corpus petition. Despite this fundamental principle, Southerland wrote: "The issue before the jury was whether the girl had consented to have intercourse with these men."[17] It is this issue Southerland and the other judicial jurors addressed and, as had the trial jurors, found the defendants guilty.

The judicial jurors' finding of guilt not only colored their consideration, but determined the resolution of the real issue before them, as Southerland himself wrote: "The question before us is whether this misconduct robbed the defendants of their fundamental right to a fair trial."[18]

The judicial jurors did not think so, finding there is not "sufficient evidence that the retyped statements differed from the original in any material matter."[19] To accept the judicial jurors' conclusion one must disregard the testimony of the three defendants and adopt as true Detective Rodenhiser's claim that the two sets of statements were identical, the same person whose conduct on the stand the judicial jurors described as "highly reprehensible."

Writing for the judicial jurors, Southerland asserted: "Moreover, there is nothing incriminating in the statements."[20] The opinion noted that Jones' statement in evidence did not include a reference to the woman who had "screamed so loud that a neighbor raised the window and threatened to call the police."[21] But attributing the statement to Jones meant accepting Officer McDermott's trial testimony to that effect when McDermott spoke to him at the time of his arrest and ignoring Jones' contrary trial testimony.[22]

Determining the truthfulness of the testimony assuredly was for the trial jurors to resolve with all the facts before them, including all the facts going to the credibility of the defendants and the police and the other witnesses including the young woman. The judicial jurors, however, took upon themselves the determination of whose testimony was credible, concluding: "And the State's evidence, together with the inherent improbability of the defendants' testimony, amply justified the verdict."[23] It was a disingenuous assertion. Were one to start with the knowledge, now a proven fact, that the police were lying and the defendants were telling the truth, *the inherent improbability* would then become *the inherent probability.* So far as the judicial jurors were concerned, the police perjury which destroyed the defendants' credibility was not significant. Southerland wrote:

Counsel argue [*sic*] that the issue made at the trial was a question of the girl's veracity against the defendants' veracity. In resolving this conflict, they say, the jury could well have believed that Rodenheiser's denial of the second statement[s] so discredited the defendants' testimony as to turn the scales against them and result in conviction. *This is too narrow a view of the matter.* The case depended not merely on the girl's testimony that she did not consent; its strength derived from the attendant circumstances above referred to. *Counsel's argument on this point is an attempt—natural enough—to magnify unduly an incident that could have wrought no serious harm to the defendants.* [Emphasis added.][24]

The argument fails because it assumes the police perjury had no effect on the jury despite the fact it made Curran, Jones, and Maguire appear to be liars. The police witnesses did not have to tell the jurors when it was so plain by inference from their testimony: if Curran, Jones, and Maguire are lying about the number of statements they signed, as we, the police, by implication say they are when we testify and tell you they each only signed one statement and those are the ones in evidence, why believe them and their eyewitnesses when they deny under oath the alleged rape?

The Supreme Court justices, however, had no way of proving their conclusion that the false police testimony had no effect on the jury's judgment of my clients' credibility. Neither the Superior Court judges nor the Supreme Court justices knew the role credibility played in the jury's finding of guilt. Only by constituting themselves as jurors could the Supreme Court justices get away with what Southerland wrote. In holding as they did, the justices never acknowledged the legal legerdemain in which they had engaged.

The now-admitted fact of the police perjury denying the existence of the second statements was of little moment to the judicial jurors. Twice in a single paragraph they found as a fact, "the issue concerning the two statements played no material part at the trial." The first time Southerland preceded his comment with "We are convinced." The second time he preceded the same comment saying, "We are satisfied. . . ."[25] But the repetition did not make the words true; it only emphasized their inaccuracy.

In support of the conclusion "that the issue concerning the two statements played no material part at the trial," Southerland emphasized that the lawyers had not argued the point to the jury.[26] Southerland, a former Delaware attorney general (1925–1929), headed Delaware's oldest and perhaps most prestigious law firm before he accepted appointment to the Supreme Court in 1951. He was too able a lawyer not to recognize the point he made to support his claim—that police perjury was not material because the defendants' lawyers did not argue in their summations there were two sets of statements—would not stand analysis. Lacking proof of the police perjury at the time of the trial, for the defense lawyers to have argued that the jury should believe the defendants rather than the police about the existence of a prior set of statements would not have helped Curran, Jones, and Maguire or their lawyers. Since the trial jurors had no reason to disbelieve the police such an argument would have emphasized precisely what the police wanted to accomplish: the jurors should not believe the defendants. Hy Young, who led the defense effort, would never have done what Southerland implied he should have done in his summation at trial. I can only conclude the Supreme Court's goal, eight years after the trial, was to justify its denial of relief, despite the now-admitted fact of police perjury.

Moreover, in his belated, implied, gratuitous advice to Young and his colleagues that they should have argued the two statements issue to the jury, the Chief Justice ignored the fact that the defense lawyers did not have available to them the information contained in McCool's Report when they prepared their cross-examinations and summations for one simple reason: there was no such report at the time of the February 1948 trial. *Even when McCool's Report came into existence within weeks after the trial ended, no one provided a copy to the trial judges, or to Curran, Jones, and Maguire, or to their lawyers.* All the defending lawyers knew about two statements was what Jones had told Young, to which Jones testified early in the trial when the state successfully sought to introduce his second statement into evidence. Young, Reinhardt, and Hagner learned that Curran and Maguire had also each signed twice only when those defendants so testified at the tag end of the trial. Although Young had tried to establish the police perjury when he cross-examined Detective Rodenhiser, Rodenhiser thwarted him as is clear from the trial transcript and confirmed by the courts.[27]

The Chief Justice knew that each defendant took the stand and, under oath, claimed the woman consented and denied raping her. If the trial jurors believed the sworn testimony of the defendants, they could not have found them guilty. Therefore, the police perjury about the number of statements had to have adversely affected the accuseds' credibility before the trial jurors. But the defendants' testimony under oath at trial meant nothing to the Supreme Court justices who, acting as jurors, were "convinced" and "satisfied that the issue of the two statements played no material part in the case."[28]

If, as Chief Justice Southerland suggested, there was nothing incriminating in the statements, which at the least placed the defendants in Woodlawn Park with the young woman, why did the police and the state's lawyers spend so much time at the trial to introduce them? Why did the police lie about the number of statements, a lie the judicial jurors knew took place? Why did the state put back on the stand as final rebuttal witnesses the two policemen, Rodenhiser and Emering, who swore that the three statements in evidence were the only statements the three defendants signed? The 1948 trial jurors did not know that the officers' testimony was false but the 1956 judicial jurors knew. Why did the police fail to tell the trial jurors that the three statements in evidence were not the statements read to the defendants at the 7:00 a.m. line-up on October 30 and, indeed, did not exist at the time of the line up? The trial jurors were unaware of those facts but the judicial jurors knew them. Whether the statements were incriminating was for the trial jurors to determine. Had they known when and where the statements were signed and, most significantly, that these statements were not the only statements the defendants signed, as the police claimed, but were in fact the second statements the defendants signed without reading, as they claimed, the trial jurors' decision might have been different.

Given the numerous portions of the transcript addressing the statements, the state's calling of police witnesses in rebuttal who continued to deny the testimony of the accused, and the applicable case law, it is difficult to accept the Supreme Court's conclusion that "the two statements [issue] played no material part at the trial." *In writing as he did, Southerland treated the police perjury as if the police officers and the prosecution had admitted the existence of the second set of statements at trial.* But they had not. Only long after the 1948 trial was it established there had actually been two sets of statements.

Charles Lane, author of the TRB column in *The New Republic,* in the February 9, 1999 issue, wrote about the then ongoing effort to oust President William J. Clinton from office. In turning to Speaker of the House Henry Hyde's basing the case for impeachment upon the oath one takes as a witness, Lane emphasized the importance of cross-examination in ferreting out perjury and its effect upon jurors once they perceive one side is lying:

Yes, Hyde is correct in noting that the swearing in of witnesses and the attendant sanction of perjury play a deterrent role against false testimony. But, if oaths are the rule of law's last line of defense, as Hyde says, then our legal system is already in deep trouble. It is precisely because oaths are so often violated that criminal and civil procedure include other safeguards—among them, cross examination, which is how most attorneys smoke out false testimony, and the jury system itself. If a witness for either side in a case provides testimony that strikes the jury as false, that side will lose. This is the ultimate sanction against lying under oath, and by and large it works.[29]

But if the safeguard of cross-examination fails, as it did at *The Rape Case* trial, the jurors are left, as the jurors were at *The Rape Case* trial, with the impression the other side—Curran, Jones, and Maguire's side—was lying. Therefore, the trial jurors declared the defendants the losers. Lane's conclusion was "by and large [the ultimate sanction, i.e., losing,] works."[30] But the "by and large" exception within which Curran, Jones, and Maguire fell consigned them to life terms in the New Castle County Workhouse.

Turning to my reliance on *Equitable Trust Co. v. Gallagher*, Southerland disposed of my position summarily, writing:

Counsel argues that the destruction of the original typed copies is a badge of fraud, and raises a presumption that the statements were different. *Equitable Trust Co. v. Gallagher*, 32 Del.Ch. 401, 102 A.2d 538, is cited. That was a case of the destruction of all existing copies of a contract, and is not in point here. If manufactured evidence had been the purpose of the second statements, why did they not include something incriminating?[31]

After the trial Rodenhiser claimed four times that the two sets of statements were identical: in his interview with Superintendent Kavanaugh; in his statement to Inspector McCool; in his testimony in response to my questions at his deposition; and in his testimony at the hearing in December 1954.[32] But Rodenhiser's claim does not negate the applicability of *Equitable Trust Co.*

v. Gallagher to *The Rape Case.* The distinction the Chief Justice sought to make, that *Gallagher* involved "the destruction of all existing copies," fails to distinguish *Gallagher* from *The Rape Case. The fact is the police finally admitted they had destroyed all of the original statements.*

Despite their condemnation of Rodenhiser's conduct, the Chief Justice and his colleagues chose not to accept the possibility, let alone the probability, that Rodenhiser eliminated material facts helpful to Curran, Jones, and Maguire from the second set of statements. Surely it was not beyond possibility that the police excised any reference to the three eyewitnesses from Jones' and Maguire's second statements, thus casting doubt upon Curran's claim in his statement that the six men were together that night. Certainly if those two statements had contained references to the three other men in the car, the state would not have been able to question the presence of the three eyewitnesses at the scene and their testimony as Duffy did in his reply summation to the jury.[33]

Southerland also took up an argument Hamilton had raised in the first oral argument before Judge Layton. Apart from arguing the Superior Court should dismiss the habeas corpus petition because the defendants had not first exhausted their remedy under Rule 35, Hamilton urged Judge Layton to dismiss the petition because the petitioners had not alleged the prosecuting attorneys knew the police were committing perjury. The perjury of a witness, including that of a policeman, Hamilton argued, is insufficient as a legal ground to support relief unless the prosecuting attorneys know of the perjury. The Supreme Court endorsed Hamilton's position despite claiming to the contrary:

It is not necessary in this case to decide whether this is a sound general rule for our courts in reviewing a conviction under Rule 35. It is conceivable that a case might be so shot through with perjury, though unknown to the prosecuting officer, as to lead to the conclusion that the prisoner had never had the semblance of a fair trial. But no such case is made here. Due process does not and cannot guarantee to a defendant complete immunity from false testimony; and hence false testimony of a witness is not in itself ground for the conclusion that fundamental constitutional rights have been violated. To warrant relief under Rule 35, much more must be shown than appears in this case.[34]

The Delaware justices committed error when they decided that Curran, Jones, and Maguire were guilty of the charge of rape, an issue not before them; the Rule 35 Motion was not to determine their guilt or innocence. The issue was whether the state was holding them illegally by its failure to accord them their constitutional right to a fair trial, a trial free of police perjury. Once the state deprived them of that right by introducing testimony now proven false, no sophistry or legal casuistry could circumvent the constitutional protection of due process of law.

Unlike the Superior Court judges, the Supreme Court justices had before them the case law and the analysis of the record. So far as I was concerned, the members of the Delaware Supreme Court departed from their oaths as lawyers as well as their oaths of office as judges.[35] They understood precisely what they were doing. At *The Rape Case* trial, the state had recalled Detective Rodenhiser to the stand in rebuttal as the last witness the jury would hear before the charge and before the jurors started deliberations. The prosecution recalled him knowing he would testify again that there was only one set of statements. The state's purpose was to have Rodenhiser repeat his earlier testimony. Given the now judicially determined fact that Rodenhiser lied at trial, it was a callous disregard of due process for the Supreme Court to conclude Curran, Jones, and Maguire had "failed to show any violation of their constitutional rights at their trial."[36]

Because they made no reference to either *Bowen* or *Moore,* the

Supreme Court avoided having to address directly the false standard of those cases *Morgan* so thoroughly repudiated. But in holding as they did, Chief Justice Southerland and his colleagues expressed a low standard for the meaning of due process.[37] The fact the false testimony was that of a high ranking police officer adversely and deliberately affecting the credibility of the accused was not enough for them.

In denying relief, no judge of either the Superior Court or the Supreme Court ever asked why Rodenhiser and the other officers lied about the number of statements Curran, Jones, and Maguire had signed. If the lie about the number of statements was, indeed, innocuous and "could have wrought no serious harm to the defendants," as Southerland for himself and his colleagues concluded, the only explanation for Rodenhiser and the others to lie was to hide the truth and make it appear the defendants were liars.[38]

By the time the Delaware Supreme Court ruled, not a single state judge who had participated in the rulings followed the course fairness and constitutional due process required. To have done so would have meant finding my clients were entitled to relief and a new, fair trial. The six Delaware judges who ruled on the Rule 35 Motion's merits were no better in their way than the police officers were once they decided Curran, Jones, and Maguire were guilty.

I now had to explain to my clients that the Delaware judges had failed them for the fifth time. If I had had any doubt about the error of the courts, I would have dreaded being the bearer of bad news. But all I was doing was reporting the latest instance of judicial failure to recognize how perjury had violated their constitutional rights.

Even though I went promptly to the Workhouse every time there was something to report, I frequently found my clients already knew the news. How they so rapidly acquired the information I never discovered. Each time they reacted stoically to the defeat and retained confidence in their optimistic lawyer.

Before me loomed the problem of demonstrating to the satisfaction of an impartial judge or judges that the perjurious police testimony at *The Rape Case* trail resulted in unconstitutional convictions and warranted relief. My next step was to apply to the United States Supreme Court by a petition for certiorari. I had to persevere.

Chief Judge Paul Leahy
Courtesy of the Delaware Public Archives

Irving Morris with his wife, **Doris** and their daughter, **Deborah Lynne** in December, 1954
Courtesy of The Sunday Star

Irving Morris during the time of The Rape Case trial

Mugshots of the defendants: **Francis J. Curran, Ira E. Jones,** and **Francis J. Maguire**
Courtesy of The Wilmington Police Department and Mayor James M. Baker

Mrs. Edward Maguire, Mrs. Francis M. Curran, and **Mrs. Jayne Stigliano**
Courtesy of The Sunday Bulletin, Philadelphia, October 1954

Francis J. Curran and **Ira F. Jones**
Courtesy of The Sunday Bulletin, Philadelphia
October 1954

Warren E. Schueler, Sr.
Courtesy of Warren E. Schueler, Sr.

Officer James A. Nagle Jr.
Courtesy of The Wilmington
Police Department and
Mayor James M. Baker

Superintendent Andrew J. Kavanaugh
Courtesy of The Wilmington Police Department and Mayor James M. Baker

Detective John A. Rodenhiser
Courtesy of The Wilmington Police Department and Mayor James M. Baker

Sergeant John Emering
Courtesy of The Wilmington Police Department and Mayor James M. Baker

Officer Edward Mazewski
Courtesy of The Wilmington Police Department and Mayor James M. Baker

H. Albert Young, taken in the late 1940s
Courtesy of the Estate of H. Albert Young

Leonard G. Hagner
Courtesy of The News-Journal

David Reinhardt
Courtesy of the Reinhardt Family

Albert James, Attorney General at the time of trial
Courtesy of the Morris James law firm archives

C. Edward Duffy
Courtesy of the Delware Public Archives

Herbert L. Maris
Courtesy of The Courier Post
Camden NJ, September 5, 1959

Steve Hamilton
Courtesy of Richards, Layton & Finger

Chief Justice Charles S. Richards (top)
Courtesy of Morris, Nichols, Arsht & Tunnell LLP,
Justices Charles L. Terry, Jr. (middle) and **James B. Carey** (bottom)
Courtesy of Young Studios

Chancellor Collins J. Seitz
Courtesy of the Delaware Lawyer

Chief Judge John Biggs, Jr.
Courtesy of the Delaware Public Archives

Clerk Edward G. Pollard
Courtesy of the Delaware Public Archives

**Justice Daniel F. Wolcott, Chief Justice Clarence A. Southerland, and
Justice James M. Tunnell Jr., 1954**
Courtesy of Young Studios

**Justice Daniel F. Wolcott, Chief Justice Clarence A. Southerland, and
Justice Howard W. Bramhall, 1956**
Courtesy of Young Studios

Chief Judge Caleb M. Wright
Courtesy of the Delaware Lawyer

21

The Double Standard

I tried hard to understand why the Delaware judges failed to recognize my clients' entitlement and grant the relief I sought for them. As time passed, it became clear the Supreme Court had a double standard in its approach to *The Rape Case*. The proof came when the Supreme Court decided *In re Bennethum* four years after *The Rape Case*. There a member of the Bar not only failed to file federal income tax returns but aggravated his misconduct by giving false testimony and fabricating evidence.[1] The court unanimously held that disbarment was required. The Supreme Court did not countenance the continued presence at the Bar of a member who would lie, as Chief Justice Southerland wrote:

Here the Committee's findings of fact, which we uphold, are that [Bennethum's] testimony that he filed his federal return was false, and that the written evidence submitted for the years 1953 and 1954 was fabricated. Such conduct has been repeatedly held to constitute evidence of moral unfitness to practice the profession, and to require disbarment, even though the offense was not committed in the practice of law. If the facts are clear, no prior conviction of false swearing is a prerequisite to disciplinary action.[2]

Yet the same three justices, Southerland, Wolcott, and Bramhall, who decided *Bennethum*, ruled against granting relief to

Curran, Jones, and Maguire despite the proven police perjury. The different results implied a distinction between, on the one hand, a false statement "even though . . . not committed in the practice of law," and, on the other hand, false statements by police officers under oath at trial in a case charging the accused with a crime carrying upon conviction the possibility of a death sentence. It was maddening that both a majority of the Superior Court and a unanimous Supreme Court recognized the false police testimony at *The Rape Case* trial but concluded they had to sustain the convictions of Curran, Jones, and Maguire.[3]

In *Bennethum* the Supreme Court's immediate condemnation of the lies and its prompt action to address the wrongdoing by one of their own stands to this day in sharp contrast to the willingness of the same judges to tolerate the police perjury in *The Rape Case*—clearly, a double standard. Worse yet, the Superior Court judges masked their toleration of the police perjury in *The Rape Case* by eschewing the use of the word "perjury" to describe Rodenhiser's lies. Judge Carey wrote:

Regardless of the category into which this testimony should be placed, nevertheless the witness was certainly guilty of conduct of a censorable [*sic*] character, regardless of its actual effect upon the outcome of the trial. If we pass this sort of thing in silence, we may be thought to give our sanction to such conduct.[4]

In order for "perjury" to occur, there must be deliberate false testimony under oath in a judicial proceeding and, moreover, the false testimony must be material to the proceedings. "Material" as applied to *The Rape Case* means the perjury, with its effect on the jury, had to have affected the outcome.

Sir William Blackstone, the English jurist, defines perjury as an offense against public justice and adopts the definition of Sir Edward Coke that "perjury is a crime committed when a lawful oath is administered, in some *judicial* proceeding, to a person who swears *willfully, absolutely* and *falsely,* in a matter material to the issue or point in question."[5]

When they decided not to declare the police officers' testimony as perjury, the Superior Court judges circumvented the need to treat Curran, Jones, and Maguire with fairness and justice. In their majority opinion, both Carey and Terry believed it was unnecessary to do anything more than criticize Detective Rodenhiser.[6] Taking a different tack, Chief Justice Southerland avoided the problem of finding the police guilty of perjury by substituting a euphemism, "false testimony." In his view the police lies did not constitute "perjury" since as "false testimony," they were not "material." His reasoning was circular but effective and accomplished the Supreme Court's goal.[7]

22

The Naysayer

One day in 1956, well after I had assumed sole responsibility for *The Rape Case*, I was in the prothonotary's office completing a title search on a property a client of Cohen and Morris had contracted to purchase. In our two-person firm, I had to scramble to accomplish my work. Thus the fact I was in the prothonotary's office doing a title search was not remarkable. In addition to the regular workload of the office and my work on *The Rape Case*, I also volunteered to help in the activities of Congregation Beth Shalom, the fund-raising efforts of the Young Adult Division of the Jewish Federation of Delaware, and the work of the Anti-Defamation League of B'nai B'rith in Delaware. The most time-consuming aspect of my pro bono work was serving as secretary of the Delaware State Bar Association from 1953 to 1957, a time when the association conducted its affairs without a professional staff. My effort on behalf of Curran, Jones, and Maguire fell well within the pro bono category, since neither the men nor their families could afford a lawyer.

As I pored over the columns of names and references to record entries, a lawyer younger than I sidled up to me and started to talk about *The Rape Case*. It was not a thoughtful exchange. Rather, he shared with me his personal judgment: I did not stand

269

a chance of securing the release of my clients on the basis of police perjury at their trial. "You won't get anywhere with that theory," was his unequivocal and final comment before he walked away. I doubt he paused to consider the effect of his words upon my morale. I was too stunned to respond. The young lawyer, a protégé of Hy Young, obviously did not think Irving Morris could possibly accomplish what the famed H. Albert Young had failed to do.

Through the years, I crossed paths with many others who thought I was chasing a will-o'-the-wisp. But in all that time the young lawyer was the only person who told me to my face I would not succeed. He had not read the trial transcript nor had he interviewed my clients and others. He had not researched the law nor acquired knowledge of the facts any more than had the guest lawyer on Joe Pyne's show. If I had been less certain of the state's injustice to my clients or less determined to persevere in my clients' cause, the young lawyer's opinion might have been even more devastating. As it was, his remark spurred me on.

As I contemplated seeking a review by the United States Supreme Court, I did not know if I could ever convince its members to reverse the Delaware Supreme Court's denial of relief. What I did know was I could not walk away from the task of demonstrating how wrong the Delaware courts had been. It took time for me to work up the energy to prepare the petition for certiorari, but finally I turned to the task.

I wanted to sign the petition for my clients as a member of the Bar of the United States Supreme Court in my own right rather than have some other member sign for me. Accordingly, I prepared an application for admission and asked Aaron Finger, a member of the United States Supreme Court Bar and a legendary lawyer at the Delaware Bar, to move my admission.[1] He agreed and signed my application.

Shortly before the date of my appearance, I was keenly disappointed when Mr. Finger told me he would be unable to make the trip to Washington. In his stead, he arranged for a member of Sutherland and Asbill in Washington, D.C., to move my admission. The Sutherland firm was the corresponding firm for Richards, Layton & Finger with its name upon the firm's stationery in those years.

With the necessary fee, my application went forward. When the Supreme Court convened on June 4, 1956, I was present along with many others who had business before the Court that day. Mac Asbill Jr. accompanied me. As we waited for the clerk to call my name, Mac wryly reassured me: "I have not yet lost one of these motions." When the clerk called my name, Mac and I went forward to stand in the well of the Court. Once Mac recited the brief, formal words moving my admission, Chief Justice Earl Warren smiled broadly at me and welcomed me to the Bar of the Court. The sincerity in his voice conveyed the distinct impression that up to that moment the Court had barely managed; now his hearty welcome assured everyone, and particularly me, that a new day had arrived because Irving Morris had become a member of its Bar.

I could now personally sign the petition for my clients.

23

Chancery Joins the Rest
(The Fifth Defeat)

fter the 1948 trial, Detective John Rodenhiser rose to the
rank of lieutenant and thereafter was demoted to sergeant. About the time the Delaware Supreme Court had
the *Rape Case* before it, several articles about John Rodenhiser
appeared in the local papers.[1] The Wilmington Department of
Public Safety, through the Police Department Board, had initiated disciplinary proceedings to oust Rodenhiser from the police
force for various alleged acts of misconduct. I played no part in
bringing the charges, initially or subsequently, placed against
him. None of the original accusations were related to his perjury
at *The Rape Case* trial.

According to the articles, Rodenhiser had submitted to an examination by Dr. M. A. Tarumianz, known as "Dr. T," the State
Superintendent of Mental Health Services.[2] Rodenhiser's lawyer
thought he could secure a medical discharge if he could show
the detective had a mental problem. A medical discharge would
guarantee Rodenhiser's pension rights and, of course, terminate
the department's inquiry since he would no longer be a policeman. Dr. T's report was not public. I thought if the report were
thorough, it could not help but describe Rodenhiser as a person

who had some significant mental problems. When I deposed him, he was abusive, arrogant, and without remorse for his misdeeds. The department's charges confirmed what I thought. Detective Rodenhiser was a martinet, abusing his power over subordinates while remaining obsequious to those with higher rank. When the department amended its charges to include his perjury in 1948 at *The Rape Case* trial I thought it ironic.

I tried informally to secure a copy of Dr. T's report, but with no success. I could not ask the Superior Court since it no longer had any jurisdiction after the case went on appeal to the Supreme Court of Delaware. Moreover, my petition for certiorari meant the case was now within the United States Supreme Court's jurisdiction. Accordingly, I filed a petition in the Court of Chancery of the State of Delaware in and for New Castle County seeking to compel Attorney General Craven, who had Dr. T's report, to turn a copy over to me.

In preparing the petition, I emphasized the destruction of petitioners' credibility by the false testimony and unlawful conduct of Wilmington police officers. On information and belief, I claimed Dr. T's report contained information which would show Rodenhiser did not testify truthfully at trial. In addition, I asserted Dr. T's report might well indicate the Delaware courts were in error in accepting Rodenhiser's denial of differences between petitioners' initial voluntary statements and the statements introduced in evidence.

Under Craven's direction, Chief Deputy Attorney General O'Donnell moved to dismiss the petition on the ground the Court of Chancery had no jurisdiction over a criminal proceeding and, moreover, the Court of Chancery had no power to act since the merits were before the United States Supreme Court on the pending petition for certiorari. The state's position brought home to me again the deep gulf between a Rule 35 Motion and a habeas corpus proceeding. Since my Rule 35 Motion was brought under the Criminal Rules, it was, indeed, a criminal proceeding. But habeas corpus was a civil proceeding. Curran, Jones, and Maguire were entitled as a matter of right to the use of discovery proceedings under the Civil Rules. As Judge Layton correctly said in 1953 after re-argument early on in my effort to secure relief: "Presumably, an application for *habeas corpus,* being a civil remedy, relators would clearly have the right to the discovery proceedings under our Civil Rules."[3]

During the argument on September 24, 1956, Chancellor Collins J. Seitz was not receptive to my position. My application, as the state correctly claimed, was to assist me in supporting my motion under Criminal Rule 35. In his customary quiet way, Seitz pressed me about jurisdiction, noting that Chancery from its earliest beginnings in England did not interfere with criminal matters. It was clear I was battling uphill against his unwillingness to permit Chancery to become involved in a criminal proceeding.

If my application had come before the Court of Chancery in the context of a habeas corpus proceeding, a civil matter, and not as a Criminal Rule 35 motion, Seitz could not have so easily decided against me. This he did with dispatch on September 26, 1956, within two days of the argument, holding, as he had signaled from his questions at the argument, Chancery does not interfere with criminal proceedings.[4]

Seitz quoted the petition at length in his opinion thus avoiding any claim he did not understand the facts and the theory I was presenting to justify the relief I sought.[5] On the underlying, substantive facts, Seitz accepted as true "that Rodenhiser did not testify fully and truthfully at the original trial, at least in some particulars. Both the Superior Court and the Supreme Court of Delaware concluded, however, that Rodenhiser's false testimony did not deprive petitioners of a fair trial and thus they refused to grant any relief." [Citations omitted.][6]

Concerning my argument that I needed the contents of Dr. T's report about Rodenhiser to place the information before the United States Supreme Court, Seitz said he was "unwilling to assume that either our Superior Court or our Supreme Court would not find a way to make such information available to [Curran, Jones, and Maguire] upon a proper application. Certainly, in any event, the U.S. Supreme Court would find a way."[7]

He suggested that I could ask the United States Supreme Court to remand the case so that my clients would have "an opportunity to bring this matter before the Delaware courts having jurisdiction of criminal matters of this type."[8] But the last thing I wanted to do was delay the progress of the petition for certiorari pending before the Supreme Court, the only way to cut through the delay in freeing my clients. Thus, I did not act upon Seitz's suggestions. Instead, after receiving his opinion, I forwarded my typed reply brief to the United States Supreme Court and waited for it to act on my petition.

My bright idea to repair to the Court of Chancery yielded yet another defeat in the courts of Delaware.

24

The First Denial of *Certiorari* (The Sixth Defeat) Leads to the District Court

The ninety–day deadline for seeking review from the Delaware Supreme Court's April 16, 1956, adverse opinion was rapidly running out before I summoned the energy to act. Now a member of the Bar of the United States Supreme Court, albeit an inexperienced one, on July 5, 1956, I signed and filed the petition for the issuance of a writ of certiorari seeking review of the denial of relief from the constitutional unfairness at trial. Since neither my clients nor their families could afford the printed briefs ordinarily required, I accompanied my petition with a motion to file in forma pauperis (i.e., as a pauper). The Supreme Court granted the petition enabling us to avoid the prohibitive printing costs.

Securing the assent of four members, the required minimum number of the Justices of the United States Supreme Court to review a lower court decision, is much like trying to win a lottery. Many try; few win. But I thought I had a good chance, because the record now showed the egregious lies at trial. I filed my brief on time, emphasizing that six of the seven judges who had had the facts before them clearly found that Detective Rodenhiser's testimony at the trial was "untrue" and/or "evasive" and/or "censorable[sic]" and, indeed, "highly reprehensible" and that he "did not testify fully and truthfully."[1] The state in turn filed its answering brief signed by Attorney General Craven and Deputy Attorney General O'Donnell.

As the weeks passed without a ruling, I began to think the Supreme Court might grant the certiorari petition. But it was not to be. The Supreme Court denied the petition on November 13, 1956, a disappointing but not unexpected result, given the paucity of cases where certiorari is granted.[2] The denial of review had only one redeeming virtue: it removed the last obstacle for me to seek relief under habeas corpus in the United States District Court for the District of Delaware. Unlike the state judges, who I thought displayed an ardent desire to defend and sustain my clients' convictions, the federal judges would not bring a predetermined bias to their consideration of the fairness of the trial.

The judges who sat on Delaware's Superior and Supreme Courts served twelve-year terms by appointment of the governor, subject to confirmation by the state senate. State judges who, by their rulings, fell out of favor with the public or with the politicians risked losing reappointment and reconfirmation. In contrast, the federal judges, Delawareans as federal law required, had lifetime appointments that provided independence and insulated them from the parochial concerns constraining the state judges.

In going forward I retained my optimism based on my conviction that the unfair trial, permeated by the police perjury, could not stand as the last word on my clients' guilt or innocence. Only a new trial free of a constitutional violation could accomplish that. Guided by that standard, I prepared the Petition for Writ of Habeas Corpus and filed it on February 6, 1957.

The Rape Case deserved the designation of "a hot potato." Surely, it would cause the presiding judge to get burned were he to grant relief. The lawyers' gossip at Jack Conrad's coffee shop in the United Cigar Store on the ground floor of the North American Building where lawyers routinely gathered, was that the federal judge, whoever he might be, would find a way to make the petition unceremoniously go away. After all, the Delaware Supreme Court had no apparent difficulty in denying relief. Moreover, the federal judge who found merit in the petition would have to overrule six judges of the Delaware courts, none of whom thought Curran, Jones, and Maguire had made a case for relief. Overruling state court judges was not something federal judges delighted in doing, and certainly not in Delaware. There was no history of feuding among the few men who comprised the state and federal benches, all of whom knew each other. (No woman had ever sat on the Superior Court or Supreme Court of Delaware or the federal District Court in Delaware as of that time.) Moreover, the Supreme Court's denial of certiorari was not helpful. Although the denial did not reach the merits, it did reflect the fact that four justices did not think the petition worthy of review, the standard the Supreme Court followed in passing upon certiorari petitions.[3]

When I filed, I did not pause to consider which judge would hear my case. The District Court then had two active judges: my mentor, Chief Judge Paul Leahy, and Judge Caleb M. Wright. I knew it would not be Leahy because of our friendship and the numerous discussions where I shared my arguments with him over the years, to say nothing of his own participation leading to my involvement in the case. He would, of course, recuse himself. (In one of our discussions after my second defeat in the Delaware Supreme Court, Leahy recognized my frustration and wryly suggested I file a habeas corpus petition before him so he could grant relief. It was an invitation neither of us regarded as serious.)[4]

Consequently, only Wright was available to hear my petition, unless a judge outside of Delaware were designated to preside. But Wright was not one to shirk his judicial duty. He had no reason to avoid sitting. Initially I thought having Wright as my judge did not augur well. He was a product of conservative downstate Delaware, as were Richards, Terry and Carey, who had sat at the 1948 trial and at the hearing in December, 1954. All the Delaware judges had sided with the state. Moreover, Wright, whose service began August 4, 1955, was the junior judge on the District Court bench.

I knew him only slightly. Our only conversation of any length had been at Picciotti's, a restaurant specializing in steaks then located on the northeast corner of Fourth and DuPont in Wilmington. The newly appointed judge and his wife, Katie, were at an adjoining table to where Doris and I sat one weekday night. It was happenstance, since Doris and I seldom ate dinner out during the week. I knew he was also a graduate of the Yale Law School, a fact giving rise to some hope of success before him.

Along with a petition for leave to proceed in forma pauperis, which Wright granted on February 6, 1957, I submitted the habeas corpus petition. It was only seven pages long, including the affidavit of my clients "that the facts set forth in the foregoing petition are true and correct to the best of their knowledge, information and belief." I expressed the essential basis of my clients' claim for relief, stressing how the deliberate false testimony of police witnesses coupled with the police destruction of the first statements ruined the defendants' credibility. In addition, although I asserted my clients' claim of their innocence, I emphasized that in considering the constitutionality of the conviction, the court should not evaluate the guilt or innocence of the accused. I detailed the unconstitutional police actions, particularly Rodenhiser's.

I then turned to the factual findings of the state judges, in essence holding the police conduct "highly reprehensible" as Chief

Justice Southerland had said.[5] My brief argued the judges had substituted their opinion for the verdict of a jury. Further, I argued that the trial court's charge instructed the jury that they were free to consider petitioners' unlawfully impaired credibility and to reject any or all of the remainder of petitioners' testimony. I told Judge Wright that the petitioners' conviction was now founded on the decision of the Delaware judges instead of on a verdict reached after deliberation by an impartial trial jury not prejudiced by police officers' "highly reprehensible" conduct under oath.

On February 20, 1957, Craven and O'Donnell filed an entirely unexpected response. They submitted not only an answer to the petition but also a motion seeking its dismissal without a hearing on the ground the court should not grant relief as a matter of law.

By filing the petition, my clients and I had assumed the burden of proving their entitlement to relief. By the state's motion to dismiss, it assumed the burden of convincing Judge Wright to summarily dismiss the petition "without a hearing," since the state asserted its contention as a matter of law. Shifting the burden was significant. By its motion, the state would have the advantage of filing two briefs, thus giving the state the first and last word, an advantage I thought was more than offset by the fact the state now bore the burden of convincing the court it was right as a matter of law. Almost sixty years later, the only explanation I have for the state's action is that Craven and O'Donnell thought Wright would slavishly follow Southerland's opinion. In their judgment, his opinion had "answered" all the arguments I had raised.

But assuming the burden of proof was not the only help the state provided. In its answer, the state admitted all or part of five of the seven substantive paragraphs of the petition. The state claimed the other two were "argumentative" and "not an allegation of fact" and, therefore, did not require an answer. The state admitted paragraph 2 of the petition where I asserted: "The issue at petitioners' trial was one of credibility, either the jury would believe petitioners and find them innocent, or believe the prosecuting witness and find them guilty." By its response to paragraph 3, the state admitted that Wilmington police officers had unlawfully destroyed the defendants' credibility by their testimony and unlawful conduct at trial. Thus by its own admissions, the state conceded the importance and the materiality of the police perjury, and—of even greater significance—the importance of the issue of credibility at trial.

In responding to paragraph 4, the state continued to help by admitting "[f]or purposes of this answer that: (1) . . . Rodenhiser gave false and evasive testimony at the trial; (2) . . . a draft of a typewritten statement was destroyed; and . . . (3) . . . Rodenhiser did not tell the jury that an earlier draft of the statements admitted in evidence had been destroyed."

Between accepting the burden of proof and admitting the factual predicate for the relief I sought, the state had unexpectedly delivered itself into my hands. My clients were delighted with what the state had done when I explained its meaning. I thought our chances of success before Judge Wright were now much improved and shared my optimism with them. Given the prior instances when my optimism had led them to believe we would succeed followed by my subsequent reports of defeat, I would not have been surprised if they had expressed skepticism.

25

Ships in the Night

Frank O'Donnell was a careful lawyer. He had been a good student at Salesianium High School in Wilmington and at both Temple University and its law school in Philadelphia. His preceptor at the Bar was E. Ennalls Berl, who, along with Clarence A. Southerland and William S. Potter, ran Southerland, Berl and Potter, Delaware's oldest firm.[1] It was a solid, staid firm, recognized for its attention to detail. But as I read his briefs before the District Court and tried to account for the state's motion to dismiss as a matter of law, it was evident he had taken Chief Justice Southerland's opinion affirming the Superior Court as if it were Holy Writ. He expected Judge Wright to accept the Supreme Court of Delaware's conclusions without question.

At the argument on April 16, 1957, O'Donnell orally embraced Southerland's euphemism of "false testimony" and rejected categorizing the lies of the police officers, particularly Detective Rodenhiser's, as perjury.[2] To O'Donnell, the lies were not perjury because they did not directly concern the main issue the jury had to decide at trial. As O'Donnell saw it, ". . . the ultimate dispute turned on the very narrow question of whether a criminal connection was made with her because the [defendants] said: 'While she consented we still didn't make a criminal connection.'"[3]

O'Donnell took great comfort from Southerland's dismissal of my theory of the case as "an attempt by counsel—natural enough—to magnify unduly a matter that had little or no consequence to the outcome of the case."[4] O'Donnell did not hesitate in his argument before Wright to repeat the slur about me Southerland had first articulated.[5]

Moreover, O'Donnell initially referred to the Chief Justice as "Chief Justice Southerland." But the longer he argued, the more frequently he said "Southerland" or "Mr. Southerland" instead of "Chief Justice Southerland." Eight times O'Donnell repeated "Southerland" or "Mr. Southerland."[6] Failing to give the chief justice his title seemed a jarring omission of his status. O'Donnell certainly would not have been intentionally disrespectful. The likely explanation for his calling the chief justice "Mr. Southerland" had to have come from how O'Donnell, as a young associate, spoke to or about Clarence A. Southerland when he was "Mr. Southerland" at Southerland, Berl and Potter.

My response to O'Donnell's charge, which adopted Southerland's argument of "immateriality" was, first, to rely upon the number of pages of the trial transcript containing references to the statements, a count I had provided in my briefs both to the Supreme Court of Delaware and to Judge Wright. I argued that just as I could not prove to the court that the perjury had made a difference in the outcome of the trial, so, too, the state could not assure the court that the perjury had no effect on the outcome of the trial.[7] The fact the police had concealed their perjury, I urged, had to tip the balance in favor of accepting the petitioners' position that the trial itself was unfair.

. . . I cannot say to the Court that without any shadow of a doubt [the police perjury] is what convicted Curran, Jones and Maguire. . . . But I say to Your Honor that neither the judges who sit upon the State Supreme Court of Delaware, nor the judges who sat at the hearing under Rule 35 [and] who also sat at trial, nor the present Attorney General's office, can with any greater certainty than I can deny it, state to Your Honor that it had no effect. And, Your Honor, when we have a situation where the court cannot resolve it, and no court can, then it is petitioners' contention that such a doubt must be resolved on the side of justice, on the side of equity, and that side would mean that this Court should grant relief here. Let there be another trial. Let these men have their day in court. But don't have upon them and have upon the conscience of the State of Delaware, a conviction where admittedly. . . . there was police false testimony, evasive testimony, perjured testimony in the conviction itself.[8]

Despite my argument, O'Donnell constantly and consistently failed to address the effect of the perjury upon the jury's decision. He did his best to reiterate Chief Justice Southerland's claim that the record contained other facts upon which, apart from the statements, the jury could have relied to find the defendants guilty. He tried to make much of the medical testimony about a "ruptured hymen."[9] In doing so, as I told Judge Wright when my turn came to argue, O'Donnell ignored the testimony of the police physician who had examined the woman shortly after she made her charge of rape and found no evidence of spermatozoa in her vagina. It was only in an examination taken hours later, by her family physician from which he testified he found evidence of spermatozoa in a broken down condition.[10]

Moreover, in talking about a "ruptured hymen," O'Donnell ignored the woman's own trial testimony that Curran "pulled on my insides."[11] Curran's version was "the only part of my person that went in her was my finger."[12] In responding to O'Donnell's point about the "ruptured hymen," I assured Judge Wright I was not arguing the guilt or innocence of my clients, an issue separate and apart from a habeas corpus or a Rule 35 Motion proceeding, both of which regarded guilt or innocence as beside the point. Both proceedings required a petitioner to demonstrate a violation of his rights resulting in the state's holding him unlawfully. As I told the judge, the medical testimony was "irrelevant and immaterial to the issue . . . before this court." He agreed.[13]

Early in the argument Judge Wright had focused upon what he thought was the significant issue. It was not the differences in the statements. As he said: "Isn't the issue a very narrow one as to whether or not the perjured testimony, the admitted perjured testimony of Rodenhiser, to the effect that there was only one statement taken, what effect that had on the jury with respect to the credibility of the defendants? Isn't that the issue in a nutshell?"[14]

In my argument I presented the issue, the credibility of the defendants in the minds of the jurors, and Judge Wright saw it. He was the first judge to recognize that credibility was at the heart of the matter. I argued that the statements were incriminating in the context in which they were presented at the trial.

In response to the Delaware Supreme Court's assertion that the police could have put into the statements damaging material, I argued that that approach ignores what is more to the point: if those statements were, indeed, unchanged, why didn't Rodenhiser and the other police officers testify at trial that the first statements were soiled, they had marks on them, and, therefore, "we destroyed them after comparing them or showing them to the men before we got the men to sign new ones." The police had the opportunity; they didn't take it. But what they did do was tell the jury, not in express words but in a way the jury could not mistake, that the three defendants were liars, and if they had lied about statements, why shouldn't the jury conclude that they were lying about the central issue before the trial court: did the young woman consent to what took place in the park?

At that point Judge Wright interrupted to say: "We get back again to credibility." I agreed and told him "that is the key to our case." I went on to explain that the issue could not be resolved as

our state judges had done by assuming the guilt of the petitioners. If the men are to be convicted of this crime, I told Judge
Wright, "they should be convicted after a fair trial, [a trial] they
have yet to have." I concluded that they would not be convicted
at a fair trial.[15]

The critical moment for me in the argument occurred when
Judge Wright asked me a hypothetical question as his last query:

JUDGE: Suppose these had not been police officers,
    Mr. Morris?

The unexpected question enabled me to drive home the significance of the police perjury warranting relief:

If the witnesses with respect to these statements had not been police
officers, we would not have a case before Your Honor with respect to
a violation of the Fourteenth Amendment. That's as pure and simple
as I can state it. . . . What makes this conviction bad is the fact that
these men are policemen, they are agents of the State, they are arms of
the State, doing society's will but doing it in as foul and as degrading a
fashion as they could possibly think of in this case.[16]

Time moved slowly after the argument. No lawyer can predict
with absolute confidence when a court will deliver its opinion
on a matter taken under advisement. Newton White, who had
considered taking *The Rape Case* years earlier, told me that Judge
Wright said he was impressed with my argument. The court reporter, Harry Blam, also told me he thought I did well. I thought
so, too.[17]

In my over fifty years of practice, I never met an experienced
lawyer who claimed he was without concern during the period
after a court took a matter under advisement and before the
opinion came down. The wisdom was it was not in a client's interest to spark the court. Nevertheless, in late summer 1955 I had

approached Superior Court Judges Richards, Terry, and Carey seeking a decision. I do not claim there was a cause and effect relationship, but the fact was I did not win before them. Now I knew my clients and I would just have to be patient while Judge Wright determined what to do.

The clients' families had more difficulty waiting. Jayne Stigliano, Sonny Jones' sister, thought the court's silence unbearable. On many occasions she called me at home to protest the delay. In her judgment, her brother was innocent. She reminded me her vow to her mother was still outstanding. I do not know if Jayne ever understood or, indeed, desired to understand, that my effort was to prove the unfairness of the trial and not Sonny's innocence, the latter point being a contention beside the point to the constitutional issue I had raised. Her calls persisted, often after midnight during the heat of the summer, awakening both Doris and me. The calls had a pattern. She would tell me she had decided to write to President Eisenhower to request he remove Judge Wright for failure to perform his judicial duties responsibly. I then would dissuade her from any such effort. Her next tack was to threaten to protest directly to Judge Wright. From the sound of her voice, I thought she had been drinking. Not until after I told her any such call could boomerang would she desist and agree not to follow through.

Jayne's calls continued for months, as did the silence from the court.

26

Crossing the Line of Tolerable Imperfection (The First Victory)

Finally, a call from Theodore "Ted" Beauchamp, a Deputy Clerk to Edward G. Pollard, the Clerk of the District Court, broke the silence on August 15, 1957. Ted told me Judge Wright had filed an opinion and directed its release to the parties, so I could pick up a copy. I asked him what the judge had ruled. Ted said he could not tell me but added, "I think you will be pleased." I walked over to the District Court and brought the opinion back to my office, reading as I walked.

We had won!

Judge Wright went immediately to the heart of the issue, the one I had raised for my clients before the state judges:

The issue presented is whether false and evasive testimony of a police officer in a criminal case deprives defendants of constitutional due process when such testimony serves the threefold function of being cumulative evidence of the State's case-in-chief, of suppressing evidence which the defense was entitled to use as it saw fit, and finally, of impeaching the credibility of the defendants. The issue is not one of guilt or innocence of the defendants.[1]

288

Recognizing that the issue of Curran, Jones, and Maguire's guilt or innocence was not relevant to the habeas corpus petition before him, Judge Wright wrote that what he had to determine was "... whether that degree of 'fundamental fairness essential to the very concept of justice' as required by the Due Process Clause of the Fourteenth Amendment was achieved in the rape trial of these defendants."[2]

In ruling as he did, Judge Wright disagreed with six state judges who had denied relief to my clients.[3] Although what Judge Wright wrote was an "opinion," it still reads much more like an answering brief when parsed against the Delaware Supreme Court's opinion. Point by point Judge Wright answered the arguments Chief Justice Southerland had put forth.

The critical distinction between the two opinions was in the poles-apart approach each of the courts had taken. To the Supreme Court, the task was to search the record to find justification for the convictions without regard to the effect of the admittedly false police testimony. Southerland concluded that the police perjury was insufficient to vacate the original trial, since he did not think the lies affected the outcome of the trial. Wright, on the other hand, based his granting of relief upon the unfairness the police perjury caused at trial.

With Richards the only exception, the state judges condemned Detective Rodenhiser in unmistakable terms for his false testimony.[4] But Judge Wright went further. To him, the only way to correct a conviction in an unfair trial resulting from state action was to set the conviction aside and grant a new trial.

I had hoped Judge Wright would regard the references to the statements in the record as the answer to the Delaware Supreme Court's opinion where Southerland had gratuitously written that whether there was one statement or two was not "material" to the outcome. Wright did not disappoint me. He seized upon my page count to dispute the Supreme Court's finding. Using the count from my brief, he supported his conclusion that the police testimony about the statements and its effect upon the credibility of the defendants was material and relevant to their convictions. He confronted and convincingly answered the Supreme Court's arguments:

It has been argued the lack of overwhelming convincing evidence that the two statements differed, coupled with the non-incriminating nature of the statements and the failure of counsel to argue the point before the jury, rendered the statements unimportant to the outcome of the case. The court cannot agree. Of the 1,085 pages of trial record, 175 pages concern the statements. Of the 1,085 pages of trial record, 920 pages consist of testimony and comment by court or counsel in the presence of the jury. Of these 920 pages, 124 pages concern the statements. It is true, the larger percentage of these 124 pages was concerned not with whether there were one or two statements but with whether the statements were voluntary. Nonetheless, the State deemed the issue of the number of statements so important that it recalled Detective John Rodenhiser in rebuttal as the last witness to be heard before the case went to the jury. Rodenhiser again laid particular stress upon the fact that there was only one statement and that the only statement taken was the one in evidence.[5]

As he continued, Judge Wright saw most clearly the effect of the police perjury upon the defendants' credibility:

When reviewed in the context of the proceedings at trial, the strength of the State's position with respect to the false testimony and its effect on the jury's decision is placed in serious doubt. The court cannot be a vehicle to resolve state conjecture caused by a state wrong. *Where there is false and evasive testimony resulting in suppression of evidence possibly vital to the defense, and which is relevant to the State's case and defendants' credibility, it is not the court's function to speculate on whether the prejudice knowingly injected into the case by a police officer caused a conviction.*

Whenever a defendant takes the stand in a criminal trial his credibility is put in issue, and in every such case if there is a conviction the testimony of the defendant has been successfully discredited. . . .

Although the testimony of a witness may be upon a collateral issue and seemingly of little or no significance or help in reaching the conclusion of guilt or innocence, the standing of the witness in his community or his connection with a law enforcement agency of the State or City may magnify the importance of the testimony to a jury. Where the false and evasive testimony is that of a high ranking police officer in active charge of the criminal investigation, this court cannot say the testimony was immaterial to the outcome. [Emphasis added.][6]

Only a courageous judge, secure in his own judgment, could have written as Wright did. His confidence in the law he cited, his recognition of the unfairness of the police perjury upon the defendants' credibility, and his sense of fairness convinced him the trial had crossed "the line between tolerable imperfection and fundamental unfairness. . . ."[7] He ruled unequivocally the state had violated the constitutional rights of my clients by allowing perjured police testimony at *The Rape Case* trial. Accordingly, Wright granted the writ of habeas corpus I had sought.[8]

I called the families and reported my first victory in over four and a half years of litigation. I then visited Curran, Jones, and Maguire at the Workhouse. They greeted my report of our success with what I thought was restraint. But as I walked away, I heard their whoops of joy as they returned to their cells.

On August 16, 1957, the headline in capital letters on the front page of the *Morning News* spread over four columns heralded our victory: "THREE SERVING LIFE IN RAPE WIN CHANCE FOR ANOTHER HEARING." Accompanying the article were the mug shots of my clients taken by the police at the time of their arrest on October 30, 1947. The photographs would not arouse any sympathy either for them or their cause as they stared out at the public.

At the time of Judge Wright's ruling, Curran, Jones, and Maguire had served almost ten years in jail from the time of their arrest and incarceration in October 1947. With Judge Wright's decision in hand, I considered seeking their immediate freedom by applying for their release on the posting of bail, but I decided against it, because I did not think Judge Wright would order their release. After all, he had not found them innocent; he had only held their trial was not fair. He could have ordered their release, since his ruling erased their conviction. But even he balked at enforcing his ruling in full. Instead of immediately releasing my clients in keeping with the literal meaning of the Latin habeas corpus (you may have the body), he concluded: "The writ should issue. The issuance of the writ, however, does not preclude a new trial or the taking of proper steps to hold the defendants in custody pending such a new trial."[9]

Promptly upon his return from vacation, Attorney General Craven in a press release announced he would seek a review before the Third Circuit. In the order Judge Wright entered on August 27, 1957, he recognized the state's planned appeal to the United States Court of Appeals for the Third Circuit. After granting my clients' habeas corpus petition and ordering their release from the custody of the Board of Corrections, Judge Wright further provided: ". . . the execution of the foregoing order directing the release of the petitioners be stayed pending an appeal of this matter by the State of Delaware to the United States Circuit Court of Appeals."

The fact my clients were still in custody despite the state's violation of their rights might itself have a helpful effect upon the thinking of the appellate judges as they considered the state's appeal. I decided against filing our own appeal to the Third Circuit claiming Judge Wright had erred in failing to grant immediate release. Given Wright's recognition of the state's right to hold my clients in custody pending a new trial or, at least, the state's decision not to retry them, the Circuit Court judges might regard any appeal by Curran, Jones, and Maguire to be without merit. And, worse, the appellate judges might think I was trying to use our victory to confront the state judges, a perception which, however much without foundation, might cause the appellate judges to defend the state judges by reversing Judge Wright.

Even though, as a practical matter, I believed we would not succeed either in seeking immediate release on bail or in taking an appeal, the decision not to seek the men's release weighed heavily upon me. If I did nothing, they would remain in custody. Obviously, it is one thing to dwell upon litigation tactics. It is quite another to do time behind bars. From my experience as a prisoner of war of the Germans in World War II, I knew what it meant to be in custody and, indeed, in jail.[10] To this day, I am not certain I made the right decision even though Bud, Sonny, and Reds supported it. At the time, I think they would have agreed to almost anything I urged given my success, the first since their arrest almost a decade earlier.

27

The Planted Note

J udge Wright's remarkable opinion, at least remarkable in my judgment, deserved a comment or note in one of the law reviews or law journals most law schools published. Comments and notes in the 1950's and to this day are the work of law school students who serve as board members of the publications. Comments are much longer than notes, but both are at the cutting edge of the law. Most notes address decisions of lower courts while they are on appeal to higher courts, including the United States Supreme Court. The editors make the final decision about which cases of interest are potential subjects for publication. The period between the search for a case of interest and the publication of the student's analysis and conclusion is relatively short. If the note does not appear before a court resolves the matter, it would vitiate the writer's and the law journal's aim to influence the outcome. Accordingly, I wanted a note about *The Rape Case* to appear while it was still undecided before the Third Circuit.

The highest accolade a comment or note achieved then or now was a reviewing court's adopting the student's thinking and suggested conclusion in commenting on a lower court opinion. Many a practicing lawyer tries to plant the seed for a note in the minds of law journal editors seeking the benefit of the law students' research as well as the publication of a note favorable to the lawyer whose case is under review. To plant the seed for a note about *The Rape Case*, I turned to my law school classmate and close friend, Melvin G. Shimm, faculty advisor to the *Duke Law Journal*, published twice yearly at that time.

I had discussed *The Rape Case* with Mel more than once. I gave him my brief in the District Court to read when he visited me in the summer of 1957. When Judge Wright granted the writ of habeas corpus on August 15, 1957, I sent the newspaper clipping to Mel with a covering letter on August 19: "If you think the matter worthy of a note, let me know and I shall forward to you any additional information you might desire which I have."[1] At that time, the briefing and argument on my appeal were months ahead.

My suggestion resulted in the publication of a note in the *Duke Law Journal's* Spring 1958 issue, entitled "Perjured Testimony: Its Effect On Criminal Defendants' Constitutional Rights."[2] Less than five pages long, including fourteen footnotes chocked full of authority, the note first focused upon the Delaware Supreme Court's view of *The Rape Case* and summarized its holding in these words: "that the defendants were not . . . deprived of a fair trial [by police perjury] and interpreted the *Mooney v. Holohan* rule to require that perjury, in order to constitute a denial of due process, must be, 'brought home to the prosecuting officer.' "[3] But the Delaware Supreme Court had not been as explicit as the note asserted. After first defining the federal rule, Chief Justice Southerland concluded: "It is not necessary in this case to decide whether this is a sound general rule for our courts in reviewing a conviction under Rule 35."[4]

The note writer then referred to my successful petition for habeas corpus before Judge Wright and his holding that such perjury as the police had committed "constitutes fundamental unfairness in the trial of a criminal case."[5] The author praised Judge Wright's holding in these words: "This decision, unique in that it marks the first time a court has explained, without equivocation, that the *Mooney* rule extends to state agents other than the prosecuting attorneys, suggests that a close reappraisal of that doctrine is necessary."[6] Judge Wright's opinion, even after *Mooney v. Holohan* and *Pyle v. Kansas,* remained the definitive holding that fairness and constitutional rights will not tolerate the perjury of any state agent, including policemen.[7]

The careful author disclosed the surprising aftermath of *Pyle v. Kansas,* the case Judge Wright cited and relied upon in his opinion, following the United States Supreme Court's decision.[8] A footnote discussed *Pyle v. Amrine,* the follow-up case to *Pyle v. Kansas:*

There the Kansas court interpreted *Pyle v. Kansas* to mean that "in order to constitute grounds for release on a writ of *habeas corpus* it must appear that the officers in charge of the prosecution knew it to be false." If any ambiguity remained after that decision it vanished when, four years later, the same Kansas court cited *Pyle v. Amrine* to stand for the proposition that the prosecutor must know of the perjury. *Townsend v. Hudspeth,* 167 Kan. 366, 205 P.2d 483 (1949). *Thus, if Pyle v. Kansas had extended the rule it went unnoticed by the very court directly affected by it.* [Emphasis added.][9]

Whether Judge Wright was aware of the subsequent history of *Pyle v. Kansas,* I do not know; he did not refer to it in his decision. For my part, I was not aware of the post *Pyle v. Kansas* decisions. To my discredit, I had not done the research the thorough Duke Law School note author did to learn that even the Kansas courts did not follow the broad principle I thought the High Court had held in *Pyle v. Kansas.* The note's conclusion was right on target:

Nevertheless, the customary narrow construction of *Mooney v. Holahan* is apparently relaxing, and new limitations will, of necessity, have to be formulated. A workable solution might be to expand the meaning of the term "prosecution authorities" to include all employees of the state directly connected with bringing a particular defendant to justice, rather than to disturb the language of the general rule. This would permit judicial flexibility and would more nearly afford the defendant the protection against prejudicial state action, to which he is constitutionally entitled.[10]

By the time the note appeared, it was too late for me to mention it in my answering brief in the Third Circuit or refer to it at the oral argument on February 20, 1958. Still, the fact a note in the *Duke Law Journal* endorsed the view I had taken pleased me immensely. Although, I did not bring the note to the Third Circuit's attention, I hoped the court would learn of the note and take the positive parts of it into account when the court reviewed the state's attempt to reverse Chief Judge Wright's holding. I no longer recall whether I believed I had no right to do so since the court had already taken the case "under advisement" or because the note itself was not a reported decision or since I thought emphasizing the "unique" holding might cause the Third Circuit to shy away from affirming the ground-breaking rule of Chief Judge Wright, a ruling I wanted to stand as unassailable.

28

Affirming the Obvious
(The Second Victory)

Throughout my years of practice, I received assistance from many sources. In representing Curran, Jones, and Maguire, on several critical occasions, the help was inadvertent and inexplicable. What occurred in the Third Circuit on the state's appeal from Judge Wright's order illustrates the point. After the state filed its opening brief in support of its appeal, I submitted an answering brief. The state then had the right to file a reply brief. Time passed but the state did nothing. On December 17, 1957, Frank O'Donnell Jr., by then chief deputy attorney general and in charge of *The Rape Case* since Steve Hamilton's departure, wrote to the Third Circuit advising the court: "The appellant in the above matter will not file a reply brief."[1]

The opportunity of having the last word is not one to be idly rejected. Why O'Donnell decided to forego a response was, and remains, a mystery. It could not have been because he had nothing to say; certainly he was not reticent at the subsequent oral argument. Perhaps other duties in the attorney general's office prevented him from writing the brief. But *The Rape Case* was too important to ignore. Perhaps he thought his not filing a reply would indicate to the Third Circuit judges the state's disdain for the position I had taken. If so, this was a serious error of judgment. After Judge Wright's decision, my position was no longer a lonely lawyer's cry that justice be done. Judge Wright was too able for his views to be ignored. Still, O'Donnell's silence for the state could not hurt me. It meant my words for my clients would constitute the last written word the Third Circuit would receive from the lawyers as the judges prepared for the oral argument. I was sanguine the Third Circuit would affirm.

Neither O'Donnell nor I was the equal of his predecessor Steve Hamilton, either in brief writing or arguing. In fairness to O'Donnell, few lawyers brought to their advocacy Hamilton's talents. He was my nemesis in the early years of the case, turning aside all my efforts for my clients while he, with Vincent A. Theisen, the chief deputy (whose help to Hamilton, I believe, was minimal), was nominally in charge for the state during Young's tenure as attorney general. I never won anything in court against Hamilton. But O'Donnell was a good, solid lawyer, trained in the tradition of Berl, Potter and Anderson. He continued Hamilton's winning ways for a while. He defeated my appeal to the State Supreme Court in 1956, but in Southerland, Wolcott, and Bramhall he had a receptive audience. While my 1956 petition for certiorari was pending, O'Donnell fended off my effort in the Court of Chancery before Chancellor Seitz to secure Dr. T's report about Detective Rodenhiser. O'Donnell also had done the work for the state leading to the United States Supreme Court's denial of my petition for certiorari.

The briefs O'Donnell and I submitted to the Third Circuit both made the same arguments we had raised before. At that time, the Third Circuit held oral argument before three judges in every appeal when a party requested it. (Today the court has strict rules limiting oral argument to those cases where the court itself decides it wants to hear the parties.) Both O'Donnell and I sought argument.

Unlike our dull briefs, the oral argument on February 20, 1958, before the three-judge panel consisting of Chief Judge John Biggs and Judges Herbert Goodrich and Harry Kalodner, was spirited. Biggs and Goodrich peppered me with questions.[2] None proved troublesome. Judge Kalodner sat silent and inscrutable throughout the argument, perhaps because the others asked all his questions. Then again it may have been that the oral arguments and the lawyers' responses to the questions from Biggs and Goodrich removed Kalodner's doubts.

My own assessment was that I had made an excellent argument demonstrating not only my knowledge of the facts of my case and the law applicable to it, but, moreover, my commitment to the principle that my clients had a constitutional right to a fair trial. As I sat in the courtroom, I regretted not having arranged to have the argument either recorded or transcribed. Based on the oral argument, I thought the Third Circuit would surely affirm Chief Judge Wright and dispense with the need to write an opinion. Wright had said it all.

But I did not take into account John Biggs' ego. Apparently he wanted to put his imprint on *The Rape Case* and say the state was wrong in *his* way. Thus, instead of the prompt unanimous affirmance Wright's opinion warranted and I expected, the Third Circuit, in an unanimous opinion by Biggs which paraphrased the same thoughts Wright had logically and elegantly expressed, upheld Chief Judge Wright seven months later on September 29, 1958.[3]

Whether Biggs, Goodrich, Kalodner, or any other member of the Third Circuit bench (a panel opinion goes to all members of the court before it is released) learned of the *Duke Law Journal* note before the Third Circuit announced its opinion I do not know. The opinion did not cite to the note. Nonetheless, the note writer and the editorial board of the *Duke Law Journal* and its faculty adviser, Mel Shimm, had to have been as pleased as I was, when the Third Circuit affirmed Judge Wright's ruling.

Chief Judge Biggs' favorable opinion came with a cost: not only increased anxiety about the outcome between the February argument and his September opinion but, more importantly, continued imprisonment for my clients despite the unconstitutionality of their trial. Even with the Third Circuit's unanimous approval of Chief Judge Wright's courageous act in granting the writ of habeas corpus, I knew, as did my clients and their families, the state intended to ask the Supreme Court to review the Third Circuit's decision. On October 1, 1958, the day after he learned of the Third Circuit's opinion, Attorney General Craven released a statement to the press in which he sought to justify seeking the Supreme Court's review. The *Journal-Every Evening* account read:

"I feel it incumbent upon me," Craven said in a prepared statement, "in view of the findings of our state courts that the defendants were not deprived of any constitutional rights, to ask the U.S. Supreme Court to pass finally on this question."

Craven said he and other state attorneys general are "disturbed" by federal court actions in similar cases.

"The federal courts had no facts before them which were not considered by our Superior and Supreme Courts," he said, adding:

"I, along with most attorneys general in the United States, have been disturbed by the increasing tendency of federal courts to alter or override the decisions of state courts by issuing writs of *habeas corpus* in cases similar to this one."[4]

Absent from Craven's press release was any recognition of the police perjury at the trial, testimony now found by all the state and federal judges, to be false. Nor did Craven say one word about the adverse effect of the police perjury on the jury's acceptance of my clients' testimony. All he had done was repeat Chief Justice Southerland's conclusion. He even attacked the way federal courts reviewed state court decisions on claims of constitutional violations. Along with most other attorney generals and many state court judges throughout the country, he claimed habeas corpus proceedings in federal courts to review state court convictions were burdening the administration of justice. I held the view it was better for our system to have prisoners attempting to write their way out of jail than attempting to break out with the risk of violence and injury. The "increasing tendency" to which Craven adverted was rhetoric not in accord with the facts: "The reports of the Administrative Office [of the United States Courts] indicated that 98 petitioners were successful [in securing release] in the district courts from 1946 through 1957."[5] I expected the Supreme Court would deny the state's petition, just as it had denied mine two years earlier.[6]

Armed with the Third Circuit's agreement with Chief Judge Wright, I no longer had any doubt about making the effort to secure my clients' release on bail. Two federal courts had held the state had violated their constitutional rights. A court, not a lawyer's litigation tactics, would have to deny Curran, Jones, and Maguire their freedom this time. I prepared a motion to set bail for their release. On October 6, 1958, I served my motion on the state and filed it with the Third Circuit. It evoked an immediate response from my old boss, Attorney General Craven, who opposed the granting of bail. The issue before the Third Circuit on my motion for bail was whether the April 2, 1958, change in Delaware law doing away with capital punishment was applicable. The old law imposed the death sentence for rape absent a jury's recommendation of mercy and the trial court's acceptance of the recommendation.[7] The new law no longer regarded rape as a capital offense.[8]

On the morning of October 8, the Third Circuit heard argument on the bail issue from Deputy Attorney General Richard J. Baker and me. (Craven had assigned responsibility for the case to Baker when O'Donnell resigned to return to full-time private practice.) The panel members this time were Judges Goodrich, Gerald McLaughlin and Austin L. Staley. Judge Staley asked whether the abolition of capital punishment in Delaware, thus making the crime of rape a bailable offense at this time, would benefit a person who was alleged to have committed the crime of rape in 1947 when the crime was not a bailable offense. I replied that I thought any benefit to a person in custody resulting from a change in legislation after his arrest would inure to the benefit of such a person under general principles of the common law. I further said the Delaware statute was silent on this point. Both Baker and I told the Court we did not know of any applicable Delaware case.

On my return to Wilmington after the argument, I found what I believed was controlling Delaware authority answering Judge Staley's question.[9] Based on the unreported case of *State of Delaware v. Thompson,* I prepared a letter to the clerk of the Third Circuit. "Applying the Thompson result to the Curran case, the answer to Judge Staley's question to me at argument is that there is authority in Delaware (the Thompson case) which holds squarely that the benefit from the change in the Delaware law will be applied in favor of an accused person."[10]

I did not know if I even had a right to submit such a letter. Almost always, when I have been uncertain about what to do, I have found calling and speaking to either the clerk or a member of the staff of the court in which my matter is pending most helpful in yielding the answer to my question or, at the least, in providing greater insight. In this instance, I called Ida O. Creskoff, the able, astute, long-time Clerk of the Third Circuit. When I told her my quandary, she suggested I should wait at least overnight before taking any action. She also made it clear that my determination and not any suggestion from her should govern what I should do. I believed her suggestion was sensible, but I was loath to do nothing. I sent the letter to the Third Circuit by hand-delivery that day.

After my letter was on its way, but before the afternoon was over, I received word by telephone that the court had entered its order setting bail for my clients' release. Clerk Creskoff was right yet again. The next morning I received a copy of Judge Goodrich's order entered late in the day on October 8. It began by saying, "Upon consideration of the motion of Irving Morris" and then went on to order "that Francis J. Curran, Francis J. Maguire and Ira F. Jones, Jr., be admitted to bail in the sum of five thousand dollars ($5,000.00) each. . . ." It concluded by providing "that the bail is to be approved by the clerk of the United States District Court for the District of Delaware."[11]

The document was curious. Never before had I seen an order describing a motion or petition assigning ownership to the lawyer instead of the client. According to the Third Circuit, what it had before it was "the motion of Irving Morris." More and more people thought of the case as my case. I welcomed the perception. Whatever its form, Judge Goodrich's order delighted me, and I promptly reported the good news to the families. In my reading and reporting, I did not realize how important the provision providing for bail "to be approved by the clerk of the . . . District Court" would turn out to be.

29

The Hair Tonic Bond

Once we learned of the Third Circuit's order on October 8, the families and I immediately set about securing the $5,000 bail. I was determined my clients would not spend one more night unjustly confined. I encouraged their families to secure from family members and friends deeds to real estate, typically acceptable collateral in Delaware's courts for bail bonds. Arranging for the bail occupied me well past midnight and into the early morning hours of October 9.

When I spoke to Reds Maguire's parents, they assured me that among family members and friends there was sufficient real estate equity to cover the $5,000. Sonny Jones' sister, Jayne Stigliano, told me she would have no problem, since her husband, Carmen Stigliano, was a friend of Frank L. Ferschke. Ferschke and his brother, William, owned all the shares of William J. Ferschke, Inc., a private company, founded by their father, that made hair tonic using a secret formula. Jayne thought Ferschke, as a favor to Carmen, would put his shares up as collateral to help with Sonny's bail. She promptly reported he had agreed to do so.

Bail for Bud Curran was a different matter. Francis and Nellie Curran with their nine daughters and another son, the youngest child, were always hard-pressed for money. Since they did not own their home, they had no deed to post as bail. I decided to ask Jayne Stigliano if she would help Bud Curran and his family by asking Ferschke to provide Bud's bail. She raised no objection, and said she would speak to Carmen who, in turn, would speak to Ferschke. As soon as she had an answer, she would let me know. I told her I would wait in my office for her call. It was past midnight when I heard from her. Jayne told me Ferschke was prepared to help but, since he did not know Bud Curran, he wanted me to speak to his lawyer, A. James Gallo, and secure his approval. Jim Gallo had been involved briefly in *The Rape Case* as the lawyer for Maguire at the preliminary hearing. He had the largest divorce practice in Delaware. The bulk of the balance of his practice was trial work representing defendants in criminal cases. He was known for his skill in plea bargaining.

I then began the search to find Jim Gallo at that late hour. It took several telephone calls before I located him playing cards in what I learned was his regular game at the Hotel Olivere at 7th and Shipley Streets. Jim interrupted to talk to me. Given his experience, I did not have to explain much. His question to me was whether or not I could assure him Bud Curran would stay in the community and appear when ordered. I had no hesitation in assuring Jim. Based on my word, Jim said he would tell Ferschke to help Bud Curran as well as Sonny Jones.

In those days, so many matters went forward upon a simple reliance on one's word. Today, possibly because of our increasing capability to reduce agreements almost immediately to writing through word processing and to transmit them by facsimile or e-mail "one's word" has given way to "one's writing." I do not hold the view that people are less reliable today. Until I learn otherwise, I am still willing to rely upon the word of most people with whom I deal.

With the bail arrangements complete, I was elated. I called the Currans, and then went home. I looked forward to the release of all three men later that morning. Everything seemed in order. Or so I thought.

Acting through the attorney general's office, I alerted the appropriate people at the New Castle County Workhouse to move Curran, Jones, and Maguire to the office of Edward G. Pollard, the Clerk of the District Court, by 9:00 a.m. At the appointed time, the Maguires assembled the people who were going to sign bonds with the deeds to their houses as collateral. Through Jayne Stigliano, I had arranged for Ferschke to bring his stock certificates to the clerk's office. I then called Ed Pollard to report my success.

Ed was an awesome person with a unique intellect. I had first met him in February 1951 when I began working for Chief Judge Leahy as his law clerk. By that time Ed had served almost nine years as Clerk of the District Court at Judge Leahy's appointment and pleasure. As a young man, Ed, from his own description, had been a wild fellow. His family came from Virginia and he still retained an easy southern drawl. Without completing high school, he had joined the Army. According to his account of his military experience, peacetime service in our Army consisted of one barroom brawl after another. A Sunday at the shore in Wildwood, New Jersey, with Ed and his family bore witness to the truth of his stories; Ed's body was covered with jagged scars. The sharp edges of broken beer bottles do not carve with the precision of a surgeon's scalpel. After his military service, Ed married a Wilmington girl, Marie Casey, and converted to her Catholic faith. He became active in Democratic politics and ultimately became administrative assistant to Senator James M. Tunnell Sr. When Judge Leahy asked Ed to assume the position of clerk of the District Court upon the Judge's swearing in as its sole judge on February 2, 1942, Ed willingly gave up the arduous daily trips to Washington during the Senate sessions. It was not a difficult decision for Ed, devoted family man that he had become. As clerk he could now be home with his family every night. More-over, his tenure in his new post was no longer subject to political uncertainty.

After I began my service as law clerk, I quickly realized Ed knew more about the Federal Rules of Procedure, both civil and criminal, than anyone I had ever met, with the possible exception of J. W. Moore, my law school procedure professor and the author and editor of *Moore's Federal Practice*, then recognized as the authoritative text on the Federal Rules of Civil Procedure. Ed was entirely self-taught. He was also one of the most fiercely loyal people I have ever had the delight to know. Any lawyer who sought to share with Ed his criticism of one of Judge Leahy's decisions ran into a firestorm. An unhappy lawyer who did so did not do it twice. From my personal experience, I knew how much the judges of the enlarged District Court bench relied upon Ed's knowledge and wisdom.

So it was with more than a fair degree of pride I reported to Ed Pollard in detail how I had secured bail for each of my clients. I told him the collateral I had arranged to post consisted of the equity value of real estate members of the Maguire family and friends owned and, in the case of Jones and Curran, I had the assurance Frank Ferschke would deposit with Ed his valuable, unencumbered shares in the Ferschke Hair Tonic Company. Thus, I told Ed, everything was in order for the release of my clients. Ed responded that was great and he would expect me in a little while. Within a few minutes, he called back. He first observed that I must have checked it out and found everything I was doing was fine, implying I was right and it was he who had made a mistake. He went on to say he had just looked at the statute covering the posting of bail in a federal court and it appeared to him that only cash or government securities were acceptable as collateral.

My immediate response was silence. However acceptable as

collateral for bail in the courts of Delaware, neither real estate deeds nor the hair tonic company stock not publicly traded, or even capable of ready valuation, met the standard of the statutory language Ed called to my attention. I had been so taken with my success in the Third Circuit, I never thought to look for a federal statute controlling bail. Knowing my collateral did not meet the statutory requirement, Ed broke the embarrassing silence by saying gently, "Of course, I could be wrong." Ed's reputation at the Bar was legendary for being able to correct and educate a lawyer while at the same time making the lawyer believe he, and not Ed, was the source of the knowledge. It was quite clear to me Curran, Jones, and Maguire would not "hit the bricks" that day short of a minor miracle.

Ed could not have been surprised when I told him Curran, Jones, and Maguire and their respective families had neither cash nor government securities to post as bail. I did not have to tell Ed how heartbreaking it would be to my clients and their families to come so close to freedom after almost eleven years in custody only to be turned aside because of the lack of money. Neither he nor I mentioned my embarrassment in having to tell my clients and their families the bail consideration, which they had arranged with my approval and encouragement, did not meet the requirements of a statute I had not even thought to look for, let alone to consult.

Ed then told me what we were going to do. Since the United States Court of Appeals for the Third Circuit, in its October 8, 1958 order granting bail, had entrusted to him as "the clerk of the United States District Court for the District of Delaware" the responsibility for approving the bail for the future appearance of Curran, Jones, and Maguire, he considered it well within his discretion to determine what was or was not acceptable as bail. He ended our conversation by telling me he expected to see my clients and me at the appointed time, then but a few minutes away.

I gathered my papers and walked from my office to the District Court then housed in the Federal Building at 11th and Market. In the clerk's office, I found the Currans, with Bud's aunt and uncle, Mr. and Mrs. Francis X. McHugh (another brother to Nellie Curran). Unbeknownst to me, the McHughs had agreed to put up their house as collateral for Bud's bail, making reliance upon the Ferschke stock unnecessary. Sonny Jones' sisters, Virginia McKinley and Jayne Stigliano, Jayne's husband, Carmen, and Frank Ferschke were there. The Maguires, Reds' brother, Edward Maguire, along with Joseph V. Segner, a friend of Reds' father, who joined with young Ed Maguire to provide the collateral for Reds' bond, completed the group.

From the family members, I learned my clients were already in United States Marshal Herbert Barnes' custody in the lockup at the end of the corridor on the second floor. Guards from the New Castle County Workhouse had brought them there to await the proceedings before Ed Pollard. I met with Ed in his office. On his desk were the various deeds he had collected even before I arrived so he could complete the paper work in his customary efficient style. I witnessed Ferschke's signature to the bond Ed had prepared and Ferschke executed, assigning to Ed as clerk of the District Court Ferschke's "250 shares of the capital stock of William J. Ferschke, Inc." to bind Sonny Jones' appearance.

Even before my arrival, Ed had opened a new page in the Miscellaneous Docket and made the entry to reflect the action he was taking. He then called the marshal's office and instructed the marshal to bring Curran, Jones, and Maguire to his office so they could sign the papers promising to appear upon command of the court. When they arrived, Ed explained the procedure to them, including the meaning of the promise they were each about to make by signing the papers he had prepared. Failure to appear upon the court's command would result in forfeiture of bail with a catastrophic effect upon the families and friends who trusted them. Ed was fastidious in explaining obligations and rights.

As reporter and columnist William P. Frank recounted in an article he wrote about the case and the release of my clients on bail, which appeared in the *Morning News* on October 10, 1958, Reds Maguire, as he waited his turn to sign the papers, fished in his pocket for a pack of cigarettes. Before he lit the cigarette he asked a guard if it was all right for him to smoke. The guard answered: "You do as you please. You're on your own now."[1] Obviously it would take some time for my clients to acclimate themselves to life outside of jail free of its compulsory rules, regulations, and constant supervision.

Within a few minutes after signing their names, the three men walked from Ed's office to the outer office of the clerk where their families awaited them. It had to have been an emotional time for all of them. I did not witness the reunion because I thought I should allow them to embrace each other in privacy. I left Ed's office by the corridor door and walked back to my office. As I did I was satisfied, although "a lot of 'ifs' [were] still pending," as Bill Frank wrote, "with having accomplished what had been regarded as 'the impossible.'"[2]

On the day of their release from custody, Curran, Jones, and Maguire had each spent twenty days shy of eleven years behind bars for a crime they denied under oath ever having committed and the state had never proved at a fair trial.

Still ahead was the outcome of the state's filing a petition to the United States Supreme Court for the issuance of a writ of certiorari to review the action of the Third Circuit, which Attorney General Craven had publicly committed to do. My clients' promises, secured by the bail, to respond to the District Court's command to appear were not idle ones. Even if the state did not file for certiorari or was unsuccessful with its petition for certiorari, the state still retained the right under Judge Wright's order to retry them on the rape charge.

Throughout my years of work to set aside their convictions, I knew the best result I could achieve for them, were we to succeed, would only reverse their convictions and sentences. The state could still retry them. If *State of Delaware v. Theodric Thompson* were followed (as I expected it would be), my clients would no longer face the death penalty should they be convicted at a retrial.[3] But they would face a return to prison and their life terms. Never once did Curran, Jones, and Maguire flinch from pursuing a new trial even when they knew, prior to *Thompson,* the death penalty would confront them upon subsequent conviction. For now, with their bail posted, my clients were back with their families and beginning the task of rebuilding their lives while the possibility of further prosecution still hung over their heads like the sword of Damocles.

Ed Pollard dutifully reported to Clerk Ida Creskoff on October 9, 1958, that Curran, Jones, and Maguire had come before him "with their sureties and I approved the bail" in a letter that was not as detailed as it might otherwise have been:

Re: *Curran, et al. v. State of Delaware*
    Habeas Corpus No. 12
    <u>Circuit Court No. 12,397</u>

Dear Mrs. Creskoff:

In accordance with the Circuit Court's order of October 8, 1958, the above defendants were brought before me today with their sureties and I approved the bail. I understand from Mr. Morris that you stated you had no facilities for keeping securities, etc. Accordingly, I assume you would want me to retain the bail bonds and any securities that were pledged. If I am incorrect in this assumption and you should want the bonds sent to you, I would appreciate your so informing me.

I acted on an uncertified order. If you think a certified copy of the order is necessary, I would appreciate your sending me one.

Yours truly,
/s / Edward G. Pollard
Clerk[4]

But the Third Circuit's order did not request detail nor did Mrs. Creskoff. The court left the matter to Ed's good judgment.

I knew I had disappointed Ed by not checking the statute. A thorough lawyer would never have assumed anything of value would qualify as bail. For his part, Ed knew there was no way, even if I had read the statute, that I could have done anything to secure the immediate release of Curran, Jones, and Maguire given the unequivocal language of the statute. Cash to meet the required $15,000 total bail was beyond the collective means of the three families. Neither my clients nor their families knew about government bonds (except, of course, the war bonds of World War II). Surely, I could not have met my goal of securing the release of my clients that day. Under no circumstances would I have suggested to Ed Pollard that he accept as bail property outside of the statutory language defining permissible bail in 1958.

Ed said nothing to my clients or their families of my failure to know the law and, worse, my failure to take the few minutes to do the research to learn what it was. So far as I know, Ed never told anyone how he saved the day for me.

My clients' release on bail on October 9, 1958, meant I was responsible that year for over twenty-five percent of all state prisoners released by federal court orders throughout the country. In 1958, Curran, Jones, and Maguire were three of the total of eleven persons falling within Attorney General Craven's claim of "increasing tendency" in his statement of October 1, 1958, following Judge Biggs' opinion. [5]

With their futures uncertain, my clients each tried to pick up his life. Sonny Jones had learned the plumbing trade while in jail. Through a relative he readily secured employment in Daniel Rappa's plumbing business. Reds Maguire took a job delivering milk for a local dairy. In jail Bud Curran learned to be an electrician, but upon his release he had no union card and no job prospects. Just as the impecunious circumstances of the Curran family had presented a problem in securing bail, so they were roadblocks in Bud's path to employment. I offered to help.

Although I did not know any electricians to whom I could turn, I was slightly acquainted with Benjamin Steinberg, the owner of Artcraft, an electrical supply house then located on West Fourth Street between Shipley and Orange near Market. At that time, Fourth and Market was the center of downtown Wilmington. Artcraft did exceedingly well, at least while Ben was alive and in control. What I did not know then, but came to learn through the years, was Ben Steinberg's generosity in his own way. Father Francis Tucker, the legendary priest of Wilmington's largest parish, St. Anthony's, often turned to Ben for help and always found him generous.[6] When I told Ben of Bud's predicament—he needed work but still might have to return to jail—Ben's response was to tell me to have Bud come and visit him at his store.

The upshot of the interview was four-fold: First, Bud satisfied Steinberg he was a competent electrician. Second, Steinberg called a contractor who was doing work at the Federal Building and secured a promise of a job for Bud. The building then housed the Post Office, the courtrooms and offices of the District Court and its Delaware judges, along with offices for Chief Judge Biggs, the FBI, the Internal Revenue Service, and other government agencies. Third, since Bud had neither the tools with which to practice his trade nor the money to buy them, Steinberg provided Bud with a tool box and the equipment he needed to go to work. Finally, by what he did for Bud out of the kindness of his heart, Ben Steinberg made me appear to be a miracle worker in the eyes of the Curran family.

The same day Bud started work he called in mid-morning to ask if I could meet him. Of course I said "Yes," and we arranged to do so at noon at the corner of Tenth and Market. As I crossed

Tenth Street from my office in the North American Building, I saw Bud leaning against the DuPont Building on the Market Street side. "You'll never guess what I'm doing on this job," was his greeting. I had no idea what he was doing so I asked him to tell me. Bud said the contractor who employed him at Steinberg's urging had the task of preparing quarters for the new federal judge in the Federal Building. "They have me wiring Judge Layton's chambers," Bud explained. Caleb R. Layton III, sitting as a Superior Court Judge, had been the first among the Delaware judges to deny relief for Curran, Jones, and Maguire.[7]

In jest, and with a broad smile, Bud asked me what I thought of his wiring Judge Layton's chair while he went about the other work in the prospective chambers. I urged my client to keep to himself all prior experience he had had with the good judge, an admonition entirely superfluous, but one I nonetheless expressed. Although I knew Layton from frequent appearances before him, including *The Rape Case,* I never shared with him Curran's role in the construction of the quarters he occupied for many years thereafter. I like to think Judge Layton would have found the same humor I did in the irony of Bud's wiring his new quarters.

By 1958, at the request of Judge Leahy, Mr. Cohen and I hired a young lawyer who had completed a clerkship with Judge Leahy. As I awaited the Supreme Court's action, the young lawyer told me he hoped the Supreme Court would grant the state's petition for certiorari. His reasoning was it would be quite an achievement for me at the relatively young age of thirty-two to argue a case before the United States Supreme Court. His comment reflected a good-faith belief in how my career would advance dramatically and legitimately. But his observation also reflected a skewed view of a lawyer's responsibility to his client.

In one sense he was right; the granting of the state's petition might well enable me to have the personal satisfaction of arguing a case before the nation's highest tribunal, provided I won. Given the success I had achieved in *The Rape Case* at that time, to have argued and lost would have been devastating. It was an absolute certainty that granting certiorari would expose my clients to the terrible risk of a reversal of the Third Circuit's favorable decision and their return to prison to resume serving their life terms.

On the other hand, were the Supreme Court to deny the state's petition, as I hoped it would, the state would face enormous problems in trying to return my clients to jail. The state would first have to decide to retry them almost eleven years after their arrest. To assemble the evidence and the witnesses would be a major undertaking. Moreover, and of critical importance, the state would go forward to a second trial knowing the jury would learn that the police had destroyed the first set of statements and that there had been police perjury at the first trial, as well as the police cover-up of McCool's subsequent report. In a new trial, unlike the first one, credibility would attach to my clients' testimony. The state would have to ponder long and hard before deciding to pursue a course that might well result in an acquittal.

The object of all the effort I had expended through the years was to have the authorities declare the trial constitutionally unfair, not the honor of arguing a case before the United States Supreme Court early in my career. I told the young lawyer his view placed personal aggrandizement before the welfare of the client, an impermissible position for a lawyer to take.

30

The Opposition Continues, Spite Is Thwarted, and *The Rape Case* Ends (The Third, Fourth, and Final Victories)

Although Attorney General Craven dearly wanted to serve another term, the Democratic Party denied him even the nomination as its incumbent candidate after a floor fight at its 1958 convention. Craven had offended so many people while in office there was little support for him among the delegates. The party turned to Michael A. Poppiti whose candidacy started with a rumor Albert J. Stiftel put abroad one day at the United Cigar Store at Tenth and Market Streets in Wilmington. Albert was fond of starting rumors just to see how far they would travel. Poppiti, in turn, lost to his University of Delaware classmate, Januar D. Bove, in the November 1958 election.[1]

On November 5, the day after his election as attorney general, Bove sought me out to tell me, or more accurately, to ask me whether I agreed with him *The Rape Case* could not be retried as a practical matter. I concurred. He then suggested we issue a joint statement so the public would know why the case was not being retried. I told him I would wait until I read whatever he suggested as the joint public statement. I did not tell him, so far as I was concerned, any such statement would have to include his opinion that he did not think he could prove my clients were guilty (the reason he was not going forward to trial), since if he thought otherwise he had the duty to bring them to trial. Moreover, the statement would have to reflect the current status of the matter: Curran, Jones, and Maguire were free because the state had not convicted them at a valid trial. We discussed Craven's promise back on October 1 to file a petition for certiorari to the United States Supreme Court. Although Craven still held the post of attorney general, he had not yet filed.[2] Despite Bove's talk about a joint statement, he told me he thought Craven was correct in proceeding to seek certiorari. Accordingly, he would continue seeking review until the Supreme Court acted. Bove also said he thought the likelihood of the Supreme Court granting certiorari was remote.

As I had throughout the case, I reported my conversation with Bove to our investigator, George Corbeil. By this time George was living in Schenectady, New York, with a daughter who needed his help. In the same letter, I told George about our clients: "Everything seems to be going well with the boys to the extent that they are all working. The novelty of being out I dare say is slowly wearing off. I consider this all to the good." I also kept George posted on my little family: "We are daily expecting a third addition to the family so I stay pretty close to home. Let's have you down here soon."[3] Karen Lisa was born on December 10, 1958, joining her older sister, Deborah Lynne, then five, and her older brother, Jonathan Abraham, then a little past two but with only four and a half more years to live.

On December 29, 1958, the eve of his departure from office, Attorney General Craven, assisted by Deputy Attorney General Richard J. Baker, finally filed the petition for certiorari. Since my clients lacked funds, I moved to proceed in forma pauperis to avoid the expense of printing our brief as the Supreme Court rules required. I prepared and filed a ten-page, typewritten brief in opposition to the granting of the state's petition. As much as I had hoped I could overcome the unlikelihood of the United States Supreme Court's granting my petition for the issuance of a writ of certiorari in 1956, I now hoped the Supreme Court would deny the state's application.

The state was no more successful in convincing the Supreme Court to review *The Rape Case* than I had been some two and one-half years earlier. By a collect Western Union Telegram on January 26, 1959 (cost $1.16), from James R. Browning, Clerk of the Supreme Court, to me, I learned: "Petition for certiorari Delaware against Curran denied today. Letter follows." The Supreme Court did not issue an opinion. Its action is reflected in its official reports:

No. 611. *Delaware v. Curran et al.*

The motion of respondents for leave to proceed *in forma pauperis* is granted. Petition for writ of certiorari to the United States Court of Appeals for the Third Circuit denied. *Joseph Donald Craven,* Attorney General of Delaware and *Richard J. Baker,* Deputy Attorney General, for petitioner. *Irving Morris* for respondents. Reported below: 259 F.2d 707.[4]

Although I had anticipated the denial, it was still a relief when the Supreme Court turned my hope into reality.

When Bove took control of the attorney general's office on January 2, 1959, he placed Chief Deputy Attorney General Clement C. Wood in charge of prosecuting *The Rape Case.*[5] After the Supreme Court had acted, the Third Circuit on January 30, 1959, formally notified the District Court of its September 29, 1958 order affirming Chief Judge Wright's decision concluding the writ of habeas corpus should issue.[6]

Bove and Wood now had to decide whether to bring Curran,

Jones, and Maguire to trial again on the charge of rape. Not having heard anything from Bove since our November 5 conversation about a joint statement, I decided to call him. After all, the only condition he had talked about was his need to await the United States Supreme Court's resolution of Attorney General Craven's then expected petition for certiorari. When I spoke to Bove on February 3, 1959, he told me he was "having Clem [Wood] study the record. In a week I'll let you know what I am going to do."

Even before Bove and Wood started to weigh what they should do, I had immersed myself sufficiently in the facts to believe if the state renewed its effort to retry Curran, Jones, and Maguire, I could win an acquittal. With their credibility restored, there was no reason to disbelieve the men's claim of innocence. If a new jury believed them, it would have to find that the woman had consented to what took place in Woodlawn Park. Moreover, I thought I could mount a good defense on the basis that there had been no penetration of the woman by the defendants. Without proof of penetration, the state could not prove rape. At best the state could claim assault, but assault, even if the state were to prove it, did not carry the death penalty. I had to keep well in mind, of course, the saying among lawyers, "litigation is chancy." There is no certainty once you go to trial. Fortunately, I never had to test either my belief in my theories or my prowess as an advocate.

Bove never called. He never spoke to me again about a joint press release. It was Wood who told me of the state's decision not to go forward with another trial. He too said nothing about a joint press release. All he wanted was my clients to appear in open court, first in the District Court and then in the Superior Court on the date he intended to announce the state's decision not to retry them. He could have entered a nolle prosequi, the decision not to prosecute, by so telling the courts at any time without requiring my clients' presence, a common practice. But Bove and Wood had something else in mind.

The terms of my clients' release on bail provided that they would reappear when the District Court summoned them. Accordingly, I brought Curran, Jones, and Maguire with me on February 25, 1959, the day Wood had arranged with the District Court for them to come before Chief Judge Wright, the same judge who had granted the habeas corpus petition in August 1957. Their appearing satisfied the conditions of their October 9, 1958 bonds. Wood was there as well. Given the state's decision not to retry my clients, I thought he would limit his participation to confirming my report of the decision to Wright, but Wood had his own agenda.

With my clients beside me, I told Wright the state was dropping the charges against them, a fact Wood confirmed. Thereupon Wood, without any advance notice, moved that Wright order the United States Marshal to handcuff Curran, Jones, and Maguire for the short walk from the second floor of the Federal Building at the north side of Rodney Square to Superior Court Courtroom No. 1 on the third floor of the Public Building on the east side of Rodney Square. The two buildings stood cater-corner from each other at Eleventh and King. To have my clients in manacles as they walked across the street just to hear Wood tell the Superior Court the state did not desire to retry them was a circumstance that hardly comported with an attempt to flee, the only justification to place them in handcuffs. After all, they had been free on bail for almost five months and had not fled the jurisdiction. Moreover, they had come forward immediately and appeared when the District Court commanded them.

Whether the handcuffs were Bove's idea or Wood's I do not know. The real purpose for placing them on the three men was the obvious desire to humiliate them by providing a photo opportunity for the press and thus lend credence to the claim Bove and Wood clearly intended to make, that the state had fought to the bitter end. Instead of applauding the federal courts for up-holding the constitutional mandate of a fair trial, the real mean-ing of the case as a legal matter, the prosecuting authorities of Delaware in the persons of Bove and Wood, themselves sworn to uphold the Constitution's guarantee of a fair trial, preferred to regard Curran, Jones, and Maguire as convicted felons and to use them to promote Bove and Wood. Chief Judge Wright listened to Wood and immediately refused the inappropriate, spiteful re-quest. Wright then entered the order providing Curran, Jones, and Maguire "are unconditionally released from the State Board of Corrections of the State of Delaware" and ended the session.[7]

With Chief Judge Wright's order in my hand, I walked with my clients and members of their families to the Superior Court. We took the elevators to the third floor, to the same courtroom where the trial had taken place. Presiding on February 25, 1959, a date only one week past the eleventh anniversary of the end of the trial, was Judge James B. Carey, one of the three judges who had sat at the February 1948 trial. Apart from court personnel, family members, and the press, there were few spectators in the cavernous courtroom. Although he had joined in the conclusion of President Judge Charles S. Richards' denial of relief in October 1955, Carey in his concurring opinion had been the first judge to find and declare Detective Rodenhiser had not told the truth at trial.[8]

Chief Deputy Attorney General Wood spoke first:

May it please the Court: Your Honor is referred to the cases of Fran-cis J. Curran, Francis J. Maguire and Ira F. Jones presently pending in this Court. These cases were tried eleven years ago. The defendants were convicted and had served eleven years of their sentence until a few months ago when the Federal Courts decided that they were entitled to a new trial. The State fought the efforts of these defendants for new trials through the State courts successfully, but through the Federal courts and to the Supreme Court unsuccessfully.

The passage of time has detrimentally affected the State's case in many ways. Many of the State's witnesses are dead; the recollection of others has unquestionably been dimmed. These and other difficulties, while not insurmountable, militate against a conviction if these cases are retried. Above and beyond this, however, is the fact that the prosecuting witness does not wish nor does she feel physically able to go through another trial. The family, out of regard for her, is opposed to further proceedings in these cases.

In view of all of these circumstances, I do not feel that the prosecuting witness should be forced to subject herself to the ordeal of a retrial of these cases.

The State enters a nolle prosequi in the cases of Francis J. Curran, Francis J. Maguire and Ira F. Jones. The number is 15, January Term, 1948.[9]

Wood's statement underscored the animus held by the people who had participated in the prosecution of my clients and opposed their release, even after the evidence I had adduced proved the police perjury at the trial. Wood did not express one word about how the now-established violation of their rights entitled Curran, Jones, and Maguire to a fair trial in the courts of Delaware. When Wood went on to talk about the reasons causing the state to decide not to retry them, he did not once pause to praise our system, which at last had provided relief from the unjust convictions and confinement. His claim that "[t]he passage of time has detrimentally affected the State's case" was disingenuous; the same passage of time had similarly affected my clients' case. He referred to the "many" deceased witnesses without identifying who had died. Surely Patrolman James Nagle would not have helped the state's case had he lived since Nagle, before committing suicide, told Father Francis X. Burns he had retyped two and perhaps all of the statements and had participated in perjury at the trial. Dr. Paul R. Smith, the Police Department's medical authority at trial, had died, but his trial testimony had favored the defendants. It was the personal physician for the family of the woman who gave detrimental testimony, not Dr. Smith. Wood did not accompany his reference to "other difficulties" with a description of what they were.

Wood's claim for the state "that the prosecuting witness does not wish nor does she feel physically able to go through another trial" seldom is an impediment to prosecution. Finally, Wood's personal "feeling" that the prosecuting witness should not be "forced to subject herself to the ordeal of a re-trial" is of questionable moment in guiding the judgment of a prosecutor sworn to enforce the law in the interest of all citizens.

As soon as Wood concluded, I stood and said:

May it please the Court, I represent Francis J. Curran, Francis J. Maguire and Ira F. Jones, Jr. The defendants do not object and, indeed, they have no power to object, to the entry of the *nolle prosequi* in this case by the State at this time. Since the State by the office of the Attorney General has made a brief statement concerning its action here today, I should like to have noted upon the record the position of my clients. Curran, Maguire and Jones were arrested on October 30, 1947 and charged with the crime of rape. They denied the charge and protested their innocence. They were indicted by the Grand Jury of this County and in answer to the indictments, they pled not guilty. In February, 1948, they were tried. Throughout the trial they asserted and maintained their innocence. They were convicted by a jury and sentenced by this Court each to a term of life imprisonment. They were confined in the New Castle County Workhouse where they remained for 11 years less 20 days. They continued to assert and maintain that they were innocent of the charges brought against them.

I then summarized their time in prison, concluding: "It has now been established that their trial was unfair and violative of their constitutional rights and their convictions have been set aside." I went on to say:

By the action of the State today, Curran, Maguire and Jones are free men in the fullest sense of the term, free to resume their lives as law abiding citizens. By the State's action, Curran, Maguire and Jones do not have to face again the frightful ordeal of a trial on these serious charges. For that reason alone they welcome the action of the State today. So that there may be no misunderstanding about their position, they say again this time through me as their present attorney that they were and are innocent of the charges brought against them.

Finally, in the last sentence of my statement, I spoke of the teaching of *The Rape Case*: " . . .that our institutions and government are sufficiently strong to accord to the most humble of our citizens that priceless gift of a free society, a fair trial, to the end that right be done."[10]

While I spoke, I had the impression Judge Carey was impatient, although he did not interrupt me. I do not think he favored my saying anything. Since he had permitted Wood to have his say, his sense of fairness, a hallmark of his judging, compelled him to let me speak at length. I chose my closing words "that right be done" because they are the final words of the writ of habeas corpus. I do not think many in the courtroom knew enough about the Great Writ to know the significance of those four words.

Immediately after I finished, Judge Carey uttered the final formal words in the litigation almost eleven and a half years after it had commenced and six years and two months since I had embarked on the effort to erase the convictions: "Let the *nolle prosequi* be entered." *The Rape Case* was over.

31

The Flawed Editorial

etween the arrest of Curran, Jones, and Maguire on October 30, 1947, and their conviction on February 17, 1948, the *Morning News* and the *Journal* published numerous articles about *The Rape Case*. Not a single one was favorable to Curran, Jones, and Maguire. The letters to the editors of both newspapers were almost without exception damning of all three. If adverse newspaper notoriety could convict, they had no chance of an acquittal at trial. Neither the newspapers' editorial writers nor the published letters addressed the presumption of innocence cloaking every defendant in a criminal proceeding. The police perjury causing the unfairness at the trial itself did not take place until the trial. The trial court, the jurors, and the public never learned of the proof of the police perjury until years later when my colleagues and I established it at a time when the accused were well into their sentences.

At the time of *The Rape Case* trial, The DuPont Company through the News Journal Company owned both papers. In those days, almost everyone in Delaware read either one or the other. Although both papers came off the same press in the same building on Orange Street between 8th and 9th, prior to the January 3, 1989 merger under the name *The News Journal,* each maintained its own news and editorial staff and policy. The relationship between the two was one of keen competition.[1]

The *Morning News* article on February 26, 1959, reporting the end of *The Rape Case* was balanced.[2] Reporter Tom Malone quoted liberally and fairly from what Wood and I had said in open court. Given the competition, it was not surprising when the *Journal* that night took a different tack. The *Journal's* unsigned news article quoted Wood's explanation for the state's dismissal of *The Rape Case* but completely ignored what I had said.[3] In addition, the *Journal,* the state's largest newspaper, published its lead editorial that night on the outcome of *The Rape Case.* The editorial was far worse than the abbreviated news story. Under the title, "Substantial Justice Served," the editorial read:

One of Delaware's most famous criminal cases has been wound up for good and all with the decision of the Attorney General's Office not to ask for a new trial for Francis J. Curran, Francis J. Maguire, and Ira F. Jones, Jr., on a charge of rape. No one can conceivably question the wisdom of that decision, regardless of the guilt or innocence of the three men.

It would be cruel and inhuman to drag the girl involved through old and half-forgotten horrors by asking her to go through the ordeal of another trial. And aside from this, the passage of the years, as Chief Deputy Atty. Gen. Clement C. Wood reminds us, has detrimentally affected the state's case. Many of the state's witnesses are now dead and the memory of others has unquestionably been dimmed.

It also seems likely that the ends of justice have substantially been served. The men affected have spent 11 years in jail; in a few years more they would have been eligible for parole. The safety of society is not at stake; it is most improbable that any one of them will repeat the kind of crime for which they were imprisoned.

But even if this is so, it is still possible to raise the question whether the federal courts are wise to overturn verdicts in the state courts for relatively insubstantial cause. In this case three judges of the State Supreme Court, after an exhaustive study of the trial record, agreed that the errors in the trial—and no trial is entirely free of error—were not sufficient to have denied the defendants their right to a fair trial. The federal courts have disagreed, as is their right. But we think that this is a right to be used sparingly. Defendants must be given the full protection of the Constitution but it will also serve the ends of justice ill if verdicts are set aside repeatedly for errors which cannot have seriously influenced the jury.[4]

In accepting and adopting the state's position not to retry my clients, the *Journal's* editorial also resurrected Chief Justice Southerland's erroneous view that my argument that the police perjury discredited the defendants' testimony and resulted in their convictions was "an attempt—natural enough—to magnify unduly an incident that could have wrought no serious harm to the defendants."[5] The editorial, as had Wood, said a retrial would place an unfair burden upon the woman by subjecting her to testifying, yet ignored the same burden on the defendants.

The *Journal's* editorial said nothing about the violation of Curran, Jones, and Maguire's civil rights. With smug satisfaction, it noted they had spent almost eleven years in jail and concluded "[i]t also seems likely that the ends of justice have substantially been served." Thus, the editorial continued to assume the guilt of the accused, ignoring the constitutional violation of their right to a fair trial, a right that disappeared once the police perjury came into and remained in evidence unrepudiated by the police. By failing to understand that the 1948 jury concluded the accused and the three eyewitnesses were liars, the editorial sided with Duffy's summation to the jury when he claimed the eyewitnesses were not even there.[6]

The editorial's fundamental error was ignoring the critical importance of our society's dependence upon the fairness of our judicial proceedings, the essential element of due process. We all lose once the state violates the constitutional rights of one citizen and the violation remains either publicly undiscovered or deliberately or even inadvertently suppressed. Yet neither the state before Judge Carey on February 25, 1959, when the nolle prosequi was entered, nor the *Journal* editorial on February 26, 1959, said a word about the real significance of the proceedings and the holdings of the federal courts in setting aside my clients' convictions because the state violated their constitutional right to a fair trial.

I thought whoever had written the editorial had failed to read Chief Judge Wright's District Court opinion or Chief Judge Biggs' opinion for the unanimous decision of the Third Circuit or, assuredly, what I had said in open court before Judge Carey at the final Superior Court session.[7] Moreover, the editorial writer had ignored, assuming he had even read, Tom Malone's even-handed news article that morning. Had the *Journal's* news story referred to what I had said in the Superior Court, its editorial would not have made sense. Attorney General Bove and Chief Deputy Attorney General Wood ignored the civil rights issue in explaining their decision to abandon the prosecution. The omission was disgraceful. For the supposedly disinterested press to fail to seize the opportunity to teach the public the importance of a fair trial in our system of justice was even more disgraceful.

After I read the editorial I wrote a long reply and then tore it up. I did not think I could change the minds of those responsible for the flawed editorial. I did think I ran the risk the editors would pick something from my letter out of context and publish snide remarks in response. Since the editors published daily, I could not afford the time to embark on a letter-writing campaign to correct the record. George Corbeil's outrage about the editorial led him to write an even longer letter. With my encouragement, he, too, decided not to send it.

With their convictions finally behind them, my clients were

free to resume their lives as best they could, formally relieved of their convictions but without any realistic possibility of escaping the fact each had spent twenty days shy of eleven years in the state's custody for a crime the state had not proved at a fair trial. What they never would or could overcome was how the bitter experience their long incarceration affected them and their families.

32

Praise

Although foreshadowed by Chief Judge Wright's opinion in the District Court and the Third Circuit's affirmance, the freeing of Curran, Jones, and Maguire still startled the public, as well as most of the legal community.[1] A number of my colleagues congratulated me. In the coffee shop of the United Cigar Store, Len Hagner led the other regulars in heaping praise upon me for my sustained effort now crowned with success. When I chanced upon Dave Reinhardt at the Workhouse, he too complimented me. Hy Young said nothing.

Dear, devoted teachers at the University of Delaware, Dr. Evelyn H. Clift and Dr. John A. Munroe, wrote personal notes of congratulation and approval. Dr. Clift wrote, you "have done a heroic job and I feel proud to be able to say 'he was a student of mine,' as everyone who can claim some acquaintance with you must also feel. Mother and Dad especially asked me to include their congratulations too."[2] John Munroe, soon to become the Dean of Delaware historians, congratulated me "on winning the long case we've talked about."[3]

Since I was quite full of myself, having achieved what most thought impossible or, at least, highly unlikely, I replied as modestly as I could to Eve Clift: "The outcome of the case was, of course, a wonderful thing for the boys and me, and it was good to hear from you with your words of praise. Please thank your parents for me for their congratulations also."[4]

To John Munroe I wrote: "I thank you for your note of March 4 about the Curran case. The experience of such a case is a very rewarding one for a lawyer. It becomes all the more rewarding when friends take the trouble to note the outcome." I closed with warmest personal regards to him, Dorothy, and the children.[5]

Even before the formal end of *The Rape Case,* my friend from law school, Jay H. Topkis, sent a congratulatory letter, my first fan letter: "I see by the papers that you won your rape case. It is the kind of victory that must make you feel proud to be a lawyer—and deservedly so."[6] My response was hardly self-effacing. I thanked Jay for his note and admitted, "Receiving fan mail is an altogether novel experience for me and somewhat heady. Needless to say, I am quite pleased with the present result as are my clients and it is, of course, always pleasing for a lawyer to have a satisfied client." I told him I was still waiting to hear from the new attorney general about the possibility of a trial. I included with my letter a copy of the complimentary article Bill Frank wrote at the time my clients were released on bail, telling Jay: "I've often used the alias of 'Bill Frank'."[7]

On February 26, 1959, I reported our success to Mr. Maris, the first lawyer to recognize the merit of their cause and to hold out hope of eventual release to Curran, Jones, and Maguire and their families:

I am enclosing herewith a verifax copy of the order of Chief Judge Wright of our District Court entered on February 25, 1959, over the objection of the Chief Deputy Attorney General (the State has never agreed to anything I wanted to do in this case, so therefore the objection even at the tail end seems appropriate) and a verifax copy of the transcript of the proceedings in our Superior Court before Judge Carey, at which time on February 25, the State entered a *nolle prosequi* which spells the end of the case. The boys were present both in the District Court and in the State Court.

Sincerely,[8]

Mr. Maris acknowledged receipt of my letter and the papers I included, commenting:

There are doubtless some happy young men (and their families) in Wilmington today. I am grateful for their sakes for the outcome of your fight but even more grateful that we found in Delaware a young attorney who had the courage and the brains to carry on a contest against the Courts and the Attorney General when he was, himself, convinced in the justice of his cause.

Our hats are off to you Irv Morris[9]

Months before I wrote to Mr. Maris, unbeknownst to me, Mr. Maris had written to Nellie Curran, in reply to her note thanking him and praising him when her son was released on bail in October 1958: "I do appreciate your kindly words for the part I played in the boys' case but the real credit goes to Irving Morris and I salute him not only for his legal ability and his untiring strength but as well, as a champion for justice."[10]

The praise I most treasured from lawyers knowledgeable about the Delaware legal scene came from William Prickett Sr. I had tried several cases against him, learning from him on each occasion. I had first met Prickett when as a high school student I ran errands for Philip Cohen. The two crossed swords in *Jones v. Bodley* and *Reid v. Baker*, Prickett's two most stinging defeats in his judgment.[11] Although his personality grated upon many, he had the grudging respect of every lawyer who opposed him. He trained a number of young lawyers who, upon departing his firm, established themselves as able practitioners in their own right. Jackson Raysor, Vincent A. Theisen, F. Alton Tybout, Robert Walls, Newton White, and, of course, his son and my contemporary, William Prickett Jr., among others—all had the benefit of Prickett's tutelage.

Upon the conclusion of *The Rape Case,* Prickett called and asked me to visit him. As I sat across his desk from him, he told me he had asked to see me so he could tell me personally what I had done for my clients in *The Rape Case* was "the most outstanding lawyering" he had ever witnessed in his entire time at the bar. Prickett's words were high praise. After all, he had known and seen in practice all the great Delaware trial lawyers during the time our careers overlapped: Aaron Finger, Clarence A. Southerland, Robert H. Richards Sr., Hugh M. Morris, E. Ennalls Berl, Paul Leahy, William S. Potter, H. Albert Young, Edwin D. Steel, Everett Warrington, Joseph H. Flanzer, James M. Tunnell Jr., Henry M. Canby, Richard F. Corroon, David Coxe Jr., and Edmund N. Carpenter, II.

I was on *cloud nine.*

33

Suing For Damages

S hortly after the release of Curran, Jones, and Maguire on bail, I called them to my office one evening to discuss payment of a fee for my services. Their families voluntarily had paid me a few dollars through the years. I knew that neither the three men nor their families could pay a reasonable fee for my work on their behalf. Despite this, I asked them whether they thought I was entitled to a fee. Each said he thought I was. I told them I had considered the matter and had concluded each of them should pay me $1,000 for my work, with the money to come from their own earnings and not from their families. Moreover, I told them, they only had to pay provided they did not need the money to meet their living expenses. I placed no time limit on payment of the amount each readily agreed was fair. Thereafter, Curran, the first to do so, paid me a total of $225 but nothing further. Jones made one payment of $25 and stopped. Maguire never paid anything. Even though my clients paid little, I know I have earned far beyond what I ever imagined I might receive from successfully representing them.

In *The Rape Case,* I persisted for six years at what seemed an impossible task to almost everyone I knew. Judge Leahy was an exception; from the start he thought I was right. My mentor and partner, Philip Cohen, never uttered a word of disapproval. My success in setting aside the convictions and righting the wrong of an unfair trial was a singular achievement for a young lawyer. Although I cannot equate with any precision the financial reward of any particular case with the reputation I acquired by defending Curran, Jones, and Maguire, my perseverance had to have impressed the local lawyers with whom I came to do most of my work and who concluded unless they could reach an accommodation with me, I would persevere in any cause I undertook without regard to the amount of compensation, the quantity of work, or the amount of time it took. I like to think I had acquired the reputation of a competent, creative, and tenacious lawyer. Thus, I believe, the good fortune I have enjoyed in the practice of law stems directly from my undertaking the representation of Curran, Jones, and Maguire.

With our clients' release, George Corbeil raised the possibility of an action for damages for what Delaware and certain Wilmington police officers had done to the men. Nellie Curran told me George had also spoken to Sammy Thompson about such an action. George said Sammy had some knowledge of the subject and, moreover, worked with a lawyer who had "made a specialty in this field." Accordingly, I did some preliminary research and then wrote to Sammy.[1]

At first blush, I did not think there was any basis in Delaware law that would permit my clients to sue the state to recover damages for their almost eleven years of unlawful imprisonment. The likelihood of the Delaware General Assembly enacting such legislation was almost nonexistent. I checked federal law providing for a civil action for deprivation of rights.[2] I thought the Civil Rights Act might warrant a suit in our District Court against the police officers whose lies had denied my clients a fair trial. Examination of Title 42, United States Code, Section 1983, Note 116, satisfied me the Civil Rights Act did not confine the right to sue to persons of color, the context for the original legislation. Moreover, I found one case holding that "immunity of state officials under state law from tort liability arising by performance of official duties does not extend to a claim asserted under [Section 1983]."[3] Thus, state officials were subject to suit; we could sue the Wilmington policemen under federal law without securing Delaware's prior permission.

In my letter to Sammy Thompson, I raised my main concern: the statute of limitations.[4] The denial of a fair trial occurred in February 1948, but no court recognized the unfairness until Chief Judge Wright did so in August 1957. The state never accepted the ruling. Only after the United States Supreme Court in January 1959 denied the state's petition for certiorari and the state confronted the need to retry Curran, Jones, and Maguire and secure a conviction to keep them in jail, did the state abandon prosecution. Several cases under Section 1983 made clear the applicable state statutes of limitations controlled actions under Section 1983. The Delaware statute for a tort action resulting in personal injuries was one year, and I could not find any provision in the Delaware statute extending the time.[5] A federal case in Massachusetts seemed to hold the statute of limitations might not begin to run until the plaintiff was released from prison.[6] Since Curran, Jones, and Maguire did not secure their release until October 1958, they had to act promptly if they were going to do anything. I shared my thinking with Sammy, invited a response, and waited.

I also wrote to George Corbeil and enclosed a copy of my April 16, 1959 letter to Sammy.[7] George replied telling me he had urged Sammy to respond.[8] In the meantime, I prepared a proposed bill for introduction in the state House of Representatives. It was not complicated. It provided for the State of Delaware to waive its sovereign immunity "for the sole and exclusive purpose of permitting a suit in tort against the State of Delaware by Francis J. Curran, Francis J. Maguire and Ira F. Jones, Jr., or any of them, on any cause of action against the State of Delaware arising out of their imprisonment as a result of an unfair trial violative of their constitutional rights in February, 1948."[9]

After discussing the likelihood of its passage with Senator John Riley and Representative Paul Shockley, I delayed having the bill introduced since, based upon what the legislators had said, I doubted it would pass. I wanted to avoid defeat. I so reported to Corbeil and enclosed a copy of the bill.[10] Meanwhile, I continued to wait for a response from Sammy Thompson. Even before Corbeil received my letter, Nellie Curran called him to complain Sammy had neglected to reply to me and had also ignored a telephone call she had made to Mr. Maris requesting Sammy to call her. (George later suggested Mr. Maris might not have passed the message along; "sometimes Maris forgets these days," George explained to me in a letter.)[11]

In August, 1959, Sammy finally wrote a lengthy response to my April request for help. He described two cases in which he had been involved with Joseph G. Feldman, a Philadelphia lawyer. The first, *Shuler v. The Evening Bulletin,* was a suit against a newspaper for false headlines calling Shuler a "cop killer" and "ex-convict." The headlines were false, Sammy wrote, "since *at law* he was proved not guilty of the Morrow (a police officer) murder even though he had served 12 years on his own alleged confession. Accordingly, at law Shuler had never been 'convicted' of any offense." The jury awarded $500. Unlike *Shuler,* the substance of *The Rape Case* articles was impervious to attack. From his and my reading of the press articles neither of us thought a case against the Wilmington papers would succeed. Sammy, moreover, did not find merit in a suit against the State of Delaware. The fact the state had entered a nolle prosequi did not establish innocence.

Nor did my clients' claim fit *Clancy v. Upper Darby National Bank,* the second case. Clancy, after over four years of imprisonment on a five to fifteen year sentence, proved his innocence when the police apprehended the actual culprit who had committed bank fraud by stealing checks, counterendorsing them, and depositing them in a personal savings account. The bank served as a private prosecutor. Prior to trial, the bank had in hand a detailed report establishing that Clancy had not signed the various documents. He was convicted on identification alone. Had the bank not withheld its handwriting report, Clancy would not have been convicted. Clancy's case was scheduled for trial in late September 1959. Sammy concluded: "Neither of these fit the Curran case shoes."[12]

Sammy, moreover, did not think Delaware would vote a grant of money to our clients as moral compensation for their wrongful imprisonment. He referred to several instances of failed legislation in Pennsylvania designed to provide money to persons unfairly convicted. Finally, Sammy turned to the practicality of a suit against the policemen. He did not "see any eventual material success." He thought the families should "bring some form of action against each and every one possible who were in any measure responsible for the grave wrong done" to make the conduct accountable "and so set a lesson for others in the future, that you can't get away with pulling any sort of a thing as this without being called to account and punished in the manner it hurts their kind the most—in the pocketbook!" But he prefaced his urging by recognizing the families could not afford to do so.[13] I concluded, since Rodenhiser and the other policemen had no assets making such litigation worthwhile, there was no point in initiating it. In reaching this conclusion, I failed to consider, let alone check for, any insurance covering policemen that might have provided a deep pocket from which my clients could hope to recover funds to compensate them for their lost years.

On August 20, 1959, I sent a copy of Sammy's letter to each of my clients, expressed my agreement with his conclusions but urged them to secure another opinion, assuring them of my co-operation should they elect to pursue a claim. I also urged they act promptly because of "the Statute of Limitations which, in any event, in my opinion, would run on or before October 8, 1959, which is the day prior to the anniversary date of your release from the Workhouse on October 9, 1958."[14]

Since the only purpose of any further litigation would have been to recover money, the likelihood of being successful in a suit against the *Journal,* the only deep pocket in a libel action in a practical sense, seemed remote. My clients could not prove actual damages, such as loss of income because of the content of the articles and editorial the paper had published, but would have had to rely upon general damages. The paper would have been able to point to the opinions of the District Court and the Circuit Court which did not conclude my clients were innocent even as they found the trial unfair. I did not want to tarnish the victory my colleagues and I had secured for our clients by being unsuccessful in a lawsuit seeking to recover money for them. If I could have figured out a way to achieve a favorable, guaranteed result, I would not have hesitated. But that was not the case.

In the end, Curran, Jones, and Maguire did not press a claim for damages. They were never compensated for the almost eleven years of imprisonment or for the destruction of the normal lives they otherwise would have led.[15] Just as they had never been in trouble with the law before their arrest, so they were never in trouble with the law after their release.

34

VINDICATED!

On August 21, 1938, four men, Townsend, Wamer, Poe, and Napue, entered a dimly lit cocktail lounge in Chicago, Illinois, with the intention of robbing its patrons. An off-duty policeman, a patron in the lounge, drew his service revolver and fired at them. He killed Townsend and seriously wounded Wamer. Return fire killed the officer. Napue and Poe carried Wamer to the getaway car driven by a fifth man, Webb. Upon Wamer's arrest, Illinois tried him for murder of the policeman, convicted him on his plea of guilty, and sentenced him to 199 years. When the state apprehended Poe, it tried, convicted, sentenced him to death, and executed him. Wamer was not a witness at Poe's trial.

Subsequently the state arrested, tried, and convicted Napue. The assistant state's attorney who had prosecuted Wamer needed Wamer's testimony because time had passed, dimming the recollection of witnesses still available to identify people in the darkened lounge. To induce Wamer's critical testimony, the assistant state's attorney promised him if he would testify against Napue, "a recommendation for a reduction of his sentence would be made and, if possible, effectuated."[1] At Napue's trial, Wamer denied that anyone "promised me anything" for testifying.[2] Napue was convicted and sentenced to 199 years. Wamer also testified against Webb when the state apprehended and tried him. Webb, too, was convicted and sentenced to 199 years.

After Webb's conviction, the former assistant state's attorney who had prosecuted Wamer, Poe, and Napue filed a petition on Wamer's behalf, seeking a reduction in his sentence, thus following through on his promise, a promise he freely admitted in his petition. When Napue learned of Wamer's petition, Napue filed his own. He relied on Wamer's false testimony at Napue's trial denying the fact he had been promised consideration for his testimony. Napue further relied on the assistant state's attorney's admission that he had known Wamer's testimony was false. After the Illinois courts denied relief to Napue, the United States Supreme Court granted Napue's petition for review.[3]

On June 15, 1959, less than four months after Chief Deputy Wood told the Superior Court Delaware would no longer prosecute Curran, Jones, and Maguire, the United States Supreme Court decided *Napue v. Illinois*.[4] In a unanimous opinion, Chief Justice Earl Warren wrote: "*First*, it is established that a conviction obtained through use of false evidence, known to be such by representatives of the State, must fall under the Fourteenth Amendment, *Mooney v. Holohan*, 294 U.S. 103; *Pyle v. Kansas*, 317 U.S. 213; *Curran v. Delaware*, 259 F.2d 707."[5]

Of the three cited cases, *Mooney* clearly involved a case where the prosecuting attorneys knew of the perjury. About *Pyle v. Kansas*, as noted in Chapter 27, the Kansas Supreme Court subsequently held the prosecuting attorney must know of the perjury to set aside a conviction.[6] As the author of the *Duke Law Journal* note wrote: "Thus, if Pyle v. Kansas had extended the rule [to include perjury by a policeman unknown to the prosecuting attorney] it went unnoticed by the very court directly affected by it."[7] In *Napue* itself, Wamer's lies at Napue's trial were known to the prosecuting attorney bringing the case within the holding of *Mooney*. Relying upon *Mooney* alone, the Supreme

Court could have granted relief to Napue. By citing to *Curran*, so it seemed to me, the Supreme Court had extended *Mooney* to vitiate a conviction where the perjury was known to policemen but unknown to the prosecuting attorneys and had adopted my argument that perjury by policemen, "representatives of the state," does not comport with due process under the Fourteenth Amendment. Only *Curran v. Delaware, The Rape Case,* where policemen committed perjury ostensibly unknown to the prosecuting attorneys, clearly supports the Supreme Court's extension of *Mooney.*

In *The Rape Case,* I had argued the police perjury impacted my clients' credibility, an issue *Napue* specifically addressed:

The principle that a State may not knowingly use false evidence, including false testimony, to obtain a tainted conviction, implicit in any concept of ordered liberty, does not cease to apply merely because the false testimony goes only to the credibility of the witness. The jury's estimate of the truthfulness and reliability of a given witness may well be determinative of guilt or innocence, and it is upon such subtle factors as the possible interest of the witness in testifying falsely that a defendant's life or liberty may depend.[8]

Although the Supreme Court did not cite his opinion in *The Rape Case,* Chief Judge Wright's words anticipated not only the Third Circuit's opinion but also the holding and the thrust of the Supreme Court's language in *Napue* on the issue of the effect of false testimony upon credibility.[9] More important than who *Napue* cited as between Wright and Biggs was the fact *Napue* relied upon *Curran, The Rape Case,* in support of its holding. The language of Chief Judge Wright and Chief Judge Biggs in their respective opinions and, finally, the language of Chief Justice Warren for a unanimous United States Supreme Court in *Napue* vindicated what I had argued in *The Rape Case.* Moreover, it answered the cheap shot Chief Justice Southerland took at me in the Delaware Supreme Court when, in denying substantive relief to Curran, Jones, and Maguire, he wrote for himself and his colleagues in the unanimous opinion: "*Counsel's argument on this point is an attempt—natural enough—to magnify unduly an incident that could have wrought no serious harm to the defendants.*" [Emphasis added.][10]

Being the successful lawyer in a case the United States Supreme Court relied upon in establishing new law was an unexpected and welcome accolade. It justified my hard work to undo the unfairness of my clients' trial. As pleased as I was, surely the *Duke Law Journal,* its Board of Editors and its faculty adviser, Mel Shimm, took as much delight as I did in reading *Napue.* When the courts set aside my clients' convictions and sentences, it was a precious victory. But *Napue* did something more: the highest court in our land unanimously confirmed my innate sense of what was fair and my professional decision to persevere until the law recognized what I knew was right from the outset.

35

Bud Curran's Death

On Thursday, March 26, 1992, I arrived at my office later than usual but still an hour or so before the expected arrival of Robert I. Harwood of New York. We planned to work on drafting an amended complaint in the Community Psychiatric Centers litigation we had filed together in California. As I walked past our receptionist, Lee Monroe, she told me that Kitty Curran was calling. I continued walking toward our conference room (I had so cluttered my own office it was impossible to work there, a frequent occurrence; I preferred the large table in the conference room anyway), when I heard Lee say, "She said you would know her by the name Kitty Curran." For the moment, I could not recall that I knew any "Kitty Curran." Then it registered: Kitty was one of Bud Curran's sisters, who with their parents had surrounded their brother with so much love and affection during his time in prison. I told Lee to put the call through to me in the conference room.

For a few minutes, Kitty and I exchanged words of delight in talking to each other after so many years. She told me that she had moved away from Wilmington but had returned a few years ago. She had a daughter who was a lawyer, a son who was a dentist, and her youngest, a daughter, was working as a banker with an income of over $50,000 a year. When I asked her about her brother, she shared with me the sadness of his illness. He was in the Christiana Medical Center recovering from a heart attack. Earlier, he lost a foot to diabetes. She went on to say Bud experienced periods of disorientation; when he awoke from sleep, he frequently thought he was back in jail. She was calling now to seek my advice.

Because of Bud's periodic lack of awareness about where he was, the hospital authorities scheduled a psychiatrist to visit with him. Bud insisted that Kitty not tell the psychiatrist and, indeed, any hospital personnel, that he had been in jail. Because it was Bud's request, Kitty had agreed. But she had misgivings about her decision. She discussed it with her sisters and they shared the same lingering doubt: they were not being fair to Bud by withholding a key fact that could affect the judgment of the medical people about how best to help him. In their discussions, my name had come up as a person the family could turn to for help, as they had done many years before. Her purpose in calling, Kitty said, was to ask whether the family should let the psychiatrist know Bud had been in jail.

I had no hesitation in telling Kitty she should inform the psychiatrist (Dr. Neil Kaye) but, in doing so, she should tell the full story, stressing Bud's conviction had been wiped out after a long struggle and the state's decision not to retry *The Rape Case*. I reminded Kitty of what I had told the three men and their families many years earlier: the state's decision not to continue the prosecution reflected the weakness of the case against them. I also suggested that she give Dr. Kaye my name and tell him he should not hesitate to call me should he have any question.

In the same conversation, Kitty told me Reds Maguire had died a year or so earlier. She had little other information except he had remarried. Kitty said Sonny Jones suffered from emphysema and was not well. His marriage to a woman guard he had met while in jail did not endure. He had remarried but had no children. I mentioned I was writing the stories of some of my cases and asked her whether she thought Bud would mind if I wrote about the most famous and satisfying case of them all. She said she certainly did not think so.

I told Kitty I would like to visit Bud at the hospital, and she replied he would be pleased to see me. I assured her I would do so sometime over the weekend. The next afternoon, I received a second call from Kitty. With obvious concern, she told me Bud had suffered yet another heart attack (his third) and was now in the intensive care unit. When I said I did not want to impose upon the family's limited time to spend with him in the ICU, she protested it would be good for his morale to see me. She said she would leave word with the hospital personnel to allow me to visit. I told her I would try to do so on Saturday.

By Saturday afternoon, I knew I would not be able to keep my promise that day. I called the hospital and was able to speak to Kitty. When I told her I could not visit that day, she said she understood. I assured her I would come by on Sunday afternoon.

I found Bud Curran in his room in the east wing of the Christiana Medical Center. In appearance, he was no longer the strapping, over six feet, black-haired young fellow I had known years before. He was now gaunt and gray and showed the ravages of time and ill-health. Yet it was apparent he had as much delight in seeing me as I did in visiting with him. We reminisced.

He told me he had kept fit in jail by using the track which then existed at the old Workhouse. Every day he would sprint the mile-and-one-eighth course, keeping an excellent pace. When we spoke of Reds Maguire, he told me Reds had died in Tennessee. He did not recall any local newspaper article at the time of Red's death. (A member of the Maguire family subsequently told me Reds died in Middletown, Delaware, and had worked as a security guard.) Bud was fearful that when he died there would be an article describing him as a rapist. He also told me Sonny Jones was dying. He said whenever he called Sonny and Sonny's wife answered, she would berate him, since she considered Bud the source of all of Sonny's problems.

Bud said the woman who had accused them lived a short distance from the Christiana Medical Center. In answer to my question, he told me she had never married. He then said, "You know, she followed me away from the direction to her home." It would have been a telling point to have made to an untainted, objective jury.

Bud spoke of wanting to return home where he lived alone. His son, Franny, Bud told me, was just like him, over six foot four and a bachelor. Bud longed for a family for his son. He wanted grandchildren. When I asked him if he had a television, he told me he did and pointed to the television behind my back. I asked him what it cost and he told me $3.25. Mistakenly, I thought it was a weekly charge. Before I left Bud, an elderly woman who represented the television firm came by to ask Bud if he wanted to renew the TV contract. It turned out the charge was $3.25 a day! Bud renewed it for two weeks, and the lady said she would come by the next day to pick up the money for the renewal. I asked her if the TV firm was a private company and she assured me it was. When I said at the rate of $97.50 a month a patient could buy a television and bring it in, she told me hospital regulations did not permit use of private TVs in the hospital. After the lady left, I told Bud of my friend and client, Leon Tanzer and his Tel-A-Rent operation of years past. He had earned a good livelihood renting and servicing televisions in all of the local hospitals at a rate far less than the current charge.

Bud then talked of his younger sister, Suzanne, who had become a member of the Bar. When I said I did not know her, Bud told me that years before he had called to tell me she had passed the Bar. I had no recollection of the call. Bud said he had encouraged Suzanne to call me for advice about a job, but she was unwilling to do so because she did not think I would hire a non-Jew. Bud protested, but unsuccessfully. She subsequently practiced with a group of local lawyers. The January 1, 1980 announcement of her association proclaimed her pride in the Curran name:

BADER, DORSEY & KRESHTOOL
Are Pleased To Announce That
THOMAS STEPHEN NUEBERGER
Has Become A Member Of The Firm
And That
AIDA WASERSTEIN
TERRY CURTIS SENINGEN
And
SUZANNE CURRAN DONOVAN
Have Become Associated With The Firm
January 1, 1980

The "Bader" was the same John Merwin Bader who had sat in for me from January to June 1955 as the attorney for Curran, Jones, and Maguire while I served as a deputy attorney general. Bud said his sister did not enjoy being part of the practice. Tragically, at age thirty-nine, Suzanne Curran Donovan died of bronchitis. Bud still mourned her.

I turned the conversation to his sister, Kitty. He told me of the success of her children. Even though Kitty had reported it all, I let Bud tell me proudly of their accomplishments. He spoke glowingly of how Kitty would do anything in the world for him. I spoke of Bud's parents who never lost faith in him and his innocence.

The visit stretched far longer than I had intended. I thought it was tiring Bud for me to stay longer. When we parted, I knew I would not be a daily visitor. A month later Kitty Curran called again, this time to tell me Bud had died on April 28, 1992. She needed my help again. She asked how she could keep the fact of Bud's conviction out of the newspaper obituary. I asked whether she or the family cared if no obituary appeared. When she said, "No," I told her to tell the funeral director not to report Bud's death to the newspaper. The *News Journal*'s policy of noting deaths depended almost entirely upon a report coming to the newspaper from the funeral director. Only rarely did the news of a death die along with the deceased. Absent a report, however, it was not likely that the newspaper would learn of Bud's death. If no obituary appeared, the newspaper could not drag Bud's name through the mud again. And so it was. The *News Journal*'s predecessors never had befriended Bud in his lifetime. Neither he nor his family had any obligation to provide a story at his death.

Epilogue

Caleb M. Wright

The hero of *The Rape Case* is Judge Wright. When the petition for habeas corpus seeking relief claiming the trial was constitutionally unfair came before him, it carried baggage: the history of the trial, the convictions, the sentences of life imprisonment for the three petitioners, the absence of any appeal from the jury's verdicts, the subsequent unsuccessful proceedings in the Delaware courts, and the United States Supreme Court's denial of the petition for certiorari. In the state proceedings six judges, including the three justices of Delaware's now separate Supreme Court, had denied relief, leaving to stand the jury's verdicts of guilty. What troubled Wright was that five of the six judges had clearly found that the state had introduced false police testimony at trial but, nonetheless, denied relief.

Years after *The Rape Case* was over I invited Chief Judge Wright to lunch with me at the Rodney Square Club. By this time he had taken senior status, but he continued to carry a full workload as his standards required. Although we were never close friends, I respected him for his courage and his sense of fairness. I knew I had his respect; in 1969 a decade after the end of *The Rape Case,* Judge Wright appointed me special master in the *Montecatini* patent litigation concerning the invention of polypropylene.[1] Absent *The Rape Case,* I doubt he would have thought of me, let alone appoint me. (A special master sits as a

351

judge for a specific purpose. In *Montecatini* I supervised depositions the parties took in Duisburg, Germany, and Milan, Italy.)

Our conversation ranged over a number of topics before Wright brought up *The Rape Case*. He prefaced his remarks with the comment he had never told anyone what he was about to say. He then told me that after *The Rape Case* was pending before him following the argument on April 16, 1957, he had tried to write the opinion "both ways." The first opinion would have denied relief. He said no matter how hard he tried, he could not write an opinion adverse to granting relief that comported with his sense of constitutional fairness. His second opinion was favorable to granting the writ of habeas corpus I sought for my clients.

Although he thought the Delaware Supreme Court was wrong in its thinking and in its conclusion, Wright never uttered a word of disparagement about any member of the court. To him, the issue was neither a matter of personalities nor a matter of state versus federal relations. He had no doubt concerning his jurisdiction over the habeas corpus petition before him. Resolving the issue was a matter of fairness and intellectual honesty. As he had made plain in his opinion, the state had crossed the line between "tolerable imperfection and fundamental unfairness" in permitting police perjury at the trial. Thus, the convictions of Curran, Jones, and Maguire could not stand.[2]

Wright went on to relate that Wolcott would not speak to him for quite some time after he filed his opinion. Even when he finally did, Wolcott did not hide his disapproval of Wright's decision. I knew full well Wolcott did not approve of Wright's ruling. In *Williams v. State*, decided December 8, 1964, my friend, David Snellenberg II, in support of his client's appeal in a criminal case, had cited and relied upon Wright's opinion.[3] Writing for a unanimous court, Wolcott affirmed the conviction, using caustic words to express his disdain for what Wright had held more than seven years earlier. He demonstrated both his animus toward

Wright and his own continued failure to understand the fundamental point *The Rape Case* raised. Echoing Chief Justice Southerland's attitude, he wrote "The case is therefore entirely dissimilar to *Curran v. State of Delaware*, D.C., 154 F.Supp. 27, *if that case be sound law,* where it appeared that there had been a deliberate concealment of fact upon a minor point by a police detective on the witness stand." [Emphasis added.][4]

Not only were the words, "if that case be sound law," a personal attack on Wright, but Wolcott went further. When he cited *The Rape Case* he departed from accepted practice and deliberately omitted the citations to the Third Circuit's unanimous opinion affirming Wright and the United States Supreme Court's denial of the state's petition for certiorari.[5] By his omissions, Wolcott appeared to want to keep secret the action of the Third Circuit and the Supreme Court leaving Judge Wright's order in place. To my surprise, Wright said he was not aware of what Wolcott had said in the *Williams* case before I referred to it at our luncheon.

In 1992, The Historical Society for the United States District Court for The District of Delaware published *Federal Justice In The First State,* a laudatory book about the federal judiciary in Delaware. Dr. Carol E. Hoffecker, then a professor of history at the University of Delaware, wrote the text with the acknowledged assistance of a research committee, cochaired by Richard R. Cooch and James T. McKinstry and consisting of twenty-four other lawyers, many of whom had served as law clerks to the federal judges, who helped in the research and writing about the eighteen men and one woman who had served as District Court judges in Delaware between 1787 and 1992.

Dr. Hoffecker, assisted by Lewis S. Black Jr., who had been Chief Judge Wright's law clerk from 1963 to 1965, well after *The Rape Case,* wrote about it extolling Judge Wright for his courage in ruling as he did:

The first major case to confront Judge Caleb M. Wright when he joined the court was that of *Curran v. State of Delaware*. This was an emotion-laden case that concerned three men who had been convicted of rape in the state courts in 1948. . . . Years after the trial evidence was found that corroborated the convicted men's testimony and they petitioned the district court for a writ of *habeas corpus*. Judge Wright demonstrated his mettle as an interpreter of the U.S. Constitution when he issued the writ. The existence of the second statements was unlikely to demonstrate that the petitioners were innocent of the crime for which they stood convicted, but the new evidence did have a potential bearing on the outcome, Judge Wright said. "Whenever a defendant takes the stand in a criminal trial his credibility is put in issue," Wright wrote, and he went on to note that "the concept that the use of perjured testimony is a denial of due process" was a well established rule of jurisprudence. Therefore, the judge reasoned that the conduct of the petitioners' trial had denied them their right to due process and that this "fundamental unfairness" must be redressed by a new trial.[6]

The comment, "[t]he existence of the second statements was unlikely to demonstrate" the defendants' innocence, was the authors' opinion. Judge Wright did not make such a finding. Their opinion may well have its roots in a reading of the Delaware Supreme Court's opinion.[7] The chapter does not mention either the Third Circuit's opinion affirming Wright, or the United States Supreme Court's denial of the state's petition for a writ of certiorari, or *Napue*.[8]

State v. Parson

My success in *The Rape Case* brought with it many opportunities throughout the rest of my career for me to involve myself in cases defending the civil liberties of the clients I undertook to represent. One was *State v. Parson*, a notorious 1966 case in Sussex County. *Parson* also illustrates that whatever animus Wolcott held against Wright for his ruling in *The Rape Case*, he did not maintain any hostility toward me.

In *Parson* the state charged Norman Benjamin Parson with rape and murder. Unlike Curran, Jones, and Maguire's denial of guilt in *The Rape Case,* Parson did not deny that he had sexually assaulted and killed sixteen-year-old Kathleen Maull after entering a house where she was babysitting. His defense was he was so drunk he had no memory of what he had done. Since the jury did not accompany its guilty verdict with a recommendation of mercy, the law at that time mandated the death sentence.

Two *Journal* editors, Martin A. Claver and Anthony Higgins, knowing of my work in *The Rape Case,* called me the morning after the verdict. They told me their stringer in Georgetown had reported Parson did not have a fair trial because of the incompetency of the court-appointed counsel, Jackson Raysor and Ralph Baker. At their urging, I agreed to look into the matter. I called my friend Jack Raysor, who welcomed my call and offer to help. I did not mention the call from Claver and Higgins.

After a meeting with Parson in the New Castle County Workhouse, I questioned whether he really could understand the charges against him. When I reported my concern to Jack, he told me for the first time that with his assent the state's psychiatrist had examined Parson but his report was inconclusive about Parson's mental capacity. There had not been any further examination of Parson. Neither the prosecution nor Raysor or Baker pursued the matter. These facts were not known to the jury. With Jack's agreement I hired Dr. Irwin Weintraub, a psychologist, who examined Parson and concluded he lacked the mental ability to assist counsel in his own defense. I prepared the motion to have Judge John J. McNeilly Jr., the judge of the Superior Court who had appointed Jack and Baker to represent Parson and who had presided at the trial, set aside the jury's verdict on the ground the state had not seriously explored the accused's mental ability to determine his capacity to understand what was happening and to assist his lawyers at trial. Jack signed it. Mc-Neilly denied the motion.

Since, according to Raysor, Baker's help in Parson's defense had been minimal, Jack, without any prior discussion with me, asked Judge McNeilly to appoint me to replace Baker. McNeilly immediately did so. I did not welcome the appointment. Although I wanted to help Jack and assure his client a fair trial, I wanted to do my work behind the scenes. Like Jack, I had no desire to be the lawyer in a case where, at its conclusion, the state would execute my client. Neither Jack nor I held out any hope to Parson that he would walk away a free man.

By 1966 Daniel Wolcott was Chief Justice of the Delaware Supreme Court, the court that would pass on Parson's forthcoming appeal. Even before I learned of my appointment, Wolcott called me to say he was pleased to note it, since, he said, "I am now satisfied Parson's rights will be fully protected." He added that I should not infer from his comment he would show any preferential treatment toward Parson. I quickly told him that I did not expect he would. He did not. The Delaware Supreme Court affirmed Parson's conviction and death sentence for rape and murder.[9]

Since Jack was not admitted to the United States Supreme Court's Bar, I prepared and signed the petition for a writ of certiorari. The Supreme Court denied the petition, leaving in place the jury's verdict and the death sentence.[10] Nonetheless, I was confident we would save Parson. How, I did not know. But I knew we had to move forward.

Our next step was to file a petition for the issuance of a writ of habeas corpus in the United States District Court of Delaware. I prepared the petition and, with the assistance of my then partner, Joseph A. Rosenthal, wrote the briefs. I made the argument to Judge Caleb R. Layton III, by then a federal District Court judge, whose opinion, as a Superior Court judge, was my first defeat in The Rape Case.[11] On January 24, 1968, after reargument following his original opinion, Layton granted the writ on the

ground the record did not show that Parson understood the proceedings.[12]

Both *The Rape Case* and *Parson* are examples where the fairness of the trial was the issue—not the guilt or innocence of the
accused. The Constitution mandates the state must conduct a
fair trial; the guilt or innocence of the accused is beside the point
if the state does not do so. In *The Rape Case* the state judges let
stand the convictions despite the proof that the police committed perjury at trial. In *Parson* the state failed to insure Parson's
right to a fair trial by ignoring the unresolved issue of Parson's
ability to understand the proceedings and assist his counsel.
Consequently, Wright in *The Rape Case* and Layton in *Parson*
"reversed" both the Superior Court and the Delaware Supreme
Court.[13]

In *Federal Justice*, Dr. Hoffecker, assisted by William E. Man-
ning, Roderick R. McKelvie, and Anthony G. Flynn, each of
whom had served as a law clerk to Judge Layton, wrote about his
service on the federal bench. They discussed the *Parson* case at
length, describing it as "[o]ne of the greatest tests that Judge Layton ever faced on the bench . . . ," concluding, "His opinion in
the Parson case should rightly be viewed as an act of personal
courage on behalf of the Constitution that he had sworn to defend."[14] I cannot help but think if Judge Layton in 1953 had applied the same courage and understanding to *The Rape Case* as
he later did in *Parson*, my clients would not have spent almost
eleven years in jail before their release on bail.

Murray M. Schwartz

Murray M. Schwartz was Chief Judge Wright's law clerk at the
time of his decision in *The Rape Case*. In 1974 President Richard
M. Nixon appointed Schwartz to the vacancy on the District

Court when Wright took senior status.[15] In May 1976, a majority of a three-judge panel court in the Delaware school desegregation litigation, in an opinion by Wright followed by an order, desegregated eleven school districts in New Castle County, including Wilmington, effective on all grade levels in September 1978. The court then disbanded itself.[16] Schwartz, the junior member of the District Court, then volunteered to carry out the remedy of busing the majority had ordered, thus relieving Wright of a serious burden. With patience and wisdom, Judge Schwartz implemented the order to desegregate the schools. During this time he received death threats but continued to do his duty. He has deservedly received honors for his courage. Although the remedy and the necessary busing were not of his making, in the public mind Schwartz became forever associated with the imposition of "forced busing" in New Castle County.[17] With others, I represented the plaintiff school children and their parents. *Federal Justice* also praises Judge Schwartz's role in the Delaware desegregation litigation.[18]

But even Schwartz misstated the facts of *The Rape Case* when he wrote an article in 2009 extolling Judge Wright. In referring to *The Rape Case* to illustrate Judge Wright's integrity, Schwartz wrote: ". . . in a high-profile criminal case three men had raped a woman." I called his attention to the fact Judge Wright's opinion held Curran, Jones, and Maguire had not had a fair trial and the convictions could not stand. The effect was that no one could or should say they "had raped a woman." In response Schwartz wrote: "Your criticism is both warranted and correct. The objectionable portion of the sentence should have stated '. . . in a state criminal case three men were indicted and charged with raping a woman.'"[19] Regrettably, he never corrected the error publicly.

In discussing the courage and wisdom displayed by Judge Wright in *The Rape Case,* Judge Layton in *Parson,* and Judge Schwartz in the desegregation litigation, *Federal Justice* does not identify me as the successful lawyer common to all three litigations. The master fact is that in order for judges to demonstrate "courage and wisdom" they need lawyers to bring the cases.

Chief Justice Wolcott's Death

Yet another exchange between Chief Justice Wolcott and me had its painful irony. He called me late in the afternoon on July 10, 1973, from the St. Francis Hospital where he was recovering from a heart attack. As I was then president of the Delaware State Bar Association, he wanted my help in planning a memorial session the Supreme Court and the Bar would hold in memory of Chief Justice Southerland, who had died less than a month earlier on June 16, 1973. We discussed the date, who would speak, and as many other details as we each could think of. That same night around 7:30 p.m., a newspaper reporter called me at home and sought a comment from me as president of the Bar on Chief Justice Wolcott's death. I was shocked. I told the reporter I would call him back. I then composed a brief comment the *Morning News* published on July 11, 1973:

> He was always a sensitive man, concerned about people. . . . As lawyer, judge of the Superior Court, chancellor, and chief justice, he served the people of our state ably and faithfully. He has left us a legacy of high achievement.
> Mr. Chief Justice Wolcott committed himself fully to the law, without regard to his personal health. We are richer by his service to us and we [are] poorer by his passing. . . . [20]

With Daniel L. Herrmann as Chief Justice, the Supreme Court and the Bar convened on September 25, 1973, in a special session to honor the memory of both Chief Justice Southerland and Chief Justice Wolcott, colleagues in the practice of law and on the bench. I later learned from William S. Potter, a partner of both, that on his way home he had stopped to see Wolcott and was the person who found him dead. Our conversation to plan the memorial session for Chief Justice Southerland was probably the last Supreme Court business Wolcott conducted. He planned the memorial session without recognizing it would be for himself as well.[21]

Collins J. Seitz

Chancellor Seitz, who denied the relief I sought in the Court of Chancery, was a remarkable jurist. He ruled in 1954 in *Belton v. Gebhart* that the disparity of the facilities between white and black public schools in Delaware violated the Equal Protection Clause of the Fourteenth Amendment and ordered immediate relief.[22] Seitz's ruling preceded the United States Supreme Court's unanimous decision two years later in the landmark case of *Brown v. Board of Education,* where Chief Justice Earl Warren quoted from *Belton* in holding segregation *per se* of students on racial grounds unconstitutional.[23] Seitz subsequently served as an Associate Judge and then Chief Judge of the United States Court of Appeals for the Third Circuit.[24]

H. Albert Young

At the time of the judicial victories in *The Rape Case,* the release on bail of Curran, Jones, and Maguire, and the state's abandonment of any further prosecution, Hy Young did not congratulate me. Given his 1954 comment that I should have waited to secure relief for my clients until he was out of office, he obviously thought he should have been the one to secure their release. Had he done so, he would have vindicated himself and his work at the 1948 trial. Hy mellowed in his later years. In 1981, my election and admission to the Delaware chapter of the American College of Trial Lawyers, a prestigious honor, was the result of Hy Young's urging. He, Victor F. Battaglia Sr., and I were a frequent threesome at Bar events downstate, and on many occasions we were the only upstate lawyers present. Together we attended funerals, inductions of judges, and other gatherings. Those journeys, with Vic driving, Hy sitting beside him in front, and I in back, brought forth from Hy and me our penchant for telling stories, much to the amusement of our younger colleague.

Long after Young's death in 1982, I came to realize how important he and his family considered *The Rape Case* to his career. In 1999 his law firm and his family created the H. Albert Young Fellowship in Constitutional Law at the Widener University School of Law. The brochure for the formal session at the school, announcing the first professor who was to hold the fellowship for the first two years, included this statement: "In other noted cases, Mr. Young represented one of the defendants in a sensational and racially charged rape trial, broke down the barriers to women serving on Delaware juries in *State v. Jones,* and obtained the first Delaware Supreme Court decision establishing the right to peaceful picketing in the *Rialto Theater* case." I doubt the career summary would have pleased Hy. He did not like to lose a case or, worse yet, even to refer to his lost cases, however few in number they were. As a stickler for accuracy, he certainly knew that however "sensational" *The Rape Case* was, it assuredly was not "racially charged." The three defendants, the alleged victim, the fifty-eight witnesses, the twelve jurors, the three prosecuting attorneys, the three lawyers representing the three defendants, and the three judges were all white. Subsequent brochures corrected the error.[25]

When all is said and done, it was Hy Young's persistence in

going after Rodenhiser which laid the basis for my claim of unfairness resulting ultimately in the release of Curran, Jones, and
Maguire.

Leonard G. Hagner

After the trial of *The Rape Case,* Len Hagner, Curran's lawyer,
served as United States Attorney for the District of Delaware
from 1953 to 1961 by appointment of President Dwight D. Eisenhower. In other jurisdictions, holding the posts Hagner did—
assistant city solicitor, deputy attorney general, part-time judge,
and, finally, full-time United States Attorney—would have given
assurance of the incumbent's ability to represent well a person
accused of a capital crime. But Delaware, at that time, was different. The posts Hagner occupied were held by persons available
and willing to take them, while the more celebrated lawyers remained in private practices far more remunerative than any of
the various public posts Len occupied.

David J. Reinhardt Jr.

Only a short time after the end of *The Rape Case* trial, David
Reinhardt, Maguire's lawyer, pleaded guilty on October 2, 1950,
in the Court of General Sessions and received a four year sen-
tence for fraudulent conversion and misapplication of more than
$12,000 from two estates. Francis A. Reardon represented him.
Attorney General James and Deputy Attorney General Vincent
A. Theisen presented the case. Chief Justice Richards and Judges
Carey and Layton sat in judgment.[26] The Supreme Court rejected
Reinhardt's offer to resign and disbarred him on October 20,
1950. While still in prison, Reinhardt embarked on a second ca-

reer rehabilitating alcoholics among prisoners. Governor Elbert N. Carvel, on the recommendation of the Board of Pardons (where Len Hagner represented Reinhardt), commuted his sentence to one year. In September 1951, Reinhardt became a case worker at the Workhouse. He subsequently worked at the Governor Bacon Health Center and the Prisoners Aid Society. For nearly twenty years Reinhardt compiled an exceptional record: only one of every fourteen he counseled was rearrested, while two of every three who did not receive his counseling wound up back in jail. In October 1957 Governor J. Caleb Boggs, again on the Board of Pardons' recommendation, granted Reinhardt a full pardon. He died in August 1970.[27]

Warren F. Schueler

Schueler, one of the three eyewitnesses the jurors erroneously believed Hy Young had paid to testify falsely to help their friends, became a member of the Delaware State Police Department, retiring with the rank of lieutenant colonel in 1971. He was an active member of the Masonic Order, a 33 degree Scottish Rite Mason, and by 1999 served as the Masonic Deputy for Delaware. I find it ironic that Captain McCool became one of Schueler's instructors at the State Police Department Academy.[28]

Joe Pyne

Cancer struck Joe Pyne and he lost a leg to that scourge while still in Wilmington, but that did not stop either his career or the enthusiasm he brought to his work. From his success in Wilmington, he moved to Los Angeles and achieved prominence as a talk-show host there. When Phil Donahue announced his retirement after almost thirty years as a talk show host, a critic wrote in *The New Republic* that Donahue had "invented the genre," a claim which elicited this letter:[29]

No. Phil Donahue didn't invent the genre, as Howard Kurtz states ("Father of the Slide," February 12). There was, way before him, Joe Pyne. I was on his very popular television talk show program, taped at KTLA-TV . . . in Los Angeles, back in November 1966. On the show, we spoke about theism versus atheism and whether prostitution should be legal. Although sometimes he had guests on who claimed to have had lunch with Jesus up on Mars, he also had a bunch of people with whom he simply argued some issue of general interest.[30]

Joe Pyne died a relatively young man without ever commanding the national audience Donahue and others acquired.

Edward G. Pollard

Not until the Bail Reform Act of 1966 did Congress, led by Senator Sam Ervin, strike down "the chief evil of the old bail system [with its] automatic reliance on monetary bail with the result that indigent defendants remained in custody while their wealthier counterparts were set free."[31] As in so many other areas, District Court Clerk Ed Pollard was ahead of his time in accepting the hair tonic stock as part of the bail consideration for Sonny Jones. In 1999 I shared an earlier version of *The Hair Tonic Bond* chapter with my friend, the late Bernard D. Fischman, who perceptively commented: "Ed Pollard is the deserved hero of the piece. The fact is that there are no more Ed Pollards in the legal system. Every court clerk, even the good compassionate clerks, spend their lives making it impossible to show any human qualities. Those who would want to help, like Ed Pollard, are afraid to do so."[32]

Herbert L. Maris

Mr. Maris' unusual career finally came to the attention of a television producer who developed a series called *Lock Up*, using Mr. Maris' cases as the source for the episodes and starring Mac-Donald Carey as Maris.[33] As part of the publicity for the series, Charles Shaw of NBC interviewed Mr. Maris. My wife Doris saw an announcement of the interview. We gathered our little family on Sunday, May 31, 1959, to watch. Generous man that he was, Mr. Maris did not hesitate to refer to me and the *The Rape Case* in the course of the interview. I promptly wrote to thank him:

I enjoyed thoroughly your appearance on my television screen on Sunday. My wife had mentioned . . . that you were scheduled to appear and I, of course, made certain to listen and watch. . . . I enjoyed your remarks thoroughly including the suggestion that a panel be established of disinterested responsible citizens who would be called in when a confession was about to be made by an accused. I have often thought that this simple procedure in which I am certain many citizens would be willing to cooperate would put an end to the many abuses associated with "voluntary confessions" presently admitted into evidence.

Your mention of my name, of course, added immeasurably to my enjoyment of the program. I might add that hearing my name on television impressed my children immensely. I thank you not only for your kindness in mentioning me in such glowing terms but also for impressing the children. For a brief moment at least, I am on a par with Sallie [*sic*] Starr.[34]

After the TV series was underway for a while, I reported to Sammy Thompson an amusing exchange I had with one of the clients of Cohen and Morris:

Many thanks for forwarding the copy of *True Man's Magazine* containing the article about Mr. Maris. To show how Mr. Maris' fame is growing . . . , I make mention of the fact that the other day one of my clients who did not know that I had any association with Mr. Maris asked me, based upon his view of the television series, "Don't you want to be like Mr. Maris?" I allowed as how nothing would please me more.[35]

Toasting the Victory

After the victory before Chief Judge Wright, George Corbeil gave me an aged, expensive bottle of a rare cognac. I told him we would not drink from that bottle until we freed Curran, Jones, and Maguire from jail. Only after the state had declined to prosecute our clients again did George and I open the bottle and toast our success and the health of our clients.

I promised George I would save the balance of the cognac to toast future, significant events in my practice of the law. I fully intended to keep my promise. When I turned to the cognac to celebrate a professional success a few years later, I found to my dismay the rare liquor was almost gone. I thought perhaps it had evaporated. I even succumbed to the thought one of the ladies who helped with housework from time to time had decided to imbibe some. My wife Doris was not a drinker and accordingly escaped any suspicion. But when I mentioned the nearly empty bottle to her, she provided the answer. Doris was a gourmet cook. She reminded me that several years after the end of *The Rape Case*, three young men, all Mormons, retained my firm to represent them in a corporate matter. With her prior assent, I invited them to dinner at our home. Among the splendid dishes she prepared was a sweet potato dish laced with the expensive cognac. She told me it was the only potable she thought appropriate for her dish from among the bottles in our small liquor cabinet. I told her she should not have used any liquor at all, given the abstinence the Mormon religion requires of its adherents. They were entitled to full disclosure from us before they ate of any dish containing liquor. Doris' rejoinder was all the alcohol had burned off before my clients partook of the sweet potatoes. In any event they were glorious sweet potatoes.

Seeking Praise

As a young lawyer wanting to leave my mark on the law, I wanted to make the most of my victory in *The Rape Case.* After the state entered the nolle prosequi, I made two efforts to do so. I first called Fred Hartman, a reporter for the *Journal* and a stringer for *Time Magazine.* I urged him to consider reporting the outcome of *The Rape Case* to *Time.* No mention of it appeared, and Fred never told me why. Perhaps neither he nor *Time* understood its significance.

I also thought the outcome would be newsworthy to *The Reader's Digest* because of the role Frederic Sondern Jr.'s article about Mr. Maris in the January 1948 issue had played in leading to the freedom of Curran, Jones, and Maguire. On March 16, 1959, I wrote to the magazine, calling attention to the original article (I enclosed a photocopy) and the eventual successful outcome. I concluded: "It was my distinct honor to have been associated with Mr. Maris in the case and I endorse each and every fine thing that Mr. Sondern had to say about Mr. Maris over ten years ago and assure you that the same is true today."[36] I sent a copy to Mr. Maris who immediately responded:

I was surprised and, frankly, pleased with copy of letter received this morning which you have taken upon yourself to write The Editor of The Readers [*sic*] Digest. I am taking it home to Mrs. Maris this evening. She will be especially elated by your most kindly words.

The Readers Digest article manifested itself in many commendable ways, so many in fact it would take days to recount—from the mother in despair in California to the wrongfully imprisoned police officer in West Virginia, from the Bronx boy trying to make good in Florida to Joe Chapman awaiting the electric chair in Rockview—but of them all, the toughest case was the Curran-Jones-Maguire, and these young men would be imprisoned today for many years to come were it not for Irving Morris. The Readers Digest and Herb Maris merely got him started. It was he who did the real work and won, deservedly, against strenuous odds.[37]

DeWitt Wallace, founder and legendary editor of *The Reader's Digest,* also acknowledged my letter:

It looks as if the recent verdict in the Curran, Maguire and Jones case was a personal victory for you and congratulations are in order. Naturally we were interested in this sidelight on the Herbert Maris story "He Frees the Innocent" . . . and I want to thank you for your thoughtfulness in sending the Wilmington News story about the men's release and verifax copies of the court order and proceedings. The staff is always pleased to know when Digest material has especially benefited someone.

You were very kind to write.[38]

I doubt my writing warranted Mr. Wallace's use of the word "kind." While I wanted *The Reader's Digest* to know of its role and Mr. Maris' in securing the freedom of Curran, Jones, and Maguire, I also wanted the magazine to recognize what I had done. I wanted more than bringing "pleasure" to the staff. But it was not to be. *The Rape Case* received national recognition only once: in the United States Supreme Court's reference in *Napue* in 1959.

Academic Approval

In 1960, Curtis R. Reitz, then an assistant professor at the University of Pennsylvania Law School, analyzed thirty-five cases, among them *The Rape Case* (to which he referred as *Curran*). He concluded: "These 35 cases demonstrate the urgent necessity for the present federal habeas corpus jurisdiction."[39] After he summarized the proceedings and rulings in *The Rape Case*, Reitz commented on the thirty-five cases generally: "The significance of the constitutional rights involved goes beyond a simple technical requirement of compliance with procedural rules. The purpose of the guarantees of due process and equal protection in the ultimate is to prevent conviction of the innocent."[40] He noted specifically about *The Rape Case*, "the possibility of Supreme Court review was not reduced by the quality of the proceedings in the state courts. The Delaware courts in the *Curran* case . . . had given plenary consideration to the asserted federal questions. *The reason, or reasons, why [Curran] did not win the votes of four of the Justices to grant certiorari cannot, of course, be known.* [Emphasis added.]"[41]

Reitz's view was that the thirty-five cases revealed

. . . the lack of merit in the proposition that federal constitutional rights of state prisoners can be protected adequately by Supreme Court review of the judgments of state courts, the proposition put forward by those who favor abolition or sharp delimitation of the federal *habeas corpus* jurisdiction. The fact of the matter is that, with very minor exception, the Supreme Court was powerless to review the state judgments. Nevertheless, the state prisoners obtained relief in a subsequent federal *habeas corpus* proceeding.[42]

Reitz's final reference to *The Rape Case* was in his consideration of the nine instances in which states petitioned for certiorari from the nineteen courts of appeal judgments in favor of a state prisoner. He noted: "*The Supreme Court refused to grant review of any of them* [including *Curran*], *even though some of the decisions below broke new and important ground in the matter of constitutional law* [citing *Curran*] or evolved [*sic*] novel and questionable theories of what constitutes exhaustion of state remedies." [Emphasis added.][43]

Napue v. Illinois

For almost five decades, I remained convinced my participation in *The Rape Case* had contributed, in the words of the late William E. Wiggin, the Editor of *The Delaware Lawyer,* to "one of the most important advances in the criminal jurisprudence of [Delaware]" if not the United States.[44] In 2007, in order to determine how many times courts had cited to *Napue* and *The Rape Case,* I asked R. Michael Lindsey, an able young lawyer in the firm my daughter, Karen L. Morris, continued after I retired, to do the research. In his thorough memorandum, he concluded I had overstated the holding of *Napue* despite the fact that both *Napue* and *The Rape Case* were each "still good law."[45] In *Napue* "the prosecutor in fact knew that [Wamer's] testimony was false and failed to correct the record. The precise holding of [*Napue*] therefore is that a conviction obtained through perjured testimony, *known by the prosecutor to be false,* violated the defendant's federal due process right to a fair trial." [Emphasis added.][46]

Lindsey's analysis of the cases led him to conclude: ". . . my research concerning [*The Rape Case*] indicated that while the Second, Third, and Fourth Circuits hold that a police officer's knowledge of perjured testimony by police is attributed to the prosecution, for the purpose of a *Napue* claim, the Fifth and Tenth Circuits refuse to attribute such knowledge to the prosecution."[47]

Lindsey took up "as a final wrinkle" the position of the Ninth Circuit. Relying upon a provision of a 1996 federal law, the Antiterrorism and Effective Death Penalty Act, the Ninth Circuit held, in connection with a habeas corpus petition, that the rule requiring imputation of the police officer's knowledge of perjury is not "clearly established federal law as determined by the United States Supreme Court and therefore must fail under U.S.C. § 2254 (d)(1), 'which provides that [a]n application for a writ of habeas corpus on behalf of a person in custody pursuant to the judgment of a state court shall not be granted with respect to any claim that was adjudicated on the merits in State court proceedings unless the adjudication of the claim . . . resulted in a decision that was contrary to, or involved an unreasonable application of, clearly established Federal law, as determined by the Supreme Court of the United States.' "[48]

As Linda Greenhouse, then *The New York Times* senior reporter covering the Supreme Court, has noted, the Act "raised the bar against federal court review of state prisoners' petitions for writs of habeas corpus."[49]

Lindsey's memorandum sharply reduced my opinion of my contribution but not my belief that I was right from the outset.

Teachings for Lawyers from *The Rape Case*

The most important lesson *The Rape Case* teaches is the importance of perseverance in each task a lawyer undertakes. Prior to my success on the habeas corpus petition before Chief Judge Wright, I had lost in every state court. When the Delaware Supreme Court affirmed the Superior Court's denial of the petition, heard by the same three judges who sat at the trial, I could have abandoned the fight and accepted the judgment of the justices of Delaware's highest court, each of whom was new to the merits of *The Rape Case*. One could argue that they were disinterested in the outcome of the proceedings and, accordingly, their unanimous opinion was entitled to the respect it deserved as the last word. But I was convinced that the trial court's verdict, founded, as it was, on the police lies, could not, and assuredly should and would not, stand "as the last word." So I persevered in my clients' cause to the eventual victory despite the Delaware Supreme Court's affirmance.

The second lesson I suggest from *The Rape Case* is that a lawyer/judge should not ignore the obvious. In *The Rape Case*, Hy Young among the lawyers recognized the police officers were lying and did his best to bring the perjury to light. But the police perjury thwarted his effort. In contrast to Young, Hagner and Reinhardt did not appear to recognize the perjury and its potential for significant adverse effect on the defendants' credibility, however obvious it now appears. Reinhardt, in particular, never grasped the impact of the perjury even after his client Maguire testified that he had signed two statements each at a different time. The trial judges who heard the merits about the two statements as Superior Court judges were equally oblivious to the obvious fact that the police perjury destroyed the defendants' credibility and, in the process, any semblance of their right to the fair trial the Constitution requires. The justices of the Delaware Supreme Court recognized the obvious, but then proceeded to ignore it claiming it was "too narrow a view of the matter."

A third lesson is the importance of cooperation among lawyers where multiple parties are involved. The fact, as I believe it to be, that Hagner and Reinhardt were not aware that their respective clients had, like Jones, signed two statements until Curran and Maguire so testified, is the result in part that the lawyers did not share with each other what they had learned from their clients. Even if Young hoped to separate his client from the other defendants, once Young had his client testify early in the trial and then cross-examined the police officers (Rodenhiser and Mazewski) about Jones' signing two statements, there was every reason for the three defense lawyers to discuss these facts among themselves. For Hagner and Reinhardt not to have learned about the two signings from their clients, as appears to me to be the fact, seems inexplicable.

The fourth lesson is that lawyers should keep in mind that less can be and frequently is more. It is perhaps the hardest lesson for a trial lawyer to act upon in the heat of a trial. Having studied the summations, I suggest Reinhardt and Young would have served their clients better by listening to Hagner and then foregoing making any summation themselves. The aggressive rhetoric they used provided Duffy the opportunity not only to assert his case but, moreover, to ignore the serious questions Hagner had so effectively and elegantly raised.

The fifth lesson for lawyers is to beware of the contentious nature of our adversarial system and its consequences. The premise of our system is the belief that contention will yield the truth. But in too many instances the contention succumbs to the desire "to win" no matter the cost. The desire to win should not impair any lawyer's duty to do what is right.

Based on my more than fifty years of litigating cases throughout our country, I believe our justice system is outstanding. As *The Rape Case* illustrates, however, the system is not perfect. The sixth lesson I suggest *The Rape Case* teaches is that this imperfect system requires that lawyers and judges keep in mind the obvious fact that judges are human beings subject to all human frailties. *The Rape Case* was a high profile case. I cannot help but think that the state judges, convinced of the defendants' guilt despite the proven police perjury, permitted their conviction to dominate their judgment.

The seventh lesson is that lawyers have an obligation to defend unpopular defendants and causes, especially when fundamental rights are at stake. When lawyers fail to come forward in defense of those fundamental rights of our citizens, even those accused of heinous crimes, we as a people risk the loss of the liberties for which our country so proudly stands.

The Rape Case's **Effect on My Career**

By the time *The Rape Case was* over, I was well into representing plaintiffs in corporate class and derivative litigation, a boutique practice in which Robert C. Barab, Judge Leahy's first law clerk, involved me in August 1955, less than six months before his sudden and tragic death in January 1956 at the age of thirty-nine, leaving a widow and three young sons.[50] His untimely death expanded my caseload, because many of the out-of-state lawyers who had forwarded cases to Barab now turned to me as local counsel. As Barab had done, I took the cases on a contingency. But unlike *The Rape Case* where I knew there would never be a pot of gold at the end of the trail, the corporate cases held out the promise of substantial rewards if my advocacy proved successful. So it was. But no success in the corporate cases ever brought me greater satisfaction than wiping out the convictions of Curran, Jones, and Maguire and achieving their release from jail and further prosecution.

Every lawyer starting out in the practice should be so fortunate as to have the opportunity to undertake the equivalent of *The Rape Case.* My successful representation of Curran, Jones, and Maguire made me known and respected at the Bar. After all, who wants to argue with a lawyer who is willing to undertake, with little compensation, to undo an injustice in what appears to be a hopeless cause and who diligently and vigorously pursues it to a successful conclusion?

Acknowledgments

When the editorial board of the University of Delaware Press unanimously accepted my book for publication, Dr. Donald C. Mell, chairman of the board, suggested I employ an editor to reduce the number of pages and focus the story I wanted to tell. As a result I sought and secured the assistance of the Press' only staff person, Karen G. Druliner, as my editor. In the years I worked with Karen she never lost patience with me although I tried it mightily as I stubbornly resisted many changes she suggested. She followed the current directives of *The Chicago Manual of Style* and *Merriam-Webster's Collegiate Dictionary* as if they were Holy Writ. To the extent I listened to her, the work you have read improved immensely and I am indebted to Karen.

In expressing my gratefulness to Karen, I hasten to recognize the help I received from Don Mell, Karen's boss, who kept a weather eye out for my project from the time the book came within his jurisdiction to its conclusion.

Another significant way I benefited was Jonathan Ari Zakheim's decision to delay a year after his graduation magna cum laude from George Washington University before entering the University of Pennsylvania Law School. Not only did my oldest grandchild participate actively in the editing process, but, moreover, it was his vote that broke many a dispute between Karen Druliner and me, more often than not in Karen's favor, putting at risk his inheritance. To boot, his research and analysis made the end product accurate and readable. I am much indebted to Jon.

I am grateful to Vicki Thomas, senior paralegal at the Dover, Delaware law firm Schmittinger and Rodriguez, who assembled the reported decisions of the Supreme Court of Delaware in the ten-year period before Delaware adopted a separate Supreme Court in 1951, and in the first year and a half of its existence. Her work enabled Jonathan and me to come upon the critical improvement in Delaware jurisprudence resulting from the abandonment of the leftover justices system and the creation of the separate Supreme Court.

Although I noted in the text the contributions of the late Melvin G. Shimm, my law school classmate, and R. Michael Lindsey, the young lawyer who works for my daughter Karen L. Morris, I think they deserve mention again. Accordingly I recognize them again for their special work on *Napue*.

In the publication of a book a lawyer's services are frequently essential. In my case I had the help of Karen L. Morris, our youngest daughter and senior partner in Morris and Morris. Karen negotiated the publication contract and attended to sundry other details for which I am grateful.

Bernard J. O'Donnell of Delaware's Public Defender's office educated me on the impediments now in the law given the Antiterrorism and Effective Death Penalty Act, which would make highly unlikely any replication of the success I achieved in *The Rape Case* were it to be brought today. He continues to fight for the rights of defendants, particularly in capital cases.

I am grateful to Geoffrey Gamble, a past president of the Delaware State Bar Association, for his modern translation of the Magna Carta provision concerning habeas corpus I have used in the epigraph.

When I was in the midst of reviewing my correspondence,

pleadings, and other records of *The Rape Case* years later while writing this book, I came upon the reel court reporter Harry Blam had given me after the argument before Judge Wright. I had played it and then put it aside. Wanting to listen to the argument again, with the help of Paul Collins and James Mullins, I was able to have the material on the reel transferred to a cassette and then onto two micro-cassettes. My secretary before I retired, A. Lynn Krayer, then transcribed the argument. Without the reel and the transcription I would not have been able to quote the arguments Frank O'Donnell and I made nor Chief Judge Wright's comments and questions as I do in Chapter 25. On listening more than forty years later, I still thought I had made a good argument.

I acknowledge my debt to the able staff members at Delaware institutions who were helpful and magnanimous to me whenever I came calling: The Widener University Law School and its archivist, David K. King; the Delaware Supreme Court and its Court Administrator, Stephen D. Taylor; The News Journal Company and its "morgue" staff, particularly Charlotte Walker and Anne Haslam, and its long-time columnist, Harry Themal; The Wilmington Institute Library and its research staff, particularly Thomas Morabito and Benedict Prestianni; the Historical Society of Delaware and its staff, particularly Connie Cooper; the Jewish Historical Society of Delaware and its archivist, Gail M. Pietrzyk.

This book contains numerous notes, surely a distraction. I gave thought to eliminating them as my mentor, the late John Harvey Powell, did in his classic, *Bring Out Your Dead*, the story of the 1793 yellow-fever plague that devastated Philadelphia then the capital of our country. I decided to include the notes for two reasons: (1) to assure the reader there is a source for what I represent are "the facts"; (2) there is something of interest which did not make the cut for inclusion in the text of the book but which appears in the notes from time to time. Once I decided to retain the notes (urged to do so by Anita Seltzer), I needed a bright, persevering person to do the tedious task of insuring that the citation in the notes supported the assertions in the text. My second oldest grandchild, my grandson Adam Zakheim, Jon's younger brother, performed that necessary responsibility for me and I am exceedingly grateful to him not only for doing so but, moreover, for the suggestions he made along the way which improved the book.

In addition to Karen Druliner, Jonathan Zakheim, and Adam Zakheim, the following friends and family members (listed in alphabetical order) permitted me to impose upon them to read the book or portions of it at various stages of my writing: Victor F. Battaglia Sr., my friend of many years whose comments led me to lessen the vitriol in the book; Joan DelFattore, who urged me to take my book for publication to the University of Delaware Press; Joshua Kutinsky, who sharply edited my article on the role of Delaware lawyers in the school desegregation litigation and brought his editing insights to bear on *The Rape Case*; Abraham L. Morris, my nephew who bears my father's name, who took time from his business affairs to share his comments; Anita Seltzer, who made precise comments critical to the improvement of the end product; Jea P. Street, who was by my side in the 1990 and 1991 school desegregation trials and whose suggestions led me to remove ugly observations better left unsaid; the late William E. Wiggin, editor of *The Delaware Bar Journal*, who read early drafts and kept after me to write *The Rape Case*; Rabbi Herbert Yoskowitz, who made gentle comments; Deborah M. Zakheim, my oldest child, who took precious time from her own writing and painting to read what her father had written; and three anonymous persons who read the draft as first submitted to the Press and made perceptive comments (sometimes at odds with each other), which the Press made available to me in confidence. I learned from each reader's suggestions. To the extent I was sufficiently thoughtful to accept them, they improved the book; to the extent I rejected them, assuredly errors remain and, of course, are all my responsibility.

I owe special thanks to Sue Scarpitti-Lucy, who put my words into the computer and patiently made the countless revisions without a single complaint while holding a full-time job and raising and mentoring her and Mark's six children.

Finally, I acknowledge my debt to the late H. Albert Young whose singular effort at trial to establish the police perjury laid the basis for my being able to prove the unfairness of the trial of Curran, Jones, and Maguire and to write *The Rape Case.*

Abbreviations of Sources Frequently Cited

Bowen

> *United States v. Bowen,* 94 F. Supp. 1006 (N. D. Ga.), affirmed, *Bowen v. United States,* 192 F.2d 515 (5th Cir. 1951), certiorari denied 343 U.S. 943, rehearing denied 343 U.S. 988.

Curran I

> *Curran v. Wooley* [*sic*], 101 A.2d 303 (Del. Super. 1953).

Curran II

> *Curran v. Woolley* 104 A.2d 771 (Del. 1954).

Curran III

> *State v. Curran,* 116 A.2d 782 (Del. Super. 1955).

Curran IV

> *Curran v. State,* 122 A.2d 126 (Del. 1956).

Curran V

> *Curran v. Craven,* 125 A.2d 375 (Del. Ch. 1956).

Curran VI

> *Curran v. State of Delaware,* 352 U.S. 913 (1956).

Curran VII

> *Curran v. State of Delaware,* 154 F.Supp. 27 (D.C. Del. 1957).

Curran VIII

    Curran v. State of Delaware, 259 F.2d 707 (3d Cir. 1958).

Curran IX

    Delaware v. Curran, et al., 358 U.S. 948 (1959).

Defense Fails

    "Defense Fails to Weaken Girl's Story in Rape Case," *Journal,* Feb. 11, 1948.

Delaware Bar

    Winslow, Helen L., Anne E. Bookout, and Patricia C. Hannigan, eds. *The Delaware Bar in the Twentieth Century,* eds. (Wilmington, Del. Delaware State Bar Association, 1994).

Hoffecker

    Hoffecker, Carol E. *Federal Justice in the First State: A History of the United States District Court for the District of Delaware* (Wilmington, Del.: The Historical Society for the United States District Court for the District of Delaware, 1992).

Hr'g Tr.

    Transcript of the December 1–2, 1954 hearing in *The Rape Case* on the Rule 35 Motion in the Superior Court. Unpublished copy in the author's possession.

Journal

    Journal-Every Evening Delaware's evening newspaper published in Wilmington, Delaware, and distributed throughout the state during the time of *The Rape Case.* Its successor paper is *The News Journal.*

Kavanaugh Deposition

    Deposition of Andrew J. Kavanaugh, Superintendent of the Department of Public Safety, taken August 6, 1954. Unpublished copy in the author's possession.

McCool Deposition

> Deposition of Detective Charles F. McCool, taken July 28, 1954. Unpublished copy in the author's possession.

McCool's Report

> Captain Charles F. McCool's undated post-trial report of his investigation of *The Rape Case* ordered by Andrew J. Kavanaugh, Superintendent of the Department of Public Safety. Unpublished copy in the author's possession.

Moore

> *United States v. Moore,* 166 F.2d 102 (7th Cir. 1948).

Morning News

> *Wilmington Morning News,* self-described as "Delaware's Morning Paper," published in Wilmington, Delaware, and distributed throughout the state during the time of *The Rape Case.* Its successor paper is *The News Journal.*

Napue

> *Napue v. Illinois,* 360 U.S. 264 (1959).

OAT

> Transcript of the April 16, 1957 oral argument before Judge Wright in the District Court. Unpublished copy in the author's possession.

PHT

> The transcript of the preliminary hearing in *The Rape Case,* November 12, 1947, in the Municipal Court of the City of Wilmington, State of Delaware, No. 139, October Term, 1947. Unpublished copy in the author's possession.

Polk's Directory

> *Polk's Wilmington City Directory, 1946–47.* (Richmond, Va: R. L. Polk & Co., 1947).

Preparations Made

"Preparations made for Jury in Rape Trial on Feb. 10," *Morning News,* Jan. 23, 1948.

Reitz

Reitz, Curtis R. "Federal Habeas Corpus: Postconviction Remedy for State Prisoners," 108 *University of Pennsylvania Law Review* 461 (1960).

Rodenhiser Deposition

Deposition of Detective John A. Rodenhiser, July 28, 1954. Unpublished copy in the author's possession.

Russ

Russ, Jonathan S. *Young Conaway Stargatt & Taylor, LLP: in Celebration of the First Forty Years.* Edited by William D. Johnston (Wilmington, Del.: Young Conaway Stargatt & Taylor, 1999).

The 1935 Code

The Revised Code of Delaware, 1935. (Wilmington, DE: Star, 1936).

Thomas and DePrisco Interview

Thomas, Catherine "Kitty" Curran and Helen Curran DePrisco. Interview by the author, May 15, 1997, Wilmington, Del.

Trial

The transcript of the trial in The Rape Case held February 10–17, 1948, in the Court of Oyer and Terminer of the State of Delaware in and for New Castle County sitting in Wilmington, Delaware. Unpublished copy in the author's possession.

Notes

Preface

1. "Three Found Guilty of Rape, But Jury Recommends Mercy," *Morning News*, Feb. 18, 1948, 1, 4. Trial, 1045.

2. "Three Men Get Life Sentences in Attack Case," *Morning News*, Mar. 17, 1948, 1.

3. On December 7, 1787, Delaware ratified the Constitution of the United States, the first of the former thirteen colonies to do so, thereby securing its place as the First State in the Union.

4. Delaware ratified the Thirteenth, Fourteenth and Fifteenth Amendments on February 12, 1901 (the 92nd anniversary of President Abraham Lincoln's birth), when the Senate Pro Tempore and the Speaker of the House of Representatives of Delaware's General Assembly officially signed Senate Joint Resolution No. 13. The Senate unanimously adopted the resolution on January 30, 1901, and the House without dissent on January 31, 1901, with two members of the House absent. Delaware thus ratified the three amendments long after their effective dates. Delaware General Assembly, *Enrolled Bills* (February 12, 1901), 1:33; Delaware General Assembly, *Journal of the State Senate* (Milford, DE: Milford Chronicle Publishing, 1901), 222; Delaware General Assembly, *Journal of the House of Representatives of the State of Delaware* (Dover, DE: S. & J. Adams, 1901), 355–56.

5. Thomas B. Malone, "Rape Case Ends; Defendants Freed," *Morning News*, Feb.26, 1959, 1.

6. *Napue v. Illinois*, 360 U.S. 264, 269 (1959).

Chapter 1. For Want of a Match

1. Trial, 754–55.

2. Throughout the Trial transcript Schueler's name is mistakenly spelled as "Schuler."

3. Trial, 755.

4. Although Curran testified Jones sat beside him in the front seat (Ibid., 757), Maguire placed Masten in the front with Jones in back (836). Fahey (565–66), Schueler (621–22), and Jones (911) agreed with Maguire. Masten was not asked where he sat (493–546).

5. 755–56; 496.

6. 834.

7. 905. Contemporary descriptions of the defendants are from Ellen H. Crossman, "Whitefaced Girl on Stand Sways by Her Simplicity," *Sunday Star,* Wilmington, Del., Feb. 15, 1948, 9.

8. Trial, 856.

9. Ibid., 752–53 (Curran); 905 (Jones); 835 (Maguire).

10. 835.

11. 563–64 (Fahey); 515 (Masten); 752 (Curran). Author interviews with Carmen N. Stigliano, Wilmington, Del., August 21, 1996; November 18, 2002; and November 11, 2004. Author interview with Martin Golden, Wilmington, Del., Aug. 3, 2006.

12. 855–56.

13. Statement of Patrolman James A. Nagle Jr. in McCool's Report, 54.

14. Trial, 747. Although her parents named her "Jane," by the time I knew her she spelled her first name "Jayne." Accordingly, I use her preferred spelling. When she died on December 23, 1992, at age 71, the obituary carried her name as "Jane Jones Stigliano." Obituary of Jane Jones Stigliano, *News Journal,* Dec. 25, 1992, B5. When her husband, Carmen N. Stigliano, died on May 18, 2006, his obituary referred to her as "Jayne." Obituary of Carmen N. Stigliano, *Sunday News Journal,* May 21, 2006, B5.

15. Trial, 722. Bud Curran was his parents' second child. He had yet another sister, Ann Marie, who had died in 1938 at age 9. See list of Curran's siblings in the author's possession.

16. Trial, 757 (Curran). Each of the other five men in the car testified Curran asked for a match. Ibid., 550–51 (Fahey); 497 (Masten); 620–21 (Schueler); 836 (Maguire); 908–09 (Jones).

17. 497.

18. 757.

19. 757, 759.

20. 552–53.

21. 759–60, 792–94.

22. 760, 794, 797–98.

23. 501; 760–61, 798, 839.

24. 795–97.

25. 839–40.

26. 841–43.

27. 841, 843, 851.

28. 187–93.

29. 201–2.

30. 843.

31. 843–44, 916–17.

32. 844–45.

33. 561–62 (Fahey); 512–15, 542, 544–46 (Masten); 653–58 (Schueler); 916, 919, 963 (Jones).

34. 632, 689.

35. 777–78.

36. 779.

37. 778–79, 781–82.

38. 897–98.

39. 853–54.

40. 920–22; 924–25. At trial the young woman testified she did not remember saying this. 68, 114.

41. 781.

42. 851.

43. 782–83, 851, 921.

44. 851–52, 893.

45. Ibid.

46. 922–23.

47. 924–25.

48. 920.

49. 130–31. *Curran IV,* 127. In note 1, Chief Justice Southerland for the Supreme Court wrote: "This statement was not before the jury; but it appears to us to be admissible as a part of a spontaneous exclamation."

50. Trial, 139–40.

51. Ibid., 140–41.

52. 142. Jones testified she said, "There is no trouble. It is just family trouble." 928.

53. 142–43 (Officer Allen's quote appears on 143).

54. 277. In 1947, Wilmington's Central Police Station was located on the ground floor on the French Street side of Wilmington's Public Building.

55. McCool's Report, 33, 36.

56. Trial, 252–54; 722–23 (Nellie G. Curran), 726 (Helen A. Curran) (Curran); 852, 897 (Maguire).

57. Ibid., 339–40, 342–43, 353.

58. 249–52. State's Exhibit No. 10. McCool's Report, 44.

59. McCool's Report, 32–33, 45.

60. Trial, 24, 59 (Curran); 24 (Maguire); 24, 63 (Jones).

61. Ibid., 20–23 (Curran); 24 (Maguire); 27 (Jones).

62. 354; 365. State's Exhibit No. 11.

63. 365–66; McCool's Report, 34–35, 46.

64. Trial, 366–68.

65. Ibid., 811–13 (Curran); 329; 969–70 (Jones); 853, 895–96 (Maguire). Maguire said he signed the second statement "about four o'clock the next day in the afternoon." Given the unanimity of the others, I think Maguire was mistaken in his recollection. McCool's Report does not resolve the issue.

66. 811 (Curran); 969–70 (Jones); 895–96 (Maguire).

67. *Miranda v. Arizona,* 384 U.S. 436 (1966). Rodenhiser did not even tell Jones any statement he gave could be used against him. Trial, 335–36. The record is silent about any warning of a constitutional right to remain silent given by police to Curran and Maguire.

68. Trial, 783–84, 811 (Curran); 335; 930, 935–36, 937, 969 (Jones); 853, 890–91 (Maguire).

Chapter 2. The Preliminary Hearing

1. Trial, 747–48; *Polk's Directory*, 448.

2. In my brief period at the Bar at the time of *The Rape Case*, I had twice bested Young in litigation in *Sayer Brothers v. Landy* and in a mechanic's lien case I brought on behalf of workmen. Although neither case went to trial, my clients in each case secured in settlement everything I could have obtained for them with a victory at trial.

3. *Russ*, 6.

4. Ibid., 8–9.

5. Years after *The Rape Case*, Albert "Bert" Jenner of Jenner and Block, the firm Jenner founded with Sam Block in Chicago, retained Young as the local lawyer for Jenner's client, Hallmark, Inc. (the watch company, not the card company), when I had to withdraw as Hallmark's lawyer and Jenner succeeded me. Jenner described Young's fee charging with the descriptive phrase: "Hy has a heavy foot on the gas pedal."

6. Carmen N. Stigliano is the source of the information regarding payment of Young's fee. See chapter 1, note 11. The sum of $5,000 in November 1947 would have the purchasing power of almost $45,000 in April 2007 according to the formula the Consumer Price Index of the Bureau of Labor Statistics uses. Alan D. Levenson, Chief Economist of T. Rowe Price of America, memorandum to the author, Aug. 19, 2007. Original in the author's possession.

7. Trial, 720–21.

8. "Court Appoints Youth Counsel," *Journal*, Nov. 17, 1947, A1.

9. *Polk's Directory*, 533.

10. Trial, 750.

11. Ibid., 680.

12. PHT, 2.

13. Ibid., 1, 23–24, 71. The charge of rape, a capital offense, was not a bailable offense except that "the court of General Sessions, when in session, or any Judge thereof in vacation, may admit to bail a person accused of such offense before indictment found, if upon full inquiry, it appears that there is good ground to doubt the truth of the accusation." The 1935 Code, Sec. 4480. With its 185 chapters and its black

numbered 6,308 sections, *The 1935 Code* housed all of Delaware's laws "general and permanent in their nature in force on [July 1, 1935]" in one volume. Ibid., iv.

14. PHT, 3.

15. Ibid., 5–12.

16. 12–21.

17. 23–31.

18. 31.

19. 31–32.

20. 24.

21. *State v. Hawkins,* 183 A. 626 (Del. Gen. Sess. 1936).

22. PHT, 29.

23. Ibid., 33–51.

24. 51–52.

25. 55–63.

26. 63.

27. 66–67.

28. 66–68.

29. 68–70 (the quotation appears at page 70).

30. 71.

31. *State v. Francis J. Curran, Francis J. Maguire and Ira F. Jones, Jr.,* True Bill, Docket Entry No. 1 (filed Nov. 17, 1947). In an early phase of *The Rape Case,* Young took the lead for the defendants, as he almost always did throughout the trial, to move on behalf of Jones to quash the Grand Jury's indictment of Curran, Jones, and Maguire on the ground that the New Castle County Jury Commissioners did not impanel any woman on the grand jury indicting them. Docket Entry No. 2 (filed Nov. 14, 1947). The attorneys for Curran and Maguire filed a similar motion five days later. Docket Entry No. 3 (filed Nov. 19, 1947). In an opinion by Chief Justice Richards, sitting with Judges Terry and Carey, the court denied Young's motion. Docket Entry No. 4 (filed Dec. 23, 1947). The court held since the petitioners were all males they had no standing to raise the point. *State v. Jones,* 57 A.2d 109 (Del. Oyer & Terminer 1947). But Young won the day when the state by Chief Deputy Attorney General C. Edward Duffy agreed with him and did not oppose the action of the jury commissioners to in-

clude women for service on juries. The court did not interfere with this practical result. Two women sat on the Grand Jury which reindicted Curran, Jones, and Maguire. Two women, including the forelady, served on the jury in *The Rape Case.* The commissioners' reason for not previously impaneling women to serve as jurors was the lack of women's restroom facilities in the jury room. "Attack Case Plea Studies by Court," *Morning News,* Nov. 20, 1947, A1 and A4.

Chapter 3. The Trial

1. *The 1935 Code,* Sec. 5166.
2. Ibid. Sec. 4305; Trial, 1–1085.
3. Delaware Constitution of 1897, Art. IV, Section 13. The Constitutional Amendment, effective June 1, 1951, created a three-person, separate Supreme Court of Delaware displacing the old system fraught with self-interest and mischief. For a trenchant analysis and history of the leftover judges system and its elimination see Maurice A. Hartnett, III, "Delaware Courts' Progression," in *Delaware Supreme Court,* 13–14, 16–21; see also Henry R. Horsey and William Duffy, "The Supreme Court Until 1951, The 'Leftover Judge' System," in *The Delaware Bar,* 364–65; Preparations Made, 4.

> Originally scheduled for the January term of court were Judges George Burton Pearson, Jr., and Caleb R. Layton III. However, Judges Terry and Carey heard the original arguments in the case, a factor that would eliminate them from sitting on the Supreme Court bench should the defendants be found guilty and an appeal granted to the higher court. Likewise, Judges Pearson and Layton, should they sit with the Chief Justice during the trial, would be eliminated from the Supreme Court bench in the case of an appeal.
>
> This would leave only one judge—Chancellor W. W. Harrington—to sit during a Supreme Court hearing, and three judges are necessary. Therefore, under the present setup, Judges Pearson and Layton will be available should the necessity of carrying the case to the Supreme Court materialize. "Preparations Made," 4.

4. Ibid.
5. Trial, 777–79 (Curran); 920,922 (Jones); 848–49, 897–98 (Ma-

guire); 552–562 (Fahey); 501–515 (Masten); 623–30, 632–34 (Schueler); 21–28 (the woman's denial).

6. "Court Appoints Youth Counsel," *Journal,* Nov. 17, 1947, A1.

7. Trial, 69.

8. Ibid., 6–18.

9. Defense Fails, 1, 4; Trial, 18–19.

10. Trial, 8–9.

11. Ibid., 9–13.

12. 13–14.

13. Ibid.

14. 250–52 (statement of Francis J. Curran).

15. 350–52 (statement of Ira F. Jones).

16. 356–58 (statement of Francis J. Maguire).

17. Statement of the young woman attached as an exhibit to McCool's Report at 72–73, 72. See note 157.

18. Trial, 14.

19. PHT 17–18.

20. Trial, 15.

21. Ibid., 16.

22. 16–17.

23. 18.

24. 16–17.

25. 18.

26. 22–23.

27. 23.

28. 30–31.

29. 31.

30. 24 (Curran); 24 (Maguire); 27, 30 (Jones); and see PHT 16–20.

31. Trial, 26.

32. Ibid., 849.

33. 30, 31–2.

34. Attorney General James on direct first asked: "I will ask you to look upon the three defendants and state if they are the three men who assaulted you and attacked you the night [*sic*] of October 30, 1947, in Woodland Park [*sic*]." She answered "Yes." Ibid., 35. On redirect James corrected his errors and the witness testified it was the morning of October 30, 1947, and the place was Woodlawn Park. 128–29.

35. Rule 16(a)(A).

36. Trial, 366–68.

37. Compare James' direct examination, thirty pages (Ibid., 6–36), with Young's cross-examination, eighty-three pages (36–68, 76–127).

38. 36–7.

39. 37.

40. 38–9.

41. 39.

42. 39–40.

43. 40–1.

44. 41–2; 13–14.

45. 46.

46. 47.

47. 47–48.

48. 109.

49. 119–20.

50. 123–24.

51. 66–8

52. 13–14.

53. 48.

54. 50.

55. 16–17 ("and so I walked up Bancroft Parkway with him.").

56. 122.

57. 759.

58. 552–53.

59. 500, 522–24.

60. 837–38.

61. 620–23.

62. 125–26.

63. 126–27.

64. 127–28.

65. 128–29.

66. Defense Fails, 1, 4.

67. Trial, 923–25 (Jones).

68. Ibid., 927 (Jones); 66 (the woman); 781 (Curran).

69. 722–23, 726 (about Curran); 852, 685 (about Maguire).

70. 244–48.
71. 248–49.
72. 249–52; State's Exhibit No. 10 appears at 250–52.
73. 252.
74. Ibid.
75. 277–78.
76. 278.
77. 278–79.
78. 280–81.
79. 278–93; the suggestion is at 292–93.
80. 285.
81. Ibid.
82. 280,285.
83. 293–94.
84. 294.
85. Ibid.
86. 295. Compare Young's question with Duffy's at 278–279.
87. 302, 311, 315–16, 334.
88. 315, 325–26, 329.
89. 315.
90. 315–16.
91. 318–20.
92. 325.
93. 326.
94. 326–27.
95. 329.

96. 329–30. Although Jones first testified the signing was "the next afternoon," I think he misspoke. On October 30, the day of his arrest, he had been awake for more than twenty-four hours. Subsequently on cross-examination on the trial's sixth day, Jones corrected himself and testified he signed the second statement "at four o'clock, that afternoon." 969. Maguire, too, said he signed the second statement about four o'clock the next day in the afternoon. 895–96. I think he, too, misspoke. McCool's Report does not resolve the issue, but it does include Mazewski's disclosure that "sometime later" on October 30, 1947, at Rodenhiser's direction, he brought a statement to Maguire in the cellblock for him to sign. McCool's Report, 40–41.

97. Trial, 331.

98. Ibid., 332–33.

99. 333–36.

100. 338–39.

101. 340–41.

102. 342–43.

103. 348–49.

104. 349–52.

105. 354.

106. 355.

107. 355–56. The transcript occupies seventy-three pages (276–349) before Duffy read the Jones paper, State's Exhibit No. 11, to the jury in contrast to the three pages (353–55) before Duffy read the Maguire paper, State's Exhibit No. 12. Reinhardt's statement appears on 355.

108. 356–58.

109. 365–68.

110. 811–13 (Curran); 329, 969–70 (Jones); 853, 895–96 (Maguire); and see *Curran IV,* 129; *Curran VII, 29; Curran VIII, 710.*

111. Trial, 751–832.

112. Ibid., 811.

113. 834–898.

114. 853 (direct), 895–96 (cross).

115. 899.

116. 899–900.

117. 900.

118. 903–04.

119. 1009–11.

120. 1007–08.

121. 1008.

122. 1009.

123. Ibid.

124. 1010.

125. 1011.

126. 1007–08 (Emering about Curran); 319, 342–43 (Mazewski about Jones); 245–48 (Nagle about Curran); 293–94, 315, 332–33, 339, 1009–10 (Rodenhiser about Jones); 353–54, 1010 (Rodenhiser about Maguire). The state did not call Officer Angelo Delloso who also was a

witness to Curran's statement in evidence. Delloso Deposition, taken July 28, 1954, 96, 101–02. Compare the police trial testimony with the condemnation by both the state and federal judges who reviewed the police testimony in the light of the facts I adduced during the course of my effort to secure a new trial free of the police perjury. *Curran III,* 786; *Curran IV,* 128–29; *Curran VII,* 29–31; *Curran VIII,* 709–711.

127. State's Exhibit No. 10; Trial, 250–52 (Quotation appears at 250.)

128. Ibid., 549–50 (Fahey); 495–96 (Masten); 617, 622, 627 (Schueler).

129. 550–51 (Fahey); 494–500 (Masten); 618,619,620–23 (Schueler); 755–57 (Curran); 906–11 (Jones); 835–38 (Maguire).

130. 350; State's Exhibit No. 11 (the text appears at 350–52) (Jones); 356; State's Exhibit No. 12 (the text appears on 356–58) (Maguire); 249; State's Exhibit No. 10 (the text appears on 250–52) (Curran); 552–58, 560–62 (Fahey); 501–15 (Masten); 620–26, 629–30, 632–34 (Schueler); 830–32 (Curran).

131. 830.

132. 930–31.

133. 940–41.

134. 892.

135. 548–63, 614 (Fahey); 493–515 (Masten); 617–34 (Schueler).

136. Years later when Young and I walked together into town after morning services at Congregation Beth Shalom at Eighteenth and Baynard Boulevard, Young told me of the difficulty he had in securing their testimony.

137. Trial, 591 (Fahey); 503–05 (Masten).

138. Ibid., 556 (Fahey); 501, 502, 505, 509, 510–11 (Masten); 623–26, 629–30 (Schueler).

139. 555–57, 560–61 (Fahey); 504, 511, 512 (Masten); 629–30 (Schueler).

140. 557–61 (Fahey); 502, 507, 513–14 (Masten); 632–33 (Schueler).

141. 556, 561–62 (Fahey); 502–03, 507, 514 (Masten); 632–34 (Schueler).

142. 557, 561–62 (Fahey); 514 (Masten); 632 (Schueler).

143. Defendants' Exhibit No. 13, 678–79.

144. 770–71.

145. 771.

146. 776.

147. 686.

148. 686–89.

149. 689–91.

150. 1008–09 (Emering about Curran); 1010 (Rodenhiser about Jones); 1010–11 (Rodenhiser about Maguire).

151. Duffy summation, 43. Superintendant of Public Safety Andrew J. Kavanaugh at his deposition claimed the three eyewitnesses had "all perjured themselves" and the Department had proof: "Statements from their parents [and] others that these boys weren't there, definitely." Hr'g Tr., 171–2. By my agreement with Hamilton, the Kavanaugh Deposition was included in the transcript of the December 1954 hearing at 139–206. The page numbers of the Kavanaugh Deposition are to the pages as they appear in the Hr'g Tr.

152. Trial, 830 (Curran); 930–31 (Jones); 892 (Maguire).

153. Ibid., 249–52 at 251, State's Exhibit No. 10 (Curran); 350–52 at 351, State's Exhibit No. 11 (Jones); and 356–58 at 357, State's Exhibit No. 12 (Maguire).

154. 251, State's Exhibit No. 10.

155. 351, State's Exhibit No. 11.

156. 357,State's Exhibit No. 12.

157. Her statement is attached to McCool's Report, 72–73. Kavanaugh believed the young woman used the word "moaning" in her statement. When shown her statement and reading it at his deposition he testified: "I don't see it in her statement." Hr'g Tr. 198. The state did not introduce the woman's statement at trial.

158. Trial, 783–84, 813–14 (Curran); 932 (Jones); 898 (Maguire).

159. Ibid., 249 (Curran's statement admitted without objection as State's Exhibit No. 10 without any questions by Hagner, Reinhardt, or Young); 355 (Maguire's statement admitted without objection as State's Exhibit No. 12 without any questions by Reinhardt, Hagner, or Young).

160. 811, 812, 813 (Curran); 329; 969–70 (Jones); 853, 895–96 (Maguire).

161. 329.

162. 149; "Curran Story in Evidence at Rape Trial," *Morning News,* Feb. 12, 1948, 1.

163. Trial, 249.

164. Ibid., 751–832.

165. 811–13.

166. Thomas and DePrisco Interview.

167. Trial, 831–32.

168. Ibid., 294–303, 315–16, 325–26.

169. 355.

170. Ibid.

171. 853.

172. 834–98; 895–96 (Duffy's follow-up questions).

173. Years later on one of our walks to town from Congregation Beth Shalom after morning services, Young told me his opinion was that Jones, his client, was innocent and "the other two were guilty."

174. See above Chapter 3 Section, "The Police Commit Perjury."

175. Trial, 329 (Jones).

176. Ibid., 895 (Maguire).

177. 812–13 (Curran).

178. 315–16, 341.

179. 1007–09 (Emering about Curran); 1009–10 (Rodenhiser about Jones); 1010–12 (Rodenhiser about Maguire).

180. 280; and see also 285.

181. *Polk's Directory,* 448.

182. Author interview with Carmen J. Stigliano, Nov. 18, 2002.

183. Around 4 p.m. on October 30, 1947, Lieutenant Egnor assigned Detective George W. Kienberger to go to the homes of Curran, Jones, and Maguire to obtain clean shorts and trousers for each man. By 5:30 p.m. Kienberger was back at the police headquarters with the articles. McCool's Report, 16, 65, 66–7.

184. Dr. Tiffany was the "official chemist for [Wilmington], the state attorney general's office, the coroner's office, and the Internal Revenue Service." He founded and contemporaneously owned and maintained Wilmington Testing & Research Laboratories, a private enterprise. "Doctor Tiffany Dies at Age 72," *Journal,* May 5, 1954, 1.

185. Trial, 386 (Maguire's shorts); 383–84 (Curran's shorts).

186. Ibid., 393. Jones' shorts were subsequently admitted into

evidence as State's Exhibit No. 15. 395.

187. 388 (direct) and 392 (cross).

188. 392.

189. 407.

190. 413.

191. Author interview with Carmen J. Stigliano, Nov. 18, 2002.

192. Trial, 204–06, 235.

193. Ibid., 677–680 (Quotation appears on 679). Defense Exhibit No. 13.

194. Trial, 698–702.

195. Ibid., 738–39.

196. 739.

197. 388 (McCool). But post-trial McCool wrote: "Spots and soiled marks were found on the shorts and trousers of all three of these defendants." McCool's Report, 15. At the time of the trial, Young was totally unaware that McCool would contradict his trial testimony in a report not prepared until after the trial, and even then never shown to Young. Trial, 413 (Tiffany).

198. Trial, 834–1013.

199. "Jury Charge In Rape Case To Come Today," *Morning News,* Feb. 17, 1948, 1, 4. I have never seen a copy of James' opening statement. The lengthy quotations in the text are attributed to James in the cited article. I think they are accurate since the article's quotes from the Hagner, Reinhardt, Young, and Duffy summations match the transcripts of these summations, copies of which are in the author's possession.

200. Hagner Summation, 2.

201. Ibid.

202. 2–3.

203. 3.

204. 4.

205. 4–5.

206. 5.

207. 5–6.

208. 6.

209. 6–7.

210. 7.

211. 7–8.
212. 8.
213. 8–9.
214. 9.
215. Reinhardt Summation, 2.
216. Ibid., 3.
217. Ibid.
218. 4.
219. Ibid.
220. Ibid.
221. 4–5.
222. 5.
223. 6.
224. 6–7.
225. 8.
226. Ibid.
227. 8–9.
228. 9–10.
229. 11.
230. Trial, 1042
231. Ibid., 105, 111, 119–20, 122–24.
232. Young Summation, 3.
233. Ibid., 4.
234. 7.
235. Ibid.
236. 17.
237. 25–26.
238. 28.
239. 6.
240. 8–15.
241. Reinhardt Summation, 4; Young Summation, 8.
242. Hagner Summation, 4.
243. Ibid., 5–6; Reinhardt Summation, 4, 5–6; Young Summation, 13–15.
244. Young Summation, 26.
245. PHT, 24.
246. Trial, 126.

247. Young Summation, 30–31.

248. Ibid., 31.

249. 31–32.

250. Duffy Summation, 33–34. It is bound together with the Young Summation and the page numbers follow consecutively.

251. Ibid., 34.

252. *State of Delaware v. Ira F. Jones, Jr.,* 57 A.2d 109 (Court of Oyer and Terminer 1947).

253. Duffy Summation, 35.

254. Ibid., 36–39.

255. Trial, 757 (Curran); 836 (Maguire); 565–66 (Fahey); 621–22 (Schueler); 493–546 (Masten).

256. Duffy Summation, 43.

257. Ibid., 41.

258. Trial, 757–59.

259. Ibid., 836–38 (Maguire); 908–09 (Jones); 619–23 (Schueler); 500 (Masten); 552 (Fahey).

260. Duffy Summation, 44–45.

261. Ibid., 49.

262. Trial, 849.

263. Duffy Summation, 58. For the challenges, see Reinhardt Summation, 8 and Young Summation, 25–26.

264. See the statement of Lieutenant Bryan in McCool's Report, 64.

265. Trial, 1a.

266. Duffy Summation, 34, 35, 50, and 52.

267. Ibid., 44, 44–45, and 55.

268. 60.

269. 61.

270. 62.

271. *Morning News,* Feb. 17, 1948, A1.

272. Ibid.

273. Trial, 1047–50.

274. Ibid., 1051–54 (Curran); 1055–57 (Jones); 1054–55 (Maguire).

275. 1051.

276. 1045–72.

277. Ellen H. Crossman, "Trial Sidelights," *Sunday Star,* Feb. 18, 1948, 9.

278. Trial, 2–5.

279. Ibid., 36–68, 76–127, 127–28.

280. "Three Facing Rape Charges Open Defense," *Morning News,* Feb. 14, 1948, 1.

281. Trial, 493–515 (Masten); 617–34 (Schueler); 686–90 (Leonzio).

282. Young Summation, 3–33.

283. "3 Young Men Are Jailed For Life In Attack Case," *Journal,* Mar. 16, 1948, 1. (Hereafter cited as 3 Young Men.)

284. *The Delaware Bar,* 733; the *Atlantic Reporter* and the *Federal Reporter* for the years 1922–1947.

285. "Youths Await Ruling on New Trial Appeals," *Journal,* Feb. 18, 1948, 1; Trial, 1045.

286. Trial, 1072.

287. Ibid.

288. 1072–73.

289. 1073; "Three Found Guilty of Rape, But Jury Recommends Mercy," *Morning News,* Feb. 18, 1948. (Hereafter cited as Three Found Guilty), 1.

290. WDEL's news-director Robert Kelly's "summary of the case on his 11 o'clock broadcast" on February 17, 1948, the day of the verdict, appeared under the caption "Broadcaster's Summary of Rape Trial Wins Praise," *Sunday Star,* Feb. 22, 1948, 9.

291. Trial, 1073. In a history of the firm Young formed in 1959 with James R. Morford and H. James Conaway Jr., and renamed after Morford's death, it is asserted without citation: "As soon as the jury rendered its verdict, Young arranged for one of the co-defendants' attorneys to immediately request a poll of the jury as to whether or not they thought the three deserved death." *Russ,* 8–9. I have not found any contemporaneous account supporting the "arrangement" Russ claims. The 1948 newspaper account reported that after the forelady announced the guilty verdict: "Mr. Reinhardt stood up at once and demanded the jury be polled." Three Found Guilty, A1, 4. Kelly corroborates this version. See note 290, above.

292. Trial, 1073–74; Three Found Guilty, 1.

293. *The 1935 Code,* Sec. 5166.

294. "Youths Await Ruling on New Trial Appeals," *Journal,* Feb. 18, 1948, 4.

295. 3 Young Men, 1.
296. Ibid.

Chapter 4. The Families Suffer

1. Author interview with Joseph Matassino, Wilmington, Del., n.d.
2. Most of the material about the Curran family is drawn from testimony by family members and from the Thomas and DePrisco Interview.
3. *Polk's Directory*, 530.
4. Ibid., 862.
5. 47.
6. 895.
7. "From a Defendant's Sister," *Journal*, February 21, 1948.
8. Thomas and DePrisco Interview.

Chapter 5. Searching for a Lawyer

1. "Herbert L. Maris, Lawyer, was 80. Philadelphian Noted for His Work in Behalf of Unjustly Convicted Prisoners," *The New York Times*, Sept. 14, 1960, 43.
2. George Corbeil to author, Dec. 7, 1957. Original in the author's possession.
3. Ibid.
4. Papers of George Corbeil in the author's possession.
5. Ibid.
6. Hr'g Tr., 210.
7. Ibid.
8. 218–19.
9. 216.
10. 221.
11. 219.
12. "Former City Policeman Found Dead in Home," *Journal*, Sept. 16, 1949, 10. His last year "had been one of trouble." A bitter family

dispute led to Nagle's arrest on September 6, 1949, and a brief incarceration in the New Castle County Workhouse on charges of assault and battery, threatening to do bodily harm to his wife's sister and her husband, and carrying a concealed deadly weapon. Out on bail with the criminal charges scheduled for trial on September 20, 1949, he committed suicide. See also "Nagle Charges Continued," *Journal*, Sept. 13, 1949; "Dismissed Policeman Found Dead of Fumes," *The Philadelphia Inquirer*, Sept. 16, 1949.

13. Herbert L. Maris to Joseph Donald Craven, June 13, 1950. Copy in the author's possession. Craven had polio as a child, but he did not let it deter him from completing college. He taught social studies at Warner Junior High School while studying law. An able teacher, he inspired loyalty among his students who sang his praises long after he had turned to the practice of law in 1936.

14. George Corbeil to Joseph Donald Craven, Aug. 12, 1950. Copy in the author's possession.

15. Ibid.

16. *Delaware Bar*, 735.

17. Thomas J. Healy Jr. to George S. Corbeil, Nov. 2, 1950. Copy in the author's possession.

18. George S. Corbeil to Thomas J. Healy Jr., Nov. 6, 1950. Copy in the author's possession.

19. Herbert L. Maris to Francis Curran Sr., Nov. 6, 1950. Copy in the author's possession.

20. When I joined Philip Cohen in the partnership effective January 1, 1953, following my clerkship with Chief Judge Paul Leahy, Taylor's office was at the other end of the hall from our office on the eighth floor of the North American Building. I had many conversations with him, but Taylor never told me why he had left the Richards' firm. Although he was caustic about the other partners, he always spoke with respect and admiration about Aaron Finger.

21. Herbert L. Maris to William E. Taylor Jr., Feb. 28, 1951. Copy in the author's possession.

22. William E. Taylor Jr. to Herbert L. Maris, Mar. 2, 1951. Copy in the author's possession.

23. Ibid.

24. Herbert L. Maris to William E. Taylor Jr., Mar. 19, 1951. Copy in the author's possession.

25. Ibid.

26. William E. Taylor Jr. to Herbert L. Maris, Mar. 23, 1951. Copy in the author's possession.

27. Herbert L. Maris to William E. Taylor Jr., Mar. 26, 1951. Copy in the author's possession.

28. If Maris and the families had secured a Delaware lawyer in 1951 they could have gone ahead with the habeas corpus petition, a civil proceeding. See Chapter 9, below.

29. Newton White to Herbert L. Maris, Aug. 13, 1952. Copy in the author's possession.

30. Herbert L. Maris to Newton White, Aug. 15, 1952. Copy in the author's possession. Compare it with similar language in George S. Corbeil to Joseph Donald Craven, Aug. 12, 1950. See note 14, above.

Chapter 6. Serendipity

1. Obituary of Jane Jones Stigliano, *The News Journal,* December 25, 1992, B5.

2. Trial, 856.

3. Ibid.

4. Compare 29–30 with 849.

5. "F. J. Curran's Attorney to Get Fee of $500," *Morning News,* Mar. 31, 1948, 2.

6. The name of a third lawyer, Deputy Attorney General Joseph H. Flanzer, appears on the title page of the trial transcript. Flanzer did not examine any of the witnesses.

7. Herbert L. Maris to Francis Curran, Dec. 16, 1952. Copy in the author's possession.

8. Thomas and DePrisco Interview.

9. "Rose Richter To Be Wed," *The New York Times,* Jan. 25, 1952, 24.

Chapter 7. My Colleagues and My Clients

1. His cousin, Albert Maris, was a well respected judge of the Third Circuit Court of Appeals.

2. *State v. Hawkins,* 183 A. 626, 630 (Del. Gen. Sess. 1936).

3. Ibid.

4. 631.

5. See Chapters 9 and 10 below.

6. The grounds are summarized in *Curran I,* 304, the first opinion after I entered the case.

7. Compare the 1935 Code, sec. 5166, with the *Delaware Code Annotated.* (St. Paul: West Publishing Company, 1953), Vol. 7, Title 11, §781. Almost thirty years after *The Rape Case* trial, the United States Supreme Court by a 7–2 vote held the death penalty for rape was unconstitutional. See *Coker v. Georgia,* 433 U.S. 584 (1977).

8. After "years of agitation," the unsuccessful proponents for a state penitentiary settled for the creation of a board of trustees and the construction of the Workhouse as a county prison to replace the facility in New Castle. It opened on November 4, 1901. "Lack of Funds Big Problem at Workhouse for 50 Years," *Morning News,* Mar. 18, 1950, 1, 7. The Workhouse changed its name to the New Castle County Correctional Institution effective July 21, 1959. In 1970 the state built the Delaware Correctional Center near Smyrna, Delaware, at a cost of $11.5 million. The old Workhouse structure was finally demolished and the grounds became a public park.

9. William P. Frank, "Step Right Up, See the Prison," *Evening Journal,* Apr. 28, 1971, 31.

10. Listed in chronological order: *Curran I, Curran II, Curran III, Curran IV, Curran V,* and *Curran VI.*

Chapter 8. Picking a Judge

1. *The Delaware Bar,* 414.

2. Ibid., 414–15.

3. Irving Morris to Charles F. G. Smith, Jan. 7, 1953, Jan. 20, 1953. Copies in the author's possession. Charles F. G. Smith to Irving Morris, Jan. 13, 1953, Jan. 23, 1953, Feb. 4, 1953. Originals in the author's possession.

4. Irving Morris to Charles F. G. Smith, Jan. 20, 1953. Copy in the author's possession.

5. Charles F. G. Smith to Irving Morris, Jan. 23, 1953. Original in the author's possession.

6. Irving Morris to Charles F. G. Smith, Jan. 7, 1953. Copy in the author's possession.

7. Charles F. G. Smith to Irving Morris, Feb. 4, 1953. Original in the author's possession.

8. Charles F. G. Smith to Irving Morris, Mar. 2, 1953. Original in the author's possession.

9. Ibid.

10. Irving Morris to Francis J. Curran, Francis J. Maguire, and Ira F. Jones Jr., Mar. 11, 1953. Copy in the author's possession.

11. Irving Morris to Charles F. G. Smith, Mar. 19, 1953. Copy in the author's possession.

12. Ibid.

13. Irving Morris to Charles F. G. Smith, Mar. 30, 1953. Copy in the author's possession.

14. Irving Morris to Charles F. G. Smith, Mar. 31, 1953. Copy in the author's possession.

15. Caleb R. Layton III to Irving Morris, Jul. 13, 1953. Original in the author's possession.

Chapter 9. My Failure to Research Leads to the First Defeat

· 1. As a boy, Hamilton won the Delaware Parks tennis championship several times, and he starred as a tennis player at Cornell. One year, he was runner-up in the Eastern Intercollegiate Tennis Tournament. "Lawyer leaps to Death from Apt.," *Morning News,* Mar. 31, 1975, 9.

2. While with Simon, Hamilton successfully reversed a verdict I had obtained against him in the Superior Court before Judge Terry in my first jury trial. See *Lee Tire & Rubber Co. v. Dormer,* 108 A.2d 168 (Del. 1954).

3. See *Curran I; Curran II; Curran III.*

4. Delaware modeled its Rule 35 after Federal Statute 28 U.S.C. §2255.

5. See Chapter 2 above.

6. "Habeas Corpus Writ Filed For 3 Serving Life Terms For Rape," *Morning News,* June 17, 1953, A1.

7. George Corbeil to Joseph Donald Craven, Aug. 12, 1950. Copy in the author's possession.

8. Irving Morris to Stephen E. Hamilton Jr., June 25, 1953. Copy in the author's possession.

9. Stephen E. Hamilton Jr. to Irving Morris, July 9, 1953. Original in the author's possession.

10. *Curran I.*

11. Ibid., 305, 308.

Chapter 10. The Importance of Civil Discovery (The Second Defeat)

1. *United States v. Morgan,* 346 U.S. 502, 517 (1953) (". . . habeas corpus is a civil proceeding although most often used to obtain relief from criminal judgments."), citing *Ex parte Tom Tong,* 108 U.S. 556 (1883).

2. *Curran I.*

3. Ibid., 307–08.

4. 308, note 1.

5. 308.

6. 307, note 4.

7. *Curran II.*

Chapter 11. The Buried Report Surfaces and the Depositions Begin

1. Kavanaugh Deposition, Hr'g Tr., 139–206. The quotation appears on 142. See Chapter 3 note 151.

2. Ibid., 146–47.

3. 144.

4. 144–145.

5. 145.

6. 145–46.

7. 147.

8. 148.

9. 148, 150.

10. 148.

11. 149.

12. 143.

13. McCool Deposition, 9–10, 53. The quotation appears on 53. The McCool Deposition is found in Depositions before Hearing on Motion on Rule 35, Section I, containing the depositions of Charles F. McCool, Angelo S. Delloso, John Rodenhiser, and John W. Emering, all taken July 28, 1954. Unpublished copy in the author's possession.

14. Ibid., 10–15.

15. 10–15.

16. McCool's Report, 51–54 (the quotation appears at 53–54).

17. Ibid., 37 (Rodenhiser); 53 (Nagle's statement about retyping the Jones and Maguire statements).

18. Trial, 811 (Curran); 969–70 (Jones); 853, 895–96 (Maguire).

19. Ibid., 811, 819 (Curran); 969–70 (Jones); 895 (Maguire).

20. McCool's Report, 40–41.

21. Ibid., 42–46 (Emering); 40–41 (Mazewski); 51–54 (Nagle); 36–39 (Rodenhiser). And see also Hr'g Tr., 165–69 (where I spelled out in detail to Superintendent Kavanaugh at his deposition how the police perjury claim that Curran, Jones, and Maguire signed only one set of statements destroyed the defendants' credibility).

22. Hr'g Tr., 147–50, esp. 149; 180–81; McCool Deposition 53–54.

23. Hr'g Tr., 198.

24. Ibid., 200.

25. Rodenhiser Deposition, 109. When the Police Department in 1956 brought charges against Rodenhiser, who in the interim had been demoted to Sergeant, it eventually used his perjury at *The Rape Case* trial as one of the bases for discharging him.

26. McCool Deposition, 11, 14–15.

27. Ibid., 1.

28. See Chapter 9 for the text of Hamilton's July 9, 1953 letter.

29. McCool Deposition, 93–94.

30. Ibid., 30–31.

31. 30–42.

32. 8.

33. 45–46.

34. 72.

35. 81–82.

36. See text at note 19, above.

37. McCool Deposition, 64.

38. Ibid., 62–92.

39. 57, 79–80.

40. 81–82, 92.

41. 43–45, 64.

42. 47, 57–62; Kavanaugh Deposition, Hr'g Tr., 172.

43. Rodenhiser Deposition, 118–119.

44. Ibid., 178–79.

45. 145.

46. 118–19; 125–26; 132–33; 141–42; 145–46.

47. 141–42.

48. Trial, 899. The same quotation appears in Judge Carey's concurring opinion in *Curran III*, 786; see also Trial, 1011–12; 293–94, 315, 329, 332–35, 339.

Chapter 12. The Offer I Should Have Refused

1. 15 *Del.C*, §5021 and 5022.

2. Ibid., §1532 (a)(6) and §1533.

3. "Voting Practices In First Ward Attract Curious," *Morning News*, Nov. 3, 1954, A1.

4. Ibid.

5. In 1971, years after he departed the office, Attorney General Craven recounted the story of the 1954 election in *T'was A Famous Victory*, a book he submitted to the University of Delaware to fulfill part of the requirements for a master's degree. Because at one time the offices of the Prothonotary (the Clerk of the Superior Court), the Register in Chancery (the Clerk of the Court of Chancery), and the Regis-

ter of Wills were side by side they came to be known as "the row offices."

Chapter 13. Winning the Newspaper Decision

1. *Equitable Trust Co. v. Gallagher*, 102 A.2d 538, 541 (Del.1954).
2. See Chapter 11, above.
3. Hr'g Tr., 128–30.
4. "2nd Statement on Rape Bared," *Morning News*, Dec. 2, 1954, 1.
5. I traveled by train since Doris and I made do with our one car all through the years of *The Rape Case*. She needed the wheels far more than I did.

Chapter 14. Young's Name and My Capacity for Work

1. See Chapter 13, above.
2. Trial, 338–41; 1011.
3. House Resolution No. 207 (the third "Whereas" clause), adopted June 9, 1982, by the 131st General Assembly of the State of Delaware House of Representatives, "Mourning The Death Of H. Albert Young, Of Wilmington, A Former Attorney General Of Delaware," reproduced in the Appendix to *Russ*.
4. John A. Munroe, *History of Delaware* (Newark, Del.: University of Delaware Press. 2001), 74. Many people think the Battle of the Brandywine took place in Delaware since the Brandywine River is frequently associated with Delaware. That battle, however, took place near Chadd's Ford, Pennsylvania, just over the line.
5. The irony is that Cooch, purportedly "the better person" by reason of his Delaware birth and lineage, was among the handful of Delaware lawyers who failed to file federal income tax returns, an embarrassing development that came to light in the mid-1950s. Cooch escaped prosecution and public censure and moved from Delaware. Eisenhower was then President and the United States Attorney's office

was in control of the Republicans. By 1963, Leonard Hagner, the lawyer for Bud Curran at *The Rape Case* trial, was the United States Attorney. One would have thought the Republicans would have exploited the Democrat Cooch's misconduct. It would have been out-of-character, however, for the sweet, gentle Len Hagner to have done so even though it meant applying a double standard to the prosecution of tax offenders.

6. As we traveled, with Hensel driving, he analyzed the presidential race for me. He demonstrated his political acumen by explaining how many states whose popular vote Stevenson could lose and yet still win the presidency by capturing the most votes in the Electoral College. Listening, I became increasingly disheartened about Stevenson's chances. As Frederich Kessler, one of my law school professors, was wont to say when he heard a poor answer: "You couldn't be wronger!" I thought of repeating Kessler's remark to Hensel but decided to keep quiet. In 1952 Eisenhower and the Republicans swept the country.

7. *Jones v. Bodley*, 27 A.2d 84 (Del. Ch. 1942), rev'd, 32 A.2d 431–432 (Del. 1943), on remand, 39 A 2d 413 (Del. Ch 1944), aff'd, 59 A. 2d 463 (Del. 1947).

8. *Curran I*, aff'd, *Curran II*.

Chapter 15. The Original Talk Show Host

1. *Sheppard v. Ohio*, 352 U.S. 910 (1956).

Chapter 16. My Short-Lived Public Service

1. The State's Answering Brief, filed January 3, 1955, 7.

2. Ibid., 11.

3. The Petitioners' Reply Brief, filed January 14, 1955, 2 (hereafter cited as Reply Brief).

4. Ibid., 8. Bader inherited from me the erroneous spelling of Rodenhiser's name.

5. 102 A.2d 538 (Del. 1954).

6. Reply Brief, 8–9.

7. *Bowen,* 516, affirming *Bowen,* 1009; *Moore,* 104.

8. Reply Brief, 11–12. Bader wrote without the benefit of *United States v. Morgan,* 222 F.2d 673 (2d Cir.1955), decided four months after he filed his brief.

9. Quigley, a Democrat, served as the representative from the Tenth Representative District in the years 1940–1944 and 1950–1962. His district included New Castle. Throughout his service he unsuccessfully promoted legislation to permit dog racing at a track to be located not only in his district but, moreover, on his 112 acre property on Delaware Route 273, east of Hare's Corner. By 1996 the Quigley Farm was the last of ten working farms dating back to 1770. In February 1996 the New Castle City Council voted to annex the property to preserve its "historic character." Neil Cornish, "Quigley Farm is Annexed," *The News Journal,* Feb. 14, 1996, B3. Despite holding all sorts of legislation hostage to his dog-track dream, Quigley never achieved his goal, but not for want of trying. He held court in a room in the basement of Legislative Hall which acquired the sobriquet, "the Snake Pit." Ralph Moyed, a reporter and later a columnist for *The News Journal* who had first-hand knowledge of Speaker Quigley and his method of operation, wrote in 1999 about the need for reform in the way the Delaware legislature conducted itself and referred to the time Speaker Quigley reigned almost fifty years earlier (1950–1962):

> I bring up the hoary practices of Delaware's General Assembly because, despite cosmetic reforms such as publication of an agenda by Senate Democrats, little has changed since Legislative Hall was on my beat.
>
> The Snake Pit in the basement is gone. The former Speaker of the House, who used the pit to sell shots of whiskey in return for contributions to "The Widows and Orphans of Dead Soldiers," has been dead for many years. But the reforms needed in Dover have never come.

Ralph Moyed, "June Madness Can Wear Down an Old Idealist," *The News Journal,* June 24, 1999, A16.

10. Having acquired the Citizens Bank Building, John Kane, our client and landlord, renamed it the North American Building after his company, the North American Life Insurance Company.

Chapter 17. Something More Needs To Be Said (The Third Defeat)

1. *Curran III.*

2. Ibid., 783–86.

3. 783; "Court Appoints Youth Counsel," *Journal,* Nov. 17, 1947, A1.

4. See Chapter 3, above, the section entitled "The Failure to Object to the Admission of the Curran and Maguire Papers."

5. *Curran III,* 784.

6. Ibid.

7. 784–85.

8. 784.

9. Ibid.

10. 785.

11. Hr'g Tr., 134–35.

12. 102 A.2d 538, 541 (Del. 1954). See also Chapter 14, above.

13. *Curran III,* 785.

14. *Curran I,* aff'd., *Curran II.*

15. Although the public perception is the law provides too many protections for those accused of crime, the reality is the law has fallen short in significant ways, not the least of which is fairness in admitting statements of criminal defendants in evidence. If the law for admitting a will to probate in a will contest, a civil case, were applied to the admissibility of a confession repudiated by an accused at a criminal trial, few confessions would ever find acceptance in criminal cases. The law's drawing the dichotomy so harshly against a person accused of crime is unfair but not likely to change.

16. Judge Terry's comments appear in Chapter 13, the text at note 3, above. See also Hr'g Tr., 134–35.

17. *Curran III,* 786.

18. Ibid.

19. Ibid.

20. Ibid. One error in the opinion, the spelling of Rodenhiser's last name as "Rodenheiser," was not the Superior Court's fault. I was the culprit who inadvertently made the error in the papers I filed. The Superior Court copied my spelling.

21. 786–87.
22. 787.
23. 786.

Chapter 18. The Optimistic Brief

1. See Chapter 3, note 3, above.

2. Although neither Southerland nor Tunnell had served as judges, each had an outstanding record as a lawyer. Southerland's expertise was corporation law. Tunnell was Delaware's preeminent trial lawyer. He practiced in Georgetown with his brother, Robert, continuing the firm their father, James M. Tunnell Sr., had founded years before he was elected to the United States Senate. Wolcott moved from his post as Chancellor to the Supreme Court. When he was passed over for membership on the Supreme Court, former Chief Justice Richards became President Judge of the Superior Court. Associate Justices Terry and Carey, previously serving both on the Supreme Court and the Superior Court, became exclusively Superior Court judges. Because of the outstanding quality of Governor Elbert N. Carvel's appointments, there was no protest either from the public or the passed-over judges themselves, and the Senate easily confirmed Southerland, Wolcott, and Tunnell.

3. The comparable number of reversals, in whole or in part, among the reported decisions between June 1, 1941, and May 31, 1951, was twenty-four.

4. See *Curran III,* 787.

5. Brief On Behalf Of Appellants in the Delaware Supreme Court, 6.

6. Compare Trial, 21–28 (the young woman), with 770, 772–73, 775–76, 777–79, 780–83 (Curran); 915–16, 919, 920, 932 (Jones); 844–51 (Maguire).

7. Ibid., 811(Curran); 969–70(Jones); 853, 895–96(Maguire).

8. *Curran III,* 786–87.

9. Ibid., 786.

10. Ibid.

11. *Bowen* and *Moore.*

12. *United States v. Morgan,* 222 F.2d 673, 674–75 (2nd Cir. 1955).

13. Compare, *Ex parte Bollman,* 8 U.S. 73, 99 (1807), with *United States v. Morgan,* 222 F.2d, 675–676.

14. *United States v. DiMartini,* 118 F.Supp. 601, 602 (S.D.N.Y.1953) (the court rejected *Moore* noting "it has been severely criticized."); see also, *Leyra v. Denno,* 347 U.S. 556 (1954) (the conviction was upset since it was not obtained in accordance with due process of law, even though the accused did not even claim he had a defense to the charges).

15. *Hayward v. United States,* 127 F.Supp. 485, 488 (S.D.N.Y. 1954) (*Hayward,* 487, note 3, and 487, noted that the *Moore* case and like cases "have been sharply criticized" and the force of the *Moore* cases holding "has been impaired by the later ruling in *United States v. Morgan,* 346 U.S. 502, 74 S. Ct. 247" where the dissent relied upon the *Moore* case).

16. Note, "Post-Release Attacks on Invalid Federal Convictions: Obstacles to Redress by Coram Nobis," 115 *Yale Law Journal* 63, 119–120 (1954); *Allen v. United States,* 102 F.Supp. 866, 869 (N.D. Ill. 1952).

17. *Curran III,* 787.

18. Ibid.

Chapter 19. Unexpected Help and Surprising Praise

1. For the repetition of the Reinhardt and Young comments, compare the State's Answering Brief in the Superior Court, 7 (Reinhardt) and 11 (Young), with the State's Answering Brief in the Supreme Court, 4 (Reinhardt) and 7 (Young).

2. *Curran III,* 783. And see the State's Answering Brief in the Supreme Court, 22 (hereafter cited as State's Brief).

3. Petitioners' Reply Brief, note 3.

4. State's Brief, 15.

5. Ibid., citing to Hr'g Tr., 85, 91, 92, 93, 101, 105, 106, 108, 112, 116, 117, 120, 121, 122, 123.

6. Trial, 1009–12, esp. 1011.

7. State's Brief, 11.

8. *United States v. Morgan,* 222 F.2d 673, 674 (2d Cir. 1955).

9. State's Brief, 22.

10. Ibid.

11. Ibid.

12. Petitioners' Reply Brief, 8–9.

13. *Curran II* was the first appeal. See Chapter 10, above.

14. Apart from the two appeals in *The Rape Case,* the other two occasions were: (1) my loss to Hamilton in *Lee Tire & Rubber Co. v. Dormer,* 108 A. 2d 168 (Del. 1954); (2) my success in initially thwarting the Diamond State Telephone Company's use of land for parking next to its new exchange at Fortieth and Washington Streets in Wilmington. *Application of Emmett S. Hickman Co.,* 108 A.2d 667 (Del. 1954).

15. Justice Bramhall had succeeded Justice Tunnell in 1954 when Tunnell resigned to make an unsuccessful try to secure the Democratic Party's nomination to the United States Senate from J. Allen Frear, the incumbent. I supported Tunnell.

Chapter 20. Unfairness Affirmed (The Fourth Defeat)

1. *Curran IV,* affirming, *Curran III.*

2. *Curran III,* 784.

3. Ibid., 786.

4. *Curran IV,* 129. Throughout its opinion the Supreme Court, as had the Superior Court, repeated my error in the spelling of Detective Rodenhiser's name.

5. Ibid.

6. *Curran III,* 786–87.

7. For judges acting as jurors, *see* the dissent of Justice John Paul Stevens in *Scott v. Harris,* 550 U.S. 372, 392 (2007), about which the distinguished, perceptive former *The New York Times* Supreme Court reporter wrote: "With evident sarcasm, Justice Stevens referred to the other justices as 'my colleagues on the jury.'" Linda Greenhouse, "Court Backs Police Officers In Chase That Hurt Driver," *The New York Times,* May 1, 2007, A18.

8. *Curran IV,* 130.

9. Ibid., 127.

10. Ibid., note 1.

11. 128.

12. 129.

13. 130.

14. Ibid.

15. Trial, 175–203, esp. 201–03.

16. Ibid., 125–26.

17. *Curran IV*, 130, and see Young's agreement. Trial, 149.

18. *Curran IV*, 129.

19. Ibid.

20. Ibid.

21. 130.

22. Compare Trial, 165–66(Officer McDermott) with 920–21 (Jones).

23. *Curran IV*, 130. Here again the court ignored the testimony of the three eyewitnesses.

24. Ibid. Except in the one instance at the outset of the quoted paragraph, the opinion uses the expression "counsel argues" to denote only one lawyer for Curran, Jones, and Maguire, as was the fact by the time of the hearing in December 1964.

25. Ibid.

26. Ibid.

27. *Curran III*, 786; *Curran IV*, 129.

28. Ibid., 130.

29. Charles Lane, "Swear To God," *The New Republic*, Feb. 8, 1999, 4, 41.

30. Ibid.

31. *Curran IV*, 130.

32. See Rodenhiser Deposition, 118–19, 125–26, 132–33, 138, 141–42, 144–48, 154, 157–58, 163–67, 169, and 171–72. See also the unsigned statement of Detective John Rodenhiser, dated March 9, 1948, in McCool's Report, 36. McCool called it "Report of Detective John Rodenhiser." See Hr'g Tr., 83, 85, 92, 95, 101, 105, 106, 112, 116, 117, 120, 121.

33. See Duffy Summation, 36 (Fahey not there); 37–39 (None of the three were there). See also 43 (where Duffy eliminates the presence of Fahey, Masten, and Schueler by claiming: "Those three defendants

were cruising around to find the first girl they could see, and when they found one it was going to be too bad.").

34. *Curran IV,* 130–31.

35. The oath found in Supreme Court Rule 54 reads: "I _____, do solemnly swear (or affirm) that I will support the Constitution of the United States and the Constitution of the State of Delaware; that I will behave myself in the office of an Attorney within the Courts according to the best of my learning and ability and with all good fidelity as well to the Court as to the client; that I will use no falsehood nor delay any person's cause through lucre or malice."

36. *Curran IV,* 131.

37. Ibid.

38. 129.

Chapter 21. The Double Standard

1. *In re Bennethum,* 161 A.2d 229, on reargument, 162 A.2d 429 (Del. 1960).

2. 161 A.2d, 234.

3. *Curran III,* 786–87; *Curran IV,* 129–30.

4. *Curran III,* 786.

5. *Blackstone Commentaries,* vol. 4, 137. *Gatewood v. State,* 15 Md.App. 314, 290 A.2d 551, 553 (Ct. Special Appeals Md. 1972). *Black's Law Dictionary,* Fourth Edition (St. Paul, Minn.: West Publishing, 1951), 1125. See also *McGuire v. Gunn,* 133 Kan. 422, 300 P.654, 656 (Sup. 1931); and *Black's Law Dictionary,* 880.

6. *Curran III,* 786.

7. *Curran IV,* 129–30.

Chapter 22. The Naysayer

1. Mr. Finger's wife, Anna, had helped prepare me for my Bar Mitzvah at Congregation Beth Shalom in December 1938. The Fingers were among the five families who founded the Congregation in 1922.

Chapter 23. Chancery Joins the Rest
(The Fifth Defeat)

1. See Chapter 20, above; "Grand Jury Asks Probe of Police," *Journal*, June 15, 1956, 1 (the front page article's summary of the grand jury's actions said: "It charged there is a 'definite tie-in' between one or more policemen and known gamblers. It said it has 'grave doubts' about the general competence and fitness of the 'two top administrative officers.' It singled out the superintendent of the Department of Public Safety (Andrew J. Kavanaugh) for censure in two incidents. It said it reached its conclusions despite the 'totally unreliable' testimony of a recently demoted police officer (ex-Lt. John A. Rodenhiser)."); "Board Bars Craven from Rodenhiser's Public Trial July 9," *Morning News, June 29, 1956,* 1; William P. Frank, "'I Could Have Been Rich If I Kept Quiet,' Accused Sergeant Says," *Morning News,* June 29, 1956, 1 (Frank quoted Rodenhiser as saying: "It was soon after [the 1948 gambling probe fiasco] that I was involved in the rape case developments and accused of wrongdoing in handling statements of the three defendants." In an earlier portion of the article, Frank wrote: "[Rodenhiser] first broke into the news when he helped to investigate and handle the rape case involving three young men who are now serving life sentences in the New Castle County Workhouse. That case still echoes through City Hall—and recently was the subject of a State Supreme Court opinion which criticized Rodenhiser for the way he was supposed to have handled statements by the defendants.")

2. Dr. T ruled with an iron hand over the state's mental hospital at Farnhurst, on Route 13 south of Wilmington, including the facility housing the criminally insane. He also maintained a private practice. When he saw the remarkable advances Dr. Pasquale Beunaconte, the new administrator, brought to the care of patients at the Stokley Hospital for the Mentally Retarded, a separate, public hospital but still much under Dr. T's control, he was fearful of the "competition" or of invidious comparisons between himself and Dr. Beunaconte. To Delaware's loss, he succeeded in removing Dr. Beunaconte. I was personally familiar with Stokley and Dr. Beunaconte, having visited and reported my findings to my wife Doris as part of a volunteer project in which she participated.

3. *Curran I,* 308, n.1.

4. *Curran V,* 377. O'Donnell did the successful work for the state, although only Craven's name appeared in the reported opinion.

5. Ibid., 375 and 376.

6. 376.

7. 377.

8. Ibid.

Chapter 24. The First Denial of *Certiorari* (The Sixth Defeat) Leads to the District Court

1. The quoted words come from the following opinions: *Curran IV,* 129 (Southerland, C.J., joined by Wolcott and Bramhall, JJ.); *Curran III,* 786 (Carey, J. joined by Terry, J.); *Curran V,* 376 (Seitz, Ch.).

2. *Curran VI.* I had not sought the United States Supreme Court's review on the issue before Seitz, i.e., did Curran, Jones, and Maguire have the right to secure Dr. T's report concerning the medical evaluation of Rodenhiser for their use in upsetting their convictions? The Supreme Court did not cite Seitz's opinion denying the petition to secure Dr. T's report. The *Supreme Court Reporter,* however, did refer to the citation for Seitz's opinion as well as to the Supreme Court's and Superior Court's opinions denying relief. In citing to Seitz's opinion in *Curran VI,* the *Supreme Court Reporter* erred, since the Supreme Court did not have a word in any of the briefs the parties put before it about Dr. T's report and my effort to obtain it. *Curran v. State of Delaware,* 77 Sup. Ct. Repts. 151 (1956).

3. *Sheppard v. Ohio,* 352 U.S. 910, 910–911 (1956).

4. Judge Richard S. Rodney retired and took senior status at the end of 1956 but remained available to accept assignments. The likelihood of Rodney presiding over *The Rape Case* was remote since one of his two sons-in-law, Daniel F. Wolcott, was a member of Delaware's Supreme Court and had participated in its denial of relief. Judge Caleb R. Layton III, who succeeded to the vacancy created when Rodney took senior status, did not assume his duties until April 29, 1957, by which time Judge Wright had already heard the oral argument of the parties.

In any event, Layton would not have sat because of his participation in the state court proceedings even if the District Court had delayed action on the case until after Layton's swearing-in. The chief competitor of Judge Layton seeking to fill Rodney's seat was C. Edward Duffy, who, with Attorney General Albert James, had prosecuted *The Rape Case.* Obviously, had Senator John Williams urged Duffy's appointment to President Dwight D. Eisenhower, Duffy would have had to recuse himself from presiding. See Hoffecker, 152–55.

 5. *Curran V,* 129.

Chapter 25. Ships in the Night

 1. My mentor, Paul Leahy, was a member of that same firm when it was known as Southerland, Berl, Potter & Leahy, before Chief Judge Leahy, with E. Ennalls Berl's sponsorship, ascended the District Court Bench in February 1942. With Southerland's appointment to the post of Chief Justice of the Supreme Court of the State of Delaware by Governor Elbert N. Carvel in 1951, the firm name became Berl, Potter & Anderson.

 2. *Curran IV,* 131. OAT, 9.

 3. OAT, IV.

 4. *Curran IV,* 130.

 5. OAT, 11.

 6. Ibid., 7, 8 (twice), 11 (twice), 13, 34, 37.

 7. 25.

 8. 25–26.

 9. 11.

 10. 17.

 11. Trial, 26.

 12. Ibid., 779.

 13. OAT, 17–18.

 14. Ibid., 8.

 15. 30–31.

 16. 31–32.

 17. Neither the state nor I asked Harry Blam to transcribe the argument. Although the state was not constrained for funds, I was.

Harry, a friend from my days as a clerk for Chief Judge Leahy, gave me the reel containing the argument, but not before my careful, practical friend had filled the reel with a number of arguments other lawyers made to the court in unrelated matters. Having entered the labor market in the depths of the Great Depression, Harry followed the policy of "waste not, want not," a policy I, a child of the Great Depression, followed as well.

Chapter 26. Crossing the Line of Tolerable Imperfection (The First Victory)

1. *Curran VII*, 29. On October 8, 1957, two months after he filed the opinion, Judge Wright became Chief Judge upon Chief Judge Leahy's retirement on October 7, 1957.

2. Ibid., quoting from and citing to *Lisenba v. People of State of California*, 314 U.S. 219, 236 (1941).

3. *Curran III*, aff'd, *Curran IV*.

4. *Curran III*, 786 (" . . . it seems plain to me that there were at least three places in the questioning when a full and truthful answer would necessarily have included this information.") (Judge Carey writing for himself and Judge Terry); *Curran IV*, 129 ("The record leaves no doubt that Detective Rodenheiser's testimony was untrue.").

5. *Curran VII*, 30.

6. Ibid. And see Chief Judge Biggs' language in *Curran VIII*, 713.

7. *Curran VII*, 31.

8. Ibid., 32.

9. Ibid.

10. "Irving Morris Reported Freed," *Sunday Star*, May 18, 1945, 1. By the time the article appeared I had been liberated and had written home in a letter the article quoted in part: "Sorry that of late I haven't been keeping up with my correspondence . . . I was captured on March 14 and until just the other day I was a 'guest' of the Germans. . . . "

Chapter 27. The Planted Note

1. Irving Morris to Melvin G. Shimm, Aug. 19, 1957, copy in the author's possession.

2. 7 *Duke L.J.* 150 (1958) (hereafter cited as Duke L.J.).

3. *Mooney v. Holohan,* 294 U.S. 103 (1935); *Duke L. J.,* 150–51, citing and quoting from *Curran IV,* 130.

4. *Curran IV,* 130.

5. *Curran VII,* 31.

6. *Duke L.J.,* 151.

7. *Pyle v. Kansas,* 317 U.S. 213 (1942).

8. *Curran VII,* 31.

9. *Duke L.J.,* 153, note 13, discussing *Pyle v. Amrine,* 159 Kan. 458, 156 P.2d 509, 515 (Kan 1945).

10. *Duke L.J.,* 154.

Chapter 28. Affirming the Obvious
(The Second Victory)

1. Frank O'Donnell, Jr. to Mrs. Ida Creskoff, Clerk, United States Court of Appeals for the Third Circuit, Dec. 17, 1957. Copy in the author's possession.

2. Located then at 9th and Chestnut Streets in Philadelphia, the courthouse was an art-deco style building constructed in the 1930s under the Works Progress Administration as part of the effort to prime the pump of the Great Depression economy.

3. *Curran VIII,* affirming *Curran VII.*

4. "Craven To Go To Top Court," *Journal,* Oct. 1, 1958, A1.

5. Reitz, 479.

6. *Curran VI.*

7. Prior to the new legislation, the 1935 Code, Sec. 5166, governed the issue.

8. 51 Del. Laws, Ch. 347, §4, effective April 2, 1958.

9. *State of Delaware v. Theodric Thompson,* Cr. A. 107–1957, Superior Court of Delaware, unreported. In *Thompson* the Grand Jury of New Castle County indicted him in 1957 on the charge of murder allegedly committed in 1953. Thompson's trial took place in September 1957. The jury convicted him without a recommendation of mercy. Under the Delaware law as it then was, the conviction meant a mandatory death sentence. 11 Del.C. §781. Thompson filed a motion for a new trial. After counsel briefed the motion, but before the court de-

cided it, the General Assembly abolished capital punishment. 51 Del. Laws, Ch. 347, §4, effective April 2, 1958. On April 15, 1958, the Superior Court heard argument on Thompson's motion for a new trial. Immediately thereafter the Superior Court denied the motion from the bench and sentenced Thompson to life imprisonment. The Superior Court thus gave to Thompson the benefit of the legislative change. The judges who sat in *Thompson* were President Judge Terry and Associate Judges Carey and William Storey.

10. Irving Morris to Ida O. Creskoff, Oct. 8, 1958. Copy in the author's possession.

11. Order of the Third Circuit, Oct. 8, 1958. Copy in the author's possession.

Chapter 29. The Hair Tonic Bond

1. William P. Frank, "Lawyer's 5-Year Fight for Justice Opens Door to 3 Jailed for Rape," *Morning News,* Oct. 10, 1958, A25.

2. Ibid.

3. Cr. A. 107–957 (unreported). I discuss the ruling in *Thompson* in Chapter 28, note 9, above.

4. Edward G. Pollard to Ida O. Creskoff, Oct. 9, 1947. Copy in the author's possession.

5. *Reitz,* 461, 525–32 (*Bowers*–1; *Carmen*–1; *Curran*–III; *Dougharty*–1; *Stoner*–1; *Wade*–1; *Westbrook*–1; *White*–1; *Woods*–1). The full citation and history of each case appear in *Reitz.*

6. In later years Father Tucker was the marriage broker in the real life, fairy-tale union of Grace Kelly, the movie actress from Philadelphia, and Prince Ranier of Monte Carlo.

7. *Curran I.*

Chapter 30. The Opposition Continues, Spite Is Thwarted, and The Rape Case Ends (The Third, Fourth, And Final Victories

1. Poppiti carried the baggage that he controlled the Delaware State Alcoholic Beverage Control Commission since some charged that

an applicant had to hire Poppiti in order to secure a Delaware liquor license. Bove did not repudiate the rumor. I knew Poppiti well; upon his 1948 admission to the Bar, Francis A. Reardon had taken Poppiti into his office across the hall from Philip Cohen in the North American Building. My impression was that Poppiti spoke from experience in appearing before the Commission and not from control of it.

2. See Chapter 28, note 4, above.

3. Letter from Irving Morris to George Corbeil, Nov. 24, 1958. Copy in the author's possession.

4. *Curran IX.*

5. After returning to full-time private practice in 1955, Hy Young formed a partnership with Wood. In June 1956 the partnership of Young and Wood dissolved. "Law Firm Dissolved, New One is Started," *Morning News,* June 29, 1956, 4 (the new firm referred to the firm Wood formed with Bayard W. Allmond). On January 1, 1959, Young joined forces with James R. Morford and H. James Conaway, Jr., with the firm name of Morford, Young and Conaway. In 1964 after Morford's sudden death on July 1, 1959, the firm became Young, Conaway, Stargatt & Taylor. *Russ,* 3–20, 28.

6. *Curran VIII,* affirming, *Curran VII.*

7. I once dictated a letter to Wood and instead of "Clement C. Wood," my then secretary, Sadie Golden, typed "Clemency" Wood. He did not exhibit any clemency toward Curran, Jones, and Maguire.

8. *Curran III,* 786–87.

9. Copy of Wood's statement is in the author's possession.

10. Original of the author's statement is in his possession.

Chapter 31. The Flawed Editorial

1. Sal DeVivo, "A Publisher's Note To Readers," *The News Journal,* Dec. 17, 1988. There was one exception to their competition: both papers used the same advertising staff for many years. The policy the separate papers enforced strictly, i.e., if you wanted to advertise in one newspaper, you had to advertise in both, the United States Supreme Court outlawed in *Citizen Publishing Co. v. United States,* 394 U.S. 131 (1969).

2. Tom Malone, "Rape Case Ends, Defendants Freed," *Morning News*, Feb. 26, 1959, 1.

3. "State Drops Old Rape Case," *Journal*, Feb. 26, 1959, 2.

4. Ibid., 20.

5. *Curran IV*, 130.

6. Duffy Summation, 37–39, 43.

7. *Curran VII*, aff'd, *Curran VIII*.

Chapter 32. Praise

1. *Curran VII*, aff'd. *Curran VIII*.

2. Evelyn H. Clift to Irving Morris, Feb. 27, 1959. Original in the author's possession.

3. John A. Munroe to Irving Morris, Mar. 4, 1959. Original in the author's possession.

4. Irving Morris to Evelyn H. Clift, Mar. 30, 1959. Copy in the author's possession.

5. Irving Morris to John A. Munroe, Mar. 10, 1959. Copy in the author's possession.

6. Jay H. Topkis to Irving Morris, Feb. 4, 1959. Original in the author's possession.

7. Irving Morris to Jay H. Topkis, Feb. 9, 1959. Copy in the author's possession. William P. Frank, "Lawyer's 5-Year Fight for Justice Opens Door to 3 Jailed for Rape," *Morning News*, Oct. 10, 1958, A25.

8. Irving Morris to Herbert L. Maris, Feb. 26, 1959. Copy in the author's possession.

9. Herbert L. Maris to Irving Morris, Mar. 2, 1959. Original in the author's possession.

10. Herbert L. Maris to Nellie Curran, Oct. 10, 1958. Copy in the author's possession.

11. *Jones v. Bodley*, 27 A.2d 84 (Del.Ch. 1942), rev'd, 32 A.2d 436 (Del. 1943), on remand, 39 A.2d 413 (Del.Ch. 1944), aff'd, 59 A.2d 463 (Del. 1947); *Reid v. Baker*, 57 A.2d 103 (Del. 1948).

Chapter 33. Suing For Damages

1. Irving Morris to Samuel Thompson, Apr. 16, 1959. Copy in the author's possession.

2. Title 42, United States Code, Section 1983.

3. *Morgan v. Null,* 117 F.Supp. 11(D.C.N.Y.1953).

4. Irving Morris to Samuel Thompson, Apr. 16, 1959. Copy in the author's possession.

5. 10 Del. C. §8118.

6. *Francis v. Lyman,* 108 F.Supp. 884, 885 (D.C. Mass. 1952), aff'd on other grounds, 203 F.2d 809 (1 Cir. 1953).

7. Irving Morris to George Corbeil, May 6, 1959. Copy in the author's possession.

8. George Corbeil to Irving Morris, June 24, 1959. Original in the author's possession.

9. Draft of the proposed bill. Original in the author's possession.

10. Irving Morris to George Corbeil, June 29, 1959. Copy in the author's possession.

11. George Corbeil to Irving Morris, June 24, 1959. Original in the author's possession.

12. Samuel Thompson to Irving Morris, Aug. 18, 1959. Original in the author's possession.

13. Ibid.

14. Irving Morris to Francis J. Curran, *et al.,* Aug. 20, 1959. Copy in the author's possession.

15. Emily J. Minor, "Nothing Can Compensate for Lost Years," *The Palm Beach Post,* Apr. 19, 2007, B1.

Chapter 34. VINDICATED!

1. See the affidavit of the Illinois Assistant State's Attorney quoted in *Napue,* 266, note 1.

2. Ibid., 267, note 2.

3. I have taken the facts as set forth in the text from *Napue,* 265–69.

4. Ibid.

5. 269.

6. See Chapter 27, above; *Townsend v. Hudspeth,* 167 Kan. 366, 205 P.2d 483 (1949). See *Pyle v. Amrine,* 139 Kan. 458, 156 P.2d 509 (1945). Oddly, the Supreme Court did not elect to correct the Kansas Supreme Court when it denied certiorari. *Pyle v. Amrine,* 326 U.S. 749 (1945).

7. *Duke L. J.,*153, note 13.

8. *Napue,* 269. See *Curran VII,* 30. See also Chief Judge Biggs' language in *Curran VIII,* 713.

9. See Chapter 27, above.

10. *Curran IV,* 130.

Epilogue

1. In *Montecatini,* Chief Judge Wright particularly wanted to preserve the testimony of the two key persons involved in the dispute before him, Dr. Karl Ziegler of Germany and Professor Giulio Natta of Italy. Both were in their early seventies. Natta suffered from Parkinson's disease. They had shared the Nobel Prize for Chemistry in 1963, and, given their rivalry, each probably questioned whether the other was qualified to receive the prize. Judge Wright did not want the case to go to trial with the parties having failed to depose Ziegler and Natta and secure their critical testimony. Since the parties wanted a special master with them at their expense, Judge Wright appointed me to oversee the depositions in Europe on three separate occasions. In December 1969 I presided at the deposition of Ziegler in Duisberg, Germany, and in March 1970 (accompanied by Doris at my expense) at the deposition of Natta in Milan, Italy. Finally, in a four-and-a-half month period between June and October 1972, I again served in Milan as the special master at the depositions of other witnesses. I was not reversed on a single ruling, but, I hasten to add, no one appealed from any of my rulings.

2. *Curran VII,* 31.

3. 206 A.2d 501 (Del. 1964)

4. Ibid., 503 (Emphasis added.). Chief Justice Southerland had retired in 1963 upon the completion of his twelve-year term and, therefore, did not sit in *Williams.* But Justice Wolcott did. He had not yet succeeded to the post of Chief Justice. After some vying between Justices Herrmann and Wolcott for the appointment, the State Senate's preference for Justice Wolcott won out over Governor Elbert N. Carvel's first selection, his advisor and friend, Justice Herrmann.

5. See note 4 above.

6. *Hoffecker,* 157–158.

7. *Curran IV,* 128–31.

8. *Curran VIII* and *Curran IX.* Justice Wolcott's inability in 1964 to accept the holding in *The Rape Case* is all the more egregious since he ignored the unanimous holding of the United States Supreme Court in *Napue,* decided June 15, 1959, only four months after the state on February 25, 1959, dropped any further prosecution of Curran, Jones, and Maguire. *Napue* had specifically cited to the Third Circuit's affirmance of Judge Wright's opinion in *The Rape Case.*

9. *Parson v. State,* 222 A.2d 326 (Del. 1966).

10. *Parson v. State,* 386 U.S. 935 (1967).

11. *Curran I.* And see Chapter 9, above.

12. *Parson v. Anderson,* 280 F.Supp. 565 (D.Del. 1968).

13. Ibid.

14. *Hoffecker,* 161–162.

15. Ibid., 180.

16. 177, 179.

17. 179.

18. 180–182; and see Irving Morris, "The Role of Delaware Lawyers in the Desegregation of Delaware's Public Schools: A Memoir," *Widener Law Symposium Journal* 9.1 (2002), 33–54 (hereafter cited as Morris).

19. Murray M. Schwartz, "Judge Caleb M. Wright," *Delaware Lawyer* 27.1 (Spring 2009), 24; Murray M. Schwartz to Irving Morris, June 30, 2009. Original in the author's possession.

20. "Wolcott's Death Stuns Colleagues, "*Morning News,* July 11, 1973, A2.

21. The memorial proceedings are reported in *Delaware Reporter,* vol. 10 (St. Paul, MN: West Publishing Co., 1973) covering the Delaware decisions reported in volumes 317–328 of the *Atlantic Reporter.*

22. 87 A.2d 862 (Del.Ch.1952)

23. 347 U.S. 483, 494 n.10 (1954)

24. See Morris, 1, 6–12.

25. Compare the first brochure with the brochure in 2007.

26. "Estate Frauds Jail Attorney for 4 Years, David J. Reinhardt, Jr., Admits Spending $12,700 of Funds in His Custody," *Morning News,* Oct. 3, 1950.

27. "D.J. Reinhardt, Ex-Attorney dies," *Morning News,* Aug. 26, 1970, 39.

28. McCool Deposition, 47, 57–62.

29. Howard Kurtz, "Father of the Slide," *The New Republic,* Feb. 12, 1996.

30. See letter by Tibor R. Machan of Auburn, Alabama, *The New Republic,* Mar. 18, 1996.

31. *Allen v. United States,* 386 F.2d 634, 637 (D.C.Ct.App.1967).

32. Bernard D. Fischman to Irving Morris, Sept. 13, 1999. Original in the author's possession.

33. Interviews by Nancy C. Vantine with Carey and Maris about "Lock up" appear in "Public Defender Without Portfolio Hailed in New Real Life Series," *Courier-Post,* Camden, N.J., Sept. 5, 1959, Television and Radio Section, 1.

34. Irving Morris to Herbert L. Maris, Jun. 1, 1959. Copy in the author's possession. The February 2006 issue of *Philadelphia,* published an article "The Best of Philly" with poll results about outstanding Philadelphians over the years in various categories. In comparing Kids's Show Hosts Sally Starr and Gene London, the report read:

> Starr: "Our gal Sal" was every eight-year-old boy's busty delight-in a cowboy hat.
> London: Decades before *Queer Eye,* his fey drawings and wifty charm proved guys don't have to be macho to succeed.
> Winner: Starr, 38 percent to 34 percent. Her show's 1971 cancellation produced the most protest mail in WPVI's history. 103.

35. Irving Morris to Samuel Thompson, May 18, 1960. Copy in the author's possession.

36. Irving Morris to DeWitt Wallace, Mar. 16, 1959. Copy in the author's possession.

37. Herbert L. Maris to Irving Morris, Mar. 19, 1959. Original in the author's possession.

38. DeWitt Wallace to Irving Morris, Apr. 3, 1959. Original in the author's possession.

39. *Reitz,* 496. In the quotations from *Reitz* I have omitted citations and footnotes. All of the emphasis-added portions are mine.

40. Ibid.

41. 501.

42. Ibid.

43. 502–03.

44. See William E. Wiggin, Introduction, "The Hair Tonic Bond (1958)," *Delaware Lawyer* 17.4 (Winter 1999/2000), 1. Wiggin also wrote that the "principle [was] now the law of the land." Ibid.

45. Memorandum, Michael Lindsey, "Legal Research Concerning the Current Status of the Holdings in *Napue v. Illinois*, 360 U.S. 264 (1959), and *Curran v. Delaware*, 259 F.2d 707 (3d Cir. 1958)," 2, 4. Original in the author's possession.

46. Ibid., 1.

47. 5.

48. Ibid.

49. Linda Greenhouse, "Justices, 5 to 4, Overturn 3 Texas Death Sentences," *The New York Times*, Apr. 26, 2007, A20.

50. "R.C. Barab, Lawyer, Found Dead in Auto," *Journal*, Jan. 25, 1956, 1.

Index